Capacity Planning for Web Performance

Metrics, Models, and Methods

ISBN 0-13-693822-1

90000

9 780136 938224

Capacity Planning for Web Performance

Metrics, Models, and Methods

Daniel A. Menascé
Department of Computer Science, George Mason University, Fairfax, Virginia
menasce@cs.gmu.edu

Virgilio A.F. Almeida
Department of Computer Science, Federal University of Minas Gerais, Brazil
virgilio@dcc.ufmg.br

Prentice Hall, PTR
Upper Saddle River, New Jersey 07458
http://www.phptr.com

Menascé, Daniel A.
    Capacity planning for Web performance : metrics, models, and
    methods / Daniel A. Menascé, Virgilio A.F. Almeida.
        p.   cm.
    Includes bibliographical references and index.
    ISBN 0-13-693822-1
    1. Computer capacity--Planning. 2. World Wide Web (Information
retrieval system)   I. Almeida, Virgilio A. F. II. Title.
QA76.9.C63M463   1998
004.2--dc21   98-3499
                                                          CIP

Editorial/Production Supervision: Craig Little
Acquisitions Editor: Stephen Solomon
Manufacturing Manager: Alexis R. Heydt
Marketing Manager: Dan Rush
Cover Design Director: Jerry Votta
Cover Design: Talar Agasyan

All product names mentioned herein are the trademarks of their respective owners.

Prentice Hall books are widely used by corporations and government agencies for training, marketing, and resale.

The publisher offers discounts on this book when ordered in bulk quantities.
For more information, contact: the Corporate Sales Department at 800-382-3419, fax: 201-236-7141, email: corpsales@prenhall.com or write
    Corporate Sales Department
    Prentice Hall PTR
    One Lake Street
    Upper Saddle River, NJ 07458

Printed in the United States of America
10 9 8 7 6 5 4 3 2 1

ISBN   0-13-693822-1

Prentice-Hall International (UK) Limited, *London*
Prentice-Hall of Australia Pty. Limited, *Sydney*
Prentice-Hall Canada Inc., *Toronto*
Prentice-Hall Hispanoamericana, S.A., *Mexico*
Prentice-Hall of India Private Limited, *New Delhi*
Prentice-Hall of Japan, Inc., *Tokyo*
Simon & Schuster Asia Pte. Ltd., *Singapore*
Editora Prentice-Hall do Brasil, Ltda., *Rio de Janeiro*

CONTENTS

PREFACE

Theme and approach

The client/server model emerged out of the convergence of computers and communications, the availability of inexpensive and powerful desktop computers with Graphical User Interfaces (GUI) and multimedia presentation devices, and advanced forms of data input, including voice input. By bringing the computation closer to the user and his/her business processes and by providing richer and easier to use interfaces, client/server systems can increase productivity, increase customer satisfaction, and cut down significantly on training costs. A special and important case of client/server applications is the World Wide Web (WWW) which has been growing at an enormous pace. The number of Web sites doubles every six months. Applications such as digital libraries, electronic commerce, video on-demand, and distance learning increase Internet and Web traffic at even higher rates. Virtual stores on the Web allow you to buy cars, books, computers, and many other products and services.

As more and more businesses and government agencies rely on distributed client/server and Web-based applications, performance considerations become extremely important. Performance analysis of intranets and Web servers is unique in many senses. First, the number of WWW clients is in the tens of millions and growing. The randomness associated with the way users visit pages and request Web services makes the problem of workload forecasting and capacity planning difficult.

This book uses a quantitative approach to analyzing client/server and Web-based systems. This approach lends itself to the development of performance predictive models for capacity planning. Instead of relying on intuition, ad hoc procedures, and rules of thumb, we provide a uniform and formal way for dealing with performance problems. The performance models discussed here are based on the theory of queuing networks. Another important feature of the book is its treatment of two fundamental characteristics of WWW traffic: burstiness and heavy-tailed distributions of Web document sizes. The techniques and models presented here provide a simple and practical approach to dealing with this type of environment.

Although some of the concepts about client/server and Web architectures may be familiar to some of the readers, these concepts are revisited here in light of quantitative and performance issues. A large number of numeric and practical examples help the reader understand the quantitative approach adopted in this book. Several MS Excel workbooks supported by Visual Basic modules accompany the book. These workbooks allow the readers to immediately put into practice the methods and models discussed here.

Who should read this book

Information technology managers and related staff must guarantee that the networked services under their management provide an acceptable quality of service to their users. Managers must avoid the pitfalls of inadequate capacity and meet users' performance expectations in a cost-effective manner. System administrators, Web masters, network administrators, capacity planners and analysts, IT managers and consultants, will benefit from reading parts or the entire book. Its practical, yet sound and formal, approach provides the grounds for understanding modern and complex networked environments.

This book can be used as a textbook for senior undergraduate and graduate courses in Computer Science and Computer Engineering. At the undergraduate level, the book is a good starting point to motivate students to learn the important implications and solutions to performance problems.

At the graduate level, it can be used in conjunction with the book *Capacity Planning and Performance Modeling: From Mainframes to Client-Server Systems*, by Menascé, Almeida, and Dowdy, Prentice Hall, 1994, in System Performance Evaluation courses. The combination of these two books offers a theoretical and practical foundation in performance modeling. The present book can also be used as a supplement for systems courses, including Operating Systems, Distributed Systems, and Networking, both at the undergraduate and graduate levels.

Book organization

Chapter 1 introduces, through a series of examples, the importance of performance considerations in client/server and Web-based systems. The concepts of capacity planning, service levels, and workload evolution are defined and illustrated.

Chapter 2 presents a brief discussion on local and wide area networks and their protocols including TCP/IP, Ethernet, Token Ring, and FDDI. The chapter revisits the client server (C/S) computing paradigm and discusses several kind of servers, such as file servers, database servers, application servers, groupware servers, object servers, and Web servers. Various architectural client/server issues including fat versus thin clients, two-tier versus three-tier C/S architectures are presented. These concepts are presented in light of performance considerations and tradeoffs.

Chapter 3 investigates, in detail, the nature of the delay incurred by a typical C/S transaction through the use of communication-processing delay diagrams. This chapter shows how service times can be computed at single disks, disk arrays, networks, and routers. Queues and contention are defined more formally and some very basic and important performance results from Operational Analysis are introduced.

Chapter 4 discusses issues that affect performance of Web servers and intranets. The chapter starts by looking at the sources of delay in Web environments. After discussing the end-user perspective to the Internet and intranet performance, the chapter provides an assessment. It examines the components and protocols involved in the execution of Web services and analyzes their capacity and performance issues.

Chapter 5 introduces a step-by-step methodology to determine the most cost-effective system configuration and networking architecture. The main steps of the methodology are: understanding the environment, workload characterization, workload model validation and calibration, performance model development, performance model validation and calibration, workload forecasting, performance prediction, cost model development, cost prediction, and cost/performance analysis.

Chapter 6 describes and illustrates with examples the major steps required for the construction of workload models. The common steps to be followed by any workload characterization project include specification of a point of view from which the workload will be analyzed, choice of the set of parameters that capture the most relevant characteristics of the workload for the purpose of the study, monitoring the system to obtain the raw performance data, analysis and reduction of performance data, and construction of a workload model.

Chapter 7 presents several different standard industry benchmarks—such as TPC-C and TPC-D, SPECcpu, SPECweb, LADDIS, and WebStone—and shows how to use benchmark results as a complementary source of information to support the capacity planning methodology.

Chapter 8 starts by introducing very simple models of network-based systems. Complexity is progressively introduced and the solution to each model is presented using first principles and intuitive concepts. After a few models are presented, the approach is generalized. The models presented in this chapter are called system-level performance models since they view the system being modeled as a "black box".

Chapter 9 introduces powerful techniques to analyze the performance of intranets and client/server systems. The chapter considers the components that make up a networked system. Component-level models account for the different resources of the system and the way they are used by different requests. The solution techniques for component-level models are based on Queuing Networks (QNs). Solution methods for both open and closed QNs with multiple classes of customers are presented in this chapter.

Chapter 10 shows how the performance models discussed in previous chapters can be specialized to handle Web performance issues. The chapter also shows how certain special features common in Web workloads, such as burstiness and heavy tail distributions of file sizes, can be accounted for in performance models for the Web.

Chapter 11 discusses aspects and techniques for workload forecasting, including regression models, moving averages, and exponential smoothing. The steps of the workload forecasting process discussed here include selection of the workload to be forecast, analysis of historical data and estimation of workload growth, selection of a forecasting technique, application of the forecasting technique to the historical data, and analysis and validation of forecast results.

Chapter 12 presents a framework for collecting performance data in networked environments that use the C/S computing paradigm. Next, it discusses the main issues in the process of measuring the performance of network-based systems. The chapter does not focus on any specific product or manufacturer. Instead, it presents general procedures for transforming typical measurement data into input parameters. The procedures can be thought of as a set of major guidelines for obtaining input parameters for performance models.

Chapter 13 wraps up the book by emphasizing the approach and methods used to develop and solve analytical performance models of client/server and Web-based systems. It also provides a unified view of the entire book.

Appendix A contains a glossary of the important terms introduced in the book.

Appendix B provides a quick reference manual of the MS Excel workbooks that accompany this book and describes the C program provided to derive burstiness parameters for HTTP logs.

Acknowledgments

The authors would like to thank their many colleagues for discussions that contributed substantially to this book. Special thanks go to our co-author in the first book of this series, Larry Dowdy of Vanderbilt University, for his enthusiasm and dedication to the field. Particular thanks go to Jeff Buzen of BGS Systems, Peter Denning of George Mason University, Jim Gray of Microsoft Research, and Leonard Kleinrock of UCLA for their praise of our work and permission to quote them on the cover. Jim Gray's suggestions on the manuscript are deeply appreciated. We would also like to thank our Acquisitions Editor at Prentice Hall PTR, Stephen Solomon, his assistant, Bart Blanken, our Production Editor, Craig Little, our Copyeditor, Kathy Finch, and our Marketing Manager, Dan Rush, for their support during the preparation and production of this book. Daniel Menascé would like to thank his students and colleagues at George Mason University for providing a stimulating work environment. He would also like to thank his parents for their love and guidance in life. Special recognition goes to his wife Gilda for a life full of love and companionship and to his children Flavio and Juliana for being a constant source of joy. Virgilio Almeida would like to thank his colleagues and students at UFMG and Boston University. In particular, he wants to thank Wagner Meira, Andre Cinelli, Cristina Murta, Jussara Almeida, Mark Crovella, Azer Bestravos, David Yates, and Carlos Cunha. Finally, Virgilio would also like to express his gratitude to his family, parents (in memoriam), brothers, and many relatives and friends. His wife Rejane and sons Pedro and Andre have always been a source of love, sweetness, joy, emotional support, and continuous encouragement.

Book's Web site and authors' addresses

A Web site will be maintained at www.cs.gmu.edu/~menasce/webbook/ to keep the readers informed about new developments related to the book. The authors' e-mail and postal addresses and Web sites are:

Prof. Daniel A. Menascé
Department of Computer Science, MS 4A5
George Mason University
Fairfax, VA 22030-4444
(703) 993-1537
menasce@cs.gmu.edu
http://www.cs.gmu.edu/faculty/menasce.html

Prof. Virgilio A. F. Almeida
Department of Computer Science
Universidade Federal de Minas Gerais
P.O. Box 920
31270-010 Belo Horizonte, MG
Brazil
+55 31 499-5887
virgilio@dcc.ufmg.br
http://www.dcc.ufmg.br/~virgilio

Chapter 1

WHEN PERFORMANCE IS A PROBLEM

1.1 Introduction

The Internet has experienced exponential growth since its inception. The number of Internet hosts can be counted by the tens of millions and grows at a very high rate all over the world, according to various surveys. The World Wide Web (WWW) has been growing at an even faster pace. The number of Web sites doubles in less than 6 mon. Applications such as digital libraries, electronic commerce, video on-demand, and distance learning increase Internet and Web traffic at even higher rates. Virtual stores on the Web allow you to buy cars, books, computers, and many other products [2]. Many Government agencies are using Web servers to disseminate documents and forms to individuals, public interest groups, private companies, and other Government agencies. Interactions between Government agencies and between them and citizens are being streamlined through Web-based services. Virtual public hearings on Government policies can be conducted through the Web.

Some popular Web sites receive millions of hits per day. It is not uncommon for these sites to exhibit extremely high response times. This has been a source of frustration for many Web users and of concern to the Webmasters of many Web sites. One of the most pressing problems faced by Web server administrators is the adequate sizing of their facilities so that they can provide the quality of service required by their users. This challenge requires them to be able to monitor the performance of the Web server and the intensity of the workload, to detect bottlenecks, to predict future capacity shortcomings, and to determine the most cost-effective way to upgrade their systems to overcome performance problems and cope with increasing workload demands.

When Internet technologies and protocols are used to build a corporation's internal network not accessible to outside users, it is referred as an *intranet*. Through the use of a variety of TCP/IP Internet development tools, intranets can easily bring information services to the desktop in a platform-independent manner through Web browsers, FTP clients, and Internet Relay Chat (IRC) clients. Industry analysts such as IDC, Zona Research, and Dataquest estimate the intranet market at several billion dollars [7]. Forrester Research reports that two-thirds of all midsize and large companies either have an intranet already installed or are in the process of implementing one [1]. Intranets have been increasingly used for multimedia-based delivery of computer-based training. Many large companies with thousands of geographically dispersed employees are making the transition from disks and CD-ROMs to Web-accessible training.

The Web and almost all intranet applications are special cases of client/server (C/S) computing. In this paradigm, work is split between two processes—the client and the server—usually running on separate interconnected machines, called the client and server machines. Many organizations are converting mainframe-based applications to C/S environments, and many are integrating their existing mainframes applications with new C/S environments. Many surveys have shown that, on average, 25% of the Information Technology (IT) budgets of large companies is devoted to C/S computing [6].

This book uses a quantitative approach to analyzing client/server and Web-based systems. This approach lends itself to the development of performance predictive models for capacity planning. Instead of relying on intuition, ad hoc procedures, and rules of thumb, we provide a uniform and formal way for dealing with performance problems. The performance models discussed here are based on the theory of queuing networks (QN).

Although some of the concepts about C/S and Web architectures may be familiar to some of the readers, these concepts are revisited here in light of quantitative and performance issues. A large number of numeric and practical examples help the reader understand the quantitative approach adopted in this book. Several MS Excel workbooks supported by Visual Basic modules accompany the book. These workbooks allow the readers to immediately put into practice the methods and models discussed here.

This chapter presents situations where performance is a problem in the context of client/server environments, intranets, Web servers, and Internet Service Providers (ISPs). These examples are used to illustrate concepts such as capacity planning, saturation, service levels, and workload intensity. The presentation in this chapter assumes that the reader is familiar, at least at a very superficial level, with the Internet, client/server systems, networking, and computer systems in general. The next chapter provides a more detailed discussion on these issues for readers who need this background knowledge to read the remaining chapters.

1.2 Client/Server Performance

Consider the example of a major car rental company that decides to migrate its operations from a mainframe-based environment to a client/server operation in which regional servers will handle regional transactions. The company has a total of 500,000 vehicles available in 3,500 locations all over the country. Reservations are taken 24 h/d and 7 d/wk by 1,800 customer representatives. An average of 360,000 reservations are made daily. Sixty percent of these reservations (216,000 = 0.6 x

360,000) are made during a peak period of 12 hours. So, the average number of reservations per hour during the peak period is equal to 21,667 (= 260,000 / 12), or 6 (= 21,667/3,600) transactions per second (tps). A mainframe-based environment supports the operations of the car rental company. Each of the 3,500 car pickup locations has a certain number of terminals connected to a concentrator. The concentrator is connected to the mainframe by a serial communications link. The reservation center has 1,800 terminals, one per customer representative, connected to the mainframe.

The company decided to replace the aging mainframe-based system to reduce the high maintenance costs they were incurring. They also wanted the new application to be user-friendly and have a well-designed Graphical User Interface (GUI) to increase the productivity of the customer representatives and improve customer satisfaction. These motivations lead the company to consider a client/server system such as the one depicted in Fig. 1.1. Each car rental location has a server that stores local databases and runs the transactions submitted by the location attendants. These transactions access both local data and data stored at the database servers located at the car reservation center. Each car rental location has a local area network (LAN) connecting the various attendant workstations to the local server. A router connects the LAN at a car rental location to a Wide Area Network (WAN). The designers of the new C/S system need to ensure that the new environment will exhibit at least the same performance as the current mainframe-based platform. The reservation center handles two types of transactions: reservations and road assistance requests. Company guidelines require that the average response time for reservation and road assistance transactions does not exceed two seconds and three seconds, respectively. Car rental locations handle two major types of transactions: car rental and reservations. Average response time requirements for both types of transactions must not exceed three seconds. These upper bounds on the response time are called *service levels*. Other examples of service levels include: minimum throughput exhibited by a server (e.g., at least 80 file operations/sec), minimum server availability (e.g., server available at least 99% of the time), percent of transactions that exhibit a response time less than or equal to a certain value (e.g., 95% of the transactions must exhibit a response time not exceeding 2 seconds).

The following are some examples of important questions to be answered by the system designers to ensure that the C/S system performance will be as expected:

- What kind of servers should be used at the car rental locations? Answering this question amounts to specifying the number and type of processors to be used, the number and type of disks, and the type of operating system (e.g., Unix or NT).

- Should a transaction processing monitor (e.g., BEA's Tuxedo, Tandem's Pathway, Microsoft's Transaction Server, Transarc's Encina, and AT&T's Top End) be used?

- What type of servers and storage boxes should be used to support the database

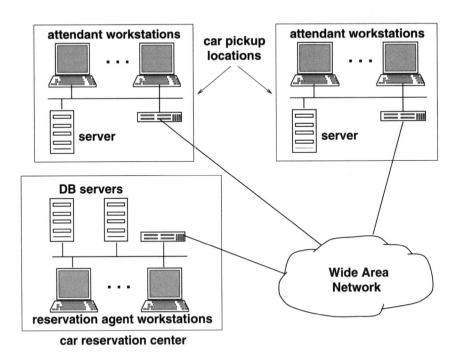

Figure 1.1. Client/server-based environment for the car rental example.

servers at the reservation center? Issues such as number and type of processors, amount of main memory, number and type of disks, database management system (e.g., Oracle, Sybase, DB/2, and Informix) to be used, and operating system must be specified.

- What kind of networking technology and bandwidth should be used at the car rental location and reservation center LANs? Some alternatives include Ethernet (10 Mbps), Token Ring (4 or 16 Mbps), and Fast Ethernet (100 Mbps).

- What should be the bandwidth of the Wide Area Network?

These are typical *capacity planning* questions. The answer to these and other questions may strongly impact the performance of the C/S system. It is also important to understand how a transaction's response time is decomposed and to identify bottlenecks for each type of transaction. Table 1.1 illustrates the percentage of the response time seen by an agent at a car rental location that is attributed to each major system component. In this example, more than 50% of the response time is dominated by the database server—the bottleneck for this type of transaction. The

Table 1.1. Response Time Breakdown for Reservation Transactions
Submitted by Car Rental Locations

Component of Response Time	Percentage of Total (%)
Client workstation at car rental location	5
LAN at car rental location	5
Application server at car rental location	25
Wide Area Network	10
LAN at the reservation center	4
Database server at reservation center	51

bottleneck is the component where a transaction spends most of its time. Response time improvements are limited by the time spent at the bottleneck.

Imagine now that the rental car company decides to launch a new promotional campaign designed to boost car rentals by 5, 10, and then 15% with respect to the current level. As a system administrator, you are asked if the system will support the corresponding increase in the number of transactions being submitted to the system, while maintaining the desired response time within the desired levels. Using the models and techniques discussed in later chapters of this book, you would be able to predict the response time of each of the major types of transactions: reservations made at car rental locations (local reservations), road assistance requests, car pickup, and phone reservations. Table 1.2 shows these response times, in seconds, for the current load and for increases of 5, 10, and 15% of the current load. Load is defined in this case as the average transaction arrival rate measured in tps.

Table 1.2 shows that the increase in response time is not linear with the load increase as depicted in Fig. 1.2. For example, a 15% increase in the arrival rate of phone reservations generates a fivefold increase in response time. In Chaps. 8 and 9 you will understand why performance of computer systems does not vary linearly with the load. An analysis of the graph of Fig. 1.2 shows that local reservations will exceed their maximum acceptable response time of 2 sec at around a 7% increase in the current load, phone reservations will be able to support a 10% increase in the current load before the 2-sec response time service level is violated, car pickup transactions will not get near their 3-sec threshold, even when the load increases by 15%, and road assistance transactions will exhibit a response time slightly higher (about 7% higher) than its 3-sec threshold when the arrival rate increases by 15%. We say that if any of the service levels has been violated, as in the case of the reservation transactions at a 15% higher load, the capacity of the system reaches *saturation*. The term saturation should not be used to indicate the case when the utilization of a device (e.g., CPU, disk, LAN segment) reaches 100%, since it is possible for service levels to be violated well before the utilization of any device reaches 100%.

Besides predicting if performance requirements will be met by either a new

Table 1.2. Response Times for Various Load Values (sec)

Transaction	Current Load	Current Load + 5%	Current Load + 10%	Current Load + 15%
Local reservation	1.28	1.67	2.45	5.06
Road assistance	0.64	0.87	1.37	3.20
Car pickup	0.64	0.76	0.94	1.23
Phone reservation	0.85	1.16	1.82	4.24

system or an existing system under a higher load situation, we have to be able to determine why performance will not be met. For instance, the predictive model we used to obtain the curves of Fig. 1.2 tells us that local reservation transactions spend 83% of their time doing input/output (I/O) at the database (DB) server located at the reservation center. Improving the DB server performance should be the first step toward ensuring that reservation transactions will meet their service level requirement of two-second response time. This can be accomplished in many ways, including spreading the same I/O load among more disks, using faster disks, or increasing the cache size at either the storage box or at the DB server.

1.3   The Capacity Planning Concept

The questions and analyses presented in the example of Sec. 1.2 are typical of capacity planning activities. Let us now introduce the concept of capacity planning in more general terms.

Capacity planning is the process of *predicting* when future load levels will *saturate* the system and of determining the most cost-effective way of delaying system saturation as much as possible. The prediction must consider the evolution of the workload, due to existing and new applications, and the desired *service levels* [5].

We would like to emphasize the importance of the term *prediction* in the definition of capacity planning. In the car rental company example, we were asked to predict what the response time would be if more reservations arrived at the system per unit time. It would not be wise to use the "wait-and-see" approach, namely let the workload intensity increase and then find out what happens to the response time.

The lack of a proactive and continuous capacity planning procedure may lead to unexpected unavailability and performance problems caused by bogged-down routers, LAN segments, servers, or other components. Down times may be financially devastating to a company. As pointed out in [3], the average down time cost per hour may range from thousands to millions of dollars depending on the type of industry. For instance, the average hourly down time cost in credit card transactions is estimated to be $6.5 million. Poor performance of a computer system may generate customer dissatisfaction and damages to the external image of the company,

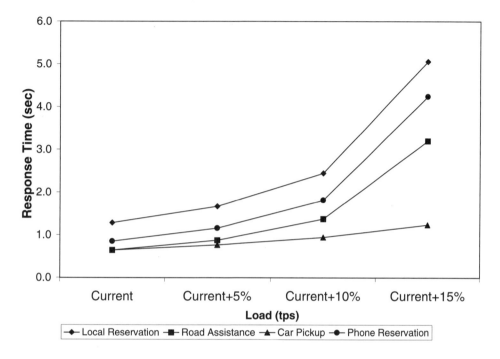

Figure 1.2. Response time vs. load for the car rental C/S system example.

leading to loss of business. Another reason for planning ahead is that solving a performance problem may not be instantaneous. Even if a company has the financial resources to buy the needed hardware and/or software to solve a capacity problem, it may take awhile until a decision is reached on the best technical approach to solve the problem, obtain quotes from vendors, go through the procurement cycle, wait for component delivery, install, and test the new components. It may also be the case that the performance problems stem from a poorly designed architecture, in which case the solution is more difficult and generally more time-consuming. This observation contradicts some people's erroneous belief that capacity planning is not important, provided one has enough money to add more hardware to the system when needed. In summary, capacity planning is important:

- to avoid financial losses

- to ensure customer satisfaction

- to preserve a company's external image

- because capacity problems cannot be solved instantaneously

The use of capacity planning techniques should not be restricted to situations where major changes are anticipated in the workload intensity or even when new applications will be deployed. There is a lot to be gained by making capacity planning a routine process carried out on a continuous basis. Many times, significant performance gains can be obtained by just reallocating servers to different LAN segments, rewriting critical portions of the C/S applications, or even creating indexes on some critical DB tables. These performance gains do not require spending money on new or faster components. However, as with any capacity planning analysis, it is important to predict ahead of time what the benefits of each alternative will be before implementing them. Prediction requires simulation or analytic models, as discussed later. Intranet- and Internet-based applications are special cases of the C/S paradigm. The importance of capacity planning in this context is illustrated in the next sections.

1.4   Web Server Performance

A virtual car dealership provides users with a Web site they can visit to search and submit purchase requests for used and new cars. The virtual dealership has 1,300 affiliated car dealers that provide information about the vehicles available on their parking lots. A full description of each vehicle, including make, model, year, accessories, mileage, price, and a photo are stored in a database accessible through the Web site. The Web server receives three types of requests:

- requests for documents, and images

- requests to search the database according to the following criteria: make, model, and distance of dealer from buyer

- purchase requests

It is important that response time at the Web server be acceptable, otherwise users will not use the service and the virtual dealership and affiliated car dealers will lose business. The virtual car dealership wants to negotiate additional partnership agreements with car dealers. This will increase the availability of makes and models and will increase the number of requests submitted to the Web site. The new agreements will be phased in gradually and are expected to increase the current arrival rate of requests by 10% at the first stage, then by 20%, and finally by 30% with respect to the current rate.

The critical request is the search transaction. It was observed that if the response time for this transaction exceeds 4 seconds but remains below 6 seconds, then 60% of the search transactions will be lost because users will abort the search and potential sales will be lost. If the response time exceeds 6 seconds at the Web Server, then 95% of the search requests will be aborted. We assume that 5% of the search transactions generate a car sale and that a sale generates US$18,000 on the average in revenues.

Management wants to answer the following questions:

- Will the Web server support the load increase while preserving the response time below 4 seconds?

- If not, at which point will its capacity be saturated and why?

- How much money could be lost daily if the Web server saturates when the load increases?

Table 1.3 summarizes the results obtained by the capacity planner by using performance models such as the ones presented later in this book. The table shows results for the current load intensity and for loads intensities 10, 20, and 30% higher than the current load. The first row shows the number of search requests submitted to the Web server per day. This number includes the searches that are aborted due to high response times. The second row indicates the predicted response time for each scenario. Note that when the load is 20% higher, the response time is in the range between 4 and 6 seconds, and therefore 60% of the transactions are lost as indicated in the third row. When the load is 30% higher the response time exceeds 6 seconds and 95% of the transactions are lost. Row four shows the actual number of vehicles sold per day, taking into account the increase in the number of search requests and the loss of sales due to aborted transactions. Row five shows the daily revenue. These values should be compared with the revenue that would be potentially obtained if the response time stayed below 4 sec (see row six). Finally, the last row shows the lost daily revenue caused by the very high response times.

Over US$102 million will be lost daily when the load increases by 30%. As the example illustrates, the consequences of not being able to predict the future

Table 1.3. Capacity Planning Results for Virtual Car Dealer

	Current	Current + 10%	Current + 20%	Current + 30%
Searches per day	92,448	101,693	110,938	120,182
Response time (sec)	2.86	3.80	5.67	11.28
Percent sales lost (%)	0	0	60	95
Sales per day	4,622	5,085	2,219	300
Daily revenue (in US$1,000)	83,203	91,524	39,938	5,408
Potential daily revenue (in US$1,000)	83,203	91,524	99,844	108,164
Lost daily revenue (in US$1,000)	—	—	59,906	102,756

performance of the Web server under a load increase can bring undesirable financial consequences.

The next section shows how performance is an important issue in intranet design and operation.

1.5   Intranet Performance

A major airplane manufacturer has 60,000 employees, including engineers, computer scientists, managers, technicians, and administrative staff. Almost every employee of the company has access to a PC or a workstation. The company is implementing an intranet to conduct business in a more efficient manner. The intranet will be used to support corporate training, for help desk support, to disseminate internal corporate news, and to handle personnel forms and memos. The first application to be implemented is help desk support.

The help desk application will be supported by a server where Frequently Asked Questions (FAQs) about common hardware and software problems will be posted. The server will also have a database of common problems and solutions to be searched via the Web. Finally, users may use a Web interface to submit their problem description if they cannot solve it through the FAQs or through the database of common problems. It is assumed that 10% of the employees, on average, submit a request to the help desk application server every day. Seventy percent of these requests fall during the peak period between 10:00 A.M. and 12:00 P.M. and then from 2:00 P.M. to 4:00 P.M. Thus the help desk server will get $4,200 \ (= \ 0.7 \times 60,000 \times 0.1)$ requests during the peak period. Since these requests come in a 4-h period, the average arrival rate is $0.29 \ (= \ 4,200/4/3,600)$ requests/sec.

The company intends to change the operating system on all its client PCs. This upgrade is likely to create a surge in the number of requests submitted to the help desk server. The company wants to predict the performance of the Web server for the help desk application as a function of the arrival rate of requests. Figure 1.3 shows that when the arrival rate of requests doubles from the current value of about 0.3 tps to 0.6 tps, the response time approaches 50 sec, more than a threefold increase from the 16-sec response time at the current load. At about 0.6 tps, we start to see a saturation on the response time value due to the fact that the number of requests in the system reaches its maximum value. Connections start to be refused, showing a very poor performance of the help desk application.

There are many possible alternatives to solve the performance problem experienced by the help desk server, including upgrading the server's CPU, adding more CPUs, more disks, or even splitting the load among more servers. These and other alternatives can be investigated with the models discussed in later chapters.

The next section presents performance issues from the perspective of an Internet Service provider.

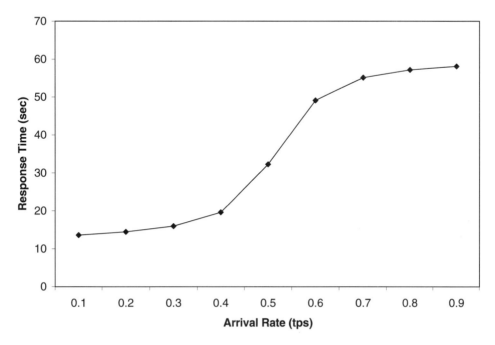

Figure 1.3. Response time at the intranet help desk server.

1.6   Internet Service Provider (ISP) Performance

An Internet Service Provider (ISP) has 100,000 users. On the average, each one establishes a session twice per day lasting for 12 min. Customers who do not find an available modem to connect, get a busy signal. The current rate structure used by the ISP is volume-based—customers have 2 h of free time per month, after which they pay by the minute of connected time. The ISP intends to change the rate structure to a flat-rate one in which customers will pay a flat fee independent of the amount of time they spend connected to the service. The ISP expects that when they make the announcement, they will get a significant boost in the number of users. They also expect users to spend more time using the service since they will not be charged by connection time.

The management of the ISP wants to know how many modems they should have in order to guarantee that the probability of a customer finding all modems busy is less than 5%. They currently have 1,500 modems. Using models to be discussed in later chapters of this book, the performance analyst was able to show what would happen with the probability that a user gets a busy signal as the number of users

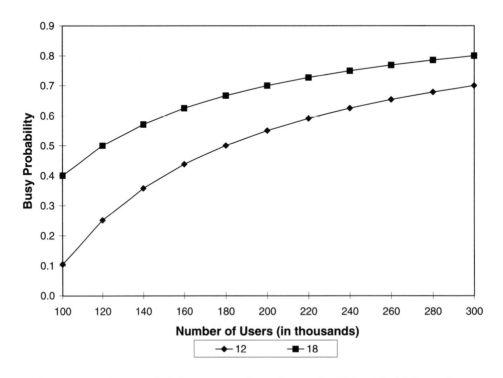

Figure 1.4. Busy probability vs. number of users for ISP with 1,500 modems.

varies. Figure 1.4 shows this probability for two values of the session duration: 12 min and 18 min. As the graph shows, if the number of users doubles, the busy probability increases to 55% for 12-min sessions and to 70% for 18-min sessions.

At this point, users would start to complaint bitterly about the quality of service they are getting. Many would likely close their accounts and some might even consider suing the ISP. Figure 1.5 shows how the busy probability varies as a function of the number of modems. The figure shows that if the ISP wants to keep a 5% busy probability, it needs 2,400 modems when sessions last 18 sec on the average.

1.7   Summary

Modern computer systems are becoming increasingly complex and dependent on networking technologies such as the ones available on the Internet. Computing is distributing between various processes such as in the client/server paradigm. Deploying applications that rely on Web servers, intranets, and client/server tech-

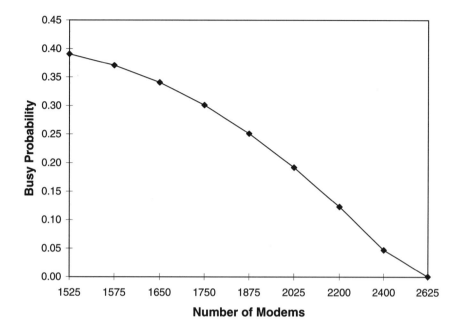

Figure 1.5. Busy probability vs. number of modems for ISP for 18-min sessions and 100,000 users.

nologies is a challenge both in assuring that the functionality will be present and in guaranteeing that the functionality will be delivered with an acceptable performance. A very nice Web server with numerous functions is of no use if takes forever to connect to it or to get useful information from it. Users tend to avoid these servers. As illustrated in some of the examples in this chapter, performance problems can bring all sorts of undesired consequences, including financial and sales loss, decreased productivity, and a bad reputation for a company.

The situations presented in this chapter emphasize the importance of being able to plan ahead for the capacity of networked systems. Capacity planning involves being able to predict when the existing applications will fail to meet the required performance levels. Performance prediction is accomplished through performance models presented in later chapters.

Capacity planning is also important when predicting the performance of a new application under development or when predicting the performance of applications that are being downsized to C/S environments [4]. An increasing number of organizations are moving mission-critical applications into client-server systems. Application designers are faced with a large number of software architectural choices that severely impact performance and cost. Examples include the distribution of work between client and server, use of three-tiered C/S architectures, distribution of functions and database tables among servers, types of clients and servers, and network connectivity. Waiting until the application goes into production may be disastrous and may require costly code redesign and rewrite. Performance models can also be applied in this context to ensure that new C/S applications meet performance requirements.

BIBLIOGRAPHY

[1] D. BAUM, Intranet politics and technologies, *Byte*, May 1997.

[2] S. HAMILTON, E-Commerce for the 21st century, *Computer*, IEEE Comput. Soc., pp. 44–47, May 1997.

[3] V. McCARTHY, Performance tools kill the gremlins on your net, *Datamation*, Sept. 1996.

[4] D. A. MENASCÉ, A framework for software performance engineering of client/server systems, *Proc. 1997 Computer Measurement Group Conf.*, Orlando, FL, Dec. 1997, pp. 460–469.

[5] D. A. MENASCÉ, V. A. F. ALMEIDA, and L. W. DOWDY, *Capacity Planning and Performance Modeling: From Mainframes to Client-Server Systems*. Upper Saddle River, NJ: Prentice Hall, 1994.

[6] A. RAI, R. PATNAYAKUNI, and N. PATNAYAKUNI, Technology investment and business performance, *Commun. ACM*, vol. 40, no. 7, pp. 89–97, July 1997.

[7] E. TITTEL and J. M. STEWART, *Intranet Bible*. Foster City, CA: IDG, 1997.

Chapter 2

WHAT ARE CLIENT/SERVER SYSTEMS?

2.1 Introduction

With the advent of computer networks in the early 1970s, the computer and communication industries started to converge, and computing paradigms started to change as a result. Several factors, such as the sharp decline in the cost per millions of instructions per second (MIP) and megabytes of RAM helped bring computing from remote mainframes to people's desktops. Moore's law, an empirical observation, has been quite accurate at predicting that the speed of microprocessors doubles every 18 mon. If this rate of growth were sustained, computers would be 11 billion times faster in 2047 when compared with 1997 performance! More conservative estimates say that computers will be 100,000 times faster in 2047 than in 1997 [3]; still quite an impressive improvement. Computers will be everywhere, including in the human body and in every single appliance. And, they will all be interconnected [5].

The client/server model emerged out of the convergence of computers and communications, the availability of inexpensive and powerful desktop computers with Graphical User Interfaces (GUI) and multimedia presentation devices and advanced forms of data input, including voice input. By bringing the computation closer to the user and his/her business processes and by providing more flexible and easier to use interfaces, client/server systems can increase productivity, increase customer satisfaction, and cut down significantly on training costs.

This chapter presents a brief discussion of local and wide area networks and their protocols, including TCP/IP, Ethernet, Token Ring, and FDDI. The chapter defines the C/S computing paradigm and discusses various kinds of servers, such as file servers, database servers, application servers, groupware servers, object servers, and Web servers. Various architectural client/server issues including fat versus thin clients, two-tier versus three-tier C/S architectures are presented.

16

2.2 The World of Networks

This section provides a brief introduction to computer networking. The origins of networking, the various types of networks, and their protocols are discussed. The common thread throughout the discussion is *performance*.

2.2.1 Genesis

The computer networks we use today have their origin in the ARPANET, a packet switched computer network, developed in the late 1960s under the leadership and sponsorship of the then Advanced Research Projects Agency (ARPA), now DARPA, of the United States Department of Defense (DoD). The first nodes of the ARPANET were delivered by Bolt, Beranek & Newman (BBN) in the early 1970s [2]. The motivation for building the ARPANET was to share resources such as the timesharing systems developed in the 1960s. However, one of the major accomplishments of the ARPANET was to demonstrate the usefulness of a computer network as a powerful tool to enhance human communication and interaction through e-mail.

Performance concerns have been present since the early days of the ARPANET. Leonard Kleinrock at UCLA led the research that developed queuing models of packet switched networks and established the measurement and network management facilities that collected and interpreted a vast array of extremely useful data used to understand and redesign the network and its protocols [12], [13].

The term *Internet* was introduced in 1983 when the ARPANET was split into two networks, a military one—MILNET—and a reduced version of the ARPANET. The Internet as we know it today is a large collection of interconnected WANs worldwide. The cornerstones of the Internet are its networking protocol, IP, and its process-to-process protocol, TCP, invented by Vint Cerf and Bob Kahn. The TCP/IP suite of protocols is discussed in Sec. 2.2.3.

The Internet has experienced exponential growth since its inception. The number of computers connected to the Internet grew from about 10 nodes in the early days of the ARPANET to almost about 100 million nodes in less than 30 yr. Currently, virtually all major companies, educational and research institutions at all levels, hospitals, and governmental agencies at the local, state, and federal levels are connected to the Internet. The number of households with access to the Internet is growing at amazing rates worldwide. As more and more people become users of the Internet and become available to participate in communications with others, and become information providers, the value of the Internet grows. Metcalfe has stated, in what is known as Metcalfe's Law, that the value of a network is proportional to the square of the number of its subscribers and the value of a network to a subscriber is proportional to the number of subscribers [3].

2.2.2 Types of Networks

Networks are usually classified as Wide Area Networks (WANs) or Local Area Networks (LANs), according to the size of the geographical area covered by the network.

Wide Area Networks (WANs)

Wide Area Networks (WANs) can span a city, multiple cities, countries, or continents [6]. The basic technology used by WANs is *packet switching*. In this technology, messages transmitted between two computers, also called *hosts*, are broken down into units called *packets*. Packets have a maximum size and have a header with fields containing the necessary addressing information to allow a packet to be routed from its source to its destination, as well as sequencing information needed to reassemble the message at the destination from its constituent packets.

The building blocks of a WAN are the *packet switches* and high-speed (e.g., from 45 Mbps to several gigabits/s) links connecting the switches. Packet switches are communication computers that store incoming packets, examine their headers, look up routing tables to make decisions for the next packet switch to send the packet on its way to the destination, and place the packet on the output queue for the selected outgoing link. This method is called *store and forward*. Some of the technologies used to build WANs include *X.25*, a standard of the International Telecommunications Union (ITU), Integrated Services Digital Network (ISDN), a service offered by many telephone companies that integrates voice and data over ordinary telephone lines, *Frame Relay*, a high-speed wide area network service offered by long-distance carriers, *Switched Multi-megabit Data Service (SMDS)*, another high-speed wide area network offered by long-distance carrier, and Asynchronous Transfer Mode (ATM), a packet switched technology that uses fixed size small packets (53 bytes), called cells, to provide fast switching to voice, video, and data over WANs [6].

Local Area Networks (LANs)

Local Area Networks are typically confined to a building or a set of closely located buildings such as in a campus of a university. There are many different LAN technologies. The most popular are 10-Mbps Ethernet [9], 100-Mbps Ethernet [10], 4- or 16-Mbps Token Ring [11], and 100-Mbps Fiber Distributed Data Interconnect (FDDI) [18].

The Ethernet technology was invented by Robert M. Metcalfe in the early 1970s and constitutes a milestone in local area networking [14]. Ethernet LANs have a bus topology (see Fig. 2.1a). All computers connect to a shared coaxial cable through a Network Interface Card (NIC). Packets transmitted by one NIC can be received by all others. This is called broadcast communication. Since packets contain the address of the destination, only the destination NIC will copy the packet to the computer's main memory. Since there is no central coordinator to decide which computer can use the shared medium, a distributed approach, called Carrier Sense with Multiple Access/Collision Detection (CSMA/CD), is used. If an NIC wants to transmit a packet it "listens" to the medium to check if there is a transmission in progress—this is called *carrier sensing*. If a transmission is in progress, the NIC waits before attempting again. It is possible, however, for two NICs that are far apart in the cable to attempt a transmission at about the same time, detect a free medium, transmit their packets and interfere with each other. This interference is

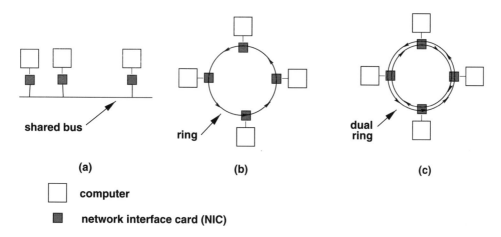

Figure 2.1. (a) Bus-based LAN. (b) Ring-based LAN. (c) Dual ring-based LAN.

called a *collision*. Ethernet NICs are equipped to detect collisions and stop transmitting a packet when collisions are detected. NICs wait for a randomly selected
time period before attempting to retransmit their packets.

As traffic on an Ethernet increases, the probability of a collision increases and
the network throughput decreases as more of the bandwidth is spent on collisions
and retransmissions.

Token Ring was invented at IBM Research Labs and, as the name says, is based
on a ring topology as shown in Fig. 2.1b. A sender inserts the bits of its packet into
the ring. The packet goes around the ring and is copied by the NIC specified in the
destination address field of the packet. The packet continues its flow around the
ring back to the sender who removes the packet and compares the received packet
with the packet sent for error control. If two or more NICs attempted to transmit
simultaneously, an interference would occur. In a Token Ring LAN, access to the
ring is controlled by a *token*, a special bit pattern that circulates through the ring.
The NIC with the token transmits. When it is done, it passes the token to the next
NIC in the ring. If an NIC does not have any packets to transmit, it just passes the
token to the next station.

As more stations are added to a Token Ring, the delay in obtaining a token
increases because the token will have to circulate through more NICs, and the
probability that the token is seized by other stations increases.

Another type of ring LAN technology is Fiber Distributed Data Interconnect
(FDDI). FDDI uses optical fibers, uses a token-passing mechanism, and improves on
Token Ring reliability by adding a second ring (see Fig. 2.1c). Data flow in opposite
directions in the two rings so that if a station fails, the hardware can reconfigure
the ring and turn it into a single functioning ring, bypassing the malfunctioning
station [6].

There are two types of limits on the number of stations that can be connected to a LAN: physical and performance limits. For example, the Ethernet standard limits an Ethernet cable to 500 m in length and requires a minimum separation of 3 m between stations [6]. Performance considerations may limit the number of stations on an LAN. To reduce traffic on a LAN and improve performance, LAN administrators segment larger LANs into LAN segments with fewer stations each. These segments are joined by connecting devices such as routers and bridges [17]. Stations that communicate more often should be in the same segment in order to decrease the load on routers and bridges. Analytic expressions for LAN performance can be found in [4].

The LAN to WAN Connection

LANs usually connect to WANs through dedicated leased lines at T1 (1.544 Mbps) or T3 (45 Mbps) speeds. The adequate sizing of the LAN-to-WAN link will be discussed in Chaps. 9 and 10, in light of performance models. Figure 2.2 shows the networking topology for a company headquartered in Los Angeles, with branches in Chicago and New York. The three locations are connected through a Frame Relay WAN. The headquarters has an Ethernet and a Token Ring LAN connected to a 100-Mbps FDDI ring backbone. The backbone connects to the Frame Relay WAN through a T1 link. The Chicago branch has two LAN segments connected by a bridge. The router to the WAN is located in one of the LAN segments. Finally, the New York branch has a single 16-Mbps Token Ring LAN connected to the WAN by a router.

The Home to WAN Connection

Currently, there are many alternatives for individuals to connect their home computers, and even their home LANs, to a WAN. The simplest and cheapest is the use of dial-up analog modems at speeds ranging from 14.4 to 56 Kbps. The next fastest alternative is ISDN Basic Rate Interface (BRI). It requires a dial-up digital modem and provides speeds of 128 Kbps. If higher speeds are required from ISDN services, one can use ISDN Primary Rate Interface (PRI) that delivers 1.544 Mbps. The same speed can be obtained by leasing a T1 line. T1-like speeds can also be obtained with High-Bit-Rate Digital Subscriber Line (HDSL) but with more flexibility. An asymmetric version of HDSL, Asymmetric Digital Subscriber Line (ADSL), provides 640 Kbps outgoing and 6 Mbps incoming. This asymmetry is advantageous for Web access, since the bandwidth requirements for fast image and video downloads are higher than for sending requests to Web servers. Finally, cable TV companies offer 10 Mbps cable modems. Some are just one-way, but some are already offering two-way communications using a two-channel modem [16].

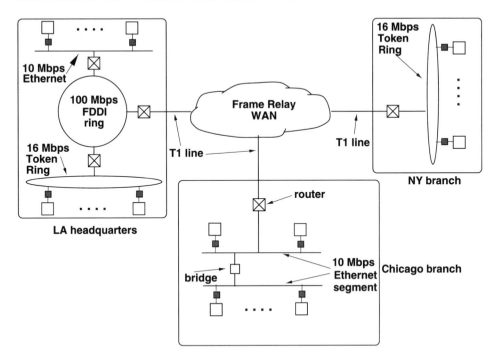

Figure 2.2. Example of LAN-WAN connectivity.

2.2.3   Protocols

The communication between two computers or two processes over a computer network is governed by a set of rules called a *protocol*. Let A and B be two entities that need to communicate over a computer network by exchanging a series of messages. A needs to address B properly so that messages from A to B arrive at the proper destination. This is accomplished by the *addressing* and *routing* functions of the protocol. Messages from A to B may be lost or become corrupted due to noise or failures in the network. The protocol must then provide *error detection*, *error recovery*, and *sequence control* functions. If A sends messages at a much faster rate than can be consumed by B, the protocol must provide *flow control* mechanisms to regulate the relative speeds of senders and receivers to avoid buffer overflows or discarded messages. So, the main functions of a protocol are: addressing, routing, error detection and recovery, sequence control, and flow control.

The interaction between two entities A and B can be *connectionless* or *connection oriented*. In the first case, messages from A to B are independent from one another and may arrive at the destination in an order different from the order in which they were transmitted. This type of protocol is good when the data to be exchanged between the two entities fit into the maximum data unit allowed by the protocol. This way, the message does not have to be fragmented into more than one data unit, and sequencing is not an issue. Connection-oriented protocols are used when messages that are much larger than the maximum data unit are to be transmitted. In this case, sequencing and error recovery are important. Before A and B start to exchange messages, a connection between them has to be established, much like when you need to talk to someone over the phone. You first dial the number of the party you want to talk to. A signal travels through the telephone network to establish a connection. If the line at the other end is not busy, a signal travels back to indicate that the conversation may start. Connection-oriented protocols are useful when large files need to be transferred between the communicating entities, because sequencing, error recovery, and flow control are important considerations for this type of application.

A protocol specification consists of two elements: the syntax and semantics. The *syntax* of the protocol specifies all messages exchanged between the entities, their formats, and the meaning of each field of the message. The *semantics* of a protocol specifies the actions taken by each entity when specific events, such as arrival of messages or timeouts, occur.

The design of a computer communication protocol may be a complex task. For this reason, protocol designers use a *layered* architecture in protocol construction. The International Organization for Standardization (ISO) defined a seven-layer model called *Reference Model for Open Systems Interconnection* [18]. The seven layers from 1 to 7 are: physical, data link, network, transport, session, presentation, and application. Each entity at layer n communicates only with remote nth-layer entities. An nth layer entity uses services provided by $(n-1)$th entities as illustrated in Fig. 2.3.

As shown in the picture, data units exchanged between nth-layer entities have to be physically processed by layers n to 1 at the sending computer, transported through the network and moved from layer 1 to n at the receiving end. Each entity at layer n exchanges a Protocol Data Unit (PDU) with a remote layer n entity. A PDU has a layer n header and a layer n data. The layer n PDU becomes layer $(n-1)$ data as shown in Fig. 2.4.

The next subsections present a brief description of the two most important protocols in the Internet: the Internet Protocol (IP) and the Transmission Control Protocol (TCP). This suite of protocols is known as TCP/IP and is at the core of the Internet. Figure 2.5 shows the layering of important TCP/IP-based protocols. The figure shows that IP is a network layer protocol on top of which we find two transport layer protocols: TCP—a connection-oriented protocol—and User Datagram Protocol (UDP)—a connectionless protocol.

HTTP (the Web protocol), the File Transfer Protocol (FTP), and TELNET (an interactive login protocol) use TCP. Network File System (NFS), Domain Name Server (DNS), and Simple Network Management Protocol (SNMP) are built on top of UDP. Note that NFS uses a Remote Procedure Call (RPC) protocol.

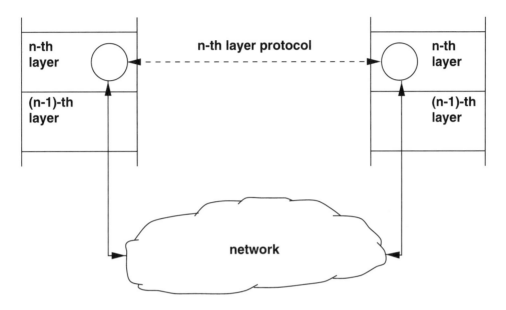

Figure 2.3. Layered approach to protocol design.

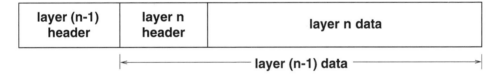

Figure 2.4. Nesting of Protocol Data Units.

Internet Protocol

IP specifies the formats of packets sent across the Internet, the mechanisms used to forward these packets through a collection of networks, and routers from source to destination [6].

Every host connected to the Internet has an address, called *IP Address*, which is unique across the Internet. This address, a 32-bit number, is usually represented by a dotted decimal notation such as 129.2.0.37, where each of the four numbers (in the range from 0 to 255) represents the value of 8 bits in the 32-bit address. The 32 bits are divided into two parts: a prefix and a suffix. The prefix is used to indicate a network and the suffix a host within the network. The number of bits allocated to the prefix determines the number of unique network numbers and the number of bits in the suffix determines the number of hosts per network.

The data unit transported by IP is called an *IP datagram*. IP is a connectionless

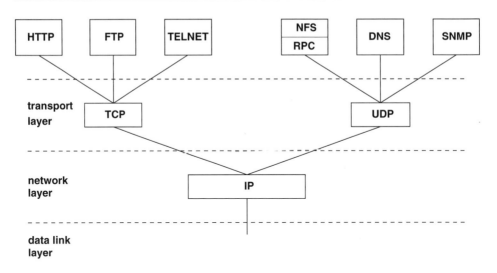

Figure 2.5. Layering of TCP/IP-based protocols.

protocol that provides no end-to-end guarantee of delivery; datagrams may be lost. IP datagrams can be delivered out of order; two datagrams sent in sequence from a source host to the same destination are routed independently, may take different routes, and may arrive out of order at the destination [19]. IP lets TCP take care of end-to-end error recovery.

The IP header is 20 bytes long. Of these, 8 bytes are used for the IP address of the source host and 8 bytes for the IP address of the destination host. An important function of IP is *routing* of datagrams from source to destination. Every host and every router on the Internet implements IP. The IP implementation at a router maintains an in-memory routing table that is used to search for the next router or host (if final destination) to forward the datagram (see Fig. 2.6).

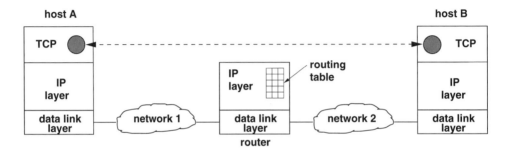

Figure 2.6. IP at hosts and routers.

The current version of IP, IPv4, with its 32-bit address field is reaching its limitations as the number of hosts connected to the Internet grows exponentially. The new version of IP, IPv6, extends the source and destination address fields from 32 to 128 bits, among other improvements including support for audio and video [6].

Transmission Control Protocol

TCP provides a connection-oriented, reliable, flow-controlled, end-to-end communication service between processes running at hosts connected through an internet. TCP guarantees that data will be delivered in the order transmitted, with no missing data. TCP allows the two end points of a connection to exchange data simultaneously, that is in full-duplex mode (see Fig. 2.6). TCP provides a stream interface, which means that it accepts a continuous stream of bytes from the application to be sent through the connection. The PDU exchanged at the TCP level is called a *segment*. The header of a TCP segment is 20 bytes long. TCP sends segments within IP datagrams.

Before data can be sent between two hosts, a connection has to be established between them. TCP implements a reliable connection establishment mechanism, called *three-way handshake* [6], [19]. Figure 2.7 shows the exchange of segments that takes place for connection establishment, data transmission, and connection termination. The vertical lines are time axes at hosts A and B. Time increases from top to bottom. Diagonal arrows indicate segments being sent between A and B.

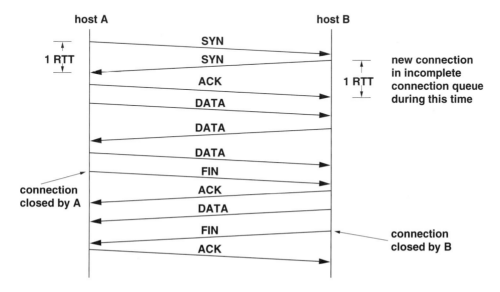

Figure 2.7. TCP connection establishment and termination.

Assume that host A establishes a connection with host B, exchanges data with B, and then closes the connection. Host A starts by sending a synchronization segment (SYN) to host B, which replies with another SYN segment. This exchange of SYN segments takes 1 RTT (round-trip time). The connection at host B is not considered complete until an acknowledgment (ACK) segment from host A arrives. During the time interval since host B sent its SYN segment to A and until it receives the ACK from A, the connection stays in a queue of incomplete connections. A connection stays in this queue for 1 RTT. If a host receives many requests to open connections from very remote servers, the incomplete connection queue may fill up, preventing the host from accepting new connections. This problem is faced by busy HTTP servers that receive many connections from remote clients [20]. When the ACK is received at host B, the three-way handshake process is complete and the connection is established. Now, data may be exchanged in both directions.

TCP connection closing is called *half-close* because when a host closes a connection, it is indicating it will no longer send data to the other host, but it is still willing to accept data. For example, in Fig. 2.7, host A closes the connection from A to B by sending a FIN segment to B, which is acknowledged by an ACK segment. When host B wants to terminate the connection from B to A, it sends a FIN segment to A, which is acknowledged with an ACK segment. So, three segments are needed to establish a TCP connection and four are needed to terminate it in both directions.

TCP uses acknowledgements, timeouts, and retransmissions for error control. Flow control is implemented by TCP through a *sliding window* mechanism [6], [19]. The window size is the maximum number of bytes that can be sent before an acknowledgement is received. Figure 2.8-a shows an exchange of three data segments with a window size of one data segment. It takes $3 \times RTT + 2 \times \delta$ to send the three segments, where RTT is a round trip time and δ is the protocol processing time at the host. For low-latency networks, $RTT \gg \delta$. So, the throughput X_1 for a window size of 1 is

$$X_1 = 3/(3 \times RTT + 2 \times \delta) \approx 1/RTT. \tag{2.2.1}$$

Figure 2.8-b shows the same exchange of three data segments with a window of size three. It takes $RTT + 2 \times \delta$ time units to send the three data segments. So, the throughput X_3 for a window size of three is

$$X_3 = 3/(RTT + 2 \times \delta) \approx 3/RTT = 3 \times X_1. \tag{2.2.2}$$

So, the throughput for a window size of three data segments is three times the throughput with a window size of one. It is clear that one cannot increase the window size continuously and obtain an ever-increasing throughput, because the bandwidth of the network limits the maximum throughput achieved in the connection [6]. So,

$$X_w = \min (B, w \times X_1) \tag{2.2.3}$$

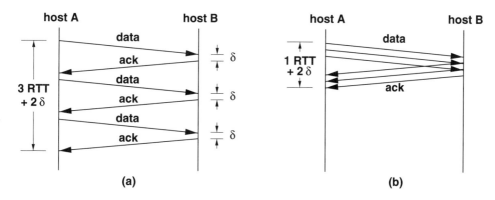

Figure 2.8. (a) TCP with window size = 1. (b) TCP with window size = 3.

where X_w is the throughput of the TCP connection in bytes per second with a window size w, and B is the bandwidth, in bytes per second, of the underlying network. Let w^* be the window size for which the throughput gain, defined as, X_{w^*}/X_1, achieves its maximum value. Then,

$$w^* = \lceil B/X_1 \rceil. \qquad (2.2.4)$$

Table 2.1 shows the maximum throughput gain X_{w^*}/X_1, the value of w^*, and the maximum throughput X_{w^*} in bytes per second for various types of underlying networks. The values of RTT and bandwidth are from [8]. As shown by the table, the benefits of large window sizes are more evident for high-bandwidth low-latency networks.

Since TCP does not know what the effective bandwidth and RTT for the network are, it uses a mechanism called *slow start* to obtain an estimate of the network performance characteristics. TCP starts the connection with a small window of size and adjusts the window size according to the rate that ACKs are received from the other side [19]. This may pose a problem for short-lived connections that may never achieve the maximum throughput under an optimal window size [8].

Table 2.1. Throughput and Window Size

Network	Bandwidth (bytes/sec)	RTT (sec)	X_1 (bytes/sec)	X_{w^*} (bytes/sec)	w^*	X_{w^*}/X_1
Ethernet	1,090,000	0.0007	1,090,000	1,090,000	1	1.000
Fast Ethernet	12,500,000	0.0007	2,085,714	12,500,000	6	5.993
Slow Internet	12,750	0.1610	9,068	12,750	2	1.406
Fast Internet	127,500	0.0890	16,404	127,500	8	7.772

2.3   The World of Clients and Servers

The next subsections describe the main features of the client/server model, discusses server types, and issues regarding client/server architectures.

2.3.1   The Client/Server Paradigm

The client/server computing model is predicated on the notion of splitting the work to be performed by an application between two processes—the *client* and the *server*. The term server should not be confused with the computer that runs the server process. We will use the term *server-class* machine or computer to designate the hardware and operating system platform used to run server processes. A client process, or simply client:

- runs on a desktop or user workstation and provides the GUI code for data capture and display

- makes requests for specific services to be performed by one or more server processes usually located at remote machines

- executes a portion of the application code

A server process, or simply server:

- runs on a machines that is usually more powerful than desktop machines, runs a multiprogrammed operating system such as Unix or Windows NT, and has more main memory and disk space than desktops have

- executes a set of functionally related services that usually require a specialized hardware/software component

- never initiates a message exchange with any client; servers are passive entities that listen to client requests, execute them, and reply to the clients

The protocol implemented between clients and servers is a *request-reply* protocol in which clients send requests and servers reply to client's requests (see Fig. 2.9). Clients and servers may run on top of TCP or on top of a connectionless protocol such as UDP.

Since a server may receive requests from many clients, a queue of requests is formed at the server. If only one request is served at a time, the resources at the server machine may be underutilized, the server throughput (number of requests served per time unit) may be low, and response time to clients will increase as the load on the server increases (see Fig. 2.10a). Most servers create multiple processes or multiple threads of execution in a single process to handle the queue of incoming requests (see Fig. 2.10b).

Using multiple threads or processes decreases the response time per request. Note that since all server processes contend for the same hardware resources (e.g.,

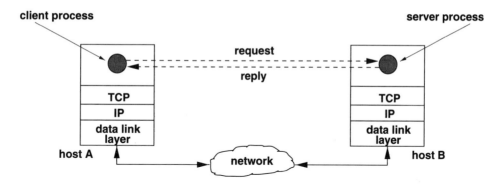

Figure 2.9. Client/server protocol: request/reply.

CPU, memory, and disks), the performance improvement saturates after the underlying hardware resources are close to being 100% utilized. Table 2.2 shows the response time as a function of the number of active threads at a server that receives requests at a rate of 2.5 requests/sec. Each request uses 0.07 sec of CPU time and 0.2 sec of disk time. As shown in the table, a significant reduction in the response time is achieved when the number of threads goes from one to two. A smaller improvement is observed when one additional thread is added. From four threads on, the improvement is negligible.

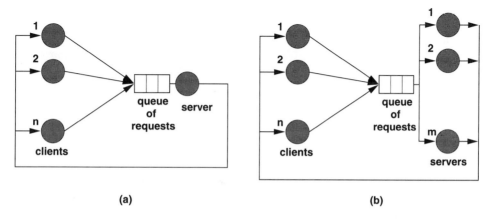

Figure 2.10. (a) Single process server. (b) Multiple process server.

Table 2.2. Server Response Time vs. Number of Threads

No. of Threads	Response Time (sec)
1	0.831
2	0.526
3	0.492
4	0.486
5	0.485

2.3.2 Server Types

The are various types of servers used in networked environments: file servers, database servers, application servers, groupware servers, object servers, web servers, and software servers [16].

File servers provide networked computers with access to a shared file system (see Fig. 2.11a). Clients make requests to look up directories, retrieve file attributes, and read and write blocks from files. One of the most popular file servers is the Network File System (NFS), which allows easy sharing of data on heterogeneous networks. The NFS protocol allows both UDP and TCP/IP to be used as a transport protocol. However, most NFS implementations use UDP.

Database servers provide access to one or more shared databases. Client requests are in the form of SQL statements—a standard language for accessing relational databases [15]. The database server receives the SQL statements and submits them to a database engine that either queries the database or updates the database, depending on the type of request. Even if the database engine has to read hundreds of records to satisfy a client query to retrieve just a few records, only the result is sent back to the client. This cuts down significantly on network traffic and reduces the number of interactions between clients and servers (see Fig. 2.11b).

Application servers provide access to remote procedures invoked by the clients through Remote Procedure Call (RPC) mechanisms. These remote procedures implement the business logic of the application and issue SQL calls to a back end database engine. So, instead of one client/server interaction per SQL call, this approach requires a single interaction per procedure invocation (see Fig. 2.11c).

As we go from Fig. 2.11a to c, we decrease the rate at which requests are sent to the server but increase the complexity of each request. There is a performance tradeoff that depends on specific values of the relevant parameters. Transaction Processing Monitors (TPMs) [1], [7] can be used to balance the load among several servers that implement the same service, provide dynamic server replication, and funnel access to database servers to improve performance. Other systems, such as Microsoft's Transaction Server, further improve performance and scalability by (1) managing a pool of threads that are allocated to service requests and returned to the pool when the service completes, and (2) establishing, at initialization time,

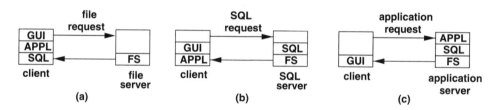

Figure 2.11. (a) File server. (b) SQL server. (c) Application server.

a pool of DB connections between the Transaction Server environment and the various databases used by the applications. This pool of pre-connected DB sessions eliminates the time required to connect to the DB during the execution of a service request.

Groupware servers provide access to unstructured and semistructured information such as text, images, mail, bulletin boards, and workflows [16]. Object servers support remote invocation of methods in support of distributed object oriented application development. Object request brokers (ORBs) acts as the glue between clients and remote objects.

Web servers provide access to documents, images, sound, executables, and downloadable applications (e.g., Java applets) through the Hyper Text Transfer Protocol (HTTP) protocol. Chapter 4 describes in more detail the anatomy of HTTP servers.

Software servers are used to provide executables to Network Computers (NCs). Network computers do not have hard drives, are connected to a network, and get the executables of commercial software packages from a software server that always has the latest version of the software.

2.3.3 Architectural Issues

A common question when designing client/server architectures is whether a two-tier or three-tier architecture should be used. In two-tier architectures, the GUI and application logic runs at the client while the SQL server runs at the server. In a three-tier organization, the GUI runs at the client, and the application logic runs at a an application server that acts as a client to an SQL server.

Another important architectural consideration is how "fat" or "thin" the client should be. Fat clients incorporate more of the transaction logic than thin clients and tend to require less interaction with the server at the expense of higher computing requirements for the client.

Requests generated from clients to servers as well as the replies that these requests generate use network bandwidth, processing, and I/O resources at the servers involved. As the load on a system increases, performance may deteriorate very fast. To improve performance and increase system scalability, one may use caches at various levels to significantly enhance the performance of client/server systems. Caches are copies of data stored at servers but kept closer to the client, sometimes at the client itself and sometimes at closer cache servers. This reduces the number of interactions needed with the server and decreases the response time. Clients may keep a cached copy of file or blocks of a file so that they do not need to access the server at every read. Servers may keep main memory caches holding copies of files or database records. Web servers closer to a set of clients may hold popular documents to avoid requesting them from remote servers, thus reducing response times and bandwidth requirements. When data are found at a cache, a *cache hit* is said to occur, otherwise we have a *cache miss*. Consider, for example, a file server that receives requests to read 8 KB file blocks at a rate of 900 requests/sec. If 30% of these requests generate a cache hit at the client, the server will be actually receiving $(1 - 0.3) \times 900 = 630$ requests/sec. If 25% of these requests can be satisfied from the file server's main memory cache, then only $(1 - 0.25) \times 630 = 472.5$ requests/sec reach the file server's disk subsystem. A price to be paid for the use of caching is that the consistency of the cached data has to be maintained. Additionally, extra processing is required in case of cache misses.

2.4   Concluding Remarks

This chapter introduced the concepts of computer networking, protocols, LANs, WANs, and described the most important features of the protocols that are at the core of the Internet and internets: TCP/IP.

The client/server model was discussed along with important architectural issues of these systems and their performance impacts. The remaining chapters of this book take a quantitative analysis of client/server system in general and of Web-based environments in particular.

More details about TCP/IP can be found in [19], [20]. A nice description of client/server systems can be found in [16]. Web servers are described in [21].

BIBLIOGRAPHY

[1] J. M. ANDRADE, M. T. CARGES, T. J. DWYER, and S. D. FELTS, *The Tuxedo System*. Reading, MA: Addison-Wesley, 1996.

[2] BBN, a history of the ARPANET: the first decade, *Tech. Rep.*, Bolt, Beranek, and Newman, MA, 1981.

[3] G. BELL and J. N. GRAY, The revolution yet to happen, in *Beyond Calculation: The Next Fifty Years of Computing*. P. J. DENNING and R. M. METCALFE, eds., New York: Copernicus Springer-Verlag, 1997.

[4] D. BERTSEKAS and R. GALLAGER, *Data Networks*. 2nd ed., Upper Saddle River, NJ: Prentice Hall, 1992.

[5] V. CERF, When they're everywhere, in *Beyond Calculation: The Next Fifty Years of Computing*. P. J. DENNING and R. M. METCALFE, eds., New York: Copernicus Springer-Verlag, 1997.

[6] D. E. COMER, *Computer Networks and Internets*. Upper Saddle River, NJ: Prentice Hall, 1997.

[7] J. GRAY and A. REUTER, *Transaction Processing: Concepts and Techniques*. San Francisco, CA: Morgan Kaufmann , 1993.

[8] J. HEIDMANN, K. OBRACZKA, and J. TOUCH, Modeling the performance of HTTP over several transport protocols, *IEEE/ACM Trans. Networking*, vol. 5, no. 5, pp. 616–630, Oct. 1997.

[9] INST. ELEC. ELECTRON. ENG., Carrier sense multiple access with collision detection (CSMA/CD) access method and physical layer specifications (ANSI), *IEEE, Standard 8802-3: 1996 (ISO/IEC) [ANSI/IEEE Std 802.3, 1996 Edition]*.

[10] INST. ELEC. ELECTRON. ENG., Supplement to carrier sense multiple access with collision detection (CSMA/CD), *IEEE, Standard 802.3u-1995*.

[11] INST. ELEC. ELECTRON. ENG., Token ring access method and physical layer specification, *IEEE, Standard 8802-5: 1995 (ISO/IEC) [ANSI/IEEE 802.5, 1995 Edition]*.

[12] L. KLEINROCK, *Queueing Systems, Vol. I: Theory*. New York: Wiley, 1975.

[13] L. KLEINROCK, *Queueing Systems, Vol. II: Computer Applications*. New York: Wiley, 1976.

[14] R. M. METCALFE and D. R. BOGGS, Ethernet: distributed packet switching for local computer networks, *Commun. ACM*, pp. 395–404, 1976.

[15] P. O'NEIL, *Database: Principles, Programming, Performance*, San Francisco: Morgan Kauffman, 1994.

[16] R. ORFALI, D. HARKEY, and J. EDWARDS, *The Essential Client/Server Survival Guide*, 2nd ed., New York: Wiley, 1996.

[17] R. PERLMAN, *Interconnections*. Reading, MA: Addison-Wesley, 1992.

[18] W. STALLINGS, *Networking Standards: A Guide to OSI, ISDN, LAN, and MAN Standards*. Reading, MA: Addison-Wesley, 1993.

[19] W. R. STEVENS, *TCP/IP Illustrated, Vol. 1*. Reading, MA: Addison-Wesley, 1994.

[20] W. R. STEVENS, *TCP/IP Illustrated, Vol. 3*. Reading, MA: Addison Wesley, 1996.

[21] N. YEAGER and R. McCRATH, *Web Server Technology*. San Francisco: Morgan Kaufmann, 1996.

Chapter 3

PERFORMANCE ISSUES IN CLIENT/SERVER ENVIRONMENTS

3.1 Introduction

Client/Server (C/S) systems are comprised of many different hardware resources including client workstations, servers with their processors and disks, LANs, WANs, and routers. Various types of software processes including applications, middleware, database management systems, protocol handlers, and operating systems share the use of the hardware resources. The shared use of these resources gives rise to contention that generates waiting queues. A C/S transaction spends a portion of its time receiving service at various resources as well as queuing for these resources.

The delays encountered by a C/S transaction may be decomposed into (1) service times: time spent using various resources such as processors, disks, and networks; and (2) waiting times: time spent waiting to use resources that are being held by other transactions. In this chapter, we investigate, in detail, the nature of the delay incurred by a typical C/S transaction through the use of communication-processing delay diagrams. We then show how service times can be computed at single disks, disk arrays, networks, and routers. Queues and contention are defined more formally, and some very basic and important performance results are introduced.

3.2 Communication-Processing Delay Diagrams

To analyze the performance of C/S systems, we need to understand what happens with a request generated by a client from the moment the request is submitted until a reply is received. For this purpose, we introduce a graphic notation, called *communication-processing delay diagrams*, to illustrate how requests spend their time at each resource including clients, servers, LAN segments, and WANs. A communication-processing delay diagram (see Fig 3.1) is a sequence of parallel time

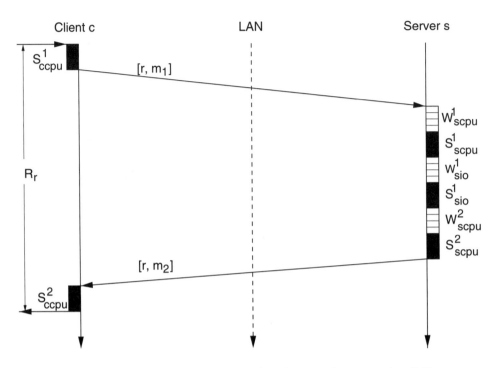

Figure 3.1. Communication-processing delay diagram for a two-tier C/S system.

axes drawn vertically with time increasing from top to bottom. There are two types of time axes:

- communication time axes (dashed lines), corresponding to time spent in LAN segments and WANs

- processing time axes (solid lines), corresponding to time spent processing elements such as client and server processors, client and server storage devices, and routers

Figure 3.1 shows time axes for a client, a server, and a LAN segment in a two-tier C/S configuration. Diagonal arrows in a delay diagram indicate requests going from clients to servers and vice versa. These arrows cross dashed lines associated with the networks traversed by the request. Requests and replies are labeled by a pair of the form $[id, m]$ where id identifies the request and its reply and m indicates the average size in bytes of the message carrying the request or reply. For example, request r in Fig. 3.1 is m_1 bytes long and its reply is m_2 bytes long. The network transmission time in seconds is equal to the message size in bits divided by the network bandwidth B in bits per second (bps). This assumes that the protocol overhead is included in the message size. Network contention time (i.e., the time needed to get access to the network) is not included in the network transmission time and will be ignored for the moment. We revisit this issue later.

The total time spent by a request at a server may be decomposed into intervals of two types: service and waiting time intervals. A *service time* interval is a period of time during which the request is receiving service from a resource such as the CPU or a disk. Service times are represented in communication-processing delay diagrams as solid rectangles placed along the processing time axes. The notation S_i^j is used to indicate service time at resource i during the jth visit to resource i. Figure 3.2 shows the graphical notation used to represent a resource i and the queue of requests waiting to obtain service from the resource.

Many requests may be contending for access to the same resources (e.g., CPU, disks, LAN segments, or communication lines), therefore waiting lines or queues are formed at each of these devices. The time spent by a request waiting to get access to resource i during the jth visit to the resource is called *waiting time* and is denoted by W_i^j. Waiting times are represented in communication-processing delay diagrams by striped rectangles along processing time axes.

The sum of all service times for a request at resource i is called *service demand* and is denoted by D_i. In the example of Fig 3.1, the service demand at the server's CPU, D_{scpu}, is $S_{\text{scpu}}^1 + S_{\text{scpu}}^2$. The sum of all waiting times at resource i for a given request is called *queuing time* and is denoted by Q_i. In Fig. 3.1, the queuing time at the server's CPU, Q_{scpu}, is $W_{\text{scpu}}^1 + W_{\text{scpu}}^2$.

The service demand, D_{LAN}, of request r at the LAN segment is the total network transmission time computed as the sum of the request and reply message sizes in bits divided by the network bandwidth B in bits per second. So, $D_{\text{LAN}} = 8 \times (m_1 + m_2)/B$.

The sum of the service demand plus the queuing time for a request at resource i is called *residence time* and is denoted by R_i'. The residence time of a transaction at a resource is the total time spent by the transaction at the resource: queuing and

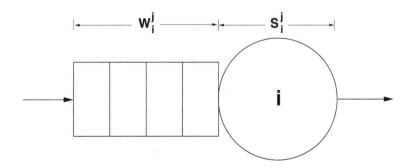

Figure 3.2. A resource and its queue.

receiving service. So, in Fig. 3.1, the residence time at the server's CPU, R'_{scpu}, is $Q_{\text{scpu}} + D_{\text{scpu}}$.

Finally, the response time of a request r, R_r, is the sum of that request's residence time at all resources. Hence, in the example of Fig. 3.1,

$$R_r = R'_{\text{ccpu}} + R'_{\text{scpu}} + R'_{\text{sio}} + R'_{\text{LAN}} \qquad (3.2.1)$$

where R'_{ccpu}, R'_{scpu}, R'_{sio}, and R'_{LAN} are the residence times at the client CPU, server CPU, server I/O subsystem, and the LAN, respectively.

In summary, we can write that

$$D_i = \sum_{\text{visits } j} S_i^j \qquad (3.2.2)$$

$$Q_i = \sum_{\text{visits } j} W_i^j \qquad (3.2.3)$$

$$R'_i = D_i + Q_i \qquad (3.2.4)$$

$$R_r = \sum_{\text{resources } i} R'_i. \qquad (3.2.5)$$

The following example illustrates the concepts of service time and service demand.

Example 3.1: Consider that a transaction t in a C/S system uses 5 msec of CPU at the client, 10 msec of CPU at the server, and reads ten 2048-byte blocks from the server's disk. So, $D_{\text{ccpu}} = 0.005$ sec and $D_{\text{scpu}} = 0.010$ sec. The average seek time at the server's disk is 9 msec, the average latency is 4.17 msec, and the transfer rate is 20 MB/sec. Thus, the average service time, S_d, at the disk is

$$
\begin{aligned}
S_d &= \text{AvgSeek} + \text{AvgLatency} + \text{TransferTime} \\
&= \text{AvgSeek} + \text{AvgLatency} + \frac{\text{BlockSize}}{\text{TransferRate}} \\
&= 0.009 + 0.00417 + 2048/20,000,000 = 0.0133 \text{ sec.}
\end{aligned}
$$

Subsection 3.3.1 provides more details on the computation of service times at magnetic disks. The service demand at the server's disk, D_d, is then equal to $10 \times S_d = 10 \times 0.0133 = 0.133$ sec. Consider that the client and the server are connected by an Ethernet with a bandwidth B of 10 Mbps and that a request going from the client to the server takes a full Ethernet packet (1,518 bytes), and that the reply from the server requires seven packets. So, $m_1 = 1,518$ bytes and $m_2 = 7 \times 1,518 = 10,626$ bytes. The total network transmission time D_{LAN} for the transaction is given by

$$D_{\text{LAN}} = 8 \times (m_1 + m_2)/B = 8 \times (1518 + 10,626)/10,000,000 = 0.0097 \text{ sec.}$$

A detailed description of how service times are computed on network segments is provided in Sec. 3.3.2. The minimum possible value for the response time, R_t, for transaction t is obtained by ignoring all waiting times. So,

$$R_t \geq D_{\text{ccpu}} + D_{\text{scpu}} + D_d + D_{\text{LAN}}$$
$$0.005 + 0.010 + 0.133 + 0.0097 = 0.158 \text{ sec.}$$

The reader should note that we have not taken into account the waiting times experienced by the transaction to get access to the network and to use the CPU and the disk at the server. The models presented in this book allow us to compute these waiting times. ∎

Consider now the three-tier C/S architecture depicted in Fig. 3.3. The client sends a request to the application server located on the same LAN (LAN 1). The application logic is executed at the application server and may require several accesses to the database (DB). Each access to the DB server has to traverse LAN 1 to reach router 1, traverse the WAN and arrive, through router 2, at LAN 2—the LAN where the DB server is located. Figure 3.4 shows a communications-processing delay diagram that illustrates the flow of a request in this C/S architecture. This diagram shows some instances of network waiting times, denoted as W_{net}, for LANs 1 and 2. The routers were not shown in the diagram to avoid cluttering.

As illustrated in Ex. 3.1, the service time, and therefore the service demand, and the network transmission time, associated with one type of request can be computed from the request characteristics and from the performance specifications of the hardware resources and networks involved. Section 3.3 describes in more detail how service times and service demands can be computed for the various resources involved in a client/server request.

To obtain the response time, we also need to compute the queuing times. This is accomplished in the remaining chapters of this book. Section 3.4 introduces the notion of queues and contention and presents some basic performance results.

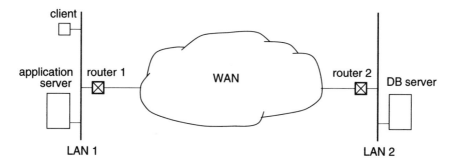

Figure 3.3. Three-tier C/S system.

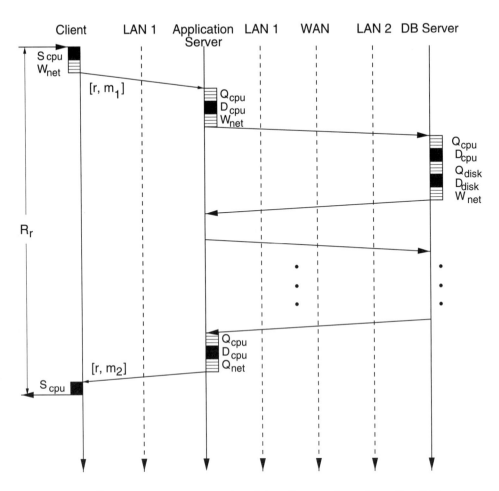

Figure 3.4. Communications-processing delay diagram for a three-tier C/S system.

3.3   Service Times and Service Demands

Consider any resource i used by a transaction in a C/S environment. The resource can be a processor at the server, any of the server disks, any of the LAN segments involved, or a router. A transaction may need to visit resource i several times before it completes. For example, a transaction may need to perform several I/Os at a given disk, use the CPU at the server several times as it is context-switched by the operating system, and use the various networks to carry the requests and replies involved in the transaction. Let V_i be the average number of visits made by a transaction to resource i, and let S_i be the average service time per visit at the resource.

The average service demand, D_i, at resource i is then the product of the average number of visits to the resource multiplied by the average time spent per visit at the resource. Thus,

$$D_i = V_i \times S_i. \qquad (3.3.1)$$

In this section we explore, in greater details, how service times can be computed for various categories of resources found in C/S systems.

3.3.1   Service Times at Single Disks and Disk Arrays

This section reviews the major elements of modern disk subsystems and identifies the contributions made by these elements to the overall service time at a disk.

Single Disks

Magnetic disks are an important component of any server and client workstation. Access times to information stored on magnetic disks is several orders of magnitude greater than access times to information stored in random access memory (RAM) due to the disk's mechanical components. A disk (see Fig. 3.5) is composed of one or more platters that rotate in lockstep, attached to a spindle. Information is magnetically recorded on both the upper and lower surfaces of each platter. The surface of a platter is divided into concentric circles called *tracks*. A read/write head, mounted at the end of an arm, is associated with each surface. Only one read/write head can be active at any time. An actuator moves all the arms together along the radius of the platters. The set of tracks located at the same distance from the center is called a *cylinder*. Tracks are divided into sectors of the same size.

To read/write to/from a magnetic disk, the actuator has to be moved to the proper cylinder. This is called a *seek*. The read/write head corresponding to the desired track has to be activated. The disk mechanism has to wait until the disk rotation brings the desired sector below the read/write head. This is called *rotational latency*. At this point, data transfer can start.

I/O subsystems involve more components than just the disks used to store information. Figure 3.6 shows the typical architecture of the I/O subsystem of a server. I/O requests are submitted to the file system. A cache at the file system stores file blocks that have been used most recently. If the desired block is in the file system cache, no disk access is needed and the request is satisfied directly from the cache. This event is called a file system *cache hit*. Otherwise, a file system *cache miss* is said to occur, and the request is sent to the device driver. The request is then queued at the device driver, which may reorder requests to optimize performance. The request is then sent to the disk controller. A cache at the disk controller (also called a disk cache) is used to match the speed between the disk and the I/O bus. The disk cache may be used for prefetching blocks that may be needed in the near future. For example, if a file is being accessed sequentially, it makes sense to bring to the cache a certain number of blocks that follow the block just requested so

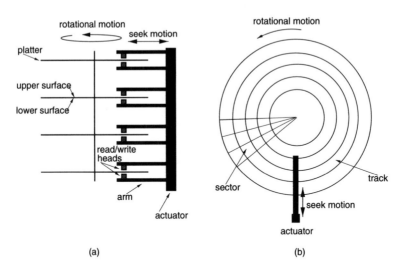

Figure 3.5. (a) Side view of a magnetic disk. (b) Top view of a magnetic disk.

that a cache hit occurs when these blocks are requested. This technique is called
read-ahead, or *pre-fetch*. The disk controller uses a disk scheduling discipline in its
queue aimed at minimizing the average number of cylinders traversed by the arm
to serve disk requests. These disk scheduling disciplines use information about the
position of the disk arm. Examples of disk scheduling disciplines include LOOK,
CSCAN, Shortest Seek Time First (SSTF), and Shortest Positioning Time First
(SPTF) [4], [9], [10].

We now provide expressions for the average service time at a disk subsystem
including the disk controller and the disk itself. More detailed models of disk access
can be found in [10]. Let

- $\overline{S}_d$: average time, in seconds, spent at the controller plus disk to access a
  block from a disk

- SeekTime: average seek time, in seconds; that is, the average time to position
  the arm at the proper cylinder

- Seek$_{rand}$: average seek time, in seconds, for a request to a random cylinder,
  provided by the disk manufacturers; sometimes, the average seek times for
  read and write requests are slightly different

- DiskSpeed: disk rotation speed, in revolutions per minute (RPM), provided
  by the disk manufacturer

- DiskRevolutionTime: time, in seconds, for a disk to complete a full revolution,
  equal to 60/DiskSpeed

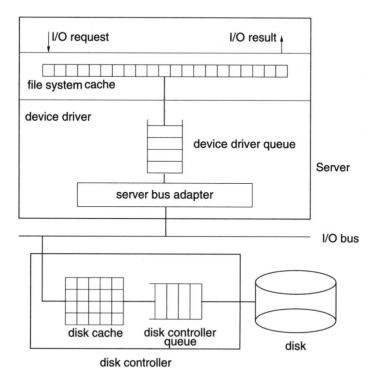

Figure 3.6. Architecture of typical I/O subsystem.

- RotationalLatency: average rotational latency, in seconds; i.e., the average time elapsed since the end of the seek until data transfer starts. This time is spent waiting for the disk to rotate until the desired sector lies under the read/write head

- BlockSize: block size in bytes

- TransferRate: rate at which data is transferred to/from a disk, in MB/sec

- TransferTime: time, in seconds, to transfer a block from the disk to the disk controller

- ControllerTime: time, in seconds, spent at the controller processing an I/O request. This includes the time to check the cache plus the time to read/write a block from/to the cache

- P_{miss}: probability that the desired block is not in the disk cache

The average access time at the controller plus disk can be written as

$$\overline{S}_d = \text{ControllerTime} +$$
$$P_{\text{miss}} \times (\text{SeekTime} + \text{RotationalLatency} + \text{TransferTime}). \quad (3.3.2)$$

The transfer time is simply the ratio between the block size and the transfer rate converted to bytes/sec. Hence,

$$\text{TransferTime} = \frac{\text{BlockSize}}{10^6 \times \text{TransferRate}}. \quad (3.3.3)$$

The cache miss probability, the average seek time, and the average rotational latency depend on the type of workload submitted to the disk subsystem. A disk workload is defined as a sequence of disk block numbers submitted to the disk subsystem. We consider two types of workloads: random and sequential. A *random* workload is one in which the blocks requested are randomly spread over the blocks on the disk. A *sequential* workload is one that exhibits subsequences, called *runs*, of requests to consecutive blocks on the disk. The workload 10, 201, 15, 1023, 45, 39, 782 is an example of a random workload and 4, 350, 351, 352, 353, 80, 104, 105, 106, 107, 108, 243 is an example of a sequential workload with two runs of length greater than one. The first (350, 351, 352, 353) has length four blocks and the second (104, 105, 106, 107, 108) has length five. Let RunLength be the average run length observed in a workload. Random workloads have RunLength = 1.

For random workloads we have that

$$P_{\text{miss}} = 1 \quad (3.3.4)$$
$$\text{RunLength} = 1 \quad (3.3.5)$$
$$\text{SeekTime} = \text{Seek}_{\text{rand}} \quad (3.3.6)$$
$$\text{RotationalLatency} = \frac{1}{2} \times \text{DiskRevolutionTime}. \quad (3.3.7)$$

Equation (3.3.7) comes from the fact that a random request may have to wait anywhere between no revolution and a full revolution. On the average, the rotational latency for a random request is half of a revolution.

The equations for sequential workloads are given below and discussed in the following paragraphs.

$$P_{\text{miss}} = 1/\text{RunLength} \quad (3.3.8)$$
$$\text{SeekTime} = \text{Seek}_{\text{rand}}/\text{RunLength} \quad (3.3.9)$$
$$\text{RotationalLatency} = \frac{1/2 + (\text{RunLength} - 1)[(1 + U_d)/2]}{\text{RunLength}}$$
$$\times \text{DiskRevolutionTime}. \quad (3.3.10)$$

Assuming that read-ahead requests are only performed on disk cache misses and that only the first request of a run will not be served out of the cache, the cache miss probability can be approximated by Eq. (3.3.8).

Equation (3.3.9) can be easily proved as follows. Consider first the following trivial relationship:

$$RunLength = NumberRequests/NumRuns \qquad (3.3.11)$$

where NumberRequests and NumRuns are the number of requests submitted to the disk in a given time interval and the total number of runs observed in the same interval, respectively. The average seek time is equal to the sum of the seek times for all requests in an interval divided by the number of requests in that interval. Only the first request of a run will require a random seek. The remaining requests of a run require a seek of length zero. So, the sum of the seek times for all requests is equal to the number of runs multiplied by the time of a random seek. Dividing the sum by the number of requests to get the average seek time per request and using Eq. (3.3.11) we get that

$$
\begin{aligned}
SeekTime &= \frac{NumRuns \times Seek_{rand}}{NumberRequests} \\
&= \frac{Seek_{rand}}{NumberRequests/NumRuns} \\
&= Seek_{rand}/RunLength. \qquad (3.3.12)
\end{aligned}
$$

Example 3.2: What is the average seek time for the workload (4, 350, 351, 352, 353, 80, 104, 105, 106, 107, 108, 243) considering that the average random seek time $Seek_{rand}$ for the disk is 9 msec?

The workload has three runs of length one—the accesses for blocks 4, 80, and 243—and two runs of length four and five: (350, 351, 352, 353) and (104, 105, 106, 107, 108). So, the average seek time for the entire workload is

$$
\begin{aligned}
SeekTime &= \frac{3}{12} \times Seek_{rand} + \frac{4}{12} \times \frac{Seek_{rand}}{4} + \frac{5}{12} \times \frac{Seek_{rand}}{5} \\
&= \frac{5}{12} \times Seek_{rand} = 3.75 \text{ msec}
\end{aligned}
$$

∎

Equation (3.3.10) is slightly more complex and is a very interesting result derived in [10]. Consider two extreme load scenarios for the disk: light load and heavy load. Under light load, i.e., a very low arrival rate of requests to the disk and therefore a very low disk utilization U_d, two consecutive requests to consecutive blocks on the disk arrive at the disk sufficiently far apart that the second request sees a random rotational latency (i.e., 1/2 of a revolution). Under heavy load, the second of two consecutive requests will be already in the queue waiting for the first request to finish. The time needed to process a request at the controller will make the second request miss a full revolution before it is able to start transferring its block. The probability that a request finds a busy disk is equal to its utilization, U_d, also defined as the fraction of time the disk is busy. Thus, a request will find an idle disk with probability $(1 - U_d)$. The fraction of a revolution seen by a request in a run is one if the request arrives at a busy disk and one-half if the request arrives at an idle disk. So, the average fraction of a revolution seen by requests in a run is

$$1 \times U_d + \frac{1}{2} \times (1 - U_d) = \frac{1 + U_d}{2}. \tag{3.3.13}$$

The average rotational latency, measured in number of revolutions, for a sequential workload can be computed as the sum of the latencies for all requests divided by the number of requests. This can also be computed as the average latency per run multiplied by the number of runs divided by the number of requests. The average latency, in revolutions, per run is given by

$$1/2 + (\text{RunLength} - 1)(1 + U_d)/2. \tag{3.3.14}$$

The first term in Eq. (3.3.14) corresponds to the first request of a run, which sees a random rotational delay. The remaining (RunLength $-$ 1) requests of a run see a latency given by Eq. (3.3.13). Finally, the average rotational latency is

$$
\begin{aligned}
\text{RotationalLatency} &= \frac{\text{NumRuns} \ [1/2 + (\text{RunLength} - 1)(1 + U_d)/2]}{\text{NumberRequests}} \\
&\quad \times \text{DiskRevolutionTime} \\
&= \frac{1/2 + (\text{RunLength} - 1)(1 + U_d)/2}{\text{NumberRequests}/\text{NumRuns}} \times \text{DiskRevolutionTime} \\
&= \frac{1/2 + (\text{RunLength} - 1)(1 + U_d)/2}{\text{RunLength}} \times \text{DiskRevolutionTime}
\end{aligned}
$$
$$\tag{3.3.15}$$

as given in Eq. (3.3.10). Equation (3.3.15) correctly reduces to the random case equation, Eq. (3.3.7), when RunLength = 1 and when the disk utilization approaches zero. Also, as the load on the disk increases, i.e., the utilization U_d approaches 100%, the rotational latency approaches a full revolution as illustrated in Table 3.1.

Note that Eqs. (3.3.9) and (3.3.10) already take into account the effect of the disk cache. Therefore, when using Eq. (3.3.2) for sequential workloads, we should only multiply the transfer time by the cache miss probability.

The curious reader may have noticed that Eq. (3.3.15) requires the disk utilization U_d. As we shall see in Sec. 3.5, the disk utilization is equal to the average arrival rate of requests to the disk multiplied by the disk average service time. But the disk average service time is a function of the average rotational latency, which depends on the utilization! It looks like we are faced with an impasse. It turns out that there is an easy way out. To compute the disk utilization, we start by using Eq. (3.3.7) for the rotational latency for random workloads. This gives, in general,

Table 3.1. Average Rotational Latency in Full Revolutions

RunLength	U_d	Rotational Latency (in revolutions)
4	0.1	0.54
4	0.5	0.69
4	0.8	0.80
8	0.1	0.54
8	0.5	0.72
8	0.8	0.85
16	0.1	0.55
16	0.5	0.73
16	0.8	0.88

a very good approximation for the average disk service time. The approximation can be improved by using the value of the service time computed this way to obtain a more accurate value for the disk utilization. This new value is used, in turn, to compute a new value for the rotational latency and therefore a new value for the disk service time. The process is repeated until successive values of the disk service time are close enough within a certain tolerance. This kind of iterative procedure is very common in solving this type of problems known as *fixed point equations*.

Figure 3.7 summarizes the formulas discussed above. Worksheet SingleDisks in the MS Excel workbook ServTime.XLS, in the disk that accompanies this book, implements these formulas as well as the iterative procedure to solve the fixed point equation for the utilization.

Example 3.3: The disk of a DB server receives requests at a rate of 20 requests/sec (0.020 requests/msec). An analysis of a trace of the requests revealed that 20% of the requests are for random blocks and 80% are for sequences of blocks or runs. The block size is 2048 bytes. The average measured run length for this workload is 24 requests. The disk rotates at 7,200 RPM, has an average seek for random requests equal to 9 msec, and a transfer rate of 20 MB/sec. The controller time is equal to 0.1 msec. What is the average disk service time?

We start by computing the average service time for random requests. Using Eqs. (3.3.5)–(3.3.7) for random requests, SeekTime $= 9$ msec, RotationalLatency $= 1/2 \times 60/7,200 \times 1,000 = 4.17$ msec, and TransferTime $= 2,048/(10^6 \times 20) \times 1,000 = 0.1$ msec. So, using Eq. (3.3.2), we get the average service time for random requests as $0.1 + 9 + 4.17 + 0.1 = 13.4$ msec.

The service time for the sequential portion of the workload can be computed using Eqs. (3.3.8)–(3.3.10). We can approximate the disk utilization U_d by the arrival rate multiplied by average random seek + average latency + average transfer

$$\text{TransferTime} = \frac{\text{BlockSize}}{10^6 \times \text{TransferRate}} \tag{3.3.16}$$

Random workloads:

$$\overline{S}_d = \text{ControllerTime} + \text{Seek}_{\text{rand}} + \frac{\text{DiskRevolutionTime}}{2} + \text{TransferTime} \tag{3.3.17}$$

Sequential workloads:

$$\overline{S}_d = \text{ControllerTime} + \frac{\text{Seek}_{\text{rand}}}{\text{RunLength}} +$$
$$\frac{[1/2 + (\text{RunLength} - 1)(1 + U_d)/2] \times \text{DiskRevolutionTime}}{\text{RunLength}} +$$
$$\text{TransferTime}/\text{RunLength} \tag{3.3.18}$$

Figure 3.7. Disk service times equations.

time. Thus

$$U_d = 0.020 \times (9 + 4.17 + 0.1) = 0.27. \tag{3.3.19}$$

The cache miss probability is $P_{\text{miss}} = 1/24 = 4.2\%$. The average seek time is $9/24 = 0.38$ msec. The average rotational latency is

$$\frac{1/2 + 23\,(1 + 0.27)/2}{24} \times \frac{60 \times 1,000}{7,200} = 5.25 \text{ msec.} \tag{3.3.20}$$

Hence, the average service time for sequential requests is $0.1 + 0.38 + 5.25 + 0.042 \times 0.1 = 5.73$ msec. So, the average service time, considering both random and sequential requests, is $0.2 \times 13.4 + 0.8 \times 5.73 = 7.26$ msec.

If we use the iterative approach discussed before to refine the service time value for the sequential workload, the procedure would converge to a value of 7.02 msec in three iterations with an absolute error of 0.01%. See the worksheet SingleDisks in the MS Excel workbook ServTime.XLS for details. ■

Disk Arrays

Reliability and increased performance in disk access can be obtained by using disk arrays, also known as Redundant Arrays of Independent Disks (RAIDs). Disk arrays can be organized in several ways. Figure 3.8 shows a disk array composed of five independent disks with their disk controllers. An array controller, with its cache and queue, controls access to the disk array. In disk arrays, data is distributed, or striped, across a set of $N - 1$ disks. Large chunks of data are broken down into $N - 1$ pieces, called *stripe units*, stored into the $N - 1$ disks. The set of these $N - 1$ stripe units is called a *stripe group*. To increase reliability, a parity block is associated

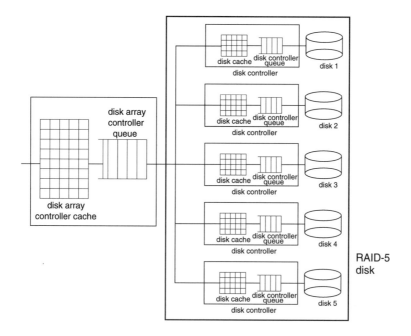

Figure 3.8. Disk array.

with each stripe group. The parity block is stored in a disk different from the $N-1$ disks used to store the stripe group. If any disk is lost due to a failure, the stripe units stored in this disk can be rebuilt from the other $N-2$ stripe units in the stripe group and from the parity block.

One of the most popular and efficient disk array organizations, called RAID-5, uses four disks for data striping and one for the parity block. The parity block is uniformly distributed, or rotated, among the five disks to avoid bottlenecks. Figure 3.9 shows how records A–E are stored in a disk array under a RAID-5 organization. Each record is striped into four stripe units. For example, record A is striped into stripe units A1 through A4 and has a parity block PA. The figure illustrates how the parity blocks are rotated among the five disks. By looking at this figure, we can derive some important performance features of RAID-5 disks:

- RAID-5 requires 25% more disk space than a non redundant disk organization.

- Large reads, i.e., reads of a full stripe group (e.g., block A in Fig. 3.9), can be done in parallel, by reading from the four disks that contain the stripe group.

- Small reads, i.e., reads of one stripe unit, exhibit good performance because they only tie up one disk, therefore allowing other small reads to other disks to proceed in parallel. For example, A1, B1, C4, D3, and E4, can all be read in parallel from drives 1, 0, 4, 2, and 3, respectively.

- Large writes, i.e., writes of a full stripe group require writing into five disks: the four data disks and the parity disk for the stripe unit.

- Small writes, i.e., writes to one stripe unit, require that the parity block for the entire stripe unit be recomputed. The new parity block can be computed from the old parity block, the old and the new values of the stripe unit being modified. Thus, a small write to a RAID-5 requires reading the stripe unit and the parity block in parallel, computing the new parity block, and writing the new stripe unit and the new parity block in parallel. For example, modifying stripe unit A2 in Fig. 3.9 requires reading A2 and PA from drives 2 and 0, in parallel, recomputing the new value of PA, and writing the new value of A2 and PA into drives 2 and 0, in parallel. Thus a write of one stripe unit requires four I/Os: two reads and two writes. This is known as the small write penalty for RAID-5 disks.

We now introduce some notation to help us discuss service times in RAID-5 disk arrays. Let

- StripeUnit: size in bytes of a stripe unit

- StripeGroupSize: size in bytes of the stripe group assumed to be a multiple of StripeUnit

- n_r: number of stripe units read by a read request

- n_w: number of stripe units modified by a write request

- λ^r_{array}: arrival rate of read requests to the disk array

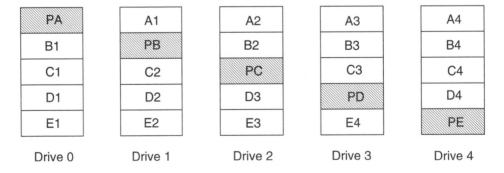

Figure 3.9. RAID-5 organization.

- λ_{array}^w: arrival rate of write requests to the disk array

- λ_{disk}^r: arrival rate of read requests to any of the disks in the array

- λ_{disk}^w: arrival rate of write requests to any of the disks in the array

- N: number of disks in the array ($N = 5$ for RAID-5)

- S_{array}^r: average service time at a disk array for read requests

- S_{array}^w: average service time at a disk array for write requests

Each read request presented to the disk array generates requests to n_r disks. The number of possible groups of n_r disks is

$$\binom{N}{n_r} = \frac{N!}{(N - n_r)! \, n_r!}.$$

Each disk in the array belongs to

$$\binom{N - 1}{n_r - 1} = \frac{(N - 1)!}{(N - n_r)! \, (n_r - 1)!}$$

groups of n_r disks. So, the fraction of read requests to the array that goes to any of the disks, assuming that requests are uniformly distributed to all disks, is

$$\frac{\binom{N - 1}{n_r - 1}}{\binom{N}{n_r}} = \frac{n_r}{N}.$$

Let $rw\,(n_w)$ be the number of stripe units read as a result of a request to write n_w stripe units. Table 3.2 shows the values of $rw\,(n_w)$ for $n_w = 1, \cdots, 4$.

Counting the reads due to read and write requests, one can write the arrival rate of disk requests at a disk as a function of the arrival rate of read and write requests to the array as,

$$\lambda_{\text{disk}}^r = \frac{n_r}{N} \times \lambda_{\text{array}}^r + \frac{rw\,(n_w)}{N} \times \lambda_{\text{array}}^w. \tag{3.3.21}$$

Table 3.2. Number of Reads Generated by Writes on a RAID-5 Device

n_w	$rw\,(n_w)$	Explanation
1	2	Read one stripe unit and the parity block
2	2	Read two additional stripe units to compute the parity
3	1	Read one more stripe unit to compute the parity
4	0	No additional reads needed

Each request to write n_w stripe units in the array requires that writes be done at $n_w + 1$ disks because the parity block has to be updated. So, the arrival rate of write requests to any disk in the array is

$$\lambda_{\text{disk}}^w = \frac{n_w + 1}{N} \times \lambda_{\text{array}}^w. \tag{3.3.22}$$

The service time at the array is equal to the maximum time spent at all disks involved in the request. The time spent at each disk of the array includes queuing plus service. So, the average service time, S_{array}^r, of read requests at a disk array is

$$S_{\text{array}}^r = \max_{i=1}^{n_r}\{R_{\text{disk } i}^r\} \tag{3.3.23}$$

where $R_{\text{disk } i}^r$ is the average response time of read requests at disk i. Expressions to compute the average response time at single disks are provided in Chap. 9. The average service time, S_{array}^w, of write requests at a disk array is

$$S_{\text{array}}^w = \max_{i=1}^{rw(n_w)}\{R_{\text{disk } i}^r\} + \max_{i=1}^{n_w+1}\{R_{\text{disk } i}^w\} \tag{3.3.24}$$

where $R_{\text{disk } i}^w$ is the average response time of write requests at disk i.

Example 3.4: Consider a medical information retrieval system that stores X-ray images as low resolution gif files in a RAID-5 disk on its server. Files are 80 KB long on the average. Each disk of the RAID-5 array has an average random seek time of 9.0 msec, a speed of 7,200 RPM, and a transfer rate of 20 MB/sec. The stripe unit size is 16 KB; therefore the stripe group size is 64 KB (= 4 × 16 KB) bytes. This means that each request to read a file generates an average of 1.25 (= 80/64) requests to the disk array. Since this number is small, i.e., close to 1, we can consider that requests to individual disks behave as random requests. This means that the average service time, S_d, to read a stripe unit at each disk is $0.009 + 0.5 \times 60/7,200 + 16,384/20,000,000 = 0.014$ sec, according to Eq. (3.3.17). The system is read-only, that is, there are no writes ($\lambda_{\text{array}}^w = 0$). Each request to retrieve a file of average size from the image server retrieves a full stripe group plus one stripe unit. So, half of the read requests to the disk array are for stripe groups ($n_r = 4$) and half for stripe units ($n_r = 1$). Using Eq. (3.3.21), we can compute the arrival rate of read requests to each individual disk as

$$\begin{aligned}
\lambda_{\text{disk}}^r &= (4/5 \times \lambda_{\text{array}}^r)/2 + (1/5 \times \lambda_{\text{array}}^r)/2 \\
&= \lambda_{\text{array}}^r/2.
\end{aligned}$$

The utilization, U_d, of each individual disk is $\lambda_{\text{disk}}^r \times S_d = \lambda_{\text{array}}^r \times S_d/2 = 0.007 \times \lambda_{\text{array}}^r$. Since the maximum utilization of any device is 100%, the maximum arrival rate of requests to the disk array is $1/0.007 = 143$ requests/sec. Since each file read corresponds to an average of 1.25 read requests to the disk array, the maximum number of X-ray images retrieved from the images server per second is equal to $143/1.25 = 114$ images/sec.   ■

Example 3.5: An Online Transaction Processing System (OLTP) is served by a DB server that uses a RAID-5 disk. Ninety percent of the requests to the DB server are for short read requests of 2 KB blocks. The remaining 10% are for write requests of 16 KB blocks. Since most RAID-5 disks allow the user to tune the stripe unit size to best fit the needs of the application, we want to investigate the influence of different stripe unit sizes in the utilization of the disks of the disk array. Assume that the component disks are the same as in Ex. 3.4. Assume that read requests to the DB server arrive at a rate of 36 requests/sec and therefore write requests arrive at 4 requests/sec. Table 3.3 shows the individual disk utilizations for several values of the stripe unit size. Before we discuss the results in the table, let us understand how the values in the table were obtained.

The number of stripe units read, n_r, is equal to the size of a DB read request divided by the stripe unit size. Since one can only read multiples of a stripe unit,

$$n_r = \lceil \text{DB read request size (in kilobytes)/StripeUnit (in kilobytes)} \rceil$$
$$= \lceil 2/\text{StripeUnit (in kilobytes)} \rceil.$$

So, if StripeUnit = 8 KB, $n_r = \lceil 2/8 \rceil = \lceil 0.25 \rceil = 1$. The number of stripe units accessed per write request to the disk array is equal to the database update request size divided by the stripe unit size. However, one cannot update more than four stripe units at a time in a RAID-5 disk. So

$$n_w = \min[4, \lceil 16/\text{StripeUnit (in kilobytes)} \rceil].$$

So, when StripeUnit = 2 KB, $n_w = \min(4, \lceil 16/2 \rceil) = \min(4, 8) = 4$.

The value of λ^w_{array} is obtained by multiplying the arrival rate, λ^w_{DB}, of updates to the DB (4 updates/sec) by the number of stripe groups involved in each update.

Table 3.3. Disk Utilization vs. Stripe Unit Size for RAID-5 Example for $\lambda^r_{\text{array}} = 36$ req/sec

λ^w_{array} (req/sec)	StripeUnit (in KB)	n_r	n_w	λ^r_{disk} (req/sec)	λ^w_{disk} (req/sec)	Percent Disk Utilization
16.00	1	2	4	14.4	16.0	40.2
8.00	2	1	4	7.2	8.0	20.2
4.00	4	1	4	7.2	4.0	15.0
4.00	8	1	2	8.8	2.4	15.2
4.00	16	1	1	8.8	1.6	14.6
4.00	32	1	1	8.8	1.6	15.4
4.00	64	1	1	8.8	1.6	17.1

The number of stripe groups per database update is equal to 16 KB divided by the number of KB accessed per write request to the disk array. This number is equal to $n_w \times$ StripeUnit (in kilobytes). Note the we need to use the ceiling function to obtain an integer number of stripe groups. So

$$\lambda_{\text{array}}^w = \lambda_{\text{DB}}^w \left\lceil \frac{16}{n_w \times \text{StripeUnit (in KB)}} \right\rceil.$$

The values for λ_{disk}^r and λ_{disk}^w are obtained using Eqs. (3.3.21) and (3.3.22). Finally, the disk utilization is computed by multiplying the total arrival rate of requests to the disk, that is, $\lambda_{\text{disk}}^r + \lambda_{\text{disk}}^w$, by the average disk service time. Note that the proper stripe unit size must be used to obtain the transfer size in each case.

Table 3.3 shows that the best stripe unit size is 16 KB because it provides the smallest utilization for each individual disk. It should be noted that as the stripe unit size increases, the total arrival rate of requests to the disks decreases or stays constant. A stripe unit size of 8 KB is worse than one of 4 KB because even though the total arrival rate is the same for both cases, the transfer time is bigger for the 8 KB case. The total arrival rate for 16 KB stripe units is smaller than for 8 KB stripe units. The total arrival rate is the same for stripe units of 16, 32, and 64 KB. However, since the transfer time increases with the stripe unit size, the disk utilization increases. ∎

The expressions for disk arrays are summarized in Fig. 3.10 and are implemented in the worksheet `DiskArrays` in the MS Excel workbook `ServTime.XLS`.

3.3.2 Service Times in Networks

A message from a client to a server has to go through several protocol layers and may have to be transmitted through one or more networks as depicted by Fig. 3.11. In this figure, a message from a client to the database server has to cross a 10-Mbps Ethernet, a 100-Mbps backbone FDDI, and a 16-Mbps Token Ring LAN. Messages generated by an application have to go through a protocol stack that involves, at least, a transport layer protocol (e.g., TCP or UDP), an internet protocol (e.g., IP or IPX), and a network protocol (e.g., Ethernet or Token Ring). Protocol entities at each layer communicate with each other by exchanging PDUs composed of a header and a data area. PDUs receive different names for different protocols and usually have a maximum size for the data area. At the network layer, the maximum size of the data area is called maximum transmission unit (MTU). As indicated in Fig. 3.11, the MTU is 1,500 bytes for an Ethernet, 4,472 bytes for an FDDI ring, and 4,444 bytes for a Token Ring. So, routers have to be able to fragment datagrams as they go through networks of decreasing MTUs. Fragments are reassembled at the IP level by the destination host. For example, a 2,500-byte packet crossing from the FDDI network in Fig. 3.11 to the Ethernet has to be fragmented into two *fragments* by router 1.

Each protocol layer adds its own header and sometimes a trailer, as explained in Chap. 2. Table 3.4 lists the PDU name, maximum size of the PDU, header plus

Arrival rate of read and write requests to component disks:

$$\lambda_{\text{disk}}^r = \frac{n_r}{N} \times \lambda_{\text{array}}^r + \frac{rw\,(n_w)}{N} \times \lambda_{\text{array}}^w \qquad (3.3.25)$$

$$\lambda_{\text{disk}}^w = \frac{n_w + 1}{N} \times \lambda_{\text{array}}^w \qquad (3.3.26)$$

Service times for reads and writes for the disk array:

$$S_{\text{array}}^r = \max_{i=1}^{n_r}\{R_{\text{disk } i}^r\} \qquad (3.3.27)$$

$$S_{\text{array}}^w = \max_{i=1}^{rw(n_w)}\{R_{\text{disk } i}^r\} + \max_{i=1}^{n_w+1}\{R_{\text{disk } i}^w\} \qquad (3.3.28)$$

Utilization of individual disks:

$$U_d = (\lambda_{\text{disk}}^r + \lambda_{\text{disk}}^w) \left[\text{Seek}_{\text{rand}} + \frac{\text{DiskRevolutionTime}}{2} + \frac{\text{StripeUnit (in bytes)}}{10^6 \times \text{TransferRate}}\right] \qquad (3.3.29)$$

Figure 3.10. Disk array equations.

trailer overhead, and the maximum size of the data area, which is equal to the maximum size of the PDU minus the overhead, for various important protocols [1], [2], [11].

The service time of a message at a network is the time it takes to transmit the message over the network. This time is equal to the ratio of the number of bytes needed to transmit the message—including protocol header and trailer overhead—divided by the network bandwidth. The protocol overhead depends on the protocols

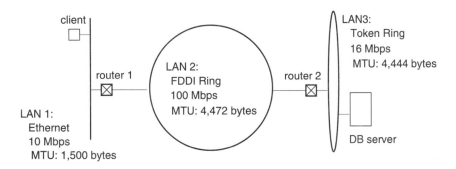

Figure 3.11. Connectivity between a client and a server.

Table 3.4. Characteristics of Various Network Protocols

Protocol	PDU Name	Max. PDU Size (bytes)	Overhead (bytes)	Max. Data Area (bytes)
TCP	Segment	65,535	20	65,515
UDP	Datagram	(*)	8	(*)
IP version 4	Datagram	65,535	20	65,515
IP version 6	Datagram	65,535	40	65,495
ATM	Cell	53	5	48
Ethernet	Frame	1,518	18	1,500
IEEE 802.3	Frame	1,518	21	1,497
IEEE 802.5 Token Ring	Frame	4,472	28	4,444
FDDI (RFC 1390)	Frame	4,500	28	4,472

(*): limited by IP datagram size.

involved and on the fragmentation that may be needed at the network layer.

To illustrate how a message service time is computed, let us consider the following example.

Example 3.6: The client of Fig. 3.12a sends a 300-byte long request to the database server and receives a 10,000-byte long reply. The interaction between the client and the server takes place over a TCP connection (see Fig. 3.12a). The request from the client to the server is placed into the data area of a TCP segment, which travels in the data area of an IP datagram. The IP datagram is encapsulated by an Ethernet frame, by an FDDI frame, and by a Token Ring frame as it travels in LANs 1, 2, and 3, respectively, as illustrated in Fig. 3.12b. So, the 300-byte request receives 20 bytes of TCP and 20 bytes of IP header, plus 18 bytes of frame overhead in LAN1, 28 bytes of frame overhead in LAN 2, and 28 bytes of frame overhead in LAN3. So, the 300-byte request becomes a 358 (= 300 + 20 + 20 + 18)-byte frame in LAN 1 and a 368 (= 300 + 20 + 20 + 28)-byte frame in LANs 2 and 3. The time to transmit a frame over a network is equal to the size of the frame in bits divide by the network's bandwidth in bits per second. So, the frame transmission time for the frames containing the client request at LANs 1, 2, and 3 are given by

$$\frac{358 \times 8}{10,000,000} = 0.000286 \text{ sec}$$

$$\frac{368 \times 8}{100,000,000} = 0.00002944 \text{ sec}$$

$$\frac{368 \times 8}{16,000,000} = 0.000184 \text{ sec.}$$

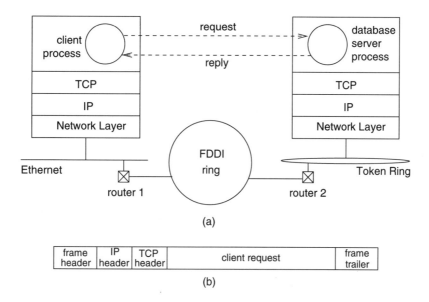

(a)

(b)

Figure 3.12. (a) Interaction between client and server over a TCP connection. (b) Frame format.

Let us now turn our attention to the reply from the server to the client. The server puts its 10,000 byte long reply in the data area of a TCP segment, which along with the 20-byte TCP header forms a 10,020-byte TCP segment that is passed to the IP level at the database server. Since a host cannot generate IP datagrams bigger than the MTU of the network to which the host is attached to, the database server generates three IP datagrams. All of them have a 20-byte IP header. The first datagram also includes the TCP header. Since the MTU for the Token Ring is 4,444 bytes, the first datagram contains the first 4,404 (= 4,444 - 20 - 20) bytes of the reply. The second datagram contains the next 4,424 (= 4,444 - 20) bytes of the reply, and the third and final datagram carries the last 1,172 bytes of the reply. Note from Table 3.4 that the header size for Token Ring is 28 bytes. So, the three frames in the Token Ring network have sizes equal to 4,472 (= 4,444 + 28) bytes, 4,472 (= 4,444 + 28) bytes, and 1,220 (= 1,172 + 20 + 28) bytes, respectively. So, the service time of the reply message in LAN 3 is $[(4,472+4,472+1,220) \times 8]/16,000,000 = 0.005082$ sec.

The three datagrams that reach router 2 coming from LAN 3 to LAN 2 do not need to be fragmented because the MTU of LAN 2 is bigger than that of LAN 3. The new size of these datagrams in LAN 2 is obtained by subtracting the overhead of the frames in LAN 3 and adding the overhead of frames in LAN 2. Since the overhead is the same for LANs 2 and 3, the frames sizes are the same. The bandwidth of LAN 2 is different from that of LAN 3. So, the service time of the reply in

LAN 2 is $[(4,472 + 4,472 + 1,220) \times 8]/100,000,000 = 0.0008131$ sec. Finally, the three fragments containing the reply reach router 1 on their way to LAN 1. The datagram sizes seen by router 1 after the 28-byte overhead from LAN 2 is eliminated are 4,444 bytes, 4,444 bytes, and 1,192 bytes, respectively. The first two datagrams have to be further fragmented because of the 1,500-byte MTU limit of LAN 1. So, each 4,444-byte datagram generates three datagrams, each with its own 20-byte IP header. The first two datagrams are 1,500 bytes long, and the last one is 1,484 bytes long. Note that $1,500 + 1,500 + 1,484 = 4,484 = 4,444 + 40$. The 40 bytes are added because fragments two and three need a 20-byte IP header each. Adding the Ethernet overhead to compute the frame size, we find that the service time of the reply at LAN 1 is $[2 \times (1,518 + 1,518 + 1,502) + 1,210] \times 8/10,000,000 = 0.00823$ sec. ∎

Current IP standards recommend that a source host discovers the minimum MTU along a path before choosing the initial datagram size [2]. This avoids fragmentation and reassembly altogether and speeds up packet processing time at intermediate routers and at the destination host. In what follows, we provide general equations for the average service time of a message at a network for the case when there is no fragmentation. The fragmentation case can be treated as discussed above.

Let

- MessageSize: size, in bytes, of a message exchanged between client and server

- MTU_n: MTU, in bytes, of network n

- TCPOvhd: overhead, in bytes, of the TCP protocol

- IPOvhd: overhead, in bytes, of the IP protocol

- FrameOvhd_n: overhead, in bytes, of the frames in network n

- Overhead_n: total overhead (TCP + IP + frame), in bytes, for all frames necessary to carry a message on network n

- Bandwidth_n: bandwidth, in megabits per second, of network n

- NDatagrams: number of IP datagrams needed to transmit a message

- N: number of networks between the client and the server

In the case of no fragmentation, the sender host (client or server) generates datagrams whose size is less than or equal to the minimum MTU over all N networks. Each datagram includes an IP header. The total number of bytes transmitted by all the datagrams is equal to the message size plus the TCP header. So, the number of datagrams needed to transmit the message over any of the N networks is

$$\text{NDatagrams} = \left\lceil \frac{\text{MessageSize} + \text{TCPOvhd}}{\min_{n=1}^{N} \text{MTU}_n - \text{IPOvhd}} \right\rceil . \tag{3.3.30}$$

The total protocol overhead involved in transmitting a message over network n is given by

$$\text{Overhead}_n = \text{TCPOvhd} + \text{NDatagrams} \times (\text{IPOvhd} + \text{FrameOvhd}_n). \quad (3.3.31)$$

Finally, the service time at network n for a message is equal to the total number of bits needed to transmit the message (including overhead) divided by the bandwidth in bits per second. Hence,

$$\text{ServiceTime}_n = \frac{8 \times (\text{MessageSize} + \text{Overhead}_n)}{10^6 \times \text{Bandwidth}_n}. \quad (3.3.32)$$

The utilization of network n is given by the arrival rate of messages to the network multiplied by the average service time of a message in the network, as shown in Sec. 3.5.1.

Example 3.7: The client in Fig. 3.11 submits transactions to the DB server at a rate of three transactions per minute, i.e, 0.05 tps. The average size of the request message is 400 bytes. Eighty percent of the replies are 8092 bytes long and the remaining 20% are 100,000 bytes long on average. Assuming that there is no fragmentation, we want to compute the average service time of requests and replies at each of the three networks as well as the utilization of each network.

Using Eq. (3.3.30), we compute the number of datagrams for requests, short replies, and long replies, as

$$\lceil (400 + 20)/(1,500 - 20) \rceil = 1 \text{ for requests}$$
$$\lceil (8,092 + 20)/(1,500 - 20) \rceil = 6 \text{ for short replies}$$
$$\lceil (100,000 + 20)/(1,500 - 20) \rceil = 68 \text{ for long replies}. \quad (3.3.33)$$

The overhead per network, computed using Eq. (3.3.31), and the average service time, computed from Eq. (3.3.32), for the request and the two types of replies are shown in Table 3.5.

The average network utilization at each network is obtained by multiplying the average arrival rate of C/S transactions by the average service time for the messages involved in a transaction. The average service time per transaction at any network is equal to the average service time for the request plus the average service time for the reply. The average service time for the reply is 0.8 times the average service time for short replies plus 0.2 times the average service time for long replies. Using the values of Table 3.5, we can compute the utilization of each network. The results are shown in Table 3.6. Network utilization values are given for various values of the number of clients. The overall arrival rate of transactions at each network is equal to the number of clients multiplied by the arrival rate of transactions per client. ■

The expressions for network service times and utilizations are summarized in Fig. 3.13 and are implemented in the worksheet `Networks` in the MS Excel workbook `ServTime.XLS` that accompanies this book.

Table 3.5. Network Computations for Ex. 3.6

		Request	Short Reply	Long Reply
LAN 1	Ndatagrams	1	6	68
	Overhead (bytes)	58	248	2604
	ServiceTime (msec)	0.366	6.67	82.1
LAN 2	Ndatagrams	1	6	68
	Overhead (bytes)	68	308	3284
	ServiceTime (msec)	0.0374	0.672	8.26
LAN 3	Ndatagrams	1	6	68
	Overhead (bytes)	68	308	3284
	ServiceTime (msec)	0.234	4.2	51.6

Table 3.6. Network Utilizations for Ex. 3.6.

	Service Times (sec)		
	LAN 1	LAN 2	LAN 3
	0.0221	0.00223	0.0140
	Percent Utilization		
No. Clients	LAN 1	LAN 2	LAN 3
40	4.4	0.4	2.8
80	8.8	0.9	5.6
120	13.3	1.3	8.3
160	17.7	1.8	11.1
200	22.1	2.2	13.9
240	26.5	2.7	16.7
280	31.0	3.1	19.5

3.3.3   Service Times at Routers

A router is a communications processor that is used to determine the route that a datagram will follow from the source host to the destination host. Datagrams incoming into a router are queued up until the router processor is available to inspect the packet. The datagram's destination address is used by the router to determine the next best outgoing link, based on routing tables at the router [8]. The datagram is then placed at the output queue for the next link in its path to the destination (see Fig. 3.14).

The time taken by a router to process a datagram is known as *router latency* and is usually provided by router vendors in microseconds per packet. The total

---

Number of datagrams generated by a message (no fragmentation):

$$\text{NDatagrams} = \left\lceil \frac{\text{MessageSize} + \text{TCPOvhd}}{\min_{n=1}^{N} \text{MTU}_n - \text{IPOvhd}} \right\rceil \qquad (3.3.34)$$

Total protocol overhead of a message over network n:

$$\text{Overhead}_n = \text{TCPOvhd} + \text{NDatagrams} \times (\text{IPOvhd} + \text{FrameOvhd}_n) \quad (3.3.35)$$

Message service time at network n:

$$\text{ServiceTime}_n = \frac{8 \times (\text{MessageSize} + \text{Overhead}_n)}{10^6 \times \text{Bandwidth}_n} \qquad (3.3.36)$$

Utilization of network n:

$$U_n = \sum_{\text{messages } j} \lambda_j \times \text{ServiceTime}_n^j \qquad (3.3.37)$$

where λ_j is the arrival rate of messages of type j and ServiceTime_n^j is the average service time for messages of type j on network n.

Figure 3.13. Network equations.

service time of a message at a router is then given by

$$\text{RouterServiceTime} = \text{NDatagrams} \times \text{RouterLatency} \qquad (3.3.38)$$

where NDatagrams is given by Eq. (3.3.30).

Example 3.8: Consider Ex. 3.7 and assume that routers 1 and 2 have a latency of 134 μsec/packet. The service time at the routers for the client request, short reply, and long reply are, respectively, $1 \times 134 = 134$ μsec, $6 \times 134 = 804$ μsec, and $68 \times 134 = 9,112$ μsec.   ∎

3.4   Queues and Contention

As already discussed, requests in a C/S system, are served by several types of resources (e.g., processors, disks, networks, and routers). Each time a request visits a resource, it may need to queue for the use of the resource. Figure 3.15a shows the graphical notation used to represent a resource (a circle) and its waiting queue (striped rectangle). The resource in the case of Fig. 3.15a could be a disk, and the striped rectangle would represent the queue of requests waiting to use the disk. In some cases, there may be multiple resources for the same queue. Consider for

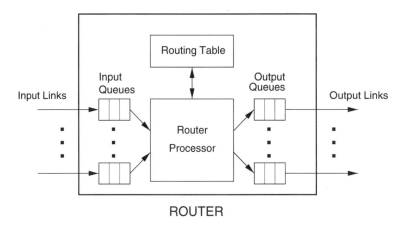

ROUTER

Figure 3.14. Router queues.

example a symmetric multiprocessor used to support a DB server. In this case, there is a common queue of processes waiting to be scheduled to any of the processors as shown in Fig. 3.15b.

There are situations where a resource is dedicated to a request or there is an

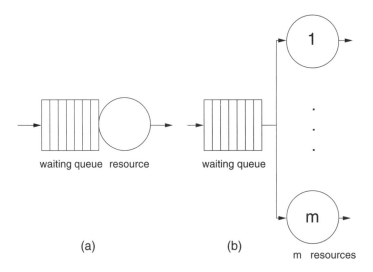

Figure 3.15. (a) Graphical notation for a resource and its queue. (b) Graphical notation for a multiresource queue.

ample number of resources, so that no queuing takes place. We call these resources *delay resources*, since they only impose a delay to the flow of a request. The graphical representation of a delay resource is a circle without the striped rectangle (the queue). Delay resources can be used to represent the time spent by a request at a client if the client does not generate another request until the previous one is completed.

As the load on a resource increases, more requests will be queued for the resource. At light loads however, the total queuing time may be negligible when compared with the service time at the resource. In these cases, we may want to represent the resource as a delay resource to simplify the model.

We now define the notation used throughout this book to represent performance variables for queues in C/S system. Some of the concepts presented here were already introduced, albeit more informally, in the previous sections.

We will call *queue* the waiting queue plus the resource or resources associated with the waiting queue. Let

- V_i: average number of visits to queue i by a C/S transaction

- S_i: average service time of a C/S transaction at resource i per visit to the resource

- W_i: average waiting time of a C/S transaction at queue i per visit to the queue

- R_i: average response time of a C/S transaction at queue i, defined as the sum of the average waiting time plus average service time per visit to the queue. So, $R_i = W_i + S_i$

- λ_i: average arrival rate of requests to queue i

- X_i: average throughput of queue i, defined as the average number of transactions that complete from queue i per unit time. We will assume that any queue is observed during a period large enough that the number of arrivals and departures to the queue are almost the same. This assumption is known as *Flow Equilibrium Assumption* [3], [7] and implies that $\lambda_i = X_i$

- X_0: average system throughput, defined as the average number of transactions that complete per time unit

- N_i^w: average number of transactions at the waiting queue of queue i

- N_i^s: average number of transactions receiving service at the any of the resources of queue i. In the case of a single resource queue (see Fig. 3.15a), N_i^s is a number between zero and one that can be interpreted as the fraction of time that the resource is busy, or in other words, the utilization of the resource

- N_i: average number of transactions at queue i waiting or receiving service from any resource at queue i. So, $N_i = N_i^w + N_i^s$

Section 3.5 establishes some important and fundamental relationships between the performance variables defined above.

3.5 Some Basic Performance Results

The relationships presented in this section are very simple and general and are known as operational results [3]. To understand the validity of these results, we do not need to resort to any complex mathematical formulation.

3.5.1 Utilization Law

Let us start with a very simple relationship called *Utilization Law*. Consider first the single resource queue of Fig. 3.15a. The utilization U_i of the resource is defined as the fraction of time that the resource is busy. So, if we monitor queue i during $\mathcal{T}$ seconds and find out that the resource was busy during B_i seconds, its utilization, U_i, is $B_i/\mathcal{T}$. Assume that during the same interval $\mathcal{T}$, C_0 transactions completed from the queue. This means that the average throughput from the queue is $X_i = C_0/\mathcal{T}$. Combining this relationship with the definition of utilization, we get

$$U_i = B_i/\mathcal{T} = (B_i/C_0) \times X_i = X_i \times S_i. \tag{3.5.1}$$

Note that in Eq. (3.5.1) we used the fact that the average time the resource was busy per transaction, i.e., the average service time S_i per transaction, is equal to the total time the resource was busy (B_i) divided by the number of transactions that were served during the monitoring period. In equilibrium, $\lambda_i = X_i$, and we can write that,

$$U_i = X_i.S_i = \lambda_i.S_i. \tag{3.5.2}$$

Example 3.9: A network segment transmits 1,000 packets/s. Each packet has an average transmission time equal to 0.15 msec. What is the utilization of the LAN segment? From the Utilization Law, the utilization of the LAN segment is $1,000 \times 0.00015 = 0.15 = 15\%$. ∎

The utilization can also be interpreted as the average number of transactions in the resource because there is one transaction using the resource during U_i percent of the time and zero transactions during $(1 - U_i)$ percent of the time. For the case of a multiple resource queue, as in Fig. 3.15b, the utilization is defined as the average number of transactions using any of the resources normalized by the number of resources. So, the utilization of an m-resource queue is

$$U_i = X_i \times S_i/m. \tag{3.5.3}$$

We will see in the next subsection why $X_i \times S_i$ is also the average number of transactions using any resource in a multiple resource queue. Since this number is less than or equal to the number of resources m, the utilization of an m-resource queue must be less than or equal to one.

3.5.2   Forced Flow Law

By definition of the average number of visits V_i, each completing transaction has to pass V_i times, on the average, by queue i. So, if X_0 transactions complete per time unit, $V_i \times X_0$ transactions will visit queue i per time unit. So, the average throughput of queue i, X_i, is $V_i \times X_0$. This simple result is known as the *Forced Flow Law* and is written as

$$X_i = V_i \times X_0. \tag{3.5.4}$$

Example 3.10: Database transactions perform an average of 4.5 I/O operations on the database server. The database server was monitored during one hour and during this period, 7,200 transactions were executed during this period. What is the average throughput of the disk? If each disk I/O takes 20 msec on the average, what was the disk utilization?

The database server throughput, X_0, is 7,200 / 3,600 = 2 tps. The average number of visits to the disk, V_d is 4.5. Using the Forced Flow Law we obtain the disk throughput, X_d , as $4.5 \times 2 = 9$ tps. To compute the disk utilization U_d we use the Utilization Law and obtain $U_d = X_d \times S_d = 9 \times 0.02 = 0.18 = 18\%$.   ■

3.5.3   Service Demand Law

The service demand D_i, previously defined as $V_i \times S_i$, can easily be related to the system throughput and utilization by combining the Utilization and Forced Flow laws as follows:

$$D_i = V_i \times S_i = (X_i/X_0)\,(U_i/X_i) = U_i/X_0. \tag{3.5.5}$$

Example 3.11: What is the service demand of the disk in Ex. 3.10? From the Service Demand Law we get that $D_d = U_d/X_0 = 0.18/2 = 0.09$ sec. Note that this is also equal to $V_d \times S_d = 4.5 \times 0.02$ sec.   ■

3.5.4   Little's Law

Our next result is probably one of the most important things you will learn in this book! It is quite simple and widely applicable. We present in what follows a very simple derivation of the result known as *Little's Law* (see [5] for a more formal derivation). Consider the box in Fig. 3.16a. This box could contain anything, from a very simple device such as a disk, or something as complex as an entire intranet. For the purpose of this discussion, we assume that "customers" that arrive at the black box spend an average of R sec in the black box and then leave. The average departure rate, that is, the throughput of the black box, is X customers/sec and the average number of customers in the black box is N. We want to show that $N = X \times R$. Consider Fig. 3.16b that shows a graph of the number of customers, $n(t)$, in the black box at time t. Suppose we observe the flow of customers from time zero to time $\mathcal{T}$. Then, the average number of customers during that interval is simply equal to the sum of all products of the form $k \times f_k$, where k is the number

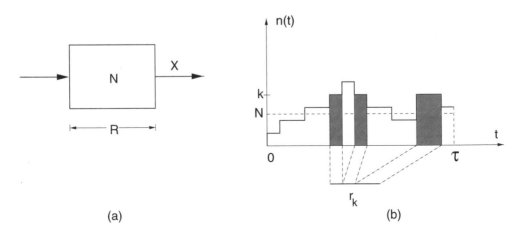

Figure 3.16. (a) Box for Little's Law. (b) Graph of n (t) vs. t.

of customers in the black box and f_k is the fraction of time that k customers are in the black box. But f_k is simply $r_k/\mathcal{T}$, where r_k is the total time that there are k customers in the black box (see Fig. 3.16b). So

$$N = \sum_k k \times f_k = \sum_k k \times \frac{r_k}{\mathcal{T}}. \tag{3.5.6}$$

Let us multiply and divide the right-hand side of Eq. (3.5.6) by the number of customers, C_0, that departed from the black box in the interval $[0, \mathcal{T}]$ and rearrange the equation. Hence,

$$N = \frac{C_0}{\mathcal{T}} \times \frac{\sum_k k \times r_k}{C_0}. \tag{3.5.7}$$

Note that $C_0/\mathcal{T}$ is the throughput X. The summation in Eq. (3.5.7) is the total number of (customer × seconds) accumulated in the system. If we divide this number by the total number C_0 of customers completed, we get the average time, R, each customer spent in the black box. So,

$$N = X \times R. \tag{3.5.8}$$

Example 3.12: An NFS server was monitored during 30 min and the number of I/O operations performed during this period was found to be 10,800. The average number of active NFS requests was found to be 3. What was the average response time per NFS request at the server?

The throughput X of the server is $10,800/1,800 = 6$ requests/sec. From Little's Law, the average response time R is N/X. So, $R = 3/6 = 0.5$ sec.   ■

Little's Law is quite powerful and can be applied to any black box provided it does not create nor destroys customers. If we now apply Little's Law to the waiting queue, to the set of m resources, and to the entire queue of Fig. 3.15b, we get, respectively, that

$$N_i^w = X_i \times W_i \tag{3.5.9}$$

$$N_i^s = X_i \times S_i \tag{3.5.10}$$

$$N_i = X_i \times R_i. \tag{3.5.11}$$

Equation (3.5.10) gives the average number of transactions at the set of m resources. So, the average number of transactions per resource, also defined as the utilization, is $X_i \times S_i/m$.

Example 3.13: Consider that router 2 in Fig. 3.11 has a latency of 200 μsec/packet. Packets flow from LAN 2 to LAN 3 at a rate of 30,000 packets/sec. What is the average number of packets in the router in transit from from LAN 2 to LAN 3?

From Little's Law, the average number of packets in router 2 in transit from LAN 2 to LAN 3 is $30,000 \times 0.0002 = 6$ packets. ∎

3.5.5   Summary of Basic Results

Figure 3.17 summarizes the main relationships discussed in Sec. 3.5. These formulas are implemented in the worksheet `BasicResults` of the MS Excel workbook `ServTime.XLS` that accompanies this book.

3.6   Performance Metrics in C/S Systems

The three most important metrics used to assess C/S systems are *response time*, *throughput*, and *cost*. We have been referring to response time and throughput since the first chapter of this book relying on the reader's intuitive understanding of these terms. In this section, we discuss in more detail the meaning of these two important measures.

In a C/S system, response time can be defined in two ways, as illustrated in Fig. 3.18. At time t_0, the client finished to receive a reply from the server. Between time t_0 and time t_1, the user is deciding what to do next and prepares to submit the next transaction . The interval between t_0 and t_1 is called *think time*. At time t_1, the client submits a new transaction to the server. The reply from the server starts to arrive at the client at time t_2 and finishes to arrive at time t_3. Both intervals $(t_2 - t_1)$ and $(t_3 - t_1)$ are usually called *response time*. To distinguish between the two, we will use the term *reaction time* to denote the interval $(t_2 - t_1)$. Consider the case of a user browsing the Web. The moment the user clicks on a link on the browser, a transaction with the server is started. This transaction may cause several files, including text and image, to be fetched from the server and displayed by the browser. As soon as the first document starts to be displayed by the browser,

Utilization of an m-resource queue:

$$U_i = X_i \times S_i/m \qquad (3.5.12)$$

Forced Flow Law:

$$X_i = V_i \times X_0 \qquad (3.5.13)$$

Service Demand Law:

$$D_i = V_i \times S_i = U_i/X_0 \qquad (3.5.14)$$

Little's Law:

$$N = X \times R \qquad (3.5.15)$$

Little's Law applied to queue i:

$$N_i^w = X_i \times W_i, \quad N_i^s = X_i \times S_i, \quad N_i = X_i \times R_i \qquad (3.5.16)$$

Figure 3.17. Basic C/S system performance results.

the reaction interval ends. When all text and image files are completely displayed, the response time interval ends. A detailed discussion of end-to-end response times in C/S systems is presented in [6].

While response time is a performance metric of interest to users, throughput, defined as the number of transactions executed per unit time, is of more interest to system administrators. The unit used to measure throughput depends on the type of C/S transaction in question. If the server is an NFS server, throughput is usually measured in NFS IOPS (NFS I/O operations per second). For Web servers, throughput is measured in HTTPops/s (http operations per second) and for

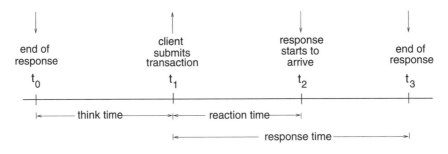

Figure 3.18. Definition of think time, reaction time, and response time

database servers, throughput is measured in tps (transactions per second). Chapter 7 discusses other measures of throughput used in industry standard benchmarks.

Cost is usually associated with some measure of performance, i.e., response or throughput, as a price-performance ratio. For example, the TPC benchmark from the Transaction Processing Performance Council (TPC), measures online transaction processing systems and provides a dollar per tps ($/tps) metric, which indicates how much needs to spent per unit of throughput. The cost figure includes both hardware and software cost.

3.7   Concluding Remarks

A C/S transaction uses various resources, including processors and disks, at the client and server, networks, and routers. The total response time of a transaction is composed of two main components: service time and waiting time. Service time includes the time the transaction spends receiving service from any of the resources (e.g., performing an I/O operation at the database server). Waiting time is the time spent waiting for a resource to become available (e.g., waiting for the CPU to become available).

This chapter presented many important concepts, such as service time, service demand, utilization, throughput, and response time. Formulas were given to obtain the average service time at single disks, disk arrays, networks, and routers. The notion of queues was introduced and formalized. Several important relationships, including the Utilization Law, Service Demand Law, Forced Flow Law, and Little's Law, were presented. Chapters 8 and 9 present models that allows us to predict the queuing time of a C/S transaction on the various resources.

The formulation presented in this chapter was coached in terms of general C/S systems, of which Web servers and intranet applications are special cases. The next chapter discusses performance issues that are more specific to these environments.

BIBLIOGRAPHY

[1] J. BLOMMERS, *Practical Planning for Network Growth*. Upper Saddle River, NJ: Prentice Hall, 1996.

[2] D. E. COMER, *Computer Networks and Internets*. Upper Saddle River, NJ: Prentice Hall, 1997.

[3] P. J. DENNING and J. P. BUZEN, The operational analysis of queuing network models, *Computing Surveys*, vol. 10, no. 3, pp. 225–261, Sept. 1978.

[4] C. C. GOTLIEB and G. H. MACEWEN, Performance of movable-head disk storage systems, *J. ACM*, vol. 20, no. 4, pp. 604–623, Oct. 1973.

[5] J. C. LITTLE, A proof of the queuing formula $L = \lambda W$, *Operations Res.*, vol. 9, pp. 383–387, 1961.

[6] M. MACCABEE, Client/server end-to-end response time: real life experience, *Proc. 1996 Comput. Measurement Group Conf.*, Orlando, FL, Dec. 8–13, 1996, pp. 839–849.

[7] D. A. MENASCÉ, V. A. F. ALMEIDA, and L. W. DOWDY, *Capacity Planning and Performance Modeling: From Mainframes to Client-Server Systems*. Upper Saddle River, NJ: Prentice Hall, 1994.

[8] R. PERLMAN, *Interconnections: Bridges and Routers*. Reading, MA: Addison-Wesley, 1992.

[9] M. SELTZER, P. CHEN, and J. OUSTERHOUT, Disk scheduling revisited, *Proc. Winter 1990 USENIX Conf.*, Washington, DC, Jan. 22–26, 1990, pp. 313–323.

[10] E. SHRIVER, *Performance Modeling for Realistic Storage Devices*, Ph.D. dissertation, Dep. Comput. Sci., New York Univ., May 1997.

[11] W. STALLINGS, *Data and Computer Communications*. New York: Macmillan, 1994.

Chapter 4

WEB SERVER AND INTRANET PERFORMANCE ISSUES

4.1   Introduction

This chapter discusses issues that affect performance of Web servers and intranets. Speed has been identified as the number one problem facing Web users [15]. They complain that it takes too long to download a page or to interact with a Web site. Thus, we start out the chapter looking at the sources of delay in a Web environment. After discussing the end user perspective to Internet and intranet performance, the chapter provides an assessment. It examines the components and protocols involved in the execution of Web services and analyzes their capacity and performance issues.

Servers, clients, and networks are the main elements of Web environments, as shown in Fig. 4.1. Servers are key components of the Internet and intranets. They deliver information upon request, in the form of text, images, sound, video, and multimedia combination of these. Web services available on the Internet and intranets are provided by many different servers using a wide variety of computers and software. Servers receive, store, and forward information on the Internet and intranets. There are several different types of servers in the Web, which come in the form of Web sites, proxy, cache, and mirror. Web servers deliver information, and it is up to clients to use it properly. Internet and intranet clients are foremost Web browsers together with other applications such as e-mail, ftp, and telnet. Browser software allows a desktop computer to communicate with any other client on a TCP/IP network and any server on the network with an HTTP address. As businesses increase their reliance on electronic commerce, Web service performance will become very important, even critical. The more information and services a company makes available on a Web site, the more hits it gets. And the more hits a Web site gets, the higher the probability that users will wait too long for a response. And in many cases, Web users or customers will compare how well the company does relative to its competitors. Dissatisfied customers switch from an unresponsive

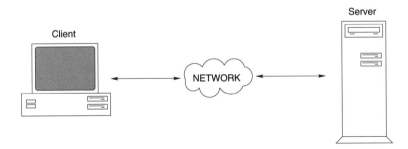

Figure 4.1. Web components.

site X to a site Z with a click of the mouse.

Performance problems on the Internet and intranets are exacerbated by the unpredictable nature of information retrieval and service requesting over the Web. At times, sites are almost idle, with no visitors. Suddenly, sometimes without warning, traffic can increase a hundredfold. This type of load spike is faced by many Web sites. During the Christmas holiday season, some electronic-commerce sites experience a dramatic rise in traffic, while remaining relatively calm the rest of the year. There are also other characteristics that distinguish Web-based systems from traditional client/server systems. For example, the size of objects (e.g., text, graphics, video, audio) retrieved from Web servers varies from 10^3 to 10^7 bytes. Compounding the problem, there is a large assortment of back-end applications running on Web servers. The combination of these unique characteristics of the Web generates several performance problems, such as server overload and network bottleneck, that have a tremendous impact on the end user perception of performance.

As the Web evolves, performance issues become one of the top management concerns. There are basically six topics to look at when analyzing the performance of Web sites: contents, server software, hardware, operating system, network bandwidth, and infrastructure. All of these issues are covered in this chapter.

4.2 More than Just Servers

Simply stated, a Web server is a combination of a hardware platform, operating system, server software, and contents, as illustrated in Fig. 4.2. All of these components have influence on the performance of Web servers and intranets. We discuss next, the specific aspects of each component that affect the operational behavior of Web servers.

HTML

Documents on the Web are written in a simple "markup language" called Hypertext Markup Language (HTML) [4]. HTML is the system used to create hypertext

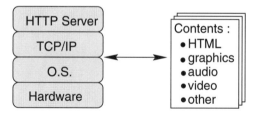

Figure 4.2. Web server elements.

documents. HTML allows one to describe the structure of documents by indicating headings, emphasis, links to other documents, and so forth. Images and other multimedia objects can be included in HTML documents. Thus, HTML allows one to integrate video, software applications, and multimedia objects on the Web. Most HTML documents consist of text and inline images. Special links point to inline images to be inserted in a document. Inline images have a great impact on server performance. When a browser parses the HTML data received from a server, it recognizes links associated with inline images and automatically requests the image files pointed to by the links. Actually, an HTML document with inline images is a combination of multiple objects, which generates multiple separate requests to the server. Whereas the user sees only one document, the server sees a series of separate requests for that document. In order to improve end user performance perception, some browsers start requesting images before the whole text has arrived at the client. In terms of system performance, it is important to understand that a single click by a user may generate a series of file requests to a server.

The Combination of HTTP and TCP/IP

The HyperText Transfer Protocol [17] (HTTP) is an application-level protocol layered on top of TCP used in the communication between clients and servers on the Web. HTTP defines a simple request-response interaction, which can be viewed as a "Web transaction." Each HTTP interaction consists of a request sent from the client to the server, followed by a response sent back by the server to the client. An HTTP request includes several pieces: the method which specifies the legal action (e.g., GET, HEAD, PUT, and POST), the Uniform Resource Locator (URL) that identifies the name of the information requested, and other additional information, such as the type of document the client is willing to accept, authentication, and payment authorization. When a server receives a request, it parses the request and takes the action specified by the method. The server then replies to the client with a response consisting of a status line indicating the success or failure of the request, meta-information describing the type of object returned and the information requested, and a file or an output generated by a server-side application (e.g., CGI). The main steps involved in an HTTP request-response interaction are:

- map the server name to an IP address (e.g., www.performance_book.com to 199.333.111.0)

- establish a TCP/IP connection with the server

- transmit the request (URL + method + other information)

- receive the response (HTML text or image or other information)

- close the TCP/IP connection

Each of these steps has an inherent cost that depends on the server and network performance, as we will see in this section.

HTTP is referred to as a "stateless protocol" because it does not include the concept of a session or interaction beyond delivery of the requested document. In the original HTTP protocol, a conversation is restricted to the transfer of one document or image. Each transfer is totally separated from the previous or next request. Considering that a Web site is accessible to millions of clients, the stateless nature of the HTTP protocol brings efficiency to the system, because servers do not need to keep track of who the clients are or what requests were serviced in the past. The other side of the coin of the stateless nature of the HTTP protocol is the performance cost. The original version of the protocol, HTTP 1.0, has several inherent performance inefficiencies. For instance, a new connection is established per request. A page with text and many small images generates many separate connections for the text and for each image. Since most Web objects are small, a high fraction of packets exchanged between client and server are simply TCP control packets used to open and close connections, as shown in Fig. 4.3a.

A key element to understand the performance of the pair HTTP-TCP/IP is the latency or the mandatory delays imposed by the protocols. Latency in this case consists of connection delay and request delay. The former is the time (measured in round-trip time [rtt]) it takes to establish a connection. The latter refers to the time it takes to complete a data transfer over an already established connection. Let us analyze the delays involved in the execution of a Web transaction.

Figure 4.3 illustrates the packets exchanged between a client and a server for an HTTP interaction over TCP [7], [14]. Figure 4.3a shows the exchange of packets that occurs in version 1.0 of the HTTP protocol, while Fig. 4.3b displays the equivalent exchange for the persistent version of the protocol, HTTP 1.1, which maintains TCP connections across HTTP requests. Horizontal dashed lines on the client side represent the mandatory round-trip times through the network, imposed by a combination of the TCP/IP and HTTP protocols. Packets represented by dotted lines are required by TCP but do not interfere with latency, because the receiver does not need to wait for them to proceed execution. The mandatory delays involved in an HTTP request-response interaction are as follows.

- The client opens a TCP connection, which results in an exchange of SYN and ACK packets (see Sec. 2.2.3).

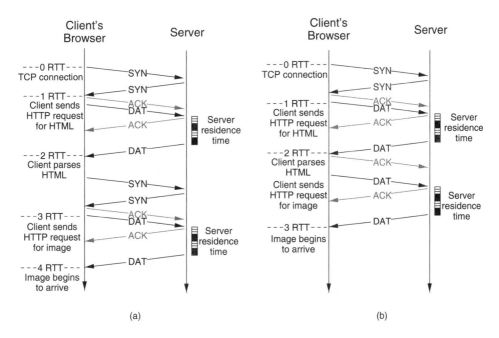

Figure 4.3.   (a) HTTP interaction in HTTP 1.0.   (b) HTTP interaction in HTTP 1.1.

- The client sends an HTTP request to the server, which parses it, executes the action requested, and sends back the response. In the case of a retrieval operation, the server has to move data from disk or cache to the client through the network. Afterward, the server is responsible for closing the connection. The FIN packets exchanged by the server and client to close the connection are not represented in Fig. 4.3, because the client does not have to wait for the connection termination to continue.

- The client parses the HTML response to look for the URL of the inline image. The client then opens a new TCP connection, that involves another three-way handshake.

- The client sends an HTTP request for the first inline image again and the process repeats itself.

For each additional request, a new TCP connection must be established and the system incurs again in a connection setup overhead. As a consequence of the combination of HTTP and TCP/IP, a client has to wait at least four network round trips before a document with one inline image is displayed by the browser. Each additional image requires at least two other round trips: one to establish a TCP connection and another to obtain the image. Furthermore, when a TCP connection is first opened, TCP employs an algorithm known as "slow start." Slow start uses the first several data packets to probe the network to determine the optimal transmission rate. Again, because Web objects are small, most objects are transferred before their TCP connection completes the slow start algorithm. In summary, most HTTP/1.0 operations use TCP inefficiently, resulting in performance problems due to congestion and overhead.

A new version of HTTP (also known as HTTP 1.1, persistent-connection HTTP, or HTTP-NG) includes features that solve part of the performance problems of version 1.0. HTTP 1.1 leaves the TCP connection open between consecutive operations, as depicted in Fig. 4.3b. This technique, called "persistent connection," uses one TCP connection to carry multiple HTTP requests, eliminating the cost of several opens and closes and minimizing the impact of slow start. Thus, multiple requests and responses can be contained in a single TCP segment. This feature also avoids many round trip delays, improving performance and reducing the number of packets exchanged. Looking at Fig. 4.3, one can see how the new HTTP protocol affects network latencies. In the case of a request for an HTML document and one inline image, the document is available to the browser after three round trips, instead of the four round trips required by the original version of HTTP. Another feature of HTTP 1.1 relevant to performance is known as "pipeline of requests." The pipelining technique in HTTP allows multiple requests to be sent without waiting for a response. It means that many requests are sent by the client over a single TCP connection, before the answer of the previous ones are received. Experimental results [13] indicate that a pipelined HTTP/1.1 implementation outperformed HTTP/1.0, even when the original version of HTTP used multiple connections in parallel over different TCP connections.

Hardware and Operating System

Web server performance depends primarily on the behavior of its basic elements: the hardware platform and the operating system. From a hardware standpoint, the performance of a server is a function of the following:

- processors: speed and number

- memory: capacity

- disk subsystem: speed and capacity

- network interface card (NIC): bandwidth

Web servers can run on top of timesharing, multiuser operating systems, such as Unix, Windows NT, and others. Reliability, performance, scalability, and robustness are some of the features that one should consider when deciding on an operating system. As described in the previous section, the TCP/IP implementation of the operating system is also a key issue for HTTP performance.

Contents

The true value of a Web site lies in the relevance and quality of the information it contains. A Web site delivers contents of many forms, such as HTML documents, images, sound, and video clips. Contents size, structure, and links affect the performance of intranets and Web servers. For example, a popular page with heavy graphics could have a strong impact on the network connection to the site. In other cases, highly popular contents may have to be mirrored on multiple servers to avoid traffic bottlenecks. Content is also a factor that influences the shape of the intranet infrastructure. As an example of the influence of content on the infrastructure, it is worthwhile mentioning the case of a major university on the west coast of the United States that electronically publishes about 100,000 pages of scientific journals. University management noted that performance hampered its ability to distribute its journals around the world. In an effort to minimize Internet response time for overseas readers, the University decided to change the information infrastructure and created a mirror Web site in Honolulu, bypassing the traffic across the U.S. Internet. Measurements indicated that the average response time dropped 164% with the creation of a mirror site [16].

4.3 Where Are the Delays?

One needs to pinpoint where the problems are before starting to change software, upgrading equipment, or installing faster lines in hope that performance will improve. In this section, we look into the execution of a generic Web transaction to identify the major sources of delays.

4.3.1 Anatomy of a Web Transaction

In distributed systems, such as the World Wide Web, when something goes wrong, the responsibility for performance is so diffuse that there is no one to blame. Thus, to fix performance problems in intranets and Web servers, the first step is to understand what happens when one clicks on a Web page link. Let us examine the anatomy of a Web transaction, as depicted in Fig. 4.4. We break a typical transaction into the major tasks performed at the three main components of a Web system: browser, network, and server.

1. Browser

   - The end user clicks on a hyperlink and requests a document.

   - The client browser looks for the requested document in the local cache and returns the document in the case of a hit. In this case, the user response time is denoted by R'_{Cache}.

   - In the case of a miss:

     – the browser asks the Domain Name Service (DNS) to map the server hostname to an IP address,

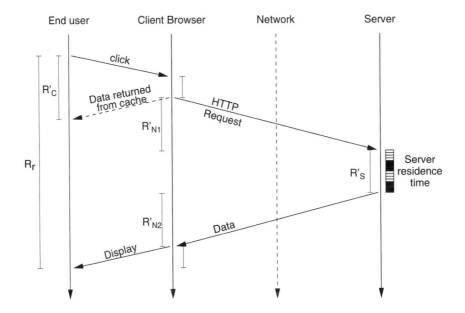

Figure 4.4. Anatomy of an HTTP transaction.

- the client opens a TCP connection to the server defined by the URL of the link, and
- the client sends an HTTP request to the server.

- Upon receiving the response from the server, the browser formats and displays the document and renders the associated images.

2. Network

- The network imposes delays to deliver information from the client to server (R'_{N1} in Fig. 4.4) and back from the server to client (R'_{N2} in Fig. 4.4). These delays are a function of the various components on the route between the client and the server, such as modems, routers, bridges, and relays. Let us denote R'_{Network} as the total time an HTTP request spends in the network. So, $R'_{\text{Network}} = R'_{N1} + R'_{N2}$.

3. Server

- A request arrives from the client.
- The server parses the request, according to the HTTP protocol.
- The server executes the method requested (e.g., GET, HEAD, etc.).

- In the case of a GET, the server looks up the file in its document tree by using the file system; the file may be in the cache or on the disks.

- The server reads the contents of the file from disk or from its main memory cache and writes it to the network port.

- When the file is completely sent, the server closes the connection.

- The server residence time, (R'_{Server}), is the time spent in the execution of an HTTP request. It includes service time and waiting time at the various components of the server, such as processor, disk, and network interface card.

When the document requested is not found in the client's cache, the response time (R_r) of a request r is the sum of that request's residence time at all resources:

$$R_r = R'_{\text{Browser}} + R'_{\text{Network}} + R'_{\text{Server}}. \qquad (4.3.1)$$

When there is a hit and data are available at the local client cache, the response time perceived by an end user is given by

$$R_r = R'_{\text{Cache}} \qquad (4.3.2)$$

where R'_{Cache} is the time spent by the browser to find and retrieve the document from its local cache. Usually, $R'_{\text{Cache}} \ll R'_{\text{Network}} + R'_{\text{Server}}$. Let us consider that the browser finds the data requested in the local cache, N_C times out of every N_T requests. The average response time, $\overline{R}_r$, over N_T requests can be written as:

$$\overline{R}_r = p_C \times R'_{\text{Cache}} + (1 - p_C) \times R_r \qquad (4.3.3)$$

where $p_C = N_C/N_T$ denotes the fraction of times that the data is found in the local cache, i.e., the probability of a cache hit.

Example 4.1: A user wants to analyze the impact of the local cache size of its browser on the Web response time that he/she perceives. The user noted that 20% of his/her requests were serviced by the local cache, and the average response time was 400 msec. The average response time for requests serviced by remote Web sites was 3 sec. The average time perceived by the user is given by

$$\begin{aligned}
\overline{R}_r &= p_C \times R'_{\text{Cache}} + (1 - p_C) \times R_r \\
&= 0.20 \times 0.4 + (1 - 0.20) \times 3.0 \\
&= 2.48 \text{ sec.}
\end{aligned}$$

Previous experiments had shown that tripling the size of the browser local cache would raise the hit ratio to 45%. Thus, the new average response time is

$$\begin{aligned}
\overline{R}_r &= 0.45 \times 0.4 + (1 - 0.45) \times 3.0 \\
&= 1.83 \text{ sec.}
\end{aligned}$$

This hypothetical example illustrates the influence of cache size on Web performance. ■

4.3.2   Bottlenecks

As the number of clients and servers grows, end-user performance is usually constrained by the performance of some components (e.g., server, network links, and routers) along the path from the client to the server. The components that limit system performance are called "bottlenecks." Bottleneck identification is a key step in performance analysis, because it indicates the component one should upgrade first to boost performance.

Example 4.2: Consider a home user that is unhappy with the access times to Internet services. She has been complaining that it takes too long to download a medium page, with an average size of 20 KB. To cut down response time, the user is considering upgrading her desktop system, replacing it by one whose processor is twice as fast. Before spending the money, she wants an answer to the following question, "What will be the response time improvement if I upgrade the speed of my desktop computer?" Let us assume that the network time to bring a medium page across the network is 7,500 msec. The average server residence time is 3,600 msec, and the time spent at the desktop system by the browser (e.g., parsing, formatting, and displaying the response) is 300 msec. Using Eq. (4.3.1), we have that

$$R_r = R'_{\text{Browser}} + R'_{\text{Network}} + R'_{\text{Server}} = 300 + 7,500 + 3,600$$
$$= 11,400 \text{ msec} = 11.4 \text{ sec}.$$

The browser time is basically CPU time. Thus, after the CPU upgrade, we can expect the browser time to be reduced to half of its original value. Thus,

$$R^{\text{new}}_{\text{Browser}} \approx \frac{1}{2} \times R'_{\text{Browser}} = \frac{1}{2} \times 300 = 150 \text{ msec}.$$

The new average response time will be

$$R_r = R^{\text{new}}_{\text{Browser}} + R'_{\text{Network}} + R'_{\text{Server}} = 150 + 7,500 + 3,600$$
$$= 11,250 \text{ msec} = 11.25 \text{ sec}.$$

Therefore, if the speed of the desktop computer were doubled, the response time would decrease from 11.40 sec to 11.25 sec, a 1.3% decrease only! The model clearly indicates that the CPU upgrade does not affect the response time significantly, because the desktop system is not the first bottleneck.   ∎

The basis for bottleneck analysis relies on the fact that the overall system throughput is limited by the throughput of the most restrictive component of the system. Thus, we only need to calculate the throughput of each component of the system and select the one that has the lowest throughput. In Chap. 9, we discuss a systematic way to determine bottlenecks as a function of the combination of workload and system configuration.

Example 4.3: A manufacturer of pharmaceuticals intends to use an intranet to disseminate graphical images of molecular structures of chemicals created by the company. The intranet will be used for online training sessions. Each class has 100 employees, and we can consider that an average of 80% of the trainees are active at a time. During the class, each user performs an average of 100 operations per hour. Each operation requests five images on the average. The average size of the requested images is 25 KB. What is the minimum bandwidth of the network connection to the image server?

There are 80 ($= 0.8 \times 100$) active users. Each user performs operations 100/3,600 operations/sec. Each operation generates $5 \times 25 \times 1,024 \times 8$ bits of data. So, the minimum bandwidth is

$$(0.8 \times 100) \times \frac{100}{3,600} \times (5 \times 25 \times 1,024 \times 8) = 2.275 \ \text{Mbps.} \qquad (4.3.4)$$

Therefore, if the network connection is a T1 line (1.544 Mbps), then the network will be the bottleneck of this intranet Web site. ∎

Example 4.3 illustrates some aspects involved in sizing an intranet. First, one needs to estimate the amount of information maintained on the server. This information includes the number of objects (e.g., documents, video, and audio) and their size. A second factor is the kind of information that the server will deliver. In other words, what is the contents available in your site? Multimedia files are 100 to 10,000 times larger than HTML pages and demand larger portions of network bandwidth. The third factor is the size of the user community. When you think of a public Web site, you may not have an idea of the number of users that will visit your site. However, when you are planning an intranet server, your community of users is somehow defined by the number of employees of your company that have access to the intranet.

4.4 Perception of Performance

Internet and intranet performance can be analyzed from different viewpoints. For instance, a Web user's perception of performance has to do with fast response time and no connections refused. On the other hand, a Webmaster's perception of performance is oriented towards high connection throughput and high availability. What is common to all perceptions of performance is the need for quantitative measurements that describe the behavior of a WWW service.

Web server performance depends on several factors: hardware platform, operating system, server software, network bandwidth, and workload. There are various well-known methodologies for performance evaluation of computer systems, described in [11]. However, Web environments have some unique characteristics that distinguish them from traditional distributed systems. Some of these characteristics have a profound impact on the performance of Web servers. First, the number of Web clients is in the tens of millions and rising. The randomness associated with the way that users visit pages makes the problem of workload forecasting and capacity planning difficult. The Web is also characterized by a large diversity of components; different browsers and servers running on a variety of platforms, with different capabilities. The variety of components complicates the problem of monitoring and collecting performance data. Finally, Web users may experience long, variable, unpredictable network delays, which depend on the connection bandwidth and network congestion.

4.4.1   Metrics

Latency and throughput are the two most important performance metrics for Web systems. The rate at which HTTP requests are serviced represents the connection throughput. It is usually expressed in HTTP operations per second. Due to the large variability in the size of Web objects requested, throughput is also measured in terms of bits per second (bps). The time required to complete a request is the latency at the server, which is one component of client response time. The average latency at the server is the average time it takes to handle a request. In summary, the most common measurements of Web server performance are:

- connections per second

- Mbits per second

- response time

- errors per second

Client response time includes latency at the server, plus the time spent communicating over the network, and the processing time at the client machine (e.g., formatting the response). Thus, client-perceived performance depends on the server capacity, the network load, and bandwidth, as well as on the client machine. Finally, increased errors per second are an indication of degrading performance. An error is any failure in attempting an interaction with the server. For example, an overflow on the pending connections queue at the server is an error. This means that an attempt by a client to connect to the server will be ignored. As a consequence, the client will retransmit the connection request until there is available space in the queue or a predefined period of time expires. Other metrics have also been used to indicate Web activity. A popular one is known as "hit," which means any connection to a Web site, including in-line requests and errors. A hit that successfully retrieves a document is called a "request." A series of consecutive requests from a user, within a given time interval, is called a "visit." Hits per day has been used as a metric to denote the popularity of a Web site.

Example 4.4: The Web site of a travel agency was monitored during 30 min and 9,000 HTTP requests were counted. The server delivered three types of objects: HTML pages, images, and video clips. It was observed that HTML documents represented 30% of the requests with an average size of 11,200 bytes. Images accounted for 65% of the requests, and their average size was 17,200 bytes. Video clips represented only 5% of the total number of requests. The average file size of video files was 439,000 bytes. What is the server throughput?

The throughput expressed in terms of connections is: $9000/(30 \times 60) = 5$ requests/second. However, this metric does not give any insight about the network bandwidth used during the observation period, nor does it give any clue about the size of the requested objects. So, to size the network bandwidth or the network interface card, we need to calculate the throughput in kilobits per second. To do that, we calculate the throughput for each class of objects as

$$\text{Class throughput} = \frac{\text{total requests} \times \text{class percentage} \times \text{average size}}{\text{observation period}}.$$

Thus,

$$\text{HTML throughput} = 9,000 \times 0.30 \times (11,200 \times 8)/1,800 = 131.25 \text{ Kbps}$$
$$\text{Image throughput} = 9,000 \times 0.65 \times (17,200 \times 8)/1,800 = 436.72 \text{ Kbps}$$
$$\text{Video throughput} = 9,000 \times 0.05 \times (439,000 \times 8)/1800 = 857.42 \text{ Kbps}.$$

The total throughput is the summation of the class throughputs, given by

$$\text{Throughput} = 131.25 + 436.72 + 857.42 = 1425.39 \text{ Kbps}.$$

To support the Web traffic, the network connection should be at least a T1 line. ∎

4.4.2   Quality of Service

When one thinks about the quality of service provided by a mobile cellular telephone company to its customers, the following indicators naturally arise:

- 24-hour-a-day uninterruptible service

- small call drop index

- large coverage

- short repair-time in case of problems

- accurate, detailed, and understandable bill

From the customer's point-of-view, the above list of service characteristics tailors the image of the company. Moreover, these indicators represent the level of service provided to customers at a given cost. The expected service levels rule the relationship between customers and the company. If the call drop index increases more than usual or repair times exceed the acceptable limit, customers will certainly complain about the quality of service provided by the phone company. The source of the problems is immaterial to customers. They do not see the switching network, base station transmitter, and the links that constitute the telephone system.

Resource utilization, blocking of handoffs, percentage of trunk blockage, and other measures of system capacity do not interest customers. What a customer sees is the level of service provided by the company.

As Web sites become a fundamental component of businesses, quality of service will be one of the top management concerns. In a Web environment, a user does not care about site failures, traffic jams, network bandwidth, or other indicators of system activities. Besides contents and aesthetics, online users want performance and security. To an online customer, quality of service means fast, predictable response time and 24 x 7 (24 hours a day and 7 days a week) uptime. Any degradation in the service level of a Web site is noted in real time. The quality in the services provided by a Web environment is indicated by the service levels. Users perceive Web services through performance metrics such as: response time, availability, reliability, predictability, and cost.

A Web site is said to be available when it is "up" and serving customer requests. Availability is the metric used to represent the percentage of time a site is available during an observation period. The longer the uptime interval, the better the availability. When a system does not correctly perform a user's request, an error has occurred in the processing of the request. Reliability measures the occurrence of failures during the processing of services. Compounding the need for high reliability and availability is the dynamic nature of the Web, which internal and external customers rely on for up-to-date business, professional, and personal information.

The problem of quality of service on the Web is exacerbated by the unpredictable nature of the interaction of users with Web services. For example, a large trade show company, may see the load of its Web site spike from an average of 250,000 hits a week during "normal" weeks to more than a million hits a day at the peak of its largest Fall show.

Companies must measure traffic, performance, and usage patterns in order to monitor the quality of service of their Web sites. After assessing the quality of service, management has to decide if additional capacity is needed to stay ahead of customer demands. Following are some typical questions, whose answers can help establish the service levels of a Web site.

- Is the objective of the Web site to provide information to external customers?

- Do your mission-critical business operations depend on the World Wide Web?

- Is the Web server usage limited to an intranet for corporate and employee information exchange?

- Do you have high-end business needs for which 24-hours-a-day, 7-days-a-week uptime and high performance are critical, or can you live with the possibility of Web downtime?

Mission-critical applications are fundamental to running the business of a company. Thus, if Web services are part of critical applications, then one has to define adequate metrics to quantify the level of service provided to users. Examples of metrics that can be used to evaluate Internet access providers and Web sites are: 1) dial-up call failure rates, 2) time it takes to log in, 3) Web site throughput, and 4) Web site time-out rate. It is also important to evaluate these metrics for different times of day. Usually, at peak time, metrics exhibit values completely different from average metrics. However, on the Web, customers want to have good services available at any time. This is why capacity planning for peak periods is so important.

4.5   Infrastructure

In modern information technology environments, a client is not tied to a specific server. Usually, a client browses from one server to another within the corporate network or in the Internet. Access to the Internet from an intranet requires that the browser is configured to go via a proxy server located behind a firewall for security. Figure 4.5 illustrates the conceptual infrastructure that underlies corporate intranets. An infrastructure includes TCP/IP, servers, desktop systems, firewalls, and networks with adequate bandwidth. From a user perspective, there is noticeable performance difference in accessing the Internet when compared with accessing a corporate network. Usually, intranets are based on LANs, whose bandwidth vary from 10 to 100 Mbps. On the other hand, Internet connections vary from 28.8 Kbps to 4.5 Mbps. This section discusses the role and performance implications of the main components of an information infrastructure.

4.5.1   Basic Components

Servers and browsers are the most popular components of a Web environment. For security reasons, a firewall is also a popular component in corporate environments. A firewall is a security mechanism used to protect data, programs, and computers on a private network from the uncontrolled activities of untrusted users and software on other computers. A firewall is a combination of system software, computer, and network hardware to screen network traffic that passes through it. While a firewall is a central point of access and control, it also represents a potential performance bottleneck because of the extra overhead it imposes on traffic. Intranet servers communicate heavily with proxy servers that act as firewall for Web pages. As a consequence, users may perceive a degradation in response time when accessing Web services via a firewall.

4.5.2   Proxy, Cache, and Mirror

Proxy, cache, and mirror are techniques used for improving Web performance and security. These techniques aim at reducing the latency of access to Web documents, the network bandwidth required for document transfers, the demand on servers with very popular documents, and the security of electronic services.

A proxy server is a special type of Web server. It is able to act as both a server and a client. Figure 4.6 shows how a proxy fits into the Web environment. A proxy acts as an agent, representing the server to the client and the client to the server. A

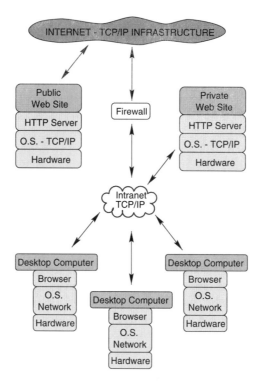

Figure 4.5. Web infrastructure.

proxy accepts requests from clients and forwards them to Web servers. Once a proxy receives responses from remote servers, it passes them to the clients. Originally, proxies were designed to provide access to the Web for users on private networks, who could only access the Internet through a firewall.   Proxy servers do more

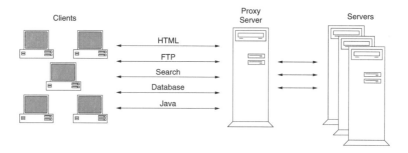

Figure 4.6. Web proxy architecture.

than merely relay HTTP responses. Web proxies can be configured to cache relayed responses, becoming then a caching proxy. In large distributed information systems, such as the World Wide Web, caching is a key issue to good performance. The basic idea in caching is simple: store the frequently-retrieved documents into local files or proxies for future use, so it will not be necessary to download the document next time it is requested. Caching minimizes access time by bringing the data as close to its consumers as possible. Thus, caching improves access speed and cuts down on network traffic, as documents often get returned from a nearby cache, rather than from faraway servers. It also reduces the server load and increases availability in the Web by replicating documents among many servers. Although caching has many advantages, it also introduces its own set of problems. For example, how can one keep a document in the cache and still be sure it is up-to-date? What documents are worth caching and for how long?

Despite its limitations, caching has a widespread use in the Web. It has been used in the Web in two forms. On the client side, browsers maintain small caches of previously-viewed pages on the user's local disk. The other form of use is in the network, where a caching proxy (also known as network caching) is located on a machine in the path from multiple clients to multiple servers, as represented by Fig. 4.6. Caching proxy servers can be located near a large community of users, such as on campus, at an intranet server, or at an Internet Service Provider (ISP) server. When a document is first requested by a client, the proxy acts as a Web client and requests the document from a remote server, returning the response to the client. Subsequent requests for the same document from any client serviced by the proxy are satisfied by the cached copy, optimizing the traffic flow and reducing bandwidth consumption. Caching effectiveness [5] can be measured by three quantities. Hit ratio is defined as the number of requests satisfied by the cache over the total number of requests. Because of the high variability of Web document sizes, it is important to have a metric that includes the size of the requested document. The byte hit ratio is equal to the hit ratio weighted by the document size. The third metric, called "data transferred," represents the total number of bytes transferred between the cache and the outside world during an observation period. Let us see how to use these new metrics.

Example 4.5: The manager of information technology of a large company decided to install a caching proxy server on the corporate intranet, which has more than 2,000 subscribers. After 6 months of use, management wanted to assess the caching effectiveness. To provide a quantitative answer for management, the system administrator wants to know what the resulting bandwidth savings after the installation of the caching server is. With the purpose of analyzing the use of cache metrics, let us consider two cases. First, we have a cache that only holds small documents, with average size equal to 4,800 bytes. The observed hit ratio was 60%. In the second case, the cache management algorithm was specified to hold medium documents, with average filesize of 32,500 bytes. The hit ratio was 20%. The proxy server was monitored during 1 hour and 28,800 requests were handled in that interval. Comparing the efficiency of the two cache strategies by the amount of saved bandwidth,

$$\text{SavedBandwidth} = \frac{\text{NoOfRequests} \times \text{HitRatio} \times \text{AverageSize}}{\text{MeasurementInterval}}$$

$$\text{SavedBandwidth \#1} = \frac{28,800 \times 0.6 \times 4,800 \times 8}{3,600} = 180 \text{ Kbps}$$

$$\text{SavedBandwidth \#2} = \frac{28,800 \times 0.2 \times 32,500 \times 8}{3,600} = 406.3 \text{ Kbps.}$$

The above results shows that, in this example, the strategy of holding larger documents saves more bandwidth. ■

Another information distribution strategy involves mirroring the site at several locations, which implies replicating the site contents at other servers. This requires regular distribution of contents updates, typically done over the Internet itself, and the use of a domain server to direct browsers to secondary sites when the primary one is busy. For example, if a company has a large base of customers that are geographically dispersed, it is difficult to service them well from a distance. The company would be better off with mirrored remotely hosted sites run by local ISPs around the world. The purpose of site mirroring is to increase availability and to balance server load, improving the quality of service.

Cost is one of the key metrics to the effectiveness of an information infrastructure. In case of Web sites and intranets, the cost × performance analysis includes new factors. For example, the location of an intranet web server in the enterprise network is important in terms of performance and the hidden infrastructure costs it can generate.

Example 4.6: Consider a large company whose manufacturing group decided to install an intranet server in the Boston area, where the group is located. The server was used for disseminating product information (e.g., catalogs, pictures, videos, and manuals). The intranet server required the installation of two T1 network connections and routers to support the estimated traffic of requests. The startup and operational costs for installing the network connection were around $50,000 for a period of 2 years. Some time after the server went into operation, management analyzed the server logs and found that 40% of the load originated from the West Coast. To save bandwidth, the company decided to analyze the cost-benefit of installing a caching server in the Los Angeles area. The cost of installing a cache proxy server in there included the cost of a workstation, software, and personnel to manage the proxy. The benefits were the response time improvement for a large group of users and the traffic reduction across the backbone in the United States.■

4.6 Web Server

The combination of server capacity and network bandwidth determines the capacity of a Web site. Web server capacity is a function of several variables, including server architecture, hardware platform, operating system, network connection, contents, and workload. This section presents specific aspects of a server's architecture and workload that affect the performance of Web services.

4.6.1 Architecture

Web server software, also known as HTTP server or HTTP daemon, are programs that control the flow of incoming and outgoing data on a computer connected to an intranet or to the Internet. Basically, a Web server software listens for HTTP requests coming from clients over the network. The server program establishes the requested connection between itself and the client, sends the requested file, and returns to its listening mode. In order to speed up the service, HTTP servers handle more than one request at a time. Usually, this is done in three different ways [17]: by forking a copy of the HTTP process for each request, by multithreading the HTTP program, or by spreading the requests among a pool of running processes.

With many sites getting millions of hits per day, traffic to a Web server may get too high for one computer to handle effectively. The obvious solution to servicing a heavy traffic load is to put more servers to work. There are a number of techniques to split the traffic across servers, but two common methods are round-robin Domain Name Server (DNS) and dynamic HTTP redirection. The latter is a technique where the server responds to a client with a new server address to which the client will resubmit the request. The redirected URL could be on the same computer as the main server or any one of several back-end mirror computers. The main server redirects the traffic to back-end Web servers, according to some load-balancing mechanism. Although the technique is transparent to users, it adds an extra connection to the original request and may, in some cases, increase the user response time and network traffic.

The DNS approach allows a site to implement the concept of server clustering. A "Web cluster" is a collection of servers and middleware technologies that allows a Web site to deliver information over the Internet or intranets. The DNS service translates a domain name to an IP address. Thus, when the DNS service receives a mapping request, it selects the IP address of one of the servers in the cluster, as depicted in Fig. 4.7. In round-robin DNS systems, the Web-server name is associated with a list of IP addresses. Each IP address on the list maps to a different server, and each server contains a mirrored version of the Web site or access to a common file system. Whenever a request is received, the Web-server name is translated to the next IP address on the list. By translating Web-server names to IP addresses in a round-robin fashion, this technique tries to balance the load among the servers. Another technique called "single-IP-image" has been used for distributing HTTP requests for a single service to different machines in a cluster [9]. Basically, the

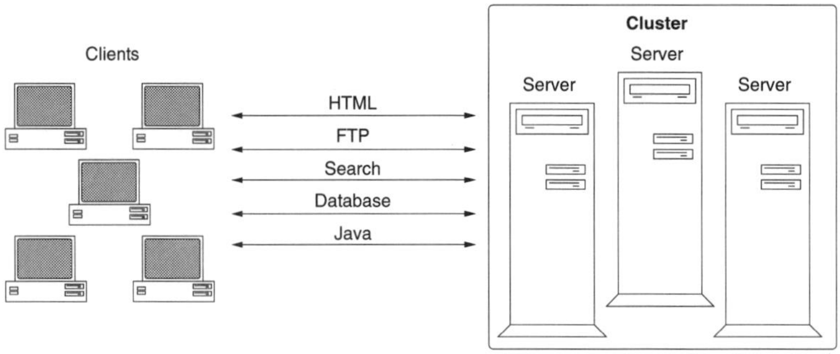

Figure 4.7. Web cluster architecture.

technique uses the address of a special TCP router as the single address of the Web cluster. Client requests are addressed to the router that, in turn, dispatches them to a server, according to some scheduling rules (i.e., server load characteristics). In order to make the dispatching transparent to users, the selected server returns the response with the router address, instead of its own address.

4.6.2　Workload

It is fundamental in evaluating the performance of Web servers to have a solid understanding of Web workload which is unique in its characteristics. For example, it is difficult to know in advance how many people will access a Web site, at what times, and what their usage patterns will be. Experimental studies [3], [8] have already identified some WWW workload properties and invariants. These properties are discussed in this section and a detailed characterization of a Web workload is presented in Chap. 6.

Dynamic Web Pages

Most Web sites do more than serve static HTML pages. A Web site becomes alive with dynamic content pages, that offer interactivity and special effects. Dynamic Web pages can be obtained by using either client-side or server-side programs. Java, ActiveX, and Dynamic HTML [10] are client-side Web technologies. With any of these technologies, special effects can be added to Web documents without relying on server-side programs. Client-side programs help reduce response times, avoiding networking and server delays. For example, Dynamic HTML achieves interactivity and special effects by automatically reformatting and redisplaying the current Web document to show modifications. These modifications can be done without the need to reload the document or to load a new document from a remote Web server.

On the server-side, interactivity can be achieved by issuing Common Gateway Interface (CGI) scripts. Servers usually interact with the user by running back-end programs or scripts. CGI is the de facto industry standard API for applications that must communicate with Web servers to execute dynamic functions associated with HTML pages. Other Web-based APIs are also in use, such as ISAPI, ICAPI, and NSAPI. A CGI program (e.g., Perl, C, or, Java) runs as a separate process outside the Web server and returns data (e.g., a dynamically generated page or the result of a search) to the Web server. Because a process is started every time a CGI is requested, this technique can be very costly. In the case of Web servers running on top of Windows NT, server-side scripting can be implemented with the Internet Server API (ISAPI) [6], which uses threads to reduce overhead cost.

In terms of performance, client-side Java shifts load off the server. On the other hand, CGI load may have a tremendous impact on the server performance, given that scripts create processes that demand operating system services and consume CPU time, memory, and disk operations. If a server has only one processor, the HTTP server and CGI scripts will share the same resources, which may slowdown the execution of HTTP requests. In many commercial Web sites, CGI programs, including search engines, represent the major part of the workload.

Example 4.7: The Web site of a virtual bookstore receives an average of 20 visitors per second. Most of the visitors only browse the books available. However, one out of ten visitors places an order for books. Each order transaction generates a CGI script, which is executed on the Web server. The Webmaster wants to know what the CPU load generated by the CGI scripts is.

We model the CGI load as follows. The average CGI CPU service demand ($D_{\text{cpu}}^{\text{cgi}}$) is 120 msec. Using Service Demand Law discussed in Chap. 3, we have that

$$U_{\text{cpu}}^{\text{cgi}} = X_{\text{cgi}} \times D_{\text{cpu}} \tag{4.6.1}$$

where X_{cgi} is the server throughput measured in CGI scripts executed per second and $U_{\text{cpu}}^{\text{cgi}}$ is the utilization of the CPU due to the execution of CGI scripts. The CGI arrival rate (λ_{cgi}) can be calculated as

$$
\begin{aligned}
\lambda_{\text{cgi}} &= \text{VisitRate} \times \text{PercentageOfOrders} \\
&= 20 \times (1/10) \\
&= 2 \text{ CGI/sec.}
\end{aligned}
$$

Assuming flow equilibrium, we have that $X_{\text{cgi}} = \lambda_{\text{cgi}}$. Thus,

$$U_{\text{cpu}}^{\text{cgi}} = 2 \times 0.12 = 0.24 = 24\%. \tag{4.6.2}$$

From the above results, we see that 24% of the CPU utilization is spent processing CGI scripts. Also, it is important to know that CGI scripts and HTTP requests are competing for the same resources: CPU, memory, and disk. Several other questions could be investigated using this simple performance model. For example, some software companies claim that Java servlets (i.e., server-side applets) have performance advantage over CGI. Performance improvement come from the fact that servlets run in the same process as the Web server, whereas CGI programs must start a new process for every request. Let us then assume that Java servlet transactions are 30% less resource-intensive than CGI applications. What would be the impact of replacing the CGI script by servlets? The CPU service demand for servlets is $D_{\text{cpu}}^{s} = D_{\text{cpu}}^{\text{cgi}} \times 0.7 = 120 \times 0.7 = 84$ msec. Using Eq. (4.6.1) again, we have that the CPU utilization due to servlets would be 16.8%. Notice that the CPU utilization was reduced from 24% to 16.8%.   ■

Novel Features

Several studies [1], [3], [8] have shown characteristics that distinguish the behavior of Web environments from traditional distributed systems. The following aspects have a profound impact on the performance of Web services. The Web exhibits extreme variability in workload characteristics. For example, it has been verified in the analysis of some popular Web sites [3] that there are very few documents whose size is less than 100 bytes. Most documents are in the range of 10^2 to 10^5 bytes, while a few files are larger than 100,000 bytes. The distribution of file sizes in the Web, including files stored on servers and files requested by clients and transmitted over the network, exhibits heavy tail, that decline via some power law (e.g., Pareto distribution). In practical terms, heavy-tailed distributions indicate that very large values (e.g., huge file sizes) are possible with non-negligible probability. Another consequence of heavy tails is that average values have a large variability, that reduces the statistical meaning of measurements. The impact of heavy tailed distributions on workload characterization will be quantitatively illustrated in Chap. 6.

A first cut approximation to represent the heavy-tail characteristic of Web workloads in performance models is to use the notion of class. Each class comprises requests that are similar with respect to the size of the document they retrieve. Thus, similar requests in terms of resource usage would be grouped together. This reduces the variability of the measurements and improves the statistical meaning of measurements. For example, one could group the HTTP requests of a workload into three classes: small pages with documents up to 5 KB, medium pages varying from 5 to 50 KB, and large pages for file sizes greater than 50 KB.

Example 4.8: A Web server was monitored for a very short period of time during which it serviced 10 HTTP requests with the following CPU demands: 0.4, 0.6, 1.5, 0.7, 1.5, 1.7, 18.1, 0.3, 0.9, and 1.4 seconds. Let us now divide the load into three classes: small, medium, and very large, according to their CPU time. Small requests demand less than 1.0 sec, medium requests demand between 1.0 and 6.0 sec and the CPU service demand for very large requests is greater than 6.0 sec. The average CPU service demands per class are 0.58, 1.53, and 18.1, respectively. If we average the service demand of the three classes, we obtain 6.7 sec. However, if we weigh the average by the number of occurrences in each class, we obtain

$$\text{AverageServiceDemand} = 0.58 \times (5/10) + 1.53 \times (4/10) + 18.1 \times (1/10) = 2.71.$$

The two averages are quite different. The one that makes sense is 2.71 sec, because it takes into account the request frequency for each class. It is then clear that the effect of a heavy-tailed distribution (represented in this example by the presence of the request with a 18.1 sec service demand) could distort performance measurements.   ■

The highly uneven popularity of various Web documents is a well-documented phenomenon [3], [8]. In several studies, it was shown that Zipf's law [18] can be used to characterize access frequency to Web documents. Zipf's law was originally applied to the relationship between a word's popularity in terms of rank and its frequency of use. It states that if one ranks the popularity of words in a given text (denoted by ρ) by their frequency of use (denoted by f), then

$$f \sim \frac{1}{\rho}. \tag{4.6.3}$$

The data shown in [1] indicates that Zipf's law applies quite strongly to documents serviced by Web servers. This means that the nth most popular document is exactly twice as likely to be accessed as the $2n$th most popular document. Results about document popularity can be used to characterize WWW workload and analyze document dissemination strategies, such as caching and mirroring.

Example 4.9: Company X considers the Internet as a medium for doing business. X is being created to sell online maps to its customers. The company expects to receive 500,000 visitors per day at the end of its first year of operation. The company anticipates that three maps will be the best sellers. The most popular document will be the site map (i.e., the home page), that shows customers how to walk through the electronic store. New York and Paris are expected to be the second and third most popular documents, respectively. The capacity planning analyst wants to estimate the number of accesses to the most popular maps, in order to place them in different disk storage units, so that I/O time is optimized. According to Eq. (4.6.3) (Zipf's Law), the frequency of accesses to a document is proportional to its popularity. Considering that the home page is hit by each customer that visits the store, we can say that its frequency of access equals one ($f = 1$). In other words, the home page is expected to receive 500,000 hits/day. The frequencies of access to the NY and Paris maps are $f_{NY} \sim 1/2 = 0.5$ and $f_{Paris} \sim 1/3 = 0.333$, according to Zipf's Law. Thus, the number of visits per day to these maps are

$$\text{NumberOfVisits} \sim f \times \text{TotalVisits}$$

$$\text{NumberOfVisitsToNY} \sim f_{NY} \times \text{TotalVisits} \sim \frac{1}{2} \times 500,000 = 250,000$$

$$\text{NumberOfVisitsToParis} \sim f_{Paris} \times \text{TotalVisits} \sim \frac{1}{3} \times 500,000 = 166,667.$$

■

4.7   Intranet and the Internet

Web servers across a company lure users with new content (e.g., graphics, audio, video), that alter the distribution patterns of network traffic. Intranets and the Internet have the potential to significantly change network traffic, causing bandwidth problems. Too much traffic on a network is always revealed by slow response times and slow transfer rates. It is clear that companies planning intranets and access to the Internet must look at their network and system infrastructure and determine whether they are adequate to support the traffic that will be created; otherwise, network performance can slow to a crawl. This section discusses network characteristics that affect Web performance.

4.7.1   Bandwidth and Latency

Latency and bandwidth are two fundamental characteristics of networks that can be analyzed quantitatively. Latency or delay indicates the time needed for a bit (or a packet) to travel across the network, from the client to the server or vice versa. To understand the issue of latency one needs to understand the route a packet takes. Between the client and the server, numerous activities take place, involving communication lines, hubs, bridges, gateways, repeaters, routers, and modems. Network latency consists of several different delays. Latency is the same thing as seek time: the minimum time between requesting a piece of data and obtaining it. A propagation delay is the time an electrical signal takes to travel along a wire or fiber. For example, for a typical LAN within a building, the propagation delay is around 1 msec. Switching delays are introduced by network devices, such as hubs, routers, and modems. In the case of shared media (e.g., Ethernet or Token Ring), packets may experience access delays. Finally, in packet-switched networks (e.g., the Internet), there are queuing delays in the packet switches. Latency influences the way that information is disseminated on the Web. Considering that everything else is equal, it is always faster to download pages that are "close," rather than far away.

Throughput or bandwidth is a measure of the rate at which data can be sent through the network. Bandwidth is usually expressed in bits per second (bps). A crucial problem of having low-bandwidth connection is the amount of time it takes to deliver documents to clients. For instance, a 56-Kbps line takes 14.3 min to transfer a 100-KB document, whereas the same document can be downloaded in 0.5 sec using a T1 line. A Web site can run on different types of network bandwidth, such as Fast Ethernet, T1 connection, and others shown in Table 4.1.

Example 4.10: What is the impact of contents on performance and infrastructure requirements? Consider Example 4.3 and assume that the training department is considering the use of video clips for improving online training. The average file size of the training videos is 950 MB. Classes have 100 students and 80% of them are active at any time. During the class, each user requests an average of two video clips per hour. Thus, the minimum network bandwidth needed to support video

Table 4.1. Network Capacity

Network connection	Theoretical bandwidth (Kbps)
28K modem	28.8
56K modem	56
ISDN 1 BRI (phone line)	64
ISDN 2 BRI (phone line)	128
T1 (dedicated connection)	1,544
T3 (dedicated connection)	45,000
Ethernet	10,000
Fast Ethernet	100,000
ATM (OC-3)	155,000
ATM (OC-12)	622,000

is $(0.80 \times 100) \times 2 \times (8 \times 950)/\, 3,600\ = 337.7$ Mbps. Looking at Table 4.1, we see that a 622 ATM network is required to support the new video objects. ∎

4.7.2 Traffic

Web traffic exhibits a bursty behavior [8]. "Bursty" refers to the fact that data are transmitted randomly, with peak rates exceeding the average rates by factors of 8 to 10 [12]. It has been also observed that Web traffic is bursty in several time scales. This phenomenon can be statistically described using the notion of self-similarity, which implies the existence of a correlational structure in traffic bursts that is retained over several time scales. A practical consequence of the bursty behavior is that Web site management has difficulty sizing server capacity and bandwidth to support the demand created by load spikes. As a result, users perceive a service performance degradation during periods of burstiness. Spikes can be characterized by the "peak traffic ratio," defined as the ratio of peak site load to average site traffic. For example, in the Web site of a cable TV network, the peak traffic ratio was 6.5 during a major boxing fight. The consequences of traffic and load spikes are tremendous on the performance of Web sites.

In some special cases, adequate capacity can be planned beforehand to handle traffic spikes. For example, during big events, such as presidential elections, the Olympic Games, the World Soccer Cup, new product releases, and the Academy Awards, a large number of people try to visit the key Web sites. Servers and Internet connections get overwhelmed with the onslaught of traffic and spikes up to eight times the average values can be observed. In an attempt to smooth the load spikes, management of Web sites set up mirror sites to take some load off the Web servers.

Example 4.11: The manager of the Web site of a large electronic publishing company is planning the capacity of the network connection. Looking at the access logs in retrospect, management noted that the site throughput was 1 million HTTP operations per day. The average document requested was 10 KB. What will be the network bandwidth needed by this site considering peak traffic?

The required bandwidth (in Kbps) is given by

$$\text{HTTP op/sec} \times \text{average size of requested documents (Kb)}$$

In our case, we have

$$1 \text{ million HTTP ops/day } = 41,667 \text{ op/hour } = 11.6 \text{ HTTP ops/sec.}$$

The needed bandwidth then is,

$$11.6 \text{ HTTP ops/sec} \times 10 \text{ KB/HTTP op} = 116 \text{ KB/sec} = 928 \text{ Kbps.}$$

Let us assume that protocol overhead is 20%. Thus, the actual throughput required is $928 \times 1.2 = 1,114$ Kbps. The network bandwidth needed by the site is 1.114 Mbps and can be provided by a T1 connection. However, management decided to plan for peak load. The hourly peak traffic ratio observed in the past was five for some big news events. The average number of HTTP ops/sec will be five times larger and therefore the required bandwidth at peak hours is also five times bigger and equal to $5 \times 1.114 = 5.57$ Mbps. Considering that each T1 line is 1.5 Mbps, the site will need four T1 connections to support the load spikes. ■

4.8   Capacity Planning

Capacity planning of intranets and Web servers can be used to avoid some of the obvious and most common pitfalls, such as Web site congestion and lack of network bandwidth. Before one starts rolling out an intranet or making a Web site available to customers, some key questions should be analyzed. The following are some of these typical planning questions.

- Is the corporate network able to sustain the intranet traffic?

- Is the installed bandwidth adequate for transmitting pictures and graphics?

- Are servers and network capacity adequate to handle load spikes?

- Will Web server performance continue to be acceptable when twice as many people visit the site?

- Does the company have tools to monitor and evaluate the effectiveness of the Web site?

Capacity planning methodologies can be used to obtain adequate answers to these questions. Web site planning should be more than a pure guesswork exercise. As businesses increase their reliance on the WWW as a real-world commercial vehicle, naive and casual approaches to sizing and planning Web sites tend to disappear.

The next chapter presents a capacity planning methodology, where the main steps are: understanding the environment, workload characterization, workload model validation and calibration, performance model development, performance model validation and calibration, performance prediction, cost model development, cost prediction, and cost/performance analysis. Workload characterization and performance models that take into consideration the unique aspects of Web environments are presented in subsequent chapters.

4.9 Summary

Performance analysis of intranets and Web servers is unique in many senses. First, the number of WWW clients is in the tens of millions and rising. The randomness associated with the way users visit pages and request Web services makes the problem of workload forecasting and capacity planning difficult.

This chapter introduced several important concepts that helps users, administrators, and managers to understand performance problems in Web environments. Performance metrics and quality of service were discussed. New concepts such as heavy-tailed characteristics, traffic spikes, and network caching and their impact on Web performance were analyzed.

BIBLIOGRAPHY

[1] V. A. F. ALMEIDA, A. BESTRAVOS, M. CROVELLA, and A. OLIVEIRA, Characterizing reference locality in the WWW, *Fourth Int. Conf. Parallel Distrib. Inform. Syst. (PDIS)*, IEEE Comput. Soc., Dec. 1996, pp. 92–106.

[2] J. ALMEIDA, V. A. F. ALMEIDA, and D. YATES, Measuring the behavior of a world-wide web server, *Seventh Conf. High Perform. Networking (HPN)*, IFIP, Apr. 1997, pp. 57–72.

[3] M. ARLITT and C. WILLIAMSON, Web server workload characterization: the search for invariants, *Proc. 1996 SIGMETRICS Conf. Measurement Comput. Syst.*, ACM, Philadelphia, PA, May 1996, pp. 126–137.

[4] T. BERNERS-LEE, R. CAILLIAU, H. NIELSEN, and A. PECRET, The World Wide Web, *Comm. ACM*, Aug. 1994, vol. 37, no. 8, pp. 76–82.

[5] A. BESTAVROS, R. CARTER, M. CROVELLA, C. CUNHA, A. HEDDAYA, and S. MIRDAD, Application-level document caching in the Internet, *Proc. Int. Workshop Distrib. Networked Environments*, Canada, 1995.

[6] M. BLASZCZAK, Writing interactive web apps is a piece of cake with the new ISAPI classes in MFC 4.1, *Microsoft Syst. J.*, May 1996.

[7] D. E. COMER, *Computer Networks and Internets*, Upper Saddle River, NJ: Prentice Hall, 1997.

[8] M. CROVELLA and A. BESTAVROS, Self-similarity in World-Wide Web traffic: evidence and possible causes, *Proc. 1996 SIGMETRICS Conf. Measurement of Comput. Syst.*, ACM, Philadelphia, PA, May 1996, pp. 160–169.

[9] O. DAMANI, P. CHUNG, Y. HUANG, C. KINTALA, and Y. WANG, One-Ip: techniques for hosting a service on a cluster of machines, *Proc. Sixth Int. World Wide Web Conf.*, Santa Clara, CA, Nov. 1996.

[10] S. ISAACS, *Inside Dynamic HTML*, Seattle, WA: Microsoft Press, 1997.

[11] D. A. MENASCÉ, V. A. F. ALMEIDA, and L. W. DOWDY, *Capacity Planning and Performance Modeling: From Mainframes to Client-Server Systems*. Upper Saddle River, NJ: Prentice Hall, 1994.

[12] J. MOGUL, Network behavior of a busy Web server and its clients, *Res. Rep. 95/5*, DEC Western Research, Palo Alto, CA, 1995.

[13] H. NIELSEN, J. GETTYS, A. BAIR-SMITH, E. PRUD'HOMMEAUX, H. LIE, and C. LILLEY, Network performance effects of HTTP/1.1 CSS1, and PNG, *Proc. ACM SIGCOMM'97*, Cannes, France, Sept. 16–18, 1997.

[14] V. PADMANABHAN and J. MOGUL, Improving HTTP latency, *Comput. Networks ISDN Syst.*, vol. 28, no. 1,2, Dec. 1995.

[15] C. M. KEHOE and J E. PITKOW, Surveying the territory: GVU's five WWW user surveys, *World Wide Web J.*, vol. 1, no. 3, 1996.

[16] J. RENDLEMAN, Reducing Web latency—Stanford University tries Web hosting to boost net access, *InternetWeek*, June 30, 1997.

[17] N. YEAGER and R. McCRATH, *Web Server Technology*. San Francisco, CA: Morgan Kaufmann, 1996.

[18] G. ZIPF, *Human Behavior and the Principle of Least Effort*. Cambridge, MA: Addison-Wesley, 1949.

Chapter 5

A STEP-BY-STEP APPROACH TO CAPACITY PLANNING IN CLIENT/SERVER SYSTEMS

5.1 Introduction

Planning the capacity of a C/S system requires that a series of steps be followed in a systematic way. This chapter starts by providing a clear definition of what adequate capacity means. It then presents a methodology that leads the capacity planner, in a step-by-step fashion, through the process of determining the most cost-effective system configuration and networking topology. Investment and personnel plans follow as a consequence. The main steps of the methodology are: understanding the environment, workload characterization, workload model validation and calibration, performance model development, performance model validation and calibration, workload forecasting, performance prediction, cost model development, cost prediction, and cost/performance analysis.

The methodology presented here requires the use of three models: a workload model, a performance model, and a cost model. The workload model captures the resource demands and workload intensity characteristics of the load brought to the system by the different types of transactions and requests. The performance model is used to predict response times, utilizations, and throughputs, as a function of the system description and workload parameters. The cost model accounts for software, hardware, telecommunications, and support expenditures.

This chapter draws in part on material presented in [7] and Chap. 2 of [8]. Various steps of the methodology are discussed in further detail in subsequent chapters.

5.2 Adequate Capacity

Many organizations invest millions of dollars to build client/server computing environments and many millions more to maintain and update the environment. In most cases, the overall capacity of the environment is unknown and capacity planning and procurement is done without a defined methodology. To complicate matters, the notion of what is *adequate capacity* is not well understood in many cases.

Figure 5.1 illustrates the three main elements used to define adequate capacity of a C/S system:

- *Service-level agreements (SLAs).* Adequate capacity has to be provided so that acceptable or desirable values for performance metrics such as response time or throughput can be achieved. Examples of SLAs include: "response times for trivial database queries should not exceed two seconds," "response times for database searches performed through the Web front-end should not exceed three seconds," "the NFS server should be able to support at least 10,000 NFS I/O operations per second with response times not exceeding 0.1 sec." The values of SLAs are specific to each organization and are determined by both management and users. Even when SLAs are not formally defined, it is possible to determine a level of acceptable service when users start to complain about poor performance.

- *Specified technologies and standards.* Providing adequate capacity to meet service-level agreements can be done in many ways by using servers and operating systems of various types and many different networking topologies. For example, it is possible for a Windows NT-based file server running on a PC-based machine to deliver the same performance as a Unix-based file server running on a RISC machine. Some organizations may prefer to use one versus the other for reasons that are not directly related to performance (e.g., ease of system administration, familiarity with the system, and number and quality of possible vendors for the underlying hardware). Users and management may also choose to adopt certain standards for network protocols (e.g., TCP/IP) and middleware, further restricting the set of solutions that can be used. Thus, users and management may specify that adequate capacity be provided with certain specified technologies and standards for reasons other than performance.

- *Cost constraints.* The problem of providing adequate capacity to meet SLAs would be somewhat easier to solve if one had unlimited monetary resources. Budget constraints are determined by management and limit the space of possible solutions. Expenditures for C/S systems include startup costs and operating costs for a defined period. Startup costs include purchase expenditures for hardware and software, installation costs, personnel costs, and initial training. Operating costs include hardware and software maintenance, telecommunications costs, and personnel costs required to maintain the system. Amortization costs may be included if they are incurred.

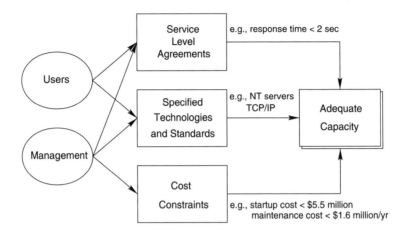

Figure 5.1. Definition of adequate capacity.

We say then that *a C/S system has adequate capacity if the service-level agreements are continuously met for a specified technology and standards, and if the services are provided within cost constraints.*

5.3   A Methodology for Capacity Planning in C/S Environments

Figure 5.2 illustrates the various steps of a capacity planning methodology for C/S systems. While these steps are essentially the same as those for capacity planning studies of mainframe-based environments, their implementation in a C/S environment is much more complex due to the heterogeneity of hardware and software components involved.

The capacity planning methodology relies on three models: a workload model, a performance model, and a cost model. The *workload model* captures the resource demands and workload intensity characteristics for each component of a global workload within a representative time frame. The *performance model* is used to predict the performance of a C/S system as a function of the system description and workload parameters. The outputs of the performance model include response times, throughputs, utilizations of various system resources, and queue lengths. These performance metrics are matched against the service-level agreements to determine if the capacity of the system is adequate. The *cost model* accounts for software, hardware, telecommunications, and support expenditures.

The following sections discuss in greater detail what is involved in each of the steps of the methodology depicted in Fig. 5.2. We will use the C/S of Fig. 5.3 to illustrate all phases of the capacity planning methodology.

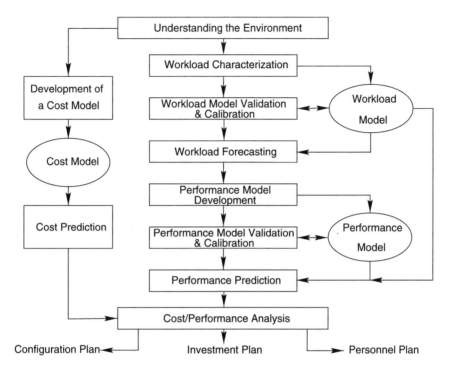

Figure 5.2. A methodology for capacity planning.

5.4 Understanding the Environment

The initial phase of the methodology consists of learning what kind of hardware (clients and servers), software (operating systems, middleware, and applications), network connectivity, and network protocols, are present in the environment. It also involves the identification of peak usage periods, management structures, and service-level agreements. This information is gathered by various means including user group meetings, audits, questionnaires, help desk records, planning documents, interviews, and other information-gathering techniques [7].

Table 5.1 summarizes the main elements of a C/S system that must be catalogued and understood before the remaining steps of the methodology can be taken.

An example of the outcome of the Understanding the Environment step for the C/S of Fig. 5.3 would be as follows.

Clients and servers. The network consists of four LAN segments (three 10 Mbps Ethernets and one 16 Mbps Token Ring) interconnected through a 100 Mbps FDDI ring. LAN 3 is connected to the Internet. LAN 1 has a Windows NT-based file server and 120 Windows NT-based PC clients. LAN 2 has a RISC-type Unix file server and 50 Unix workstations. This file server uses a storage box with several

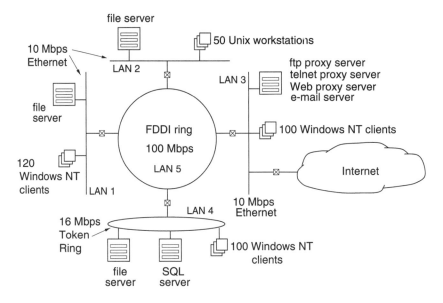

Figure 5.3. Example C/S system for capacity planning methodology.

RAID-5 disks and a capacity of 512 Gbytes. LAN 3 runs an ftp proxy server, a telnet proxy server, a Web proxy server, and the e-mail server on a Windows NT server-based dual processor high-end PC-based machine. This LAN supports 100 Windows NT clients. Finally, LAN 4 has a Windows NT-based file server and an SQL database server running Oracle to support enterprise-wide mission-critical applications. This LAN has 100 Windows NT-based clients. BEA's Tuxedo [1] is used as a Transaction Processing (TP) Monitor to support client/server transaction management.

Applications. Workstations on LAN 2 are mostly used by researchers of the R&D department engaged in running computer simulations of molecular biology experiments. These researchers store all their files in the file server in LAN 2. They use e-mail, ftp, telnet, and Web services from the proxy server on LAN 3. Clients on LANs 1, 3, and 4 split their time between running office automation applications (e.g., word processing, spreadsheets, and presentation preparation packages) and running various types of client/server transactions to support sales, marketing, personnel, accounting, and financial activities. These C/S transactions use a TP monitor and the SQL server on LAN 4. All users in LANs 1, 3, and 4 read e-mail and access the Web through the proxy server on LAN 3. The company's employees go through Web-based training courses hosted at the server on LAN 3. Most of the accesses to these applications come from clients on LANs 1, 3, and 4.

Network connectivity and protocols. The network connectivity map is

Table 5.1. Elements in Understanding the Environment

Element	Description
Client platform	Quantity and type
Server platform	Quantity, type, configuration, and function
Middleware	Type (e.g., TP monitors)
DBMS	Type
Application	Main types of applications
Network connectivity	Network connectivity diagram showing all LANs, WANs, network technologies, routers, servers, and number of clients per LAN segment
Network protocols	List of network protocols being routed
Service-level agreements	Existing SLAs per application. When formal SLAs are absent, industry standards can be used (see [4])
LAN management and support	LAN management support structure, size, expertise, and responsiveness to users
Procurement procedures	Elements of the procurement process, justification mechanisms for acquisitions, expenditure limits, authorization mechanisms, and duration of the procurement cycle

given in Fig. 5.3. The Internet and transport protocols used throughout all networks is TCP/IP.

Service-level agreements. There are no formal SLAs established, but users start to complain if response times exceed 2 sec for trivial C/S transactions and 5 sec for the more complex transactions. Response times at e-mail and Web services has not been a problem.

LAN management and support. Each of the four user LANs (LANs 1–4) have a dedicated team of LAN and system administrators. The number of system administrators for each of these LANs is 6, 3, 5, and 6, respectively. There is also a Database Administrator (DBA) for the database managed by the SQL server and three network specialists that constantly monitor the performance on the FDDI ring and are responsible for overall network management functions such as assigning IP addresses to subnetworks, managing routing tables, maintaining network security, and verifying the connection to the Internet.

Procurement procedures. As an example, procurement decisions could be made by an Information Technology Committee, headed by the Chief Information Officer (CIO) of the company and composed of four user representatives and four system administrators (one from each LAN), which reviews applications for hardware and software upgrades. Decisions are made based on budget availability and on how well the requests are justified. The average procurement cycle for items over \$5,000 is 2 mo. Expenditures below \$5,000 can be made using a much faster procedure that takes two business days on the average.

5.5   Workload Characterization

Workload characterization is the process of precisely describing the systems's global workload in terms of its main components. Each workload component is further decomposed into basic components, as indicated in Fig. 5.4, which also shows specific examples of workload components and basic components. The basic components are then characterized by workload intensity (e.g., transaction arrival rates) and service demand parameters at each resource.

The parameters for a basic component are seldom directly obtained from measurements. In most cases, they must be derived from other parameters that are measured directly. Table 5.2 shows an example of three basic components, along with examples of parameters that can be measured for each. The last column indicates the type of basic component parameter—workload intensity (WI) or service demand (SD). Values must be obtained or estimated for these parameters, preferably through measurements with performance monitors and accounting systems. Measurements must be made during peak workload periods and for an appropriate monitoring interval (e.g., 1 hour). For example, consider the "Mail Processing" basic component. Data would be collected relative to all messages sent during a 1 hour monitoring interval. Assume that 500 messages were sent during this interval. Measurements are obtained for the message size, mail server CPU time, and server I/O time for each of the 500 messages. The average arrival rate of send mail requests is equal to the number of messages sent (500) divided by the measurement interval (3,600 sec), i.e., 500/3,600 = 0.14 messages sent per second. Similar measurements must be obtained for all basic components.

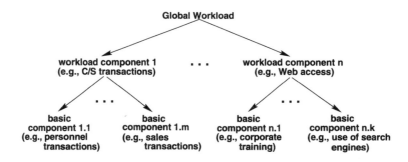

Figure 5.4. Workload characterization process.

Table 5.2. Example of Basic Component Parameters and Types
(WI = Workload Intensity; SD = Service Demand)

Basic Component and Parameters	Parameter Type
Sales transaction	
Number of transactions submitted per client	WI
Number of clients	WI
Total number of IOs to the Sales DB	SD
CPU utilization at the DB server	SD
Average message size sent/received by the DB server	SD
Web-based training	
Average number of training sessions/day	WI
Average size of image files retrieved	SD
Average size of http documents retrieved	SD
Average number of image files retrieved/session	SD
Average number of documents retrieved/session	SD
Average CPU utilization of the httpd server	SD
Mail processing	
Number of messages received per day per client	WI
Number of messages sent per day per client	WI
Number of clients	WI
Average message size	SD
CPU utilization of the mail daemon	SD

5.5.1 Breaking Down the Global Workload

When workload intensity is high, large collections of workload measures can be obtained. Dealing with such collections is seldom practical, especially if workload characterization results are to be used for performance prediction through analytic models [8]. One should substitute the collection of measured values of all basic components by a more compact representation—one per basic component. This representation is called a *workload model*—the end product of the workload characterization process.

Consider a C/S-based application that provides access to the corporate database, and assume that data collected during a peak period of 1 hour provides the CPU time and number of I/Os for each of the 20,000 transactions executed in that period. Some transactions are fairly simple and use very little CPU and I/O, whereas other more complex ones may require more CPU and substantially more I/O. Figure 5.5 shows a graph depicting points of the type (number of I/Os, CPU time) for all transactions executed in the measurement interval. The picture shows three natural groupings of the points in the two-dimensional space shown in the graph. Each group is called a *cluster* and has a *centroid*—the larger circles in the figure—defined

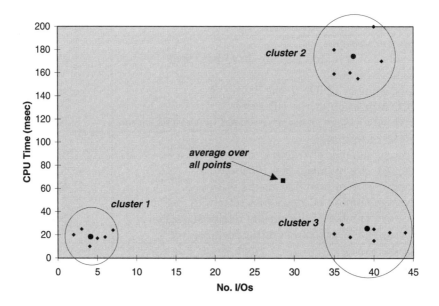

Figure 5.5. Space for workload characterization (no. of I/Os, CPU time).

as the point whose coordinates are the average among all points in the cluster. The "distance" between any point and the centroid of its cluster is the shortest distance between the point and the centroid of all clusters. The coordinates of the centroids of clusters 1, 2, and 3, are (4.5, 19), (38, 171), and (39, 22), respectively. A more compact representation of the resource consumption of the 20,000 transactions is given by the coordinates of centroids 1, 2, and 3. For instance, transactions of class 1 perform, on the average, 4.5 I/Os and spend 19 msec of CPU time during their execution.

The graph in Fig. 5.5 also shows the point whose coordinates, (28, 68), are the average number of I/Os and the average CPU time over all points. It is clear that if we were to represent all the points by this single point—the single cluster case—we would obtain a much less meaningful representation of the global workload than the one provided by the three clusters. Thus, the number of clusters chosen to represent the workload impacts the accuracy of the workload model.

Clustering algorithms can be used to compute an optimal number of basic components of a workload model, and the parameter values that represent each component. A discussion of clustering algorithms and their use in workload characterization is presented in Chap. 6.

5.5.2   Data Collection Issues

In ideal situations, performance monitors and accounting systems are used to determine the parameter values for each basic component. In reality, the tool base
required for integrated network and server data collection may not be available to
the system administrators, or they may not have enough time to deploy and use a
complete suite of monitoring tools. This is a chronic problem for many organizations. The problem is compounded by the fact that most monitoring tools provide
aggregate measures at the resource levels (e.g., total number of packets transmitted
on a LAN segment or total server CPU utilization). These measurements must be
apportioned to the basic workload components. Benchmarks and rules of thumb
(ROTs) may be needed to apportion aggregate measures to basic components in lieu
of real measurements. Figure 5.6 illustrates the range of data collection alternatives
available to a capacity manager.

In many cases, it is possible to detect a fairly limited number of applications
that account for significant portions of resource usage. Workload measurements can
be made for these applications in a controlled environment such as the one depicted
in Fig. 5.7. These measurements must be made separately at the client and at the
server for scripts representing typical users using each of the applications mentioned
above. These measurements are aimed at obtaining service demands at the CPU
and storage devices at the client and server as well as number of packets sent and
received by the server and packet size distributions. The results thus obtained for a
specific type of client and server must be translated to other types of clients and/or
servers. For this purpose, we can use specific industry standard benchmarks, such
as SPEC ratings, to scale resource usage figures up or down.

Example 5.1: Assume that the service demand at the server for a given application was 10 msec, obtained in a controlled environment with a server with a
SPECint rating of 3.11. To find out what this service demand would be if the
server used in the actual system were faster and had a SPECint rating of 10.4, we
need to scale down the 10 msec measurement by dividing it by the ratio between
the two SPECint ratings. Thus, the service demand at the faster server would be
$10/(10.4/3.11) = 3.0$ msec. Of course, the choice of which benchmark to use to

Figure 5.6. Data collection alternatives for workload characterization.

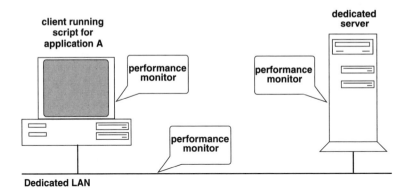

Figure 5.7. Controlled environment for workload component benchmarking.

scale measurements taken in controlled environments down or up depends on the type of application. If the application in question is a scientific application that does mostly number-crunching of floating-point numbers, one should use SPECfp as opposed to SPECint ratings.   ■

In general, the actual service demand, ActualServiceDemand, is obtained from the measured demand, MeasuredServiceDemand, at the controlled environment by multiplying it by the ratio of throughput ratings—such as the SPEC ratings—of the resource used in the controlled environment and the resource used in the actual environment:

$$\text{ActualServiceDemand} = \text{MeasuredServiceDemand} \times \frac{\text{ControlledResourceThroughput}}{\text{ActualResourceThroughput}}. \qquad (5.5.1)$$

Chapter 12 discusses in greater detail issues involved in data collection for client/server systems.

5.5.3   Validating Workload Models

In building any model, abstractions of the reality being modeled are made for simplicity, ease of data collection and use, and the computational efficiency of the modeling process. The abstractions compromise the accuracy of the model, so the model must be validated within an acceptable margin of error, a process called *model validation*. If a model is deemed invalid, it must be calibrated to render it valid. This is called *model calibration*.

Validating workload models entails running a synthetic workload composed of workload model results and comparing the performance measures thus obtained with those obtained by running the actual workload. If the results match within a

10–30% margin of error, the workload model is considered to be valid. Otherwise, the model must be refined to more accurately represent the actual workload. This process is depicted in Fig. 5.8.

5.6 Workload Forecasting

Workload forecasting is the process of predicting how system workloads will vary in the future. Through this process one can answer questions such as: "How will the number of e-mail messages handled per day by the server vary over the next 6 mo?" "How will the number of hits to the corporate intranet's Web server vary over time?" Answering such questions involves evaluating an organization's workload trends if historical data are available and/or analyzing the business or strategic plans of the organization, and then mapping these business plans to changes in business processes (e.g., staff increases and paperwork reduction initiatives will yield 50% more e-mail and Internet usage and 80% more hits on the corporate Web server).

During workload forecasting, basic workload components are associated to business processes so that changes in the workload intensity of these components can be derived from the business process and strategic plans.

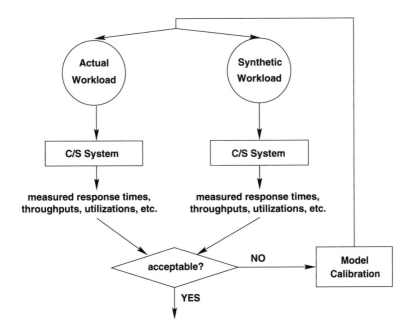

Figure 5.8. Workload model validation.

Example 5.2: Consider the C/S transactions in the example of Fig. 5.3. Assume that we plot the number of invoices issued for each of the past 6 mon, months numbered 1–6, as depicted in Fig. 5.9. By using linear regression, we can establish a relationship between the number of monthly invoices and the month number. In this example,

$$\text{NumberInvoices} = 250 \times \text{Month} + 7,250.$$

If we now need to forecast the number of invoices for the next month, we can use the above linear relationship to predict that 9,000 invoices will be issued next month. The number of invoices can be associated with the number of transactions of various types submitted to the database server. We can use regression techniques (see Chap. 11) to establish relationships between the number of invoices and the number of C/S transactions of various types, such as sales, purchase requisition, marketing, and finance. These relationships allow us to predict the arrival rate of these types of transactions. For example, if each invoice generates, on the average, 5.4 sales transactions, we can predict that next month, the database server will receive $9,000 \times 5.4 = 48,600$ sales transactions. If we divide this amount by the 22 working days of a month and by the 8 business hours of a day, we get an arrival rate of 276 sales transactions/hour. ■

Chapter 11 discusses workload forecasting techniques, such as moving averages, exponential smoothing, and linear regression, in detail.

5.7   Performance Modeling and Prediction

An important aspect of capacity management involves predicting whether a system will deliver performance metrics (e.g., response time and throughput) that meet desired or acceptable service-levels.

5.7.1   Performance Models

Performance prediction is the process of estimating performance measures of a computer system for a given set of parameters. Typical performance measures include response time, throughput, resource utilization, and resource queue length. Examples of performance measures for the C/S system of Fig. 5.3 include the response time for retrieving mail from the mail server, the response time experienced during Web-based corporate training sessions, the throughput of the file server in LAN 2, the utilization of the backbone FDDI ring, and the throughput and average number of requests queued at the Web proxy server. Parameters are divided into the following categories:

- *system parameters*: characteristics of a C/S system that affect performance. Examples include load-balancing disciplines for Web server mirroring, network protocols, maximum number of connections supported by a Web server, and maximum number of threads supported by the database management system.

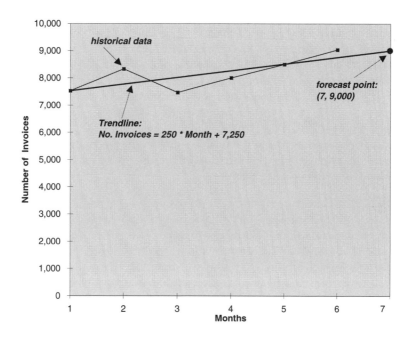

Figure 5.9. Workload forecasting.

- *resource parameters*: intrinsic features of a resource that affect performance. Examples include disk seek times, latency and transfer rates, network bandwidth, router latency, and CPU speed ratings.

- *workload parameters*: derived from workload characterization and divided into:

  - *workload intensity parameters*: provide a measure of the load placed on the system, indicated by the number of units of work that contend for system resources. Examples include the number of hits/day to the Web proxy server, number of requests/sec submitted to the file server, number of sales transactions submitted per second to the database server, and the number of clients running scientific applications. Another important characteristic of the workload is the burstiness of the arrival process as discussed in Chaps. 4 and 10.

  - *workload service demand parameters*: specify the total amount of service time required by each basic component at each resource. Examples include the CPU time of transactions at the database server, the total transmission time of replies from the database server in LAN 4, and the total I/O time at the Web proxy server for requests of images and video clips used in the Web-based training classes.

Performance prediction requires the use of models. Two types of models may be used: simulation models and analytical models. Both types of models have to consider contention for resources and the queues that arise at each system resource— CPUs, disks, routers, and communication lines. Queues also arise for software resources—threads, database locks, and protocol ports.

The various queues that represent a distributed C/S system are interconnected, giving rise to a network of queues, called a queuing network (QN). The level of detail at which resources are depicted in the QN depends on the reasons to build the model and the availability of detailed information about the operation and availability of detailed parameters of specific resources.

Example 5.3: To illustrate the above concepts we will use the notation introduced in Chap. 3 to show two versions—a high level and a more detailed level—of the QN model that corresponds to LAN 3 in Fig. 5.3, its Web server, its 100 clients, and the connections of LAN 3 to the Internet and to the FDDI ring. Figure 5.10 depicts a high-level QN model for LAN 3. The 10 Mbps LAN is depicted as a queuing resource and so is the Web server. The set of 100 Windows clients is depicted as a single delay resource because requests do not contend for the use of the client; they just spend some time at the client. The FDDI ring and the Internet are not explicitly modeled as this model focuses on LAN 3 only. However, traffic coming from the FDDI ring and from the Internet into LAN 3 has to be taken into account.

Note that the model of Fig. 5.10 hides many of the details of the Web server. As mentioned in Sec. 5.4, the Web server runs on a dual processor machine. Thus, a more detailed representation of the QN model would have to include the server

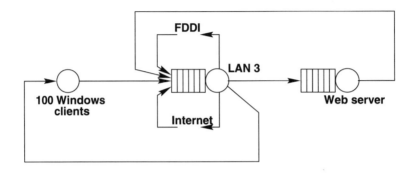

Figure 5.10. High-level QN of LAN 3.

processors and disks as shown in Fig. 5.11.   ■

Chapters 8 and 9 discuss, in detail, techniques used to build performance models of C/S systems.

5.7.2   Performance Prediction Technique

To predict the performance of a C/S system we need to be able to solve the performance model that represents the system. Analytic models [8] are based on a set of formulas and/or computational algorithms used to generate performance metrics from model parameters. Simulation models [5], [6], [9] are computer programs that mimic the behavior of a system as transactions flow through the various simulated resources. Statistics on the time spent at each queue and each resource are accumulated by the program for all transactions so that averages, standard deviations, and even distributions of performance metrics can be reported on the performance measures.

There is a wide range of modeling alternatives. As more system elements are represented in greater detail, model accuracy increases. Data gathering requirements also increase, as shown in Fig. 5.12. It is important that a reasonable balance be made between model accuracy and ease of use to allow for the analysis of many alternatives with little effort and in very little time. Analytic models are quite appropriate for the performance prediction component of any capacity management/planning study. In this book, we explore how analytic-based QN models can be used to model C/S systems, Web servers, and intranets.

Many times it is unfeasible to obtain detailed performance data. It is important to note that a detailed performance model that uses unreliable data yields nonrepresentative results.

5.7.3   Performance Model Validation

A performance model is said to be valid if the performance metrics (e.g., response time, resource utilizations, and throughputs) calculated by the model match the

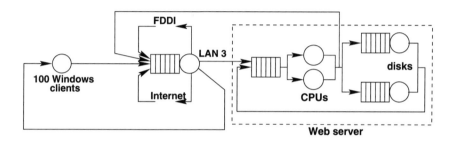

Figure 5.11. Detailed QN of LAN 3.

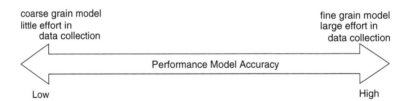

Figure 5.12. Performance model accuracy.

measurements of the actual system within a certain acceptable margin of error. Accuracies from 10 to 30% are acceptable in capacity planning [8].

Fig. 5.13 illustrates the various steps involved in performance model validation. During workload characterization, measurements are taken for service demands, workload intensity, and for performance metrics such as response time, throughput, and device utilization. The same measures are computed by means of the performance model. If the computed values do not match the measured values within an acceptable level, the model must be calibrated. Otherwise, the model is deemed valid and can be used for performance prediction. A detailed discussion on performance model calibration techniques is given in [8].

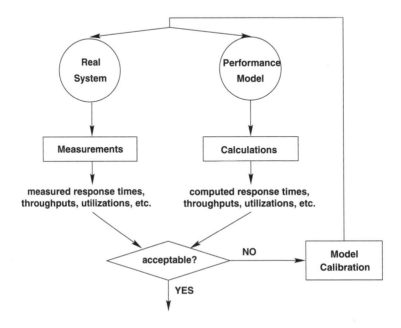

Figure 5.13. Performance model validation

5.8   Development of a Cost Model

A capacity planning methodology requires the identification of major sources of cost as well as the determination of how costs vary with system size and architecture. Costs are categorized into startup and operating costs. Startup costs are those incurred in setting up the system, while operating costs are the annual expenses incurred to maintain the system and provide upgrades in hardware and software to avoid obsolescence, performance degradation, and security vulnerabilities. Startup costs apply to hardware, software, infrastructure, and initial installation charges. Operating costs are related to hardware and software maintenance and upgrades, personnel costs, training, telecommunications services, and consulting fees.

The highly distributed nature of LAN and client/server environments is frequently responsible for a lack of knowledge of the costs incurred in maintaining these environments. A survey of 250 companies showed that fewer than 5% of U.S. corporations quantify their expenditures of PCs and LANs [4]. The same study indicates that costs associated with LAN-connected PCs range from $5,000 to $10,000 per user, making PC/LAN usage the largest undocumented IT cost in most corporations. In general, client/server costs can be divided into four major categories: hardware costs, software costs, telecommunications costs, and support cost. Hardware costs include the cost of

- client and server machines along with their disks and other peripherals, memory, and network cards

- disk storage arrays

- routers, bridges, and intelligent switches

- backup equipment

- uninterrupted power supplies (UPS)

- cabling

- vendor maintenance and technical support

Software costs account for the cost of

- server and client network operating systems

- server and client middleware (e.g., TP monitors)

- database management systems

- HTTP servers

- mail processing software

- office automation software

- business applications

- antivirus software

- security and intrusion detection software

- software development

- vendor software maintenance and upgrades

Telecommunication costs include charges for

- WAN services (e.g., Frame Relay, X.25 networks, T1, T3, ISDN)

- Internet Service Providers

Support costs include

- salaries, fringes, and benefits of all system administrators, database administrators, LAN, and Web administrators

- help desk support costs which includes salaries, fringes, and benefits of help desk staff, and their infrastructure (e.g., computers, servers, and phones)

- training costs for support staff (includes travel and time off for training courses)

- network management hardware and software

- performance monitoring software

More than one survey [2], [4] indicates that personnel costs account for a large percentage—between 60 and 70%—of client/server costs. One can be as detailed as required when accounting for costs. This increases the accuracy of the cost assessment at the expense of the time and effort needed to obtain all needed information. Alternatively, one can use more aggregated cost models that account for most of the cost elements with a reasonable degree of accuracy. When some of the cost elements are not known precisely, one can use Rules of Thumb (ROTs) to obtain a first-cut approximation to the cost model. Examples of cost ROTs are: hardware and software upgrade is 10% of the purchase price per year, system administrator costs lie between $500 and $700 per client per month, training costs range from $1,500 to $3,500 per technical staff person per year, 40% of personnel costs are in the resource management category, 40% are in applications development and maintenance, and 20% in other personnel [3], [4].

An MS Excel spreadsheet, called Cost.XLS, included in the accompanying disk, provides a template for computing startup and operating costs for C/S systems.

5.9 Cost/Performance Analysis

Once the performance model is built and solved and a cost model developed, various analyses can be made regarding cost-performance tradeoffs. The performance model and cost models can be used to assess various scenarios and configurations. Some example scenarios are, "Should we mirror the Web server to balance the load, cut down on network traffic, and improve performance?" "Should we replace the existing Web server with a faster one?" "Should we move from a two-tier C/S architecture to a three-tier one?" For each scenario, we can predict what the performance of each basic component of the global workload will be and what the costs are for the scenario.

The comparison of the various scenarios yields a configuration plan, an investment plan, and a personnel plan. The configuration plan specifies which upgrades should be made to existing hardware and software platforms and which changes in network topology and system architecture should be undertaken. The investment plan specifies a timeline for investing in the necessary upgrades. The personnel plan determines what changes in the support personnel size and structure must be made in order to accommodate changes in the system.

Some people favor the exclusive use of Return on Investment (ROI) analyses to assess the payback of migrating to a C/S system. These analyses have the drawback of looking only at the economic aspect of the issue. Other people decide to invest in client/server systems because they see them as a necessary ingredient of a company's business strategy, an enabling factor to improve customer service and product quality, and to shorten time to market of new products.

5.10 Concluding Remarks

Determining the adequate capacity of complex, distributed client/server systems requires careful planning so that user satisfaction is guaranteed, company goals are achieved, and investment returns are maximized.

This chapter presented the framework of a methodology for capacity planning of client/server systems. Chapter 6 expands on the "workload characterization" step and discusses clustering analysis techniques, data transformation, and other related issues. Chapter 7 discusses several industry standard benchmarks that can be used as an aid in the process of workload characterization in lieu of actual measurements. Techniques for measurements and data collection are discussed in Chap. 12. Chapters 8 and 9 introduce performance models. Chapter 8 looks at the issue from a systems point of view where large subsystems—a complete Web server, for example—are seen as black boxes. Chapter 9 looks at performance models that allow us to take into account the details of subsystems—the disks and processors of a Web server, for example. Chapter 10 considers performance modeling as it applies to the Web. Finally, Chap. 11 discusses various workload forecasting techniques such as linear regression, exponential smoothing, and moving averages.

BIBLIOGRAPHY

[1] J. M. ANDRADE, M. T. CARGES, T. J. DWYER, and S. D. FELTS, *The Tuxedo System*. Reading, MA: Addison Wesley, 1996.

[2] GARTNER GROUP, *The Cost of LAN Computing: A Working Model*, Feb. 7, 1994.

[3] E. HUFNAGEL, *The hidden costs of client/server, your client/server survival kit, Network Computing*, vol. 5, 1994.

[4] ITG, *Cost of Computing, Comparative Study of Mainframe and PC/LAN Installations*, Mountain View, CA: Information Technology Group, 1994.

[5] A. M. LAW and W. D. KELTON, *Simulation Modeling and Techniques*. 2nd ed. New York: McGraw-Hill, 1990.

[6] M. H. MACDOUGALL, *Simulating Computer Systems: Techniques and Tools*. Cambridge, MA: MIT Press, 1987.

[7] D. A. MENASCÉ, D. DREGITS, R. ROSSIN, and D. GANTZ, A federation-oriented capacity management methodology for LAN environments, *Proc. 1995 Conf. Comput. Measurement Group*, Nashville, TN, Dec. 3–8, 1995, pp. 1024–1035.

[8] D. A. MENASCÉ, V. A. F. ALMEIDA, and L. W. DOWDY, *Capacity Planning and Performance Modeling: From Mainframes to Client-Server Systems*. Upper Saddle River, NJ: Prentice Hall, 1994.

[9] S. M. ROSS, *A Course in Simulation*. New York: Macmillan, 1990.

Chapter 6

UNDERSTANDING AND CHARACTERIZING THE WORKLOAD

6.1 Introduction

The performance of a distributed system with many clients, servers, and networks depends heavily on the characteristics of its load. Thus, the first step in any performance evaluation study is to understand and characterize the workload. The workload of a system can be defined as the set of all inputs that the system receives from its environment during any given period of time. For instance, if the system under study is a database server, then its workload consists of all transactions (e.g., inquiry and update) processed by the server during an observation interval. Consider that a server was observed during 1 hour and 70,000 transactions were completed. The workload of the DB server during that 1-hour period is the set of 70,000 transactions. The workload characteristics are represented by a set of information (e.g., arrival and completion time, CPU time, and number of I/O operations) for each of the 70,000 DB transactions.

It is certainly difficult to handle real workloads with a large number of elements. Therefore, in order to work with practical problems, one needs to reduce and summarize the information needed to describe the workload. In other words, one needs to build a workload model that captures the most relevant characteristics of the real workload.

The choice of characteristics and parameters that will describe the workload depends on the purpose of the study. For example, if one wants to study the cost × benefit of creating a proxy caching server for a Web site, then the workload characteristics needed for the study are the frequency of document reference, concentration of references, document sizes, and interreference times. Thus, based on the percentage of documents that are responsible for the majority of requests received by the site, one can evaluate the benefits of a proxy caching server. However, if one is interested in determining the impact of a faster CPU on the response time of a Web server, a different set of information must be collected. In this case, the performance study will rely on data such as average CPU time per request, average number of I/O operations per request, and average request response time.

Although each system may require a specific approach to the analysis and characterization of its workload, there are some general guidelines that apply well to all types of systems [6]. The common steps to be followed by any workload characterization project include: (1) specification of a point of view from which the workload will be analyzed, (2) choice of the set of parameters that captures the most relevant characteristics of the workload for the purpose of the study, (3) monitoring the system to obtain the raw performance data, (4) analysis and reduction of performance data, and (5) construction of a workload model. This chapter describes and illustrates with examples the major steps required for the construction of workload models. The methodology presented here is based in part on the material described in Chap. 2 of [14].

6.2   Characterizing the Workload for an Intranet

To help us understand the problem of workload characterization for distributed systems, consider the example of an intranet environment. It is worth noting that intranets are essentially based on the client/server paradigm, and therefore this example applies well to other types of client/server systems. A construction and engineering company is planning to roll out new applications and to increase the number of employees that have access to the intranet. Between 400 and 600 employees currently have access to the corporate intranet. The goal is to give all 4,000 employees access by the end of next year. Before starting the expansion of the intranet, management wants to analyze the performance of the current applications.

The corporate intranet offers a range of applications, from simple text to sophisticated graphics. The main applications are an employee directory, the human resources system, health insurance payments, quality management, and on-demand interactive training. The intranet consists of five Web servers that are accessed by employees through a LAN, as shown in Fig. 6.1.

Users have been complaining about the response time of the human resources system. So, the starting point for the performance study is server "B", which holds the application. As we mentioned earlier, the first step in any performance evaluation project is to understand and characterize the workload. Therefore, the central question is: "How do you characterize the workload for an intranet?"

First of all, we need to define what workload we want to characterize. There are multiple and different workloads in a distributed environment. It depends on the point-of-view from which we look at the workload. The workload presented to a client desktop consists of commands and "clicks" given by a user and responses provided by servers to the user's requests. From the server standpoint, the workload is made up of all HTTP requests it receives during an observation period. A server may receive requests from all clients in the system. The load of the network is usually described in terms of the traffic (e.g., packet size distribution) and the

CLIENTS   **SERVERS**

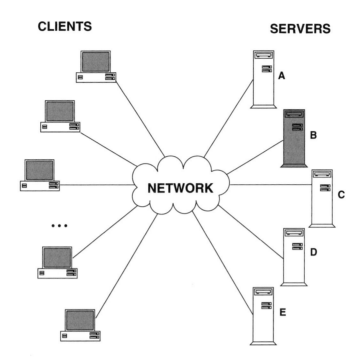

Figure 6.1. An intranet environment.

interpacket arrival time. Packets originate from HTTP interactions and e-mails.

A second question that must be answered refers to the level of the workload description. A high-level description would specify the workload from the user's point of view. For instance, one could specify the load in terms of Web transactions, such as insurance payment inquiries, document search, and interactive online training session. On the other hand, a low-level characterization would describe the user's requests in resource-oriented terms, such as average CPU time per request and number of packets exchanged between the client and server.

Let us start the workload characterization process by looking at the requests received by Web server "B", which hosts the human resources system. To simplify the example, let us consider a very short observation period. During a 1-sec interval, the server received ten HTTP document requests from clients on the local area network. What is the workload presented to the server in the observed period of time?

According to the definition in [10], the term workload designates all the processing requests submitted to a system by the user community during any given period of time. Thus, the workload in question consists of the sequence of ten requests received by the server. How could this workload be characterized? In other words, how could the workload be precisely described?

6.2.1 A First Approach

The first step in the characterization process is the identification of the basic components of the workload of a computer system. The *basic component* refers to a generic unit of work that arrives at a system from an external source. The nature of the service provided by the system determines the type of the basic component. Common types are a job, a transaction, an interactive command, a process, and an HTTP request. In client/server environments, the basic component could be a client request or the database transaction. For example, the basic component for a banking system is a transaction (e.g., savings account balance inquiry, checking account update, or loan status inquiry). The basic component of the workload presented to a file server in a distributed environment is a request for service [4]. *Read* and *Write* operations to files are the most popular requests made by a diskless workstations or network computers to a file server. These file operations received by a server from the workstations and other servers during any period of time make up the server's workload.

There are many forms of workload characterization. The one to be chosen depends on the purpose of the characterization. Basically, a characterization process yields a workload model that can be used in several activities, such as selection of computer systems, performance tuning, and capacity planning. Our interest concentrates mainly on building workload models for capacity planning purposes, as illustrated by Fig. 6.2. The characterization process analyzes a workload and identifies its basic components and features that have impact on the system's performance. It also yields parameters that retain the characteristics capable of driving performance models used for capacity planning activities.

The workload of a computer system can be described at different levels, as illustrated by Fig. 6.3. At the highest level, corporate and business plans provide

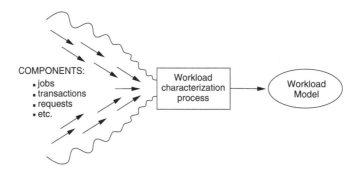

Figure 6.2. Workload characterization process.

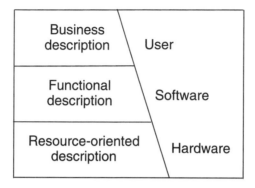

Figure 6.3. Workload description.

an initial description of the workload in terms of features of the main applications. The business workload is a user-oriented description, with business quantities such as number of employees, line items per order, and invoices per customer. At the next level, the *functional characterization* describes the programs, commands or applications that make up the workload. In our example, the workload consists of a series of Web requests. This type of characterization does not depend upon the underlying computer system, which makes the characterization system independent. However, functional description is related to software models, such as on-line transaction processing, HTTP services, and database system. For performance modeling and capacity planning purposes, though, business description and pure functional models have a serious drawback: They do not capture any quantitative information about the resource consumption behavior. This complicates the accomplishment of some basic capacity planning activities such as sizing a system or predicting the performance of a new system. These activities typically require quantitative information about the workload. For example, a request for a large graphic document with thousands of KB consumes much more CPU and I/O time than a request for a small HTML document does. Thus, in order to make the characterization useful, it is necessary to include in the model some high-level information about resource requirements. For instance, a request description would include information about the size of the document.

At the physical level, the *resource-oriented characterization* describes the consumption of the system resources by the workload. The resources to be included in the characterization are those whose consumption have a significant impact on performance [10]. The execution of a typical request by the HTTP server is simple. The server receives requests from Web clients, parses each request and determines the file corresponding to the document requested. The Web server retrieves the file (from cache or disk) and sends the document back to the client over the network. Assuming that each process servicing a request has a fixed amount of memory, we can consider that the CPU and the I/O system (i.e., disks) are the main physical resources of the server to be used in the characterization. Once the request connection has been accepted, the network itself does not influence the execution of the request, which is then characterized in terms of CPU and I/O time involved in its execution. The pair (CPU time, I/O time) can be used to characterize the execution of a request on the Web server. All major operating systems and HTTP servers provide facilities for determining how much CPU is being consumed by a particular process that runs on behalf of a request. Usually, the operating systems include accounting logs that record the hardware resource usage by each process execution. CPU time, elapsed time, total I/O operations, core memory usage, and number of page faults are examples of the type of process execution information existing in a system accounting file.

6.2.2   A Simple Example

If we assume the server of our previous example has only one size of document, the workload characterization would be as easy as pie. Let us consider that each document has the same size; for example, 15 KB. This implies having approximately the same CPU and I/O times for each of the ten executions of the HTTP requests. From data available in the system accounting files and access logs, we got the following characterization: ten requests represented by the pair (0.013, 0.09) where the first number in the pair represents the CPU service demand of a request and the second its disk service demand. Consider now a more realistic situation. We all know that Web documents have different sizes, ranging from one to several pages. This implies variable size files, leading to variations in the values of the two parameters chosen for the characterization of the workload of this example.

Table 6.1 shows the CPU, I/O, and execution times for each of the ten Web requests for documents of different sizes. The execution time corresponds to the elapsed time required by the server to service the request. The average response time equals 0.55 sec. Looking at Table 6.1, we note that each execution is represented by a different pair of values of CPU and I/O times. For instance, the pair (0.0095, 0.04) is completely different, in terms of resource usage, from (0.2170, 1.20). Which pair should be chosen as a representation for the ten executions?

A key issue in workload characterization is *representativeness*, which indicates the accuracy in representing the real workload. Bearing this in mind, the next step is to determine a characterization for the workload described by Table 6.1. The first idea that comes to mind is that of a *typical Web request*, averaged over all of the executions. Its characterizing parameters are the average CPU and I/O times. Table 6.2 shows the pair of parameters of a single command that now characterizes the workload displayed in Table 6.1. The real workload is now represented by a model composed of ten requests characterized by the pair (0.0331, 0.205), that places on the server the same CPU and I/O demands as those placed by the original requests. But how accurate is this representation?

One technique for assessing the accuracy of a workload model relies on the anal-

Table 6.1. Execution of HTTP Requests (sec)

Request No.	CPU Time	I/O Time	Execution Time
1	0.0095	0.04	0.071
2	0.0130	0.11	0.145
3	0.0155	0.12	0.156
4	0.0088	0.04	0.065
5	0.0111	0.09	0.114
6	0.0171	0.14	0.163
7	0.2170	1.20	4.380
8	0.0129	0.12	0.151
9	0.0091	0.05	0.063
10	0.0170	0.14	0.189
Average	0.0331	0.205	0.550

Table 6.2. Single-class Characterization

Type	CPU Time (sec)	I/O Time (sec)	No. of Components
Single	0.0331	0.205	10
Total	0.331	2.05	10

ysis of the effect caused on the system when a model replaces the actual workload. In a more general way, as proposed in [10], the basic tenet of the workload characterization process can be stated as: a workload model $\mathcal{W}$ is a perfect representation of the real workload $\mathcal{R}$ if the performance measures (P) obtained when running $\mathcal{W}$ and $\mathcal{R}$ on the same system are identical ($P_{\mathrm{real}} = P_{\mathrm{model}}$), as shown in Fig. 6.4. Considering that the purpose of our workload characterization is to provide information to performance models, response times can be used to evaluate the accuracy of the workload model. Thus, the characterization is accurate if the response time of the server executing the workload model is close to the average response time measured during the execution of the real workload. If the response time of the execution of the request characterized by (0.0331, 0.205) approximates 0.55 sec, then the *typical request* turned out to be a good model.

Examinations of the values displayed in Table 6.2 lead to a refinement in the characterization process. The average response time of 0.55 sec does not adequately reflect the behavior of the actual server response times. Measured response times can be grouped into three distinct classes, according to their variation range. Moreover, each class can be associated with the size of document, which is the main influence on the response time. Thus we define the following classes: small, medium, and large. Due to the heterogeneity of the components of a real workload, it is

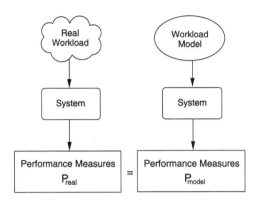

Figure 6.4. Representativeness of a workload model.

difficult to generate an accurate characterization if the workload is viewed as a single collection of requests. In an attempt to improve representativeness, the original workload is partitioned into three classes, based on resource usage, response time, and document size.

A *class* comprises components that are similar to each other concerning resource usage. The first class, named *small documents*, includes executions whose CPU and I/O times vary from 0.0001 to 0.0099 sec and from 0 to 0.05 sec, respectively. The second class, called *medium documents*, consists of those executions whose CPU time ranges from 0.0100 to 0.0300 sec and I/O times vary from 0.06 to 0.14 sec, respectively. The class of *large documents* has CPU and I/O times exceeding 0.03 and 0.14 sec, respectively. Table 6.3 presents three pairs of average parameters that now represent the original workload. Clustering the requests into three classes preserves some important features of the real workload and makes clear the distinction between requests that demand different amounts of resource time.

Let us take a look at the following example that shows the importance of classes in the context of capacity planning. In our example, suppose the small HTML pages, with text only, will be modified to incorporate a lot of graphics. The modification will increase the size of the pages and will transform all small documents into midsize documents. Before authorizing the modification to the pages, the system administrator wants to evaluate its effect on the server response time and the impact on network traffic. This kind of question could not be answered by a model with a single class, because the group of small documents is not explicitly represented. Breaking down the workload into classes increases the predictive power of a model.

Up until now, we have seen how to cluster a series of HTTP requests and represent them by one or more classes of requests. But, one factor is missing from completing the characterization: the rate at which requests arrive at the server. This rate depends primarily on the answers to two questions. What is the number

Table 6.3. Three-Class Characterization

Type	CPU Time (sec)	I/O Time (sec)	No. of Components
Small documents	0.0091	0.04	3
Medium documents	0.0144	0.12	6
Large documents	0.2170	1.20	1
Total	0.331	2.05	10

of users that generate requests to the server? How often a user interacts with the server? When a user interacts with a system, as in our example, the average think time determines the intensity of the load. *Think time*, as defined in Chap. 3, is the interval of time that elapses from when the user receives the answer from the system (e.g., UNIX's prompt or the page in the browser) until he or she issues a new request. The smaller the think time, the higher the rate at which requests arrive at the server.

The workload of our previous example is simple and small: only ten requests. In this case, if we wanted to test the performance of a faster server, it would be easier to generate the real requests for the new machine, instead of building a workload model. *Real workloads* consist of all original programs, transactions, and requests processed during a given period of time [10]. Therefore, real systems exhibit very complex workloads, composed of thousands of different programs, transactions, and requests. It would be unrealistic, even impossible, to consider the use of real workloads in capacity planning studies, where several different scenarios of hardware and software are analyzed. When a study involves comparisons of system's performance under varying scenarios, it is necessary to be able to reproduce the workload, in order to obtain the same conditions for the tests. Hence, the importance of building *workload models* that are compact, represent with accuracy the real workload, and are reproducible.

6.2.3 Workload Model

A workload model is a representation that mimics the real workload under study. It can be a set of programs written and implemented with the goal of artificially testing a system in a controlled environment. A workload model can also be a set of input data for an analytical model of a system. It would not be practical to have a model composed of thousands of basic components to mimic the real workload. Models should be compact. A compact model places on the system a demand much smaller than that generated by the actual workload. Let us take as an example the characterization of the workload of the server we described in Table 6.1. The first model we built consists of a single typical request. Thus, instead of running ten requests, the execution of the workload model with just one request would give us information to analyze the performance of the system under study. Thus, a model should be representative and compact. Workload models can be classified into categories, according to the way they are constructed. The two main categories of workload model are as follows.

- *Natural models* are constructed either using basic components of the real workload as building blocks or using execution traces of the real workload. A natural benchmark consists of programs extracted from the real workload of a system. The programs should be selected so that the benchmark represents the overall system load in given periods of time. Another natural model very often used in performance studies is the workload trace. It consists of a chronological sequence of data representing specific events that occurred in the system during a measurement session. For example, in the case of a Web server, the log access contains a line of information per request processed by the server. Among other information, each line specifies the name of the host making the request, the time stamp, and the name of the file requested. This type of log characterizes the real workload during a given period of time. Although traces exhibit reproducibility and representativeness features, they do have some drawbacks. Usually, traces consist of huge amounts of data that complicate their use. It is not that simple to modify a trace to represent different workload scenarios. Also, traces are suitable only for simulation models.

- *Artificial models* do not make use of any basic component of the real workload. Instead, these models are constructed out of special-purpose programs and descriptive parameters. We can also separate the artificial models into two classes: executable and non executable models. Executable artificial models consist of a suite of programs especially written to experiment with aspects of a computer system. The class of executable models include workloads such as *instruction mixes*, *kernels*, *synthetic programs*, *artificial benchmarks*, and *drivers*. Instruction mixes are hardware demonstration programs intended to test the speed of a computer on simple computational and I/O operations. Program kernels are pieces of code drawn out of the computationally intense parts of a real program. In general, kernels concentrate on measuring the performance of processors without considering the I/O system. Synthetic programs are specifically devised codes that place demands on different resources of a computing system. Unlike benchmarks, synthetic programs do not resemble the real workload. Benchmarks, synthetic programs, and other forms of executable models are not adequate input for performance models.

When the performance of a system is analyzed through the use of analytic or simulation models, new representations for the workload are required. Because our approach to capacity planning relies on the use of analytic models for performance prediction, we will focus on workload representations suitable for this kind of model.

Nonexecutable workload models are described by a set of mean parameter values that reproduce the same resource usage of the real workload. Each parameter denotes an aspect of the execution behavior of the basic component on the system under study. The basic inputs to analytical models are parameters that describe the service centers (i.e., hardware and software resources) and the customers (e.g., transactions and requests). Typical parameters are:

- component (e.g., transaction and request) interarrival times

- service demands

- component sizes

- execution mix (classes of components and their corresponding levels of multi-programming)

Each type of system may be characterized by a different set of parameters. As an example, let us look at a parametric characterization of a workload on a distributed system file server, presented in [4]. The study shows the factors that have a direct influence on the performance of a file server: the system load, the device capability, and the locality of file references. From these factors, the following parameters are defined:

- frequency distribution of the requests, which describes the participation of each request (e.g., read, write, create, and rename) on the total workload

- request interarrival time distribution, which indicates the time between successive requests. It also indicates the intensity of the system load

- file referencing behavior, which describes the percentage of accesses made to each file in the disk subsystem

- size of reads and writes, that have a strong influence on the time needed to service a request

The above parameters completely specify the workload model and are capable of driving synthetic programs that accurately represent real workloads. Another study [15] looks at an I/O workload from a different perspective. The workload model for a storage device (i.e., queues, caches, controllers, and disk mechanisms) is specified by three classes of parameters: time access attributes, access type (i.e., fraction of reads and writes), and spatial locality attributes. Time access attributes capture the time access pattern, which includes arrival process (i.e., deterministic, Poisson, bursty), arrival rate, burst rate, burst count, and burst fraction. Bursty workloads are discussed in Sec. 6.4. Spatial locality attributes specify the relationship between consecutive requests, such as sequential and random accesses. Due to "seek" delays, workloads with a larger fraction of sequential accesses may have better performance than those with random accesses (see Chap. 3). Thus, for a detailed model of an I/O device, it is important to include the spatial locality attributes of the workload.

Analytic models capture key aspects of a computer system and relate them to each other by mathematical formulas and/or computational algorithms, which are introduced in Chap. 8. Basically, analytic performance models require as input information such as workload intensity (e.g., arrival rate, number of clients, and think time) and the service demand placed by the basic component of the workload on each resource of the system. It is important to note that there is a difference between a high-level workload description (e.g., from the user's point of view) and the model inputs described here. Many times, one has to transform the functional level description to resource-oriented parameters, as we will see in the next section.

6.3   A Workload Characterization Methodology

Once we have discussed the main issues associated with workload characterization, let us describe the steps required to construct a workload model to be used as input to analytic models. Our approach focuses on resource-oriented characterization of workloads.

6.3.1   Choice of an Analysis Standpoint

As pointed out in Chap. 5, the global workload for a distributed environment is a combination of different workloads viewed by the different components of the system. We already know that the response time of a client/server transaction is the sum of that transaction's residence time at all resources, i.e., client desktop, network, and server. Suppose that we find the server residence time to be too high. We then begin the analysis by examining the server performance. From the server standpoint, the workload is made up of all requests the server receives from each possible client. Therefore, the first step in the workload characterization process is to establish the analysis standpoint, from which the workload will be characterized.

6.3.2   Identification of the Basic Component

In this step, we identify the basic components that compose the workload. Transactions and requests are the most usual components. The choice of components depends both on the nature of the system and the purpose of the characterization. The product of this step is a statement such as this: The workload under study consists of transactions and requests.

6.3.3   Choice of the Characterizing Parameters

Once the basic components have been identified, the next step is to choose which parameters characterize each type of basic component. In fact, the nature of the characterizing parameters is dictated by the input information required by analytic models. The parameters can be separated into two groups. One concerns the workload intensity. The other group refers to service demands of the basic components. What is missing here is the definition of which system resources are represented in the model. Usually, the chosen resources are those that most affect the performance of the target system when executing the workload under study. In summary, each component is represented by two groups of information:

- workload intensity

  - arrival rate

  - number of clients and think time

  - number of processes or threads in execution simultaneously

- service demands, specified by the K-tuple $(D_{i1}, D_{i2}, \ldots, D_{iK})$, where K is the number of resources considered, and D_{ij} is the service demand of basic component i at resource j. In the example of Table 6.1, each request is characterized by the 2-tuple (CPU time, I/O time), such as (0.0095 sec, 0.04 sec).

6.3.4 Data Collection

This step assigns values to the parameters of each component of the model. It generates as many characterizing tuples as the number of components of the workload. Chapter 12 presents techniques and tools used for data collection for client/server environments. Data collection includes the following tasks:

- Identify the *time windows* that define the measurement sessions. The time interval during which the system, the workload, and the performance indexes are observed represents the time window. Continuous observations of system behavior for days or weeks, depending on the nature of the business, allow the analyst to pick the appropriate time windows on which to base capacity planning studies.

- Monitor and measure the system activities during the defined time windows. Accounting tools available in the operating system and software monitors may be used to this end.

- From the collected data, assign values to each characterizing parameter of every component of the workload.

Many times it is not possible to obtain service demands directly from measured data. However, one can use relationships such as the ones discussed in Chaps. 3 and 12 to obtain the needed service demands from the measured data. For example, assume that we are looking for the service demand of HTTP requests to image files on the Web server's disk. An analysis of the HTTP LOG will reveal how many image files and their sizes were read during the measurement interval. This information, combined with the disk's performance characteristics, can be used to obtain the service demand being sought.

6.3.5   Partitioning the Workload

Real workloads can be viewed as a collection of heterogeneous components. Concerning the level of resource usage, for instance, a request for a video clip deeply differs from a request for a small HTML document. Because of this heterogeneity, many times the representation of a workload by a single class lacks accuracy. The motivation for partitioning the workload is twofold: improve representativeness of the characterization and increase the predictive power of the model. The latter stems from the fact that most forecasting methodologies rely on key indicators that are closely associated with specific classes of the workload, as shown in Chap. 11. Partitioning techniques divide the workload into a series of classes such that their populations are formed by quite homogeneous components. The aim is to group components that are somehow similar. But, what attribute should be used as a basis for the measure of similarity? A description of some attributes used for partitioning a workload into classes of similar components is as follows.

Resource Usage

The resource consumption per component can be used to break the workload into classes or clusters. Table 6.4 shows an example of classes of commands in a interactive environment. In this example, processor and I/O are considered the critical elements of the system. The attributes that divide the workload are the maximum CPU time and maximum I/O time required by a transaction. The *Light* class, for example, comprises transactions that demand more than 8 msec and less than 20 msec of CPU time and I/O time that varies between 120 and 300 msec.

Applications

A workload can have its components grouped according to the application they belong to. For instance, a workload could be partitioned into several classes, such as accounting, inventory, customer services, and others. Another example is based on the types of applications on the Internet. Let us consider that one wants to characterize the type of traffic that flows through the Internet connection to one's company. Due to the disparity in size and duration between most current Internet

Table 6.4. Workload Partitioning Based on Resource Usage

Transaction	Frequency	Maximum CPU Time (msec)	Maximum I/O Time (msec)
Trivial	40%	8	120
Light	30%	20	300
Medium	20%	100	700
Heavy	10%	900	1200

transactions (e.g., WWW, telnet) and newer multimedia applications (e.g., Mbone), it is critical to break the network traffic down into different applications. The Mbone traffic stems from the transmission of meetings, workshops, and video conferences that last for long periods of time. Multimedia is a bandwidth-intensive application, that has great impact on network performance. Table 6.5 shows the types of traffic and the amount of bytes transmitted during the period of observation. Applications which are neither significant in terms of resource consumption nor critical to the business can be grouped into a single class. In the example of Table 6.5, this class is called *others*.

The problem with the choice of this attribute is the existence of very heterogeneous components within the same application. We can envision coexisting in the same application a very large batch job that updates a database and trivial transactions that perform a simple query to the same database. These two types of components are completely different concerning resource usage. The same observation applies to the Web. While the retrieval of a small Web page may require a negligible amount of time at the server, a video can take several seconds of CPU and I/O time to be sent out by the server. Thus, if we group all components of the application into just one class, the values obtained for the parameters of the class would not be representative for components such as the very short requests and the video downloads.

Objects

One can divide a workload according to the type of objects handled by the applications. In the WWW, a workload can be partitioned by the types of documents accessed at the server. As an example, Table 6.6 exhibits a workload partitioned into categories of documents as proposed in [1], [8].

Geographical Orientation

A workload can be divided along lines of geography. Due to the inherent delays involved in WANs, it is important to make a distinction between requests or transactions that are serviced locally or remotely. As an example, one can split the workload up into two classes: *local* and *remote*. The location from which the re-

Table 6.5. Workload Partitioning Based on Internet Applications

Application	KB Transmitted
WWW	4,216
ftp	378
telnet	97
Mbone	595
Others	63

Table 6.6. Workload Partitioning Based on Document Types

Document Class	Percentage of Access (%)
HTML (html file types)	30.0
Images (e.g., gif, or jpeg)	40.0
Sound (e.g., au, or wav)	4.5
Video (e.g., mpeg, avi, or mov)	7.3
Dynamic (e.g., cgi, or perl)	12.0
Formatted (e.g., ps, dvi, or doc)	5.4
Others	0.8

quests are submitted is also used to define classes. Let us consider the case of a study to implement a caching strategy, dedicated to reduce response time and bandwidth consumption in the Web. Based on the observation that some documents are very popular, the study aims at replicating the most popular files to cooperative servers located in areas responsible for the greatest number of requests. In this case, the workload is partitioned according to the IP address of the machine that generated the HTTP request. One class corresponds to requests that come from the East Coast, another refers to requests that originate from the West Coast, and so forth. Table 6.7 summarizes the example and indicates the percentage of requests corresponding to each geographic region.

Functional

The components of a workload may be grouped into classes according to the functions being serviced. For instance, a Unix workload can be characterized by associating process names with functions performed in the system. As an example, we may divide the workload by command names as shown in Table 6.8. As a rule of thumb, one should try to keep the number of different classes to the minimum needed by the capacity planning study. If the initial number of classes is too large, aggregation of classes should be carried out. A helpful hint for aggregation is the

Table 6.7. Workload Partitioning Based on Geographical Orientation

Classes	Percentage of Total Requests
East Coast	32
West Coast	38
Midwest	20
Others	10

Table 6.8. Workload Partitioning Based on Functions

Classes	Number of Commands	Total CPU Time (sec)
oracle	1,515	19,350
sas	58	18,020
cp	950	7,500
date	225	26
ls	90	115
find	50	60

following: Concentrate on these classes of interest to the organization; collapse the rest into a single class. Let us assume that our interest is in analyzing the impact of predicted growth of database activities on the performance of the system. In light of this goal, the workload should be partitioned into two classes: database (e.g., oracle) and other applications. The remaining five classes would be represented by the class *Others*.

Organizational Units

A workload can be partitioned based on the organizational units of a company. This attribute may be useful for companies that have their strategic planning and growth forecasts generated on an organizational basis. As an example, a workload can be divided into classes, taking the organizational structure as attribute of similarity, such as finance, marketing, and manufacturing.

Mode

The mode of processing or the type of interaction with the system may be used to categorize the components of a workload. The mode of processing and the parameters chosen to describe them are as follows.

- *Interactive* — an online processing class with components generated by a given number of PCs, network computers, or workstations with a given think time. An interaction is a combination of waiting and thinking states. The user alternates between waiting for the response of the interaction and thinking before submitting the next command or mouse "click". An example would be a Web-based training application on a company's intranet.

- *Transaction* — an online processing class that groups components (e.g., transactions, or requests) that arrive at a computer system with a given arrival rate. An example would be the set of book orders that arrive at the Web site of a virtual bookstore.

- *Batch* — refers to components executed in batch mode, which can be described by the number of active jobs in the system. An example would be a mail daemon running at the mail server.

To be useful in performance evaluation, analytic models require classes of homogeneous components, concerning resource usage. It is clear that some attributes do not partition the workload into classes of homogeneous components. For instance, let us consider the case of a workload partitioned along geographical lines into two classes: West Coast and East Coast. However, the workload is composed of heterogeneous transactions that could be further divided into subclasses according to resource usage. Let us call these classes light and heavy. Therefore, it is desirable to partition a workload using multiple attributes.

Table 6.9 illustrates a partitioning based on two attributes: geographical basis and resource usage. Thus, we now have divided the workload into five classes, according to the source location of the transaction and the level of resource usage, such as "Heavy transactions from the West Coast."

6.3.6   Calculating Class Parameters

As we saw in Sec. 6.3.3, each component (w_i) is characterized by a K-tuple of parameters $w_i = (D_{i1}, D_{i2}, \ldots, D_{iK})$, where K is the number of resources considered and D_{ij} is the service demand requested by component i at resource j. After partitioning the workload into a number of classes, the capacity planner faces the following problem: How should one calculate the parameter values that represent a class of components? Two techniques have been widely used for this: averaging and clustering.

Averaging

When a class consists of homogeneous components concerning service demand, an average of the parameter values of all components may be used to represent the parameter values for the class. Thus, for a class composed of p components, the arithmetic mean of each parameter of the tuple $(D_{i1}, D_{i2}, \ldots, D_{iK})$ is given by:

$$\overline{D}_j = \frac{1}{p}\sum_{l=1}^{p} D_{lj}, \quad j = 1, 2, \ldots, K \qquad (6.3.1)$$

Table 6.9. Workload Partitioning Based on Multiple Attributes

Number	Type	Resource Usage
1	West Coast	Light
2	West Coast	Heavy
3	East Coast	Light
4	East Coast	Heavy
5	Others	Light

where $\overline{D}_j$ is the mean service demand of this class at resource j. The K-tuple $(\overline{D}_1, \overline{D}_2, \dots, \overline{D}_K)$ then represents a given class. To evaluate the homogeneity of a class, a capacity planner may use some statistical measures of variability, such as variance, coefficient of variation, and the relative difference between the maximum and minimum values observed in the class.

Clustering

Figure 6.5 shows a graph of the two parameters that define a given workload composed of transactions. Each point (x, y) in the graph corresponds to an execution of a transaction. The y-axis represents the CPU time demanded by an execution, whereas the x-axis depicts the I/O time.

Suppose that we want to partition the workload of Fig. 6.5 into classes of similar transactions. The question is, How should one determine groups of components of similar resource requirements? The answer lies in the *clustering analysis*. Basically, clustering of workloads is a process in which a large number of components are grouped into clusters of similar components. Although clustering analysis can be automatically performed by specific functions of some software packages, such as SPSS and SAS, it is important to be aware of the fundamentals of this technique.

Before discussing the technique in detail, let us first state the problem more

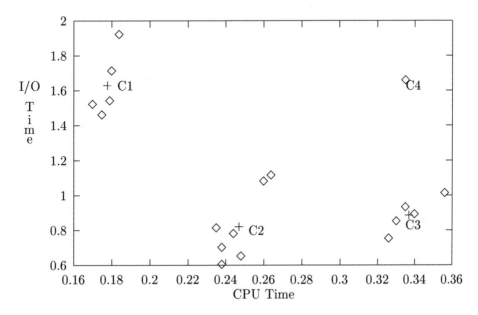

Figure 6.5. Service demands of a C/S transaction.

precisely. Let a workload $\mathcal{W}$ be represented by a set of p points $w_i = (D_{i1}, D_{i2}, \ldots, D_{iK})$ in a K-dimensional space, where each point w_i represents a component of $\mathcal{W}$, and K is the number of service demand parameters. To make the notation clear, let us revisit the example of Table 6.1 in Sec. 6.2.2. In that example, each request represents a point in the workload model. Thus, $p = 10$ and $K = 2$, because we are using just two resources (i.e., CPU and I/O) to characterize each request. For instance, using the notation proposed here, we have $w_1 = (0.0095, 0.04)$ and $w_8 = (0.0129, 012)$.

A clustering algorithm attempts to find natural groups of components based on similar resource requirements. Let the *centroid* of a cluster be the point whose parameter values are the means of the parameter values of all points in the cluster. To determine cluster membership, most algorithms evaluate the distance between a point w_i and the cluster centroids in the K-dimensional space. The point w_i is then included in the cluster that has the nearest centroid in the parameter space. As noted from Fig. 6.5, the components of the workload are naturally grouped into three clusters C_1, C_2, and C_3, whose centroids are indicated by a cross symbol. The component represented by point C_4 is called an *outlier* because it does not fit into any of the clusters within a reasonable distance.

The output of a clustering algorithm is basically a statistical description of the cluster centroids with the number of components in each cluster. For performance modeling purposes, each cluster defines a class of similar components. The characterization parameters of a class coincide with those of the cluster's centroid. The cluster analysis partitions a workload $\mathcal{W}$ into a set of R classes. If we apply a clustering method to the points of Table 6.1, we would get three clusters representing the classes displayed in Table 6.3. The centroids of the classes are the pairs of values (CPU time, I/O time) displayed in the Table 6.3. For instance, the centroid of the small documents class is the pair (0.0091, 0.04). Let us now describe the steps required to perform a clustering analysis of a given workload.

Data Analysis   The first step prepares the raw data that characterizes a workload. The input to this step consists of a set of K-tuples $(D_{i1}, D_{12}, \ldots, D_{iK})$ corresponding to the workload components. The input data analysis involves the following activities:

- sampling drawing

- parameter transformation

- outlier removal

The number of components that make up a workload is a function of the length of measurement sessions. If this number is very large, a sample should be drawn from the measured workload. The purpose is to keep the time required to perform the clustering analysis within acceptable limits. Random sampling yields representative subsets of a workload. Special situations, however, may require other sampling criteria. For example, if the Webmaster of a site is interested in knowing the effect of large video retrievals on network traffic, then the sample must include these requests.

The distribution of each parameter of a tuple should undergo an analysis to eliminate values that may distort the mean parameter value. From a frequency distribution of a parameter, one may observe very few large values that correspond to a small percentage of the components (e.g., 1% or 2%). If a histogram is unable to exhibit useful information because of a highly skewed format of a distribution, a *logarithmic* or another transformation may be required to obtain a more clear representation of the data.

Parameter values that range several orders of magnitude may lead to outliers. When examining the raw data, you should be very cautious about discarding a point considered as an outlier. The reason stems from the fact that measurements of several distributed systems (e.g., Internet, WWW, Ethernet traffic) show numbers that exhibit a pattern known as "heavy-tailed." This means that very large numbers could be present in samples of measurements, such as number of bytes transmitted, file sizes, and CPU times. These extremely large numbers do affect the performance of a system and should not be ignored. However, there are cases when you do not need to consider these very large numbers as part of the data. That is the case with some special tasks. Once in a while, a company runs a large job that reorganizes databases and disk space. Usually, these jobs take a very long time to run. Thus, depending on the time window you are analyzing, you may discard the points that correspond to those jobs, because you have control over their execution and you are able to move them out of your period of analysis.

To prevent the extreme values of a parameter from distorting the distribution, one should use some kind of transformation or scaling. One technique consists of trimming the distribution and use the 95th or 98th percentile value as the maximum value in a linear transformation such as the following:

$$D_i^t = \frac{\text{measured } D_i - \text{minimum of } \{D_i\}}{\text{maximum of } \{D_i\} - \text{minimum of } \{D_i\}} \tag{6.3.2}$$

where D_i is the original service demand parameter, D_i^t is the transformed parameter, and $\{D_i\}$ represents the set of all measured values of D_i. The above transformation maps the parameter values onto the interval from 0 to 1. Outlier analysis should be done carefully to avoid the elimination of a very few components that have great impact on system performance. As an example, jobs that reorganize large databases are among the heaviest resource consumers. Depending on how often they run, these jobs may be classified as outliers, or they may form a special class in the workload characterization. For a complete treatment of this subject see [11].

Distance Measures The distance between two points is the most common metric used by clustering techniques to assess similarity among components of a workload. A popular distance measure is the *Euclidean Metric*, which defines the distance d

between two points $w_i = (D_{i1}, D_{i2}, \ldots, D_{iK})$ and $w_j = (D_{j1}, D_{j2}, \ldots, D_{jK})$ as

$$d = \sqrt{\sum_{n=1}^{K} (D_{in} - D_{jn})^2}. \tag{6.3.3}$$

The use of raw data in the computation of Euclidean distances may lead to distorted results. For example, let us consider a three-tier C/S application that performs claim processing for a health insurance company. The user site is located in LAN A, and the application server and the DB server are both located in LAN B, which is connected to LAN A via WAN links. Users are complaining about poor performance. The analyst identified that the long response times occur with two types of transactions during the peak hour of the prime shift time period. Using network monitors and tools from the operating system, the analyst traced the execution of the transactions. It was found out that most of the transaction execution time was spent in the WAN and in the DB server. For the purpose of the study, the analyst decided to characterize the workload using two attributes: CPU time at the database server and the size of the reply message from the DB server to the client. The reply size is used to estimate the transmission delays. Table 6.10 presents the information concerning the execution of the three most popular transactions, labeled Tr1, Tr2, and Tr3, which are inquiry, update, and retrieve transactions. The sample transactions are characterized in terms of CPU time (in msec) and reply size (in bytes).

The Euclidean distances calculated according to Eq. (6.3.3) are

$$d_{Tr1Tr2} = \sqrt{(90 - 500)^2 + (13,000 - 4,000)^2} = 9,009.3$$

$$d_{Tr1Tr3} = \sqrt{(90 - 700)^2 + (13,000 - 25,000)^2} = 12,015.5$$

$$d_{Tr2Tr3} = \sqrt{(500 - 700)^2 + (4,000 - 25,000)^2} = 21,001.0.$$

We can note from the above results that point Tr1 is closer to Tr2 than to Tr3. Let us now change the unit of the parameter that represents the reply size from bytes to kilobytes. The new values of reply size for transactions Tr1, Tr2, and Tr3

Table 6.10. Transaction Execution Profile

Transaction	Server CPU Time (msec)	Reply Size (bytes)
Tr1	90	13,000
Tr2	500	4,000
Tr3	700	25,000
Mean	430	14,000
Standard Deviation	310.96	10,535.65

are 12.7, 3.9, and 24.4 KB, respectively. Thus, the Euclidean distances among the same points become

$$d_{Tr1Tr2} = \sqrt{(90 - 500) + (12.7 - 3.9)^2} = 410.1$$

$$d_{Tr1Tr3} = \sqrt{(90 - 700)^2 + (12.7 - 24.4)^2} = 610.1,$$

$$d_{Tr2Tr3} = \sqrt{(500 - 700)^2 + (3.9 - 24.4)^2} = 201.1.$$

Changing the units used to represent the parameters implied in the modification of the relative distances among points Tr1, Tr2, and Tr3. Now, point Tr2 is closer to Tr3 than to Tr1. When CPU time was specified in milliseconds and reply size in bytes, the second parameter dominated the computation of the Euclidean distance, making the effect of the first parameter on the results negligible. Scaling techniques should be used to minimize problems that arise from the choice of units and from the different ranges of values of the parameters.

Scaling Techniques   These are used to avoid problems that accrue from parameters with very different relative values and ranges. As we saw in the example of the computation of Euclidean distances, there are cases where it is desirable to work with unit-free parameters. Thus, a transformation is needed. The z score is a transformation that makes use of the mean and the standard deviation of each parameter over the values measured. The z score of a given parameter is calculated as

$$\text{z score} = \frac{\text{measured value} - \text{mean value}}{\text{standard deviation}}. \tag{6.3.4}$$

Let us now calculate the z score of the reply size parameter of Table 6.10. Both units (bytes and kilobytes) are used to show that the z score is unit-free. The mean and standard deviation for the reply size (RS) in bytes are 14,000 and 10,535.65, respectively.

$$z_{RS_{Tr1}} = \frac{13,000 - 14,000}{10,535.65} = -0.095$$

$$z_{RS_{Tr2}} = \frac{4,000 - 14,000}{10,535.65} = -0.949$$

$$z_{RS_{Tr3}} = \frac{25,000 - 14,000}{10,535.65} = 1.044.$$

The mean and standard deviation for the reply size in kilobytes are 13.67 and 10.29, respectively. So, the new z-scores are

$$z_{RS_{Tr1}} = \frac{12.7 - 13.67}{10.29} = -0.095$$

$$z_{RS_{Tr2}} = \frac{3.91 - 13.67}{10.29} = -0.949$$

$$z_{RS_{Tr3}} = \frac{24.41 - 13.67}{10.29} = 1.044$$

which are the same as before.

Clustering Algorithms   The goal of a clustering algorithm is to identify natural groups of components, based on similar resource requirements. There are various clustering algorithms available in the literature. References [2], [9] present a thorough review of clustering techniques. They can be grouped into two broad categories: hierarchical and nonhierarchical. The former includes those techniques where the input data are not partitioned into the desired number of classes in a single step. Instead, a series of successive fusions of data are performed until the final number of clusters is obtained. Nonhierarchical techniques start from an initial partition corresponding to the desired number of clusters. Points are reallocated among clusters so that a particular clustering criterion is optimized. A possible criterion is the minimization of the variability within clusters, as measured by the sum of the variance of each parameter that characterizes a point. Two widely known clustering algorithms are discussed in detail.

The minimal spanning tree (MST) method is a hierarchical algorithm that begins by considering each component of a workload to be a cluster. Next, the two clusters with the minimum distance are fused to form a single cluster. The process continues until either all points are grouped into a single cluster or the final number of desired clusters is reached. The definition of the desired number of clusters may be obtained with the help of a measure called *linkage distance*, which represents the farthest distance between a component in one cluster to a component in another cluster [5]. The linkage distance increases as a function of how different the components being combined are. If the linkage distance exceeds a given limit, the algorithm stops with the current number of clusters. Considering a workload represented by p tuples of the form $(D_{i1}, D_{i2}, \ldots, D_{iK})$, the steps required by the MST algorithm [11] are shown in Fig. 6.6.

A *k-means algorithm* is a nonhierarchical clustering technique that begins by finding k points in the workload, which act as an initial estimate of the centroids of the k clusters. The remaining points are then allocated to the cluster with the nearest centroid. The allocation procedure iterates several times over the input points until no point switches cluster assignment or a maximum number of iterations is performed. Figure 6.7 shows the steps required by the k-means algorithm to perform a clustering analysis on a workload represented by p points of the form $w_i = (D_{i1}, D_{i2}, \ldots, D_{iK}), i = 1, \cdots, p$.

A common problem found in clustering analysis is the difficulty of deciding on the number of clusters present in a workload. For practical purposes in capacity planning studies, it is desirable to keep this number small. The value depends on factors such as the goals of the study, the number of critical applications, the types of objects, and the modes of processing (e.g., transaction, interactive, or batch).

Example 6.1: To illustrate the use of clustering techniques, let us consider the example of a Web server composed of a fast processor and a large disk subsystem. The server is dedicated to deliver HTML documents on request. During a specific

1. Set the initial number of clusters equal to the number of components of the workload (i.e., $j = p$).

2. Repeat the following steps until the desired number of clusters is obtained.

3. Determine the parameter values of centroid C_j of each of the j clusters. Their parameter values are the means of the parameter values of all points in the cluster.

4. Calculate the $j \times j$ intercluster distance matrix, where each element (m, n) represents the distance between the centroids of clusters m and n.

5. Determine the minimum nonzero element (q, r) of the distance matrix. It indicates that clusters q and r are to be merged. Then, decrease the number of clusters $(j \leftarrow j - 1)$.

Figure 6.6. Minimal spanning tree algorithm.

1. Set the number of clusters to k.

2. Choose k starting points, to be used as initial estimates of cluster centroids. For example, one can select either the first k points of the sample or the k points mutually farthest apart. In this case, the distance matrix is required.

3. Examine each point of the workload and allocate it to the cluster whose centroid is nearest. The centroid's position is recalculated each time a new point is added to the cluster.

4. Repeat step 3 until no point changes its cluster assignment during a complete pass or a maximum number of passes is performed.

Figure 6.7. k-means algorithm.

time window, the access logs of the Web server recorded the execution behavior of all requests. With the purpose of keeping the example small, a random sample of the workload was drawn and seven requests were selected. The performance study aims at analyzing the cost $\times$ benefit of caching the most popular documents in main memory. In order to do that, we need to study the relationship between document size and popularity, in order to have an idea of the size of the main memory required by the document cache. Table 6.11 shows the parameters that

Table 6.11. Workload Sample

Document	Size (KB)	Number of Accesses
1	12	281
2	150	28
3	5	293
4	25	123
5	7	259
6	4	241
7	35	75

characterize the workload for the purpose of this study. As can be noted from the table, the components of this workload are not homogeneous. Therefore, we want to find out classes of similar components. A step-by-step description of the clustering process is now presented.

1. Because of the difference in magnitude in the values of document size and frequency of access, a change of scale is required. Table 6.12 shows the parameter values transformed by a $\log_{10}$ function, that is, each value y in Table 6.12 is equal to $\log_{10} x$ where x is the value in Table 6.11 corresponding to y.

2. Let us consider that our goal is to obtain three clusters. We use the Euclidean distance as the metric to evaluate distances between clusters. The MST algorithm is selected.

3. The initial number of clusters is set to seven, which is the number of components.

4. The parameter values of the centroids of each cluster coincide with the parameter values of the components, as shown in Table 6.13. In this case, each cluster has a single component.

Table 6.12. Logarithmic Transformation of Parameters

Document	Size (KB)	Number of Accesses
1	1.08	2.45
2	2.18	1.45
3	0.70	2.47
4	1.40	2.09
5	0.85	2.41
6	0.60	2.38
7	1.54	1.88

Table 6.13. Centroids of the Initial Clusters

Document	Size (KB)	Number of Accesses
C1	1.08	2.45
C2	2.18	1.45
C3	0.70	2.47
C4	1.40	2.09
C5	0.85	2.41
C6	0.60	2.38
C7	1.54	1.88

5. Let us now calculate the intercluster distance matrix, using Eq. (6.3.3). For instance, we note from Table 6.14 that the distance between clusters C5 and C6 is 0.25.

6. The minimum distance among the clusters of Table 6.14 is that between C3 and C6, i.e., 0.13. These clusters are merged to form a larger cluster C36. The coordinates of its centroid are $(0.70 + 0.60)/2 = 0.65$ and $(2.47 + 2.38)/2 = 2.43$.

7. Now, we have six clusters. We recompute the distance matrix for the new number of clusters, as shown in Table 6.15.

8. The smallest element of Table 6.15 corresponds to the distance between clusters C36 and C5 which are therefore merged. The coordinates of the centroid of cluster C356 are $(0.65 + 0.85)/2 = 0.75$ and $(2.43 + 2.41)/2 = 2.42$.

9. We now have five clusters; the distance matrix for the new cluster configuration is given in Table 6.16.

Table 6.14. Intercluster Distance Matrix

Cluster	C1	C2	C3	C4	C5	C6	C7
C1	0	1.49	0.38	0.48	0.24	0.48	0.74
C2		0	1.79	1.01	1.64	1.83	0.76
C3			0	0.79	0.16	**0.13**	1.03
C4				0	0.64	0.85	0.26
C5					0	0.25	0.88
C6						0	1.07
C7							0

Table 6.15. Intercluster Distance Matrix

Cluster	C1	C2	C36	C4	C5	C7
C1	0	1.49	0.43	0.48	0.24	0.74
C2		0	1.81	1.01	1.64	0.76
C36			0	0.82	**0.19**	1.05
C4				0	0.64	0.26
C5					0	0.88
C7						0

Table 6.16. Intercluster Distance Matrix

Cluster	C1	C2	C365	C4	C7
C1	0	1.49	0.33	0.48	0.74
C2		0	1.73	1.01	0.76
C365			0	0.73	0.96
C4				0	**0.26**
C7					0

10. The smallest element of Table 6.16 corresponds to the distance between clusters C4 and C7 which are therefore merged. The coordinates of the centroid of C47 are $(1.40 + 1.54)/2 = 1.47$ and $(2.09 + 1.88)/2 = 1.99$.

11. The number of clusters is now four, and the distance matrix for the new cluster configuration is given in Table 6.17.

12. The smallest element of Table 6.17 corresponds to the distance between clusters C1 and C365 which are therefore merged. The parameter values of the centroid of C1365 are $(1.08 + 0.75)/2 = 0.92$ and $(2.45 + 2.42)/2 = 2.44$.

13. The number of clusters is now three, and the distance matrix for the new cluster configuration is given in Table 6.18.

Table 6.17. Intercluster Distance Matrix

Cluster	C1	C2	C365	C47
C1	0	1.49	**0.33**	0.61
C2		0	1.73	0.89
C365			0	0.84
C47				0

Table **6.18.** Intercluster Distance Matrix

Cluster	C1365	C2	C47
C1356	0	1.60	0.72
C2		0	0.89
C47			0

14. The original workload given in Table 6.11 has been partitioned into three classes of similar requests. Each class is represented by parameter values that are equal to the average of the parameter values of all components of the class. Table 6.19 presents the output of the clustering process. It contains the description of the centroids that represent each cluster and its number of components. Each cluster corresponds to one class in the workload. In the example, classes are named according to their document size. For instance, the class of small documents corresponds to an average document size of 8.19 KB and an average number of accesses equal to 271.51. This class has four documents. Note that the values in Table 6.19 were scaled back to the original scale. ∎

6.4   Bursty Workloads

New phenomena have been observed in large distributed systems such as the Internet, intranets, and World Wide Web. Several studies [1], [7], [12] have revealed new properties of network traffic, such as the self-similarity. Intuitively, a self-similar process looks bursty across several time scales. A study [12] shows that total traffic (measured in bytes per second or packets per second) on Ethernet LANs and on WANs is self-similar. In another study [7], it is shown that Web traffic contains bursts observable over four orders of magnitudes. Figure 6.8 displays a plot of the Web traffic as a function of 1,000-sec time intervals. The diurnal cycle of network demand is evident as well as the burstiness of the day-day activity. The same study shows that traffic bursts are also observable when you change the time periods to

Table **6.19.** Output of the Clustering Process

Type	Class	Document Size (KB)	No. of Accesses	No. of Components
Small	C1356	8.19	271.51	4
Medium	C47	29.58	96.05	2
Large	C2	150.00	28.00	1

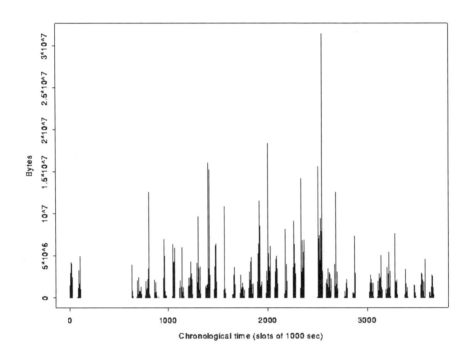

Figure 6.8. WWW traffic burst (reprinted from [7]).

100, 10, or 1 sec. What is important for us in this book is that self-similarity of network traffic (i.e., Internet, WWW, Ethernet) implies burstiness at several time scales. And burstiness has a strong impact on the performance of networked systems.

As pointed out in [3], HTTP request traffic is bursty with the burstiness being observable over different time-interval scales. Peak rates during bursts exceed the average rate by factors of 5 to 10 and can easily surpass the capacity of the server. It is also shown in [3] that even a small amount of burstiness degrades the throughput of a Web server. So, we need to include burst effects in our models. The question that arises naturally is: How can we represent burstiness in the workload characterization?

Burstiness in a given observation period can be represented by a pair of parameters, (a, b). Parameter a is the ratio between the maximum observed request rate and the average request rate during the monitoring period. Parameter b is the fraction of time during which the instantaneous arrival rate exceeds the average arrival rate. In [3], it is shown that even a small amount of burstiness ($a = 6$, $b = 5\%$) can degrade the throughput of a Web server by 12–20%. Chapter 10 presents simple analytical models that incorporate the effects of burstiness. It is important to keep in mind that the representativeness of workload models for analytic models is limited. Very often, simplifying assumptions are introduced in the workload representation so that the solution of the analytical model remains simple and efficient. To illustrate the problem, let us examine the case of modeling Ethernet environments. The workload of an Ethernet network consists of the packets transmitted by workstations on the network and can be characterized by packet length and interarrival time statistics. With the purpose of simplifying the model, many studies on workload characterization of Ethernet environments assume homogeneous arrivals of packets. However, measurement experiments described in [4] show that the packet arrival process in Ethernet environments is bursty. The packet arrival pattern follows a train model, where the network traffic consists of a collection of packet streams flowing between various pairs of workstations [11]. One of the sources of this arrival pattern stems from the fact that messages transmitted are often much larger than the maximum packet size on the Ethernet and must be partitioned into smaller units that are consecutively transmitted. This operational behavior of Ethernet networks clearly contrasts with the homogeneous arrival assumption. Although the simplifications imply loss of accuracy, they do not invalidate the use of simple models; they are still capable of capturing some fundamental performance properties of computer systems. Simple performance models are valuable tools for practitioners.

6.5 Conclusions

Understanding and characterizing a workload are key issues in any performance study. This process represents the first step for capacity planning, performance tuning, system procurement and selection, and for the design of new systems. The better one understands the workload of a system, the more chances one has to obtain the best possible level of performance, given the system's workload. Although each system may require a specific approach to the analysis of its workload, there are some common guidelines that apply well to most systems. The basic steps to perform a workload characterization are summarized as:

- selection of a point of view from which the workload will be analyzed

- identification of the basic components of the workload

- selection of the set of parameters that capture the most relevant characteristics of the workload for the purpose of the study

- monitoring the system to collect raw performance data

- partitioning of the workload into classes of similar components

- calculation of the values of the parameters that characterize each class

- construction and validation of a workload model

BIBLIOGRAPHY

[1] M. ARLITT and C. WILLIAMSON, Web server workload characterization: the search for invariants, *Proc. 1996 SIGMETRICS Conf. Measurement Comput. Syst.*, ACM, Philadelphia, PA, May 1996, pp. 126–137.

[2] M. ANDERBERG, *Cluster Analysis for Applications.* New York: Academic, 1973.

[3] G. BANGA and P. DRUSCHEL, Measuring the capacity of a web server, *Usenix Symp. Internet Technol. Syst.*, Monterey, CA, Dec. 1997.

[4] R. BODNARCHUK and R. BUNT, A synthetic workload model for a distributed file system, *Proc. 1991 SIGMETRICS Conf. Measurement Comput. Syst.*, ACM, May 1991.

[5] J. CADY and B. HOWARTH, *Computer System Performance Management and Capacity Planning.* Australia: Prentice Hall, 1990.

[6] M. CALZAROSSA and G. SERAZZI, Workload characterization, *Proc. IEEE*, vol. 81, no. 8, Aug. 1993.

[7] M. CROVELLA and A. BESTAVROS, Self-similarity in world-wide web traffic: evidence and possible causes, *Proc. 1996 SIGMETRICS Conf. Measurement Comput. Syst.*, ACM, Philadelphia, PA, May 1996, pp. 160–169.

[8] C. CUNHA, A. BESTAVROS, and M. CROVELLA, Characteristics of WWW client-based traces, *Tech. Rep. BU-CS-95-010*, Comput. Sci. Dep., Boston Univ., Boston, MA, Nov. 1995.

[9] B. EVERITT, *Cluster Analysis.* Halsted, 2nd ed. 1980.

[10] D. FERRARI, G. SERAZZI, and A. ZEIGNER, *Measurement and Tuning of Computer Systems.* Upper Saddle River, NJ: Prentice Hall, 1983.

[11] R. JAIN, *The Art of Computer System Performance: Analysis, Techniques for Experimental Design, Measurement, Simulation, and Modeling.* New York: Wiley, 1991.

[12] W. LELAND, M. TAQQU, W. WILLINGER, and D. WILSON, On the self-similar nature of Ethernet traffic (extended version), *IEEE/ACM Trans. Commun. Techno.*, Feb. 1994.

[13] S. LING, R. BUNT, and D. EAGER, Characterizing client-server workload on an Ethernet, *Proc. CMG '91*, The Computer Measurement Group, Nashville, TN, 1991.

[14] D. A. MENASCÉ, V. A. F. ALMEIDA, and L. W. DOWDY, *Capacity Planning and Performance Modeling: From Mainframes to Client-Server Systems*. Upper Saddle River, NJ: Prentice Hall, 1994.

[15] E. SHRIVER, *Performance Modeling for Realistic Storage Devices*, Ph.D. dissertation, Dep. Comput. Sci., New York Univ., May 1997.

Chapter 7

USING STANDARD INDUSTRY BENCHMARKS

7.1 Introduction

It is common sense; everyone agrees that the best way to study the performance of a given system is to run the actual workload on it and measure the results. The downside to real workloads is the difficulty of measuring and porting the programs to distributed environments. In most cases, it is not cost-effective to set up configurations of client/server systems or Web servers to run real workloads and measure their performance. A widespread alternate approach is to use benchmark results to compare the performance of different systems. Benchmarking refers to running a set of representative programs on different computers and networks and measuring the results.

Benchmark results are used to evaluate the performance of a given system on a well-defined workload. Much of the popularity of standard benchmarks comes from the fact that they have performance objectives and workloads that are measurable and repeatable. Usually, computer system procurement studies and comparative analyses of products rely on benchmarks. They are also used as monitoring and diagnostic tools. Vendors, developers, and users run benchmarks to pinpoint performance problems of new systems. Benchmarks help developers accurately test new systems or assess the impact of modifications to a system.

Benchmark results can both inform and confuse users about the real capability of systems to execute their actual production workloads. The source of confusion lies on how one interprets benchmark results. Before using benchmark results, one must understand the workload, the system under study, the tests, the measurements, and the results. Otherwise, one will not be able to interpret the benchmark results properly. Therefore, the first step is to answer the following questions.

- What is a particular benchmark actually testing?

- How close does the benchmark resembles the user environment workload?

- What is the benchmark really measuring?

Once benchmark results are well understood, one can use them to increase one's knowledge about the performance of the system under study. For example, benchmark results can be used to estimate input parameters for performance models of Web-based systems and client/server environments. Or they can give an idea about the performance of a system when processing heavy workloads. However, it is important to notice that most benchmarks are good tools for comparing systems, rather than accurate tools for capacity planning for a given customer application environment. This chapter presents several different standard industry benchmarks and discusses them in light of the above questions. It also shows how to use benchmark results as a complementary source of information to various steps of the capacity planning methodology introduced in Chap. 5.

7.2   The Nature of Benchmarks

Time and rate are the basic measures of system performance. From the user's viewpoint, program or application execution time is the best indicator of system performance. Users do not want to know if the server is next to the desktop computer on the LAN or if it is located thousands of miles away from her/his location, connected through various networks. Users always want fast response time. From management's viewpoint, the performance of a system is defined by the rate at which it can perform work. For example, system managers are interested in questions such as: How many transactions can the system execute per minute or how many requests is the Web site able to service per second? Besides time and rate, both users and managers are always concerned with cost, reflected in questions such as: What is the system's operational cost? and What is the server purchase cost? As a consequence of all these different viewpoints, the basic problem still remains: What is a good standard measure of system performance?

Computer makers usually refer to the speed of a processor by its cycle time, which can be expressed by its length (e.g., 4 nanosec) or by its rate (e.g., 250 MHz). However, one common misperception is the use of the clock speed (i.e., in megahertz or nanoseconds) to compare processor performance. The overall performance of a processor is directly affected by other architectural traits, such as caching, pipelining, and functional units [4]. In the past, a popular way of rating processor performance was MIPS (millions of instructions per second). Although MIPS had been largely employed as a basis for comparisons of processors, it is important to remind the reader about the problems with its use. MIPS is dependent on the instruction set, which makes it difficult to compare computers with different repertoires of instructions. For instance, using MIPS to compare the performance of a Reduced Instruction Set Computer (RISC) and a Complex Instruction Set Computer (CISC) has little significance. As MIPS is not defined in a domain of any specific application, its use may be misleading. Different programs running on the same computer may reach different levels of MIPS.

System performance is complex; it is the result of the interplay of many hardware and software components. Compounding the problem is the fact that every C/S system is unique in its configuration, applications, and operating systems. Furthermore, C/S systems exhibit a large variation in performance when executing different applications. No single number can represent the performance of a client/server system on all applications. In a quest to find a good performance measure, standard programs, known as *benchmarks*, have been used to evaluate the performance of systems. Benchmarking refers to running a set of standard programs on a system to compare its performance with that of others. The next section describes a hierarchy of benchmark tests used to evaluate performance of computer systems.

7.2.1   Benchmark Hierarchy

A sequence of complex tests has been designed to investigate the performance of computer systems. The plethora of existing benchmark programs can be thought of as a hierarchy, where different levels are characterized by the complexity of their programs as well as by their ability to predict actual performance. At the innermost level of the hierarchy, as shown in Fig. 7.1, are synthetic benchmarks that perform only "basic operations," such as addition and multiplication. Dhrystone and Whetstone are examples of this type of programs [1]. The former is a synthetic benchmark aimed at measuring the speed of a system on the execution of fixed point computations. Whetstone is a small program for measuring floating point calculations. These programs do not compute any real task and their utility to the comprehension of performance of practical systems is very limited. At the second level of the benchmark hierarchy are the so-called "toy benchmarks." They are very small programs that implement some classical puzzles, such as Sieve of Eratosthenes and Towers of Hanoi [4]. This type of benchmark does not help to predict the performance of real workloads and has no use in the analysis of practical problems. Kernels, the third level, are portions extracted from the code of

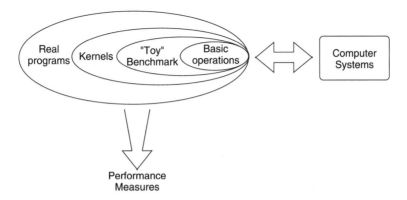

Figure 7.1. Benchmark hierarchy.

real programs. These pieces of code represent the essence of the computation, i.e., where most of the time is spent. Livermore Loops and Linpack are good examples of program kernels [1]. In general, this type of benchmark concentrates on the system's capability to execute some numeric computation and therefore measures only the CPU performance. Because they are not real programs, they provide little information about the performance perceived by end users. At the outermost level of the hierarchy is the workload composed of full-scale real programs used to solve real problems. These programs make up benchmark suites, such as SPEC, TPC, and AIM. As an example, there are some domain-oriented benchmarks that use programs such as components of the GNU C compiler, UNIX utilities for compressing and decompressing large files, and debit and credit bank transactions. They offer the most accurate picture of the system performance perceived by end users.

7.2.2   Avoiding Pitfalls

As in any performance study, the first step to safely interpret the benchmark results is to understand the environment (see Chap. 5). In other words, you need to know where and how the benchmark tests were carried out. Basically, you need information such as processor specification (e.g., model, cache, and number of processors), memory, I/O subsystem (e.g., disks, models, speed), network (e.g., LAN, WAN, and operational conditions), and software (e.g., operating system, compilers, transaction processing monitor, and database management system). Once you understand the benchmark environment, then you should consider several other factors before making use of the benchmark numbers. To avoid pitfalls, you should ask yourself some key questions to find out how relevant the benchmark results are to your particular system or application. Examples of these key questions are:

- Did the system under test have a configuration similar to my system? Examine the configuration description and compare the hardware, the network environment (topology, routers, protocols, and servers), the software, the operating system parameters, and the workload. Did the testing environment look like my system environment? Is the number of processors in your system the same as that described in the benchmark environment? What version of the OS was used in the tests? What were the memory and cache sizes of the server? These are typical questions you should answer before drawing conclusions about the benchmark results.

- How representative of my workload are the benchmark tests? For example, if your system is dedicated to order processing, then a transaction processing benchmark can give you some insight about the performance of your application. However, if you are planning a new graphical application, transaction processing benchmark results are useless, because the two workloads are very dissimilar.

As systems evolve, so must the benchmarks that are used to compare them. All standard benchmarks release new versions periodically. Therefore, when examining benchmark results, pay attention to the version used and look for new features included in the latest releases.

7.2.3 Common Benchmarks

Many benchmark tests are used to evaluate a wide variety of systems, subsystems, and components under different types of workloads and applications. Benchmarks are available from many sources, such as industry consortia, commercial sources, and universities. The most often cited are SPEC, TPC, AIM, Neal Nelson Business Benchmark (NNBB), Whetstone, Dhrystone, Linpack, and Perfect Club [1], [2]. Users groups and Web searches are good sources of updated information about several types of benchmarks. However, to be useful, a benchmark should have the following attributes [3]:

- relevant: it must provide meaningful performance measures within a specific problem domain

- understandable: the benchmark results should be simple and easy to understand

- scaleable: the benchmark tests must be applicable to a wide range of systems, in terms of cost, performance, and configuration

- acceptable: the benchmarks should present unbiased results that are recognized by users and vendors

Two consortia offer benchmarks that are common yardsticks for comparing different computer systems. The System Performance Evaluation Cooperative (SPEC) [7] is an organization of computer industry vendors that develops standardized performance tests, i.e., benchmarks, and publishes reviewed results. SPEC publishes performance results of CPU benchmarks, file server benchmarks, Web server benchmarks, and graphics benchmarks [2]. The Transaction Processing Performance Council (TPC) [9] is a nonprofit organization that defines transaction processing and database benchmarks. TPC-C and TPC-D are commonly used industry benchmarks that measure throughput and price/performance of OLTP environments and decision support systems [1], [3]. Benchmarks can be grouped into two categories: component-level and system-level. Next section discusses standard component-level benchmark tests and results.

7.3 Component-Level Benchmarks

In component-level benchmarks, a set of tests and workloads are specified to measure component or subsystem performance, such as CPU speed, disk I/O service time, or file server throughput. In this section we discuss a benchmark that measures CPU performance.

7.3.1 CPU

SPEC CPU benchmark is designed to provide measures of performance for comparing compute-intensive workloads on different computer systems. SPECxx, where xx could be 92, 95, and 98, specifies the generation of the CPU benchmark. The current generation of SPEC CPU contains two suites of benchmarks: CINT and CFP. The former is designed for measuring and comparing compute-intensive integer performance. The latter focuses on floating-point performance. Because these benchmarks are compute-intensive, they concentrate on the performance of the computer's processor, the memory architecture, and the compiler. However, they do not stress other key components, such as I/O, networking, or graphics.

Workload

The SPEC benchmark suite consists of programs selected from various sources, primarily academic and scientific. Some are reasonably full implementations and other programs are adaptations to fulfill the benchmark goal of measuring CPU. The CFP suite for measuring floating-point compute performance contains ten applications written in FORTRAN. The benchmark suite (CINT) that measures integer compute performance contains eight applications, as displayed in Table 7.1. In addition to the short description of the benchmarks, Table 7.1 also shows the SPEC reference times. SPEC CPU benchmark used the SPARCstation 10/40 (40MHz SuperSPARC) as a reference machine to normalize the performance metrics. Each benchmark program is run and measured on this machine to establish a reference time for that benchmark. These times are used to calculate the SPEC results described in the next section.

Results

The SPEC CPU benchmark results are organized along three dimensions of the compute-intensive performance domain: integer versus floating point, speed versus

Table 7.1. SPEC CINT Benchmarks

Number	Benchmark	Reference Time (sec)	Application Area
1	099.go	4,600	Artificial intelligence
2	124.m88ksim	1,900	Chip simulator
3	126.gcc	1,700	Programming
4	129.compress	1,800	Text file compression
5	130.li	1,900	Lisp language interpreter
6	132.ijpeg	2,400	Image compression
7	134.perl	1,900	Shell interpreter
8	147.vortex	2,700	Object-oriented database

throughput and peak versus baseline. The baseline results are aggregate performance statistics with minimal compiler optimizations. Peak numbers are obtained with heavy optimizations. For the purpose of measuring speed, each benchmark test, denoted by nnn, has its own ratio, defined as:

$$\text{SPECratio for } nnn\text{.benchmark} = \frac{nnn\text{.benchmark reference time}}{nnn\text{.benchmark run time}}.$$

SPECint is the geometric mean of eight normalized ratios, one for each benchmark program in Table 7.1. This metric refers to the peak results, since the benchmarks make use of many optimization tricks. SPECint_base is the geometric mean of eight normalized ratios when compiled with conservative optimization for each benchmark. For each benchmark of the CINT suite, a throughput measure is calculated. SPECrate measures the throughput as a function of the number of copies run, the time needed to complete all the copies and a reference factor. SPECint_rate is the geometric mean of eight normalized throughput ratios. SPECint_rate_base is the geometric mean of eight normalized throughput ratios when compiled with conservative optimization for each benchmark. Similar measures are calculated for the CFP suite using the individual results obtained for each of the ten programs that make up the benchmark. Table 7.2 shows the SPEC CPU performance results for system X. Benchmark results can be used to provide information to performance models to answer some typical "what if" questions, as shown in Ex. 7.1.

Example 7.1: Consider that a vendor is announcing an advanced Web server with a faster processor and a larger on-chip cache memory. The vendor says that the new technology improves performance by 60%. Before deciding on the upgrade, you want an answer to the classic question: "What if we use the new Web server?" Although the vendor does not provide specific information about the performance of Web services, he/she points to the SPECint results. In this case, SPECint is relevant because the technology upgrade reflects directly on the CPU speed. To

Table 7.2. SPEC CPU Benchmark Results for System X

Measure	Result
SPECint	15.0
SPECint_base	12.6
SPECint_rate	135.0
SPECint_rate_base	118.0
SPECfp	21.4
SPECfp_base	17.9
SPECfp_rate	180.0
SPECfp_rate_base	168.0

estimate the new server impact on the response time of HTTP requests, we can use the models described in Chap. 10. However, we need to feed the model with input data that reflect the speed of the new server. Note that the new technology basically improves the CPU performance. The SPECint for the old and new servers are 12.1 and 16.3, respectively. Therefore, we should change the CPU service demands to reflect the server upgrade. Let us denote by α the ratio between the SPECint of the two servers:

$$\alpha = \frac{\text{SPECint}^{\text{new}}}{\text{SPECint}^{\text{old}}} = \frac{16.3}{12.1} = 1.35.$$

The new CPU service demands, denoted by $D_{\text{cpu}}^{\text{new}}$, is

$$D_{\text{cpu}}^{\text{new}} = \frac{D_{\text{cpu}}^{\text{old}}}{\alpha} = \frac{D_{\text{cpu}}^{\text{old}}}{1.34}. \tag{7.3.1}$$

What Eq. (7.3.1) says is that the CPU service time of the HTTP requests will be smaller in the new processor. In other words, the CPU time dedicated to service the requests should be divided by $\alpha = 1.35$ to reflect the faster processor. Although CPU is a key component of a system, the overall system performance depends on many factors, such as I/O and networking. Performance models, such as those described in Chaps. 9 and 10, are able to calculate the effect of upgrading the CPU on the overall performance of the system using the new CPU demands.   ■

7.3.2   File Server

File server performance can be measured by synthetic benchmarks that model a workload based on an input mix of file server operations. The SPEC's System File Server (SFS) is a UNIX networking benchmark suite that measures the request response time and throughput of a server for several load levels [2]. The SFS benchmark suite is based on the LADDIS program.

LADDIS

The LADDIS benchmark measures Network File System (NFS) server performance by generating a synthetic load of NFS operations and then measuring the request response time of the server for different load levels [11]. LADDIS executes as a collection of distributed cooperating processes in a UNIX environment. These processes generate the load to the file server. A manager process controls the several steps of the benchmark and collects performance results from each LADDIS generator process to consolidate and report the final results. A series of LADDIS executions is run at increasing NFS request load levels. Each run produces an average response time, which is combined with the corresponding throughput level to form the main performance result provided by the LADDIS benchmark, as shown in Table 7.3.

Workload

LADDIS does not model any specific user application workload. When executed with the default parameter setting, LADDIS generates a workload that resembles the one generated by an intensive software development environment. The standard workload consists of a mix of operations, selected from 17 NSF operations, with five of them (i.e., read, write, lookup, getattr, readlink) making up more than 90% of the mix used in the benchmark. LADDIS parameters can be modified and adjusted to generate a workload that represents a specific user environment. The load generated by the LADDIS benchmark is viewed by the server as a steady stream of operations. This feature has been pointed out by critics as unrealistic because real file server workloads are bursty. Chapters 4 and 10 present discussions about burstiness and its influence on system performance.

Results

LADDIS reports a single figure-of-merit performance value, that is the throughput (i.e., NFS ops/sec) at 50 msec average response time. The benchmark program measures the response time of the NFS server at the load generator processes. The 50 msec value is an arbitrary reference for the maximum average response time. From Table 7.3, we note that the LADDIS result reported is 4,840 SPECnfs.

Example 7.2: A file server is planned to support a network environment with 50 telemarketing representatives. On average, each active representative issues a transaction once every 60 sec. The system should be able to process at least 50 transactions per second. Every transaction accesses the file server 30 times. In order to have fast transaction response time, the system designers have specified that each request to the file server should not take longer than 25 msec. Management wants to size the file server system. We have learned in this section that LADDIS benchmark results includes an average NFS response time versus throughput curve for various file servers. Before using the LADDIS results, the capacity-planning analyst realizes that the LADDIS workload could be used as an approximation for the application workload. Therefore, the first step is to determine the minimum throughput required from the file server. The Forced Flow Law, discussed in

Table 7.3. NFS Throughput and Response Time Results

Throughput (NFS ops/sec)	Average Response Time (msec)
400	11.5
900	15.4
1,400	18.3
1,900	22.0
...	...
4,400	41.6
4,840	50.0

Chap. 3, establishes a relationship between component and system throughput. It
states that

$$X_{\text{fs}} = V_{\text{fs}} \times X_o \qquad (7.3.2)$$

where X_{fs} is the file server throughput, X_o denotes the total system throughput and
V_{fs} is the average number of visits per transaction to the file server, also called visit
ratio. Considering that the minimum system throughput is 50 transactions/sec and
each transaction accesses the file server 30 times, we have that the minimum file
server throughput, measured in operations per second is

$$X_{\text{fs}} > 30 \times 50 = 1,500 \text{ ops/sec}.$$

By examining the LADDIS results, management found out that file server XXX is
able to handle 1,500 ops/sec with an average response time equal to 10 msec. Also,
file server ZZZ executes 1,700 ops/sec with 15 msec of average response time. Once
both file servers meet the system performance specifications, other factors such as
cost, reliability, and vendor reputation should be used in selecting the server. ∎

7.4   System-Level Benchmarks

System benchmarks measure the entire system. They measure the processor, the
I/O subsystem, the network, the database, the compilers, and the operating system.

7.4.1   Transaction Processing Systems

TPC benchmarks measure the processor, I/O subsystem, network, operating system, and database management system. They assess the performance of applications such as debit/credit transactions, wholesale parts supplier, and ad hoc business
questions (e.g., sales trends and financial analysis). TPC runs four benchmarks:
A, B, C, and D. TPC-A and TPC-B are a standardization of the Debit/Credit
benchmark. They are based on a single type of transaction that performs operations similar to a bank account update. Whereas the TPC-B benchmark focuses
on the performance of the database components of a transaction processing environment, the TPC-A benchmark also measures the network performance of OLTP
environments. The main metric reported by TPC-A and B is system throughput, measured in transactions per second (tps), under the restriction that 90% of
transactions are responded in less than 2 sec. The purpose of TPC-D is to evaluate
price/performance of a given system executing decision support applications. These
applications support the formulation of business questions solved through long and
complex queries against large databases. Decision support applications are different
from OLTP applications, which are update-intensive and consist of short transactions. TPC-D has three metrics: power, throughput, and price/performance.

TPC-C

TCP-C is an industry standard benchmark for moderately complex online transaction processing systems. It models an application that manages orders for a

wholesale supplier. TPC-C provides a conceptual framework for order-entry applications with underlying components that are typical of other transaction processing systems.

Workload The workload consists of five transactions: *New-order, Payment, Delivery, Order-Status*, and *Stock-level*, that update, insert, and delete. The five transactions have different percentages of execution time in the benchmark. *New-order* and *Payment* represent 45% and 43%, respectively, of the total transactions in the mix. Each of the other three transactions account for 4% of the load. The TPC-C workload is database-intensive, with substantial I/O and cache load. It meets Atomicity, Consistency, Isolation, and Durability (ACID) requirements and includes full-screen presentation services.

Results TPC-C yields a performance measure known as tpmC (i.e., transactions per minute). In the TPC-C terminology, throughput is the maximum number of *New-order* transactions per minute that a system services while executing the four other transaction types. TPC-C is satisfied with 90% of the *New-order* transactions responding in less than 5 sec during the test. Other transactions have different response time requirements. This property assures the service level for the *New-order* transactions, which indicates repeatable response times. For example, a 9,000-tpmC system is able to service 9,000 *New-order* transactions per minute while satisfying the rest of the TPC-C mix workload. Table 7.4 shows some of the typical results provided by TPC-C. As we can observe from Table 7.4, a price/performance measure is provided by TPC-C. The pricing methodology covers all components and dimensions of a transaction processing system. Thus, the following factors are included in the total system cost: computer system, terminals, communication devices, software (e.g., database management system and transaction monitor), and a five-year maintenance cost. Suppose that the total cost of system X is $450,000 and the throughput is 4500 tpmC. Then, the price/performance ratio for system X

Table 7.4. TPC-C Results

Platform Results	
Company	X
System	xyz
Processors	4
Disk capacity	708.33 GB
RAM	4 GB
DBMS	Microsoft SQL
Operating System	Windows NT
Total system cost	$460,220
TPC-C throughput (tpmC)	10,950.30
Price/performance	$42.03

equals \$100 per tpmC.

Example 7.3: The manager of information technology of an insurance company wants to replace its database management software. The manager is considering a new software that is said to be 30% faster than the one in use. How can the manager assess the impact of the new software on the system's order-processing application?

The TPC-C benchmark can be used to evaluate the relative performance of two different software systems on the same hardware. By examining the TPC-C results we learned that the performance measures of the current and new software are 15,000 and 18,000 tpmC, respectively. The throughput ratio of the two software systems is

$$P_x = \frac{\text{throughput of the new software}}{\text{throughput of the current software}} = \frac{18,000}{15,000} = 1.2.$$

Using the client/server models of Chaps. 8 and 9, we can calculate the transaction response time, after adjusting the DB server throughputs by P_x. To represent the new software, the throughputs of the model are related by the relationship

$$X_{\text{server}}^{\text{new}} = P_x \times X_{\text{server}}^{\text{old}}.$$

Another way of looking at the TPC-C results is to compare the price/performance of the system with the two different DB softwares. Let us assume that the numbers are \$40.12 and \$49.15 for the current and new DB software. The price/performance ratio for the new software is 22.5% higher than the current software. The question is whether the throughput and response time improvements are worth the cost for the new system and whether users want to pay more for the additional speed. ■

7.4.2   Web Servers

This section describes the two most popular Web server benchmarks: Webstone and SPECweb [10]. Both programs simulate Web browsers. They generate requests to a server, according to some specified workload characteristics, receive the responses returned by the server and collect the measurements. It is important to note that Web server benchmarks are usually carried out in small isolated LANs, with almost no transmission errors. On the contrary, Web services, offered in the "real world", are accessed through the Internet or large intranets, which involve WAN connections, gateways, routers, bridges, and hubs that make the network environment noisy and error-prone. Thus, the analysis of Web benchmark results should take this observation into account.

Webstone

Webstone is a configurable client/server benchmark for HTTP servers that uses workload characterization parameters and client processes to generate HTTP traffic to stress a server in different ways [8]. It was designed to measure maximum server throughput and average response time for connecting to the server. It makes a number of GET requests for specific documents on the Web server under study and collects performance data. The first version of the benchmark did not include CGI loads or the effects of encryption or authentication in the tests.

Webstone is a distributed, multiprocess benchmark, composed of master and client processes. The master process, local or remote, spawns a predefined number of client processes that start generating HTTP requests to the server. After all client processes finish running, the master process gathers the performance data collected by the client processes and generates a performance summary report. The user can either specify the duration of the test or the total number of iterations.

Workload There are four different synthetic page mixes that attempt to model real workloads. The characteristics of each page mix, i.e., file sizes and access frequencies, were derived from the access patterns to pages available in some popular Web sites. Webstone allows one to model user environment workloads, via synthetic loads generated according to some input parameters, specified by the user. The specification parameters are as follows.

- Number of clients that request pages. Clients request pages as fast as the server can send them back. User think times cannot be represented in the Webstone workload.

- Type of page, defined by file size and access frequency. Each page in the mix has a weigh that indicates its probability of being accessed.

- The number of pages available on the server under test.

- The number of client machines, where the client processes execute on.

Results The main results produced by Webstone are throughput and latency. The former, measured in bytes per second, represents the total number of bytes received from the server divided by the test duration. The latter measures the time it takes to complete a request from the client's viewpoint. Latency consists of three components: connection, request response time, and network latency due to WAN connections, routers, and modems. The first component reflects the time taken to establish a connection, while request response time reflects the time it takes to complete the data transfer once the connection has been established. Table 7.5 displays a summary of Webstone results for a test run of 10 min [8]. The Webstone number corresponds to the throughput measured in pages per minute. The total amount of data moved is the product of the total number of pages retrieved and the page sizes. The page size is the sum of all files associated with the page plus the HTTP overhead in bytes. The connection time refers to the time needed to establish a connection. The other results are self-explanatory.

Webstone also presents a metric called Little's Load Factor (LLF), derived from Little's Law [6]. It indicates the degree of concurrency on the request execution,

Table 7.5. Typical Webstone Results

Metric	Value
Webstone number (pages/min)	456
Total number of clients	24
Total number of pages retrieved from server	4,567
Total number of errors	0
Total number of connections to the server	12,099
Average time per connect (sec)	0.0039
Maximum time per connect (sec)	0.0370
Total number of bytes moved per client	3,076,611,677
Average throughput (bytes/sec)	215,181
Average response time (sec)	1.181
Maximum response time (sec)	18.488

that is, the average number of connections open at the Web server at any particular instant during the test. It is also an indication of how much time is spent by the server on request processing, rather than on overhead and errors. Ideally, LLF should be equal to the number of clients. A lower value indicates that the server is overloaded, and some requests are not being serviced before they time out. From Chap. 3, we know that the total number of customers in a box is equal to the throughput of the box multiplied by the average time each customer spends in the box. Thinking of the Web server as a box, we have that

$$\text{Average number of connections} = \text{Connection rate} \times \text{Average residence time.}$$
$$(7.4.1)$$

The average residence time is the average response time plus the connection time. Plugging numbers from Table 7.5 into Eq. (7.4.1), we have that

$$\text{Average number of connections} = 12,099/(10 \times 60) \times (1.181 + 0.0039) = 23.89.$$

In this example, the average number of connections (23.89) is very close to the number of clients (24).

Example 7.4: Assume that the results displayed in Table 7.5 correspond to a Webstone run with parameters configured to represent the workload forecast for the Web site of a hotel company. The capacity planner wants to size the bandwidth of the link that connects the site to the Internet Service Provider. The bandwidth of the link should support incoming and outgoing traffic. Let us consider that the average size of an HTTP request is 100 bytes. During the 10-min test, the server received 4,567 page requests. Thus, the total amount of incoming bytes in the period was $(4,567 \times 100 \times 8)/(10 \times 60) = 6,089.3$ bps. The outgoing traffic is given by the server throughput, $215,181 \times 0 - 1,721,448$ bps. Thus, the minimum required bandwidth is given by

$$\text{LinkBandwidth} > 6,089.3 + 1,721,448 = 1.72 \text{ Mbps}.$$

Therefore, in order to support the estimated demand for pages, the company's Web site should be connected to the Internet through two T1 links (2×1.544 Mbps). Because Webstone allows one to tailor the workload to represent a specific user environment, Webstone can be used as a monitoring tool. In this example, we used the performance measurements collected by Webstone during the test to size the network bandwidth.   ■

SPECweb

SPECweb is a standardized benchmark developed by SPEC to measure a system's ability to act as a Web server for static pages. It can be used to evaluate the performance of Web-server software running on UNIX or Windows NT platforms. The architecture of SPECweb consists of one or more client systems generating a workload of HTTP GET requests to a server under test. The architecture is based on the LADDIS process structure for generating workload. The "prime" client process coordinates the test execution of the client processes on the client machines. It starts child processes (or threads in the NT version) that actually generate the workload. The initial release of SPECweb concentrates on server performance for static pages. SPECweb measures the server capacity to handle HTTP GET requests. Although requests for static pages represent a large part of workloads of real Web servers, other services are important as well. For example, CGI plays an important role in e-commerce Web sites. Also, features of persistent connections available in the HTTP protocol, such as Keep-Alive [10], are not supported by the initial version of SPECweb. Unlike Webstone, the SPECweb benchmark does not allow users to change the workload.

Workload   The workload characteristics for SPECweb were drawn from the logs of several popular Web servers. Thus, SPECweb tries to mimic the accesses to the documents of a server of a typical Web service provider, which supports home pages for various companies and organizations. The SPECweb workload mixes four classes of files, according to their file sizes and access percentages, as displayed in Table 7.6. It is worth noting that the relationship established for file sizes and frequency in this workload follows the heavy-tailed distribution concepts discussed in Chap. 4. The total size of the file set of SPECweb scales with the expected throughput. The rationale for that stems from the fact that expectations for a high-end server, in terms of the variety and size of the documents available, are much greater than for a smaller server. The workload parameters are fixed by the benchmark specification and cannot be changed without invalidating the results.

Results   The server maximum throughput is the main result for SPECweb. To calculate the peak throughput, the load generator processes increase the number of requests to the server. To be a valid result, the maximum throughput must be

Table 7.6. File Sizes Per Class and Access Frequency for SPECweb

Class	File sizes (KB)	Access percentage
0	0 − 1	35
1	1 − 10	50
2	10 − 100	14
3	100 − 1000	1

within 5% of the corresponding load. SPECweb provides a full performance curve, which plots average request response time as a function of the throughput. The reported response time for SPECweb is for the server only; it does not include any delay in getting across the network. Figure 7.2 shows an example of the results of a benchmark run, comprised of several load levels. In this example, the SPECweb result is 1,400 ops/sec, which corresponds to the peak throughput measured during the run. SPECweb also generates detailed statistics about the test run, such as offered load, throughput per class, error percentage, mean response time, and standard deviation.

Example 7.5: A company is planning to roll out intranet applications to its employees, located all over the country. Some users will access the site through LANs,

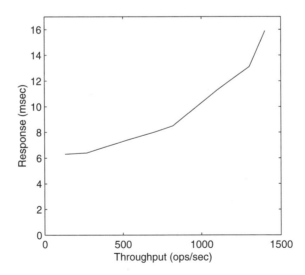

Figure 7.2. Performance curve for Web server X.

and others will go through the Internet. The system administrator considers that the SPECweb workload could be used as an approximation for the initial workload of the company Website. The system analyst estimates an average throughput of 480 requests/sec. By examining the SPECweb benchmark results, the analyst found two systems that meet the throughput requirements, as shown in Table 7.7. The SPECweb for systems A and B are 1,330 and 1,440 ops/sec, respectively. At first sight, SPECweb numbers indicate that system B has a better performance.

Before deciding which system should be selected, the IT managers want to take a look at other capacity planning issues. Due to performance problems in previous experiences with client/server computing, IT management now plans to use a service-level agreement (SLA, described in Chap. 5). Because of the distributed nature of the Web, measuring performance is inherently difficult. Thus, users and IT management agreed on defining an upper limit for Web server response time. In other words, 95% of the requests must have a server response time less than 20 msec. Furthermore, IT management wants to have enough capacity to accommodate peaks, which are 200% more than the average Web request rate. Thus, the Web server should be able to handle 1,440 (= 480 × 3) ops/sec at peak times. The detailed statistics of Table 7.7 show that throughput requirements are satisfied, but SLAs are not. The server response time for system B at 1,440 ops/sec is 33.8 msec, much greater than the 20 msec threshold agreed on between IT and users. This example shows that benchmark analysis should not be restricted to a single number. Different performance and cost aspects must be examined before selecting a given system. ∎

Table 7.7. SPECweb Benchmark Results

System A		System B	
SPECweb = 1,330		SPECweb = 1,440	
Thput (ops/sec)	Response (msec)	Thput (ops/sec)	Response (msec)
130	6.2	152	4.5
270	6.9	300	4.7
430	7.4	445	5.4
560	7.8	600	5.7
700	8.5	770	6.0
850	9.3	920	6.8
980	10.3	1,070	7.4
1,150	11.8	1,200	8.3
1,280	14.0	1,380	10.0
1,330	17.2	1,440	33.8

7.5 Conclusions

This chapter presented several industry standard benchmarks. They provide a standard yardstick for comparing performance across different systems. As pointed out in the introduction, benchmark results can both inform and confuse users about the real capacity of systems to execute their actual production workloads. It depends on how one interprets the results. Before using benchmark results, one must understand the workload, the system under study, the tests, the measurements, and the results. Standard benchmarks can be used in a variety of ways provided one understands them. For instance, benchmark results can be used for comparing different hardware systems running the same software or different software products on one system. They can also be used to compare different models of systems in a compatible family. Standard benchmark, though, is not an adequate tool for capacity planning for a system with a customized workload. However, benchmark results can be used in conjunction with performance models for capacity planning purposes. As we saw in the examples of this chapter, benchmark results can provide useful input information for performance models. Next chapters show how to construct performance model of Web, intranets, and client/server systems.

BIBLIOGRAPHY

[1] K. Dowd, *High Performance Computing.* O'Reilly & Associates, 1993.

[2] R. Grace, *The Benchmark Book.* Upper Saddle River, NJ: Prentice Hall, 1996.

[3] J. Gray, *The Benchmark Handbook for Database and Transaction Processing Systems.* 2nd ed., San Mateo, CA: Morgan Kaufmann, 1993.

[4] J. Hennessy and D. Patterson, *Computer Architecture: A Quantitative Approach.* San Francisco, CA: Morgan Kaufmann, 1996.

[5] J. Levitt, Measuring web-server capacity, *Inform. Week*, Jan. 13, 1997.

[6] D. A. Menascé, V. A. F. Almeida, and L. W. Dowdy, *Capacity Planning and Performance Modeling: From Mainframes to Client-Server Systems.* Upper Saddle River, NJ: Prentice Hall, 1994.

[7] System Performance Evaluation Cooperative, http://www.spec.org

[8] G. Trent and M. Sake, WebSTONE: the first generation in HTTP benchmarking, *MTS Silicon Graphics*, Feb. 1995.

[9] Transaction Processing Performance Council, http://www.tpc.org

[10] N. Yeager and R. McCrath, *Web Server Technology.* San Francisco, CA: Morgan Kaufmann, 1996.

[11] M. Wittle and B. Keith, LADDIS: the next generation in NFS file server benchmarking, *USENIX Assoc. Conf. Proc.*, Cincinatti, OH, Summer 1993, pp. 111–128.

Chapter 8

SYSTEM-LEVEL
PERFORMANCE MODELS

8.1 Introduction

As pointed out in Chap. 5, a performance model can be developed at different levels of detail. In this chapter, we look at performance models from a system-level point of view as opposed to a component-level point of view. A *system-level* performance model views the system being modeled as a "black box." In this case, the internal details of the box are not modeled explicitly; only the throughput function of the box is considered. The throughput function, $X_0(k)$, gives the average throughput of the box as a function of the number, k, of requests present in the box. Figure 8.1a depicts a black box view of a database server. A system-level performance model is represented by a state transition diagram (STD) that illustrates the states that a system can be found in as well as how it transitions from state to state. A detailed discussion of STDs and their use in system-level performance modeling is given in this chapter.

A *component-level* model takes into account the different resources of the system and the way they are used by different requests. Processors, disks, and networks are explicitly considered by the model. Figure 8.1b shows a component-level view of the same database server shown in Fig. 8.1a. Component models use queuing networks and are the topic of Chap. 9.

This chapter starts by introducing very simple models so that the reader can understand the approach. Complexity is progressively introduced and the solution to each model is presented using first principles and intuitive concepts. After a few models are presented, the approach is generalized. A few more examples are discussed under the more general framework.

8.2 Simple Server Model I—Infinite Population/Infinite Queue

Consider a database server accessible to a very large population. One could imagine that this is the database server of a search engine accessible to users through the WWW or the database server that supports searches for a Web-accessible bookstore.

174

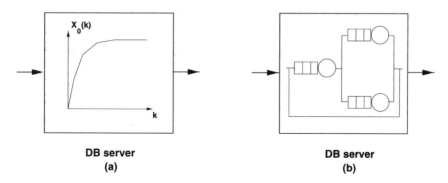

DB server
(a)

DB server
(b)

Figure 8.1. (a) System-level view. (b) Component-level view.

The number of people in the user population is unknown and very large. By "very large" we mean that the arrival rate of requests for database service is not influenced by the number of requests that arrived already and are being processed. From now on, we will refer to this as the *infinite population* case. The arrival process to the DB server is then characterized by requests arriving at an average arrival rate of λ requests/sec. We also assume that all requests are statistically indistinguishable. This implies that the requests present in the DB server are not important, only the number of requests that are present counts. This is the single class or *homogeneous workload* assumption [3].

Since this is our first and simplest example, we assume that the average throughput function is very simple. It is a constant, that is, it does not depend on the number of requests in the system. What could be simpler? So, the average throughput of the DB server is given by $X_0(k) = \mu$ requests/sec. It should be noted that the server's service rate is not just a function of its physical characteristics (e.g., processor and disk speeds and number of processors), but also of the demands of the workload (e.g., service demands of a DB request at the processors and disks).

We also assume, in this example, that the DB server does not refuse any requests. All arriving requests are queued for service. This assumption is known as *infinite queue*. We will see in the next subsections that we can as easily model finite queue situations to illustrate the case where a server can only handle a maximum number of requests—the *finite queue* case.

The analyses presented in this section and in all chapters of this book assume that the systems being analyzed are in *operational equilibrium* [1]. This means that the number of requests present in the system at the start of an observation interval is equal to the number of requests present at the end of the interval. The number of requests in the system may vary between the start and end of the interval. For reasonably large intervals, the number of departures tends to approach the number of arrivals and therefore the operational equilibrium assumption holds with negligible error.

Requests arrive at the DB server at a rate of λ requests/sec, queue for service, get served at a rate of μ request/sec, and depart. We want to compute the fraction of time, p_k, that there are k $(k = 0, 1, \cdots)$ requests in the DB server, the average number of requests present, the average response time of a request at the database server, and the server's utilization and throughput.

We start by deciding how to describe the *state* of the database server. Given the assumptions presented thus far, the state description for our DB server is a *single* parameter, the number of requests present in the server—waiting or receiving service. It turns out that by choosing such a simple state description we are implicitly making the additional assumption that old story is irrelevant. This means that it does not matter how the system arrived at a certain state k nor does it matter for how long the system has been in this state. The only thing that matters is that the system is at state k. This is also known as the *memoryless* or *Markovian* assumption.

The possible states are then given by the integers $0, 1, 2, \cdots, k, \cdots$. Due to the infinite population and infinite queue length assumptions used in this example, we have an infinite, but enumerable, number of states. We then draw a state transition diagram (STD), where each state is represented by a circle (see Fig. 8.2). Transitions between states correspond to physical events in the system and are represented by arrows between states. For example, an arrival of a new request when the server has k requests will take the server to state $k + 1$. This type of transition happens upon request arrivals, and therefore the rate at which these transitions occur is λ transitions/sec, the arrival rate. Similarly, if the database server has k requests and one of them completes, the new state is $k - 1$. These transitions occur at rate μ, the request completion rate.

We start by obtaining the values of p_k $(k = 0, 1, \cdots)$. Since we are assuming operational equilibrium, the flow of transitions going into a state k has to be equal to the flow of transitions going out of that state. For a more formal discussion on this, see [1]. This is called *flow equilibrium equation* or *flow-in = flow-out* principle and can in fact be applied to any set of states. Consider Fig. 8.3 that shows a

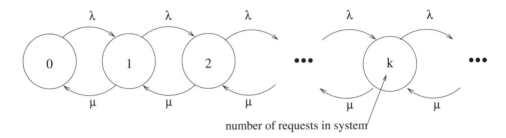

Figure 8.2. State transition diagram—infinite population/infinite queue.

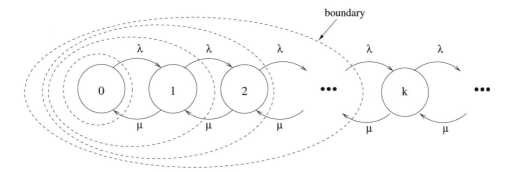

Figure 8.3. State transition diagram with boundaries.

sequence of boundaries (dashed lines) around states. Each boundary contains one more state than the previous. The first boundary contains state 0 only. The next includes states 0 and 1. The next boundary includes states 0, 1, and 2, and so on. The flow-in = flow-out principle applies to any of these boundaries.

The flow out of a boundary is computed by considering all transitions that go from a state within the boundary to a state outside the boundary. The flow into a boundary includes all transitions that come from a state outside the boundary to a state inside the boundary. The following is the set of flow-in = flow-out equations for Fig. 8.3:

$$\text{flow} - \text{in} \; = \; \text{flow} - \text{out}$$
$$\mu \, p_1 \; = \; \lambda \, p_0 \tag{8.2.1}$$
$$\mu \, p_2 \; = \; \lambda \, p_1 \tag{8.2.2}$$

$$\cdot$$
$$\cdot$$
$$\cdot$$

$$\mu \, p_k \; = \; \lambda \, p_{k-1} \tag{8.2.3}$$

$$\cdot$$
$$\cdot$$
$$\cdot$$

Note that if we combine Eqs. (8.2.1) through (8.2.3), we get

$$p_k = \frac{\lambda}{\mu} \, p_{k-1} = \frac{\lambda}{\mu} \left(\frac{\lambda}{\mu} \, p_{k-2} \right) = \cdots = p_0 \, \left(\frac{\lambda}{\mu} \right)^k , \quad k = 1, 2, \cdots \tag{8.2.4}$$

We now have p_k as a function of p_0 for all values of $k = 1, 2, \cdots$. We just need to find p_0. Our database server has to be in one of the possible states at any time. So, the sum of the fractions of time that the server is at any possible state, from 0 to ∞, equals one. Hence,

$$p_0 + p_1 + p_2 + \cdots + p_k + \cdots = \sum_{k=0}^{\infty} p_k = \sum_{k=0}^{\infty} p_0 \left(\frac{\lambda}{\mu}\right)^k = 1. \tag{8.2.5}$$

This leads to

$$p_0 = \left[\sum_{k=0}^{\infty} \left(\frac{\lambda}{\mu}\right)^k\right]^{-1} = 1 - \frac{\lambda}{\mu}. \tag{8.2.6}$$

Note that the infinite sum in Eq. (8.2.6) is the sum of a geometric series. This series only converges (i.e., has a finite sum) if $\lambda/\mu < 1$. This means that an equilibrium solution to the system can only be found if the average arrival rate of requests is smaller than the service rate. This makes a lot of sense!

Example 8.1: Requests arrive to the database server at a rate of 30 requests/sec. Each request takes 0.02 sec on the average to be processed. What is the fraction of time that k ($k = 0, 1, \cdots$) requests are found in the database server?

If the server can process μ requests in 1 sec, one request takes an average of $1/\mu$ seconds to complete. Then, the average service rate μ is the inverse of the average service time per request. So, $\mu = 1/0.02 = 50$ requests/sec. The average arrival rate is $\lambda = 30$ requests/sec. So, the fraction of time that the database server is idle, i.e., p_0, is $1 - (\lambda/\mu) = 1 - (30/50) = 1 - 0.6 = 40\%$. Then, the server is utilized $1 - p_0 = \lambda/\mu = 60\%$ of the time. The fraction of time that there are k requests at the server is given by

$$p_k = (1 - \lambda/\mu)(\lambda/\mu)^k = 0.4 \times 0.6^k \quad k = 0, 1, \cdots. \tag{8.2.7}$$

Figure 8.4 shows how p_k decays rapidly with k. This is a geometric distribution.∎

So, from what we saw in Ex. 8.1, the utilization U of the server is

$$U = 1 - p_0 = \lambda/\mu \tag{8.2.8}$$

This means that $p_k = (1 - U) U^k$ for $k = 0, 1, \cdots$. The state distribution depends only on the utilization and not on the individual values of the arrival and service rates!

Now that we know p_k, we can easily find the average number $\overline{N}$ of requests at the server by using the definition of average. Thus,

$$\overline{N} = \sum_{k=0}^{\infty} k \times p_k = \sum_{k=0}^{\infty} k \times (1 - U) U^k = (1 - U) \sum_{k=0}^{\infty} k \times U^k. \tag{8.2.9}$$

But, the summation $\sum_{k=0}^{\infty} k \times U^k = U/(1 - U)^2$ for $U < 1$. Making the proper substitutions we get

$$\overline{N} = U/(1 - U). \tag{8.2.10}$$

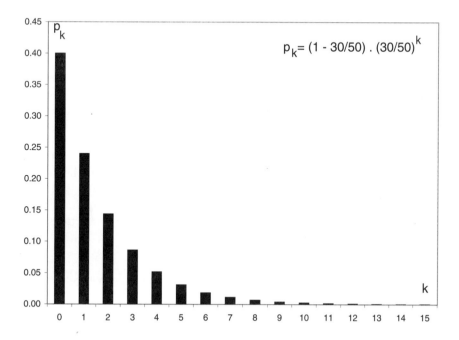

Figure 8.4. Fraction of time (p_k) vs. k for Ex. 8.1.

So, using the parameters of Ex. 8.1 in Eq. (8.2.10), we get that the average number of requests at the server is $0.6/(1 - 0.6) = 1.5$.

The throughput of the server is μ when there is at least one request being processed—this occurs during a fraction of time equal to U. The throughput equals zero when the server is idle. So, the average throughput, X, of the server is

$$X = U \times \mu + 0 \times (1 - U) = (\lambda/\mu)\,\mu = \lambda. \tag{8.2.11}$$

This is an expected result since no requests are being lost at the server. So, in equilibrium, the average arrival rate will be equal to the average departure rate.

We now compute the average response time, R, at the server by using Little's Law (see Chap. 3). The black box in this case is the server. So, given the throughput X, computed in Eq. (8.2.11), and the average number of requests $\overline{N}$, given by Eq. (8.2.10), we get that

$$R = \overline{N}/X = (U/\lambda)/(1 - U) = (1/\mu)/(1 - U) = S/(1 - U) \tag{8.2.12}$$

where $S = 1/\mu$ is the average service time of a request at the server. Let us understand what Eq. (8.2.12) is telling us. First, when the utilization of the server is very low, i.e., U is close to zero, the average response time is equal to the average service time. This is expected since no time is spent queuing due to the presence of other requests. When the utilization is very high, i.e., U is close to 1, the denominator of Eq. (8.2.12) goes to zero and R goes to infinity! In fact, R goes to infinity quickly as U gets close to 100%. Figure 8.5 shows the ratio of the average response time over the average service time as a function of the utilization.

Example 8.2: Consider again the parameters for Ex. 8.1. What is the average response time at the server? What is the average response time if the server is replaced with a server twice as fast? What would the response time be if the arrival rate doubles when the server becomes twice as fast?

Using Eq. (8.2.12), the average response time is $R = (1/50)/(1 - 0.6) = 0.05$ sec. If the server is twice as fast, $\mu = 100$ requests/second, and the server utilization becomes $U = 30/100 = 0.3$. So, $R = (1/100)/(1 - 0.3) = 0.014$ sec. So, by using a server that is twice as fast, the response time is reduced to about 28% of its original value. If both the arrival rate and the service rate are doubled, the utilization remains the same, $U = 0.6$. Using Eq. (8.2.12), we get that $R = (1 / 100)/(1 - 0.6) = 0.025$ sec. ∎

The expressions for the infinite population/infinite queue server are summarized

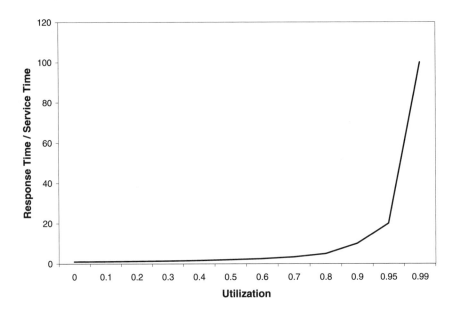

Figure 8.5. Response time/service time for infinite population-infinite queue server.

in Fig. 8.6. They are also implemented in the MS Excel workbook `SysMod.XLS` that accompanies this book.

Before we consider other situations, let us briefly summarize the steps we took in solving this problem. We will be following exactly the same steps in the rest of this chapter.

1. Determine a proper representation for the state of the system being modeled.

2. Determine the set of feasible states.

3. Determine the possible transitions between states by considering the possible events that can happen in the system being modeled. Examples of events are arrival of a request and completion of a request.

4. For each possible transition between states, determine the transition rate by looking at the event that caused the transition. For example, if the event that caused the transition from state k to state $k + 1$ is an arrival of a request, the transition rate is the rate at which requests arrive when the system is at state k.

5. Use the *flow equilibrium principle* (flow-in = flow-out) to write down equations that relate the values of p_k—the fraction of time the system is at state k. Remember that the sum of all p_ks has to be equal to one.

6. Solve for the p_ks and use them to compute performance metrics such as utilizations, throughput, average number of requests, and average response time.

8.3   Simple Server Model II—Infinite Population/Finite Queue

Consider now that the server considered in Sec. 8.2 cannot queue all incoming requests. Arriving requests that find W requests in the server—queued or being processed—are rejected. Some servers set limits on the number of requests that can be handled to guarantee a good performance for those requests in the system. Another reason for limiting the number of requests is that each request consumes system resources such as space in various system tables.

Let us now use the steps we outlined at the end of the previous section to find $p_k, U, \overline{N}$, and R for this case. Since the server refuses any additional requests when there are W requests in the system, the possible states are $0, 1, \cdots, W$. An arriving request that finds k $(k < W)$ requests in the system causes a transition to state $k + 1$ at rate λ. A completing request at state k $(k = 1, \cdots, W)$ causes a transition to state $k - 1$ with rate μ. Figure 8.7 shows the state transition diagram for this case.

If we draw the same type of boundaries as we did in Fig. 8.3, we get that

$$p_k = p_0 \ (\lambda/\mu)^k \quad k = 1, \cdots, W. \tag{8.3.1}$$

Fraction of time server has k requests:

$$p_k = (1 - \lambda/\mu)\,(\lambda/\mu)^k \quad k = 0, 1, \cdots$$

Server utilization:

$$U = \lambda/\mu$$

Average server throughput:

$$X = \lambda$$

Average number of requests in the server:

$$\overline{N} = U/(1 - U)$$

Average response time:

$$R = (1/\mu)/(1 - U) = S/(1 - U)$$

Figure 8.6. Infinite population/infinite queue server equations.

The difference now comes in the computation of p_0. We now have a finite number of states as opposed to an infinite number of states, as in the previous case. So,

$$p_0 + p_1 + \cdots + p_W = p_0 \sum_{k=0}^{W} (\lambda/\mu)^k = p_0 \left[\frac{1 - (\lambda/\mu)^{W+1}}{1 - \lambda/\mu} \right] = 1 \tag{8.3.2}$$

which implies that

$$p_0 = \frac{1 - \lambda/\mu}{1 - (\lambda/\mu)^{W+1}}. \tag{8.3.3}$$

Example 8.3: Consider again the database server of Ex. 8.1, but now assume that at most four requests can be queued at the server—including requests being

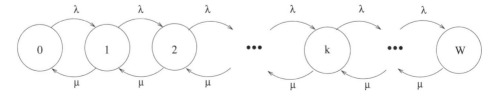

Figure 8.7. State transition diagram—infinite population/finite queue.

processed. What is the fraction of time that k $(k = 0, \cdots, 4)$ requests are found in the database server?

Using the values $\lambda = 30$ request/sec, $\mu = 50$ requests/sec, and $W = 4$, in Eq. (8.3.3), we get that

$$p_0 = \frac{1 - (30/50)}{1 - (30/50)^5} = 0.43 \tag{8.3.4}$$

and $p_k = 0.43 \times 0.6^k$ for $k = 1, \cdots, 4$.   ■

The utilization of the server is the fraction of time the server is not idle. So, as before, $U = 1 - p_0$ where p_0 is given by Eq. (8.3.3). Making the proper substitutions, we get

$$U = \frac{(\lambda/\mu)\,[1 - (\lambda/\mu)^W]}{1 - (\lambda/\mu)^{W+1}}. \tag{8.3.5}$$

In a server with a finite queue, an important performance metric is the fraction of requests that are lost because the queue is full. This is given by p_W since requests are only lost when the system is in state W. So, $p_{\text{loss}} = p_W$.

The average number of requests at the server is computed in a way similar to the previous section. Thus,

$$\overline{N} = \sum_{k=0}^{W} k \times p_k = p_0 \sum_{k=0}^{W} k\,(\lambda/\mu)^k. \tag{8.3.6}$$

But, using the fact that $\sum_{k=0}^{W} k \times a^k = [W \times a^{W+2} - (W+1)\,a^{W+1} + a]/(1-a)^2$, combined with the value for p_0 given in Eq. (8.3.3) and making the proper algebraic manipulations, we get that

$$\overline{N} = \frac{(\lambda/\mu)[W(\lambda/\mu)^{W+1} - (W+1)\,(\lambda/\mu)^W + 1]}{[1 - (\lambda/\mu)^{W+1}](1 - \lambda/\mu)}. \tag{8.3.7}$$

The throughput X of the server is μ when the server is busy and zero otherwise. The fraction of time the server is busy is its utilization. So,

$$X = U \times \mu + 0 \times (1 - U) = \frac{\lambda\,[1 - (\lambda/\mu)^W]}{1 - (\lambda/\mu)^{W+1}}. \tag{8.3.8}$$

Once more, we use Little's Law to compute the average response time R as $\overline{N}/X$, where $\overline{N}$ and X are given by Eqs. (8.3.7) and (8.3.8), respectively. So, making the proper substitutions we get that

$$R = \overline{N}/X = \frac{S\,[W(\lambda/\mu)^{W+1} - (W+1)\,(\lambda/\mu)^W + 1]}{[1 - (\lambda/\mu)^W](1 - \lambda/\mu)}. \tag{8.3.9}$$

Example 8.4: Consider the same parameters for arrival rate and service rate used in Ex. 8.1. What should the minimum value for the maximum number of accepted requests be so that less than 1% of the requests are rejected?

We want to compute the value of W such that $p_W = p_0\,(\lambda/\mu)^W < 0.01$. Using the values of $\lambda = 30$ requests/sec and $\mu = 50$ requests/sec, we get that $p_0 = 0.4/(1 - 0.6^{W+1})$ according to Eq. (8.3.3). We want the value of W such that

$$0.4 \times 0.6^W/(1 - 0.6^{W+1}) < 0.01.$$

Doing a little bit of algebra and using logarithms we find that $W \geq 8$. Alternatively, one can use the spreadsheet in the workbook SysMod.XLS and look at a table that shows the fraction of lost requests versus W and pick the correct value of W. Figure 8.8 shows how the fraction of lost requests decreases with W. As it can be seen, the drop is more substantial for smaller values of W.   ■

All equations for the case of a fixed service fixed rate server, infinite population, and finite queue are summarized in Fig. 8.9.

8.4   Generalized System-Level Models

The examples of Secs. 8.2 and 8.3 can be generalized to allow us to model other situations. We follow here the same basic approach outlined at the end of Sec. 8.2, except that we will allow the arrival and service rates to be a function of the state. This means that the arrival rate, λ_k, and the service rate, μ_k, may depend on

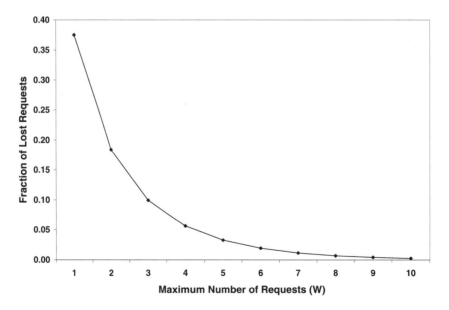

Figure 8.8. Fraction of lost requests vs. maximum number of requests (W).

Fraction of time server has k requests:

$$p_k = \frac{1 - \lambda/\mu}{1 - (\lambda/\mu)^{W+1}} \; \left(\frac{\lambda}{\mu}\right)^k \quad k = 0, \cdots, W$$

Server utilization:

$$U = \frac{(\lambda/\mu) \, [1 - (\lambda/\mu)^W]}{1 - (\lambda/\mu)^{W+1}}$$

Average server throughput:

$$X = U \times \mu = \frac{\lambda \, [1 - (\lambda/\mu)^W]}{1 - (\lambda/\mu)^{W+1}}$$

Average number of requests in the server:

$$\overline{N} = \frac{(\lambda/\mu)[W(\lambda/\mu)^{W+1} - (W+1) \, (\lambda/\mu)^W + 1]}{[1 - (\lambda/\mu)^{W+1}](1 - \lambda/\mu)}$$

Average response time:

$$R = \overline{N}/X = \frac{S \, [W(\lambda/\mu)^{W+1} - (W+1) \, (\lambda/\mu)^W + 1]}{[1 - (\lambda/\mu)^W](1 - \lambda/\mu)}$$

Figure 8.9. Infinite population/finite queue server equations.

the state k. In general, we may have infinite states. An STD for this generalized system-level model is given in Fig. 8.10.

Using the same kind of boundaries we used in the STD of Fig. 8.3 and applying the flow-in = flow-out principle, we get that

$$\lambda_{k-1} \, p_{k-1} = \mu_k \, p_k \quad k = 1, 2, \cdots \tag{8.4.1}$$

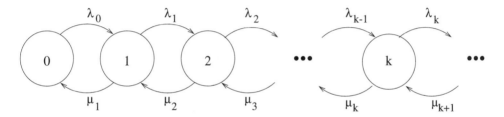

Figure 8.10. State transition diagram for generalized system-level model.

We can then write, by applying Eq. (8.4.1) recursively, that

$$p_1 = \frac{\lambda_0}{\mu_1} p_0 \tag{8.4.2}$$

$$p_2 = \frac{\lambda_1}{\mu_2} p_1 = \frac{\lambda_1}{\mu_2} \frac{\lambda_0}{\mu_1} p_0 \tag{8.4.3}$$

$$p_k = \frac{\lambda_{k-1}}{\mu_k} p_{k-1} = \frac{\lambda_{k-1}}{\mu_k} \cdots \frac{\lambda_1}{\mu_2} \frac{\lambda_0}{\mu_1} p_0 \tag{8.4.4}$$

Using a more compact notation we get that

$$p_k = p_0 \prod_{i=0}^{k-1} \frac{\lambda_i}{\mu_{i+1}}. \tag{8.4.5}$$

But, as before, the sum of all p_ks equals to one. Thus,

$$\sum_{k=0}^{\infty} p_0 \prod_{i=0}^{k-1} \frac{\lambda_i}{\mu_{i+1}} = 1. \tag{8.4.6}$$

This implies that

$$p_0 = \left[\sum_{k=0}^{\infty} \prod_{i=0}^{k-1} \frac{\lambda_i}{\mu_{i+1}} \right]^{-1}. \tag{8.4.7}$$

Equations (8.4.5) and (8.4.7) can be specialized to many different situations by chosing the proper expressions for λ_k and μ_k. We will use these results in the following sections to analyze several other client/server component models. Figure 8.11 summarizes all equations for the generalized system-level model.

8.5   Other System-Level Models

Given the generalized framework discussed in the previous section, we can consider many possible alternatives when modeling client/server systems. We consider here three dimensions to the problem:

- *population size*: we consider the infinite population case and the finite population case with M clients.

- *server service rate*: we consider fixed service rate servers, $X(k) = \mu$, and variable service rate servers, $X(k) = \mu_k$.

Fraction of time server has k requests:

$$p_k = p_0 \prod_{i=0}^{k-1} \frac{\lambda_i}{\mu_{i+1}}$$

where

$$p_0 = \left[\sum_{k=0}^{\infty} \prod_{i=0}^{k-1} \frac{\lambda_i}{\mu_{i+1}} \right]^{-1}$$

Server utilization:

$$U = 1 - p_0$$

Average server throughput:

$$X = \sum_{k=1}^{\infty} \mu_k \, p_k$$

Average number of requests in the server:

$$\overline{N} = \sum_{k=1}^{\infty} k \times p_k$$

Average response time:

$$R = \frac{\overline{N}}{X} = \frac{\sum_{k=1}^{\infty} k \times p_k}{\sum_{k=1}^{\infty} \mu_k \, p_k}$$

Figure 8.11. Generalized system-level model equations.

- *maximum queue size*: the two cases considered here are: infinite queue size and maximum queue size limited to W requests. Note that for the finite population case with M clients, a maximum queue size of M is equivalent to an infinite queue since a maximum of M requests can be in the system.

8.5.1   Infinite Population Models

Infinite population models are adequate to represent WWW environments, where the number of users is potentially very large. Secs. 8.2 and 8.3 considered two cases of infinite population models. Infinite population models are also known as *open models* and can be depicted as in Fig. 8.12.

Besides the two open models considered in Secs. 8.2 and 8.3, we consider here the cases of variable service rate with limited and infinite queue size.

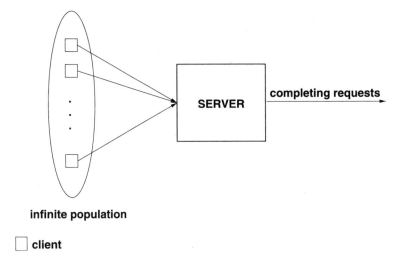

infinite population

client

Figure 8.12. Open model.

Variable Service Rate and Infinite Queue

The throughput of the server is usually a function of the number of requests present in the system. A typical throughput curve $X(k)$ is shown in Fig. 8.13. The figure shows that as the number of requests in the system increases starting from zero, the throughput increases almost linearly with the number of requests. This reflects the fact that at light loads, requests face very little congestion at the system internal queues. After some point, congestion starts to build up and throughput increases at a much lower rate until it saturates, reaching its maximum value. This maximum value is determined by the bottleneck device at the server.

We will use the generalized expressions for p_k and p_0 given by Eqs. (8.4.5) and (8.4.7). The expressions for λ_k and μ_k used in this case are $\lambda_k = \lambda$ for $k = 0, 1, \cdots$ and $\mu_k = X(k)$ for $k = 1, 2, \cdots$. Thus, making the proper substitutions, we get

$$p_k = \left[1 + \sum_{j=1}^{\infty} \frac{\lambda^j}{\prod_{i=1}^{j} X(i)} \right]^{-1} \frac{\lambda^k}{\prod_{i=1}^{k} X(i)}. \tag{8.5.1}$$

The summation in Eq. (8.5.1) has an infinite number of terms and cannot be computed for the general case where all values of the throughput are different. Fortunately, as we pointed out before, the throughput saturates after a certain value of k. Let J be the value of k after which the value of the throughput no longer changes.

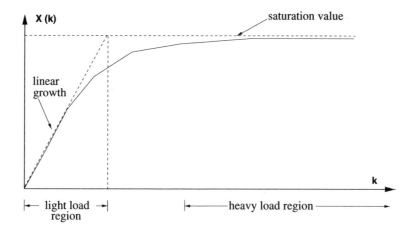

Figure 8.13. Typical throughput curve.

Now, the expression for μ_k becomes

$$\mu_k = \begin{cases} X(k) & k \le J \\ X(J) & k > J \end{cases} .$$
(8.5.2)

Using the expression of μ_k given in Eq. (8.5.2) in Eq. (8.5.1) and doing some manipulations, we get that

$$p_0 = \left[1 + \sum_{k=1}^{J} \frac{\lambda^k}{\beta(k)} + \frac{\lambda^J}{\beta(J)} \frac{\rho}{1-\rho} \right]^{-1}$$
(8.5.3)

and

$$p_k = \begin{cases} p_0 \, \lambda^k / \beta(k) & k \le J \\ p_0 \, X(J)^J \, \rho^k / \beta(J) & k > J \end{cases}$$
(8.5.4)

where $\beta(k) \stackrel{\text{def}}{=} X(1) \times X(2) \times \cdots \times X(k)$ and $\rho \stackrel{\text{def}}{=} \lambda / X(J)$. Equations (8.5.3) and (8.5.4) are only valid if $\lambda < X(J)$, that is, if the arrival rate is less than the maximum service rate.

A closed form expression for the average number of requests in the server can be found using Eqs. (8.5.3) and (8.5.4) and the fact that $\overline{N} = \sum_{k=0}^{\infty} k \times p_k$. After some manipulations, we get

$$\overline{N} = p_0 \left[\sum_{k=1}^{J} \frac{k \times \lambda^k}{\beta(k)} + \frac{\rho \, \lambda^J \, [\rho + (J+1) \, (1-\rho)]}{(1-\rho)^2 \, \beta(J)} \right].$$
(8.5.5)

The average throughput in open models with unbounded queue sizes is equal to the average arrival rate. So, $X = \lambda$. Finally, the response time R is obtained from

Little's Law as $R = \overline{N}/X$. Note that Eqs. (8.5.3)–(8.5.5) become, as expected, the equations for the infinite population, fixed service rate, and infinite queue size case when $J = 1$.

Example 8.5: A client/server system receives requests at a rate of 30 requests/sec. The throughput of the server when there is one request present is 18 requests/sec, for two requests it is 35 requests/sec, and for three or more requests is 50 requests/sec. What are the server utilization, average throughput, average number of requests in the system, and average response time?

Note that $\lambda = 30$ requests/sec, $J = 3$, $X(1) = 18$ requests/sec, $X(2) = 35$ requests/sec, and $X(J) = 50$ requests/sec. Using these values, we get that $\rho = 30/50 = 0.6$, $\beta(1) = 18$, $\beta(2) = 18 \times 35 = 630$, and $\beta(3) = 18 \times 35 \times 50 = 31,500$. Using these values in Eq. (8.5.3), we get that $p_0 = 0.16$ and, therefore, the server utilization is $U = 1 - p_0 = 0.84 = 84\%$. From Eq. (8.5.5), we get that $\overline{N} = 2.27$ requests. Since the throughput X is equal to $\lambda = 30$ requests/sec, we get that the response time is $R = \overline{N}/X = 1.77/30 = 0.076$ sec. ∎

Variable Service Rate and Limited Queue Size

The difference between this case and the previous one is that now requests can be lost if W requests are already at the server upon arrival of a new request. The expressions for λ_k and μ_k are $\lambda_k = \lambda$ for $k = 0, \cdots, W - 1$ and

$$\mu_k = \begin{cases} X(k) & k = 1, \cdots, J \\ X(J) & k = J + 1, \cdots, W \end{cases} \qquad (8.5.6)$$

The expression for p_k now becomes

$$p_k = \begin{cases} p_0 \times \lambda^k / \beta(k) & k = 1, \cdots, J \\ p_0 \times \rho^k \times X(J)^J / \beta(J) & k = J + 1, \cdots, W \end{cases} \qquad (8.5.7)$$

and p_0 is given by

$$p_0 = \left[1 + \sum_{k=1}^{J} \frac{\lambda^k}{\beta(k)} + \frac{\rho \times \lambda^J \left(1 - \rho^{W-J}\right)}{\beta(J)\left(1 - \rho\right)} \right]^{-1}. \qquad (8.5.8)$$

The fraction of lost requests is simply $p_W = p_0 \times \rho^W \times X(J)^J / \beta(J)$. The average number of request in the server can be computed as $\overline{N} = \sum_{k=1}^{W} k \times p_k$. The average throughput X is given by

$$X = \sum_{k=1}^{W} X(k) \times p_k = \sum_{k=1}^{J} X(k)\, p_k + X(J) \sum_{k=J+1}^{W} p_k. \qquad (8.5.9)$$

Finally, the response time is computed from Little's Law as $R = \overline{N}/X$.

Example 8.6: Consider the same client/server system of Ex. 8.5 except that now, the server's queue is limited to five requests. What are the new values for the the server utilization, average throughput, average number of requests in the system, average response time, and the fraction of lost requests?

Using the expressions derived in this subsection as implemented in the MS Excel workbook SysMod.XLS, we get that the server utilization is $U = 82.7\%$, the average number of requests at the server is $\overline{N} = 1.85$ requests, the average throughput is equal to 28.4 requests/sec, and from Little's Law, the average response time is $1.85/28.4 = 0.065$ sec. The fraction of lost requests is $0.053 = 5.3\%$. ■

8.5.2 Finite Population Models

Consider now the case of a database server that is accessed only by client work-stations in the same company, as in the case of an intranet. We now have a *finite population* of, say, M clients in what is also called a *closed model* (see Fig. 8.14). Each of these clients submits a transaction, waits for the response of that transaction, analyzes the response, and composes a new transaction to be submitted to the server, as explained in Sec. 3.6. As defined in that section, the time spent by the client from the time a response to a transaction is received and the next transaction is submitted is called *think time*. Let Z be the average think time, in seconds, at each client. When a client is in the think state, it submits one transaction at each Z time units. Thus, the average rate at which each client in the think state submits transactions to the server is $1/Z$. Assume as before that the state of the server can be characterized by the number k of requests in the server. The state transition diagram (STD) for a finite population model has only $M + 1$ states (from 0 to M), where M is the number of clients.

If the system is in state k, that is, transactions submitted by k of the M clients are in the server, $M - k$ clients are in the think state. Since each of these $M - k$ clients generates transactions at a rate of $1/Z$ transactions/sec, the average rate at which transactions arrive at the server when it is at state k is $\lambda_k = (M - k)/Z$ for $k = 0, \cdots, M$. Figure 8.15 shows the state transition diagram for the finite population case.

The next subsections consider the finite population case with a fixed service rate and with a variable service rate.

Fixed Service Rate

Consider, as before, that the server's service rate is fixed, that is, it is not state-dependent. So, $\mu_k = \mu$ for $k = 1, \cdots, M$. Using the proper definitions of λ_k and μ_k in Eq. (8.4.5) and (8.4.7) we get that

$$p_k = p_0 \; \frac{M!}{(M-k)! \, (\mu \, Z)^k} \quad k = 0, \cdots, M \tag{8.5.10}$$

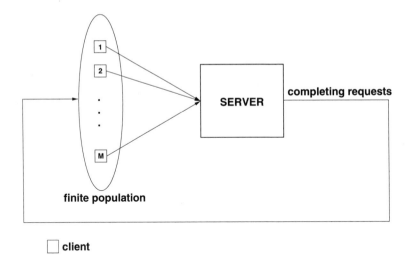

Figure 8.14. Closed model.

where

$$p_0 = \left[\sum_{k=0}^{M} \frac{M!}{(M-k)!\,(\mu\,Z)^k}\right]^{-1}. \tag{8.5.11}$$

A few words about the computations in Eqs. (8.5.10) and (8.5.11) are in order. Even though there is no closed form expression for the summation in Eq. (8.5.11), it is a finite summation and therefore can always be computed. Some numerical problems may arise in the computation of p_k and p_0 for very large values of M due to the factorials that appear in the numerator and the denominator. Imagine, for example, a client server system with 200 clients. If we used the naive approach of first computing $200! = 200 \times 199 \times \cdots 2 \times 1$, we could easily exceed the limit of the largest number that can be stored in the computer we are using to do the computation. An alternative way is to expand the factorials in the numerator and

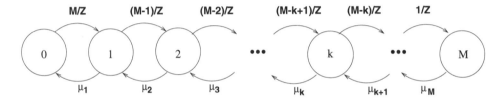

Figure 8.15. State transition diagram—finite population.

denominator and rearrange the terms as follows

$$p_k = p_0 \overbrace{\frac{M}{\mu\ Z} \cdot \frac{M-1}{\mu\ Z} \cdot \frac{M-2}{\mu\ Z} \cdot \cdots \cdot \frac{M-(k-1)}{\mu\ Z}}^{k\ \text{terms}} \qquad k = 1, \cdots, M \qquad (8.5.12)$$

and

$$p_0 = \left[\sum_{k=0}^{M} \overbrace{\frac{M}{\mu\ Z} \cdot \frac{M-1}{\mu\ Z} \cdot \frac{M-2}{\mu\ Z} \cdot \cdots \cdot \frac{M-(k-1)}{\mu\ Z}}^{k\ \text{terms}} \right]^{-1}. \qquad (8.5.13)$$

Note that once we obtain the value of p_k for $k = 0, \cdots, M$, we can compute all performance metrics of interest.

Example 8.7: A C/S application runs for 50 clients. The software that runs at the client workstation runs a local computation that lasts for 2 sec, on the average, before submitting a new request to the server. The server can process requests at a rate of 80 requests/sec. What are the average response time, average server throughput, average number of requests at the server, and the server utilization?

The number of clients is $M = 50$, the average think time is $Z = 2$ sec, and the service rate is $\mu = 80$ requests/sec. Using Eq. (8.5.13), we can compute the value of p_0 as 0.69 with the help of the spreadsheet in the MS Excel workbook SysMod.XLS. The server utilization is $U = 1 - p_0 = 0.31 = 31\%$. The average number of requests is computed as $\sum_{k=1}^{50} k \times p_k$. Again, using the same spreadsheet, we get $\overline{N} = 0.443$ requests. The server throughput is

$$X = \sum_{k=1}^{50} \mu \times p_k = \mu \sum_{k=1}^{50} p_k = \mu\ (1 - p_0) = 80 \times 0.31 = 24.8 \text{ tps.} \qquad (8.5.14)$$

Using Little's Law, we can compute the average response time as $R = \overline{N}/X = 0.443/24.8 = 0.018$ sec. ∎

Variable Service Rate

The difference between this case and the previous is that the service rate of the server is variable and given by

$$\mu_k = \begin{cases} X(k) & k = 1, \cdots, J \\ X(J) & k > J \end{cases}. \qquad (8.5.15)$$

The arrival rate λ_k is given by $\lambda_k = (M-k)/Z$ for $k = 0, \cdots, M$ as before. The expression for p_k becomes

$$
p_k = \begin{cases}
p_0 \; \dfrac{M!}{(M-k)! \; Z^k \beta(k)} & k = 1, \cdots, J \\[3mm]
p_0 \; \dfrac{M! \; X(J)^J}{(M-k)! \; [Z \; X(J)]^k \; \beta(J)} & k = J+1, \cdots, M
\end{cases}
\qquad (8.5.16)
$$

and p_0 is given by

$$
p_0 = \left[1 + \sum_{k=1}^{J} \frac{M!}{(M-k)! \; Z^k \; \beta(k)} + \frac{X(J)^J}{\beta(J)} \sum_{k=J+1}^{M} \frac{M!}{(M-k)! \; [Z \; X(J)]^k} \right]^{-1}
\tag{8.5.17}
$$

where $\beta(k)$ was defined in Sec. 8.5.1. The average number of requests at the server is given by $\overline{N} = \sum_{k=1}^{M} k \times p_k$ and the average throughput as

$$
X = \sum_{k=1}^{M} X(k) \; p_k = \sum_{k=1}^{J} X(k) \; p_k + X(J) \sum_{k=J+1}^{M} p_k.
\tag{8.5.18}
$$

Finally, the response time is computed from Little's Law as $R = \overline{N}/X$.

Example 8.8: Consider the same parameters as in the client/server of the previous example, except that now the service rate is no longer constant but is given by $X(1) = 18$ requests/sec, $X(2) = 35$ requests/sec, and $X(k) = 50$ requests/sec for $k = 3, \cdots, M$. What are the server utilization, average throughput, average number of requests in the system, and average response time?

Using the above equations, we get that server utilization is $U = 76.3\%$, the average number of requests at the server is $\overline{N} = 1.12$ requests, the average throughput is equal to 19.5 requests/sec, and from Little's Law, the average response time is $1.12/19.5 = 0.057$ sec. ∎

8.6   Concluding Remarks

The performance of servers in a client/server environment can be analyzed at a high level, from a system's point of view, or at a low level, where the various components of the system are modeled explicitly. This chapter covered the high-level view and discussed system-level models. These types of models are based on state transition diagrams that represent the states a system can be found in. State transition rates are associated with the rates at which events occur at the underlying system being modeled. By equating the flow into a state or set of states with the flow out of that set, we are able to derive a set of equations that relate the fraction of time that the system is at each state. From these fractions of time, we can obtain performance metrics of interest, such as the server utilization, average number of requests in the system, average response times, and fraction of requests rejected.

This chapter presented a general set of equations for state transition diagrams that have state-dependent arrival and departure rates. These equations were specialized to cover various cases including: infinite population/fixed server rate/infinite queue, infinite population/fixed server rate/finite queue, infinite population/variable server rate/infinite queue, infinite population/variable server rate/finite queue, finite population/fixed server rate, and finite population/variable server rate. All equations derived in this chapter are implemented in the MS Excel workbook SysMod.XLS that accompanies this book. A more formal treatment—based on the theory of stochastic processes—of the models discussed in this chapter can be found in [2].

The next chapter discusses the lower-level models, called component models, and also shows how system-level models can be combined with component-level models.

BIBLIOGRAPHY

[1] J. P. BUZEN, Operational analysis: an alternative to stochastic modeling, *Performance of Computer Installations*. North Holland, June 1978, pp. 175–194.

[2] L. KLEINROCK, *Queueing Systems, Vol. I: Theory*. New York: Wiley, 1975.

[3] D. A. MENASCÉ, V. A. F. ALMEIDA, and L. W. DOWDY, *Capacity Planning and Performance Modeling: From Mainframes to Client-Server Systems*. Upper Saddle River, NJ: Prentice Hall, 1994.

Chapter 9

COMPONENT-LEVEL
PERFORMANCE MODELS

9.1 Introduction

In Chap. 8 we looked at computer systems characterized by their throughput function $X(n)$, where n represents the load of the system in terms of the number of requests present at the system. In this chapter, we look at the components that make up a networked system and examine how we can build models that take into consideration the interaction of these components. These models are called queuing networks (QNs). We discuss solution methods for both open and closed QNs with multiple classes of customers. The MS Excel workbooks `OpenQN.XLS` and `ClosedQN.XLS` that accompany this book implement the algorithms and solution methods discussed here. We also present bounds on performance and provide models for dealing with multiple resource queues to model multiprocessor servers and other such situations. The chapter concludes with an example of a model of an intranet.

9.2 Queuing Networks

Chapter 5 introduced the notion of a queuing network (QN), as a network of interconnected queues that represents a computer system (see Sec. 5.7.1). A *queue* in a QN stands for a resource (e.g., CPU, disk, network) and the queue of requests waiting to use the resource. A queue is characterized by a function $S(n)$ that represents the average service time per request when there are n requests at the queue. Remember that the term queue stands for the waiting queue plus the resource itself; the number of requests, n, at the queue is called the *queue length*. There are three categories of resources in a queuing network and they vary according to whether there is queuing or not and whether the average service time, $S(n)$, depends on the queue length n or not. The resource types are described below. The graphical notation used to represent them as well as an example of the curve $S(n)$ is given in Fig. 9.1.

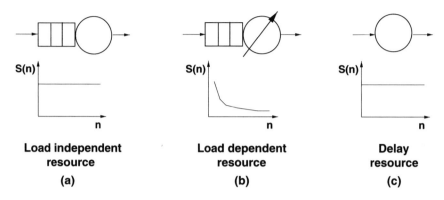

Figure 9.1. Types of resources in a queuing network.

- load-independent resources: represent resources where there is queuing but the average service time does not depend on the load; that is, $S(n) = S$ for all values of n (Fig. 9.1a).

- load-dependent resources: used to represent resources where there is queuing and the average service time depends on the load; that is, $S(n)$ is an arbitrary function of n (Fig. 9.1b).

- delay resources: indicate situations where there is no queuing. Thus, the total time spent by a request at a delay resource is the request's service time. The average service time function does not depend on the number of requests present at the resource; that is, $S(n) = S$ for all values of n (Fig. 9.1c).

Not all requests that flow through the resources of a queuing network are similar in terms of the resources used and the time spent at each resource. As pointed out in Chap. 6, the total workload submitted to a computer system may be broken down into several workload components, which are represented in a QN model by a *class* of requests. Different classes may have different service demand parameters and different workload intensity parameters. Classes of requests may be classified as *open* or *closed* depending on whether the number of requests in the QN is unbounded or fixed, respectively. Open classes allow requests to arrive, go through the various resources, and leave the system. Closed classes are characterized by having a fixed number of requests in the QN. A QN in which all classes are open is called an open QN. A QN in which all classes are closed is called a closed QN. A QN in which some classes are open and others are closed is called a *mixed* QN.

Figure 9.2a shows an example of an open QN that represents a database server with a multiprocessor with four CPUs and two disks. The set of four CPUs is represented in the QN as a single queue that acts as a load-dependent resource.

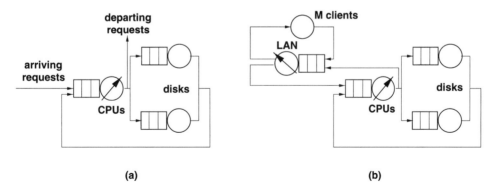

Figure 9.2. (a) Example of an open QN. (b) Example of a closed QN.

The service time function is of the form

$$S(n) = \left\{ \begin{array}{ll} 1/(n \times \alpha) & n \leq 4 \\ 1/(4 \times \alpha) & n > 4 \end{array} \right. \tag{9.2.1}$$

to indicate that the average service time decreases with the number of requests as more processors are used until all four processors are busy. Figure 9.2b illustrates the same database server receiving requests from a fixed number, M, of clients that send their requests through an Ethernet LAN. The set of clients is represented in the QN as a delay resource because a request that returns to a client does not have to queue for access to the client. The service demand at that resource is the average time spent at the client before submitting a new request to the database—the think time. The LAN is represented by a load-dependent resource to indicate that, as the load on the network increases, the throughput on the LAN decreases due to the increase in the number of collisions for access to the network medium.

In the following sections of this chapter we will be studying both open and closed queuing networks. We will show how to determine performance metrics such as throughput, response times, resource utilization, and bottlenecks.

9.3   Open Systems

Consider first the case of single-class open queuing networks and then generalize for the case where multiple classes are considered.

9.3.1   Single-Class Open Queuing Networks

Let us examine first the case of a single open class QN where all resources are either delay- or load-independent resources. Consider the following notation.

- λ: average arrival rate of requests to the QN

- K: number of queues

- X_0: average throughput of the QN. In the case of open systems with operational equilibrium, the average throughput is the same as the average arrival rate. So, $X_0 = \lambda$

- V_i: average number of visits to queue i by a request

- S_i: average service time of a request at queue i per visit to the queue

- W_i: average waiting time of a request at queue i per visit to the queue

- X_i: average throughput of queue i

- R_i: average response time of a request at queue i, defined as the sum of the average waiting time plus average service time per visit to the queue. So, $R_i = W_i + S_i$

- R_i': average residence time of a request at queue i. This is the total waiting time (i.e., the queuing time) plus the total service time (i.e., the service demand), over all visits to queue i. So, $R_i' = Q_i + D_i = V_i \times R_i$

- R_0: average response time; equal to the sum of the residence times over all queues. So, $R_0 = \sum_{i=1}^{K} R_i'$

- n_i: average number of requests at queue i waiting or receiving service from any resource at queue i

- N: average number of requests in the QN

We start by obtaining the average response time R_i at queue i. We note that the average response time is equal to the average service time S_i plus the average waiting time of a request. The average waiting time is equal to the average number of requests *seen* at queue i by an arriving request to the queue multiplied by the average service time S_i per request. An important result, known as the Arrival Theorem [7], [10], applied to open QNs, says that the average number of requests seen upon arrival to queue i is equal to the average number, n_i, of requests in the queue. Thus,

$$R_i = S_i + n_i \times S_i. \tag{9.3.1}$$

But, from Little's Law, $n_i = X_i \times R_i$. Combining this result with Eq. (9.3.1) and noting from the Utilization Law that $U_i = X_i \times S_i$, we get that

$$R_i = S_i/(1 - U_i). \tag{9.3.2}$$

From Eq. (9.3.2), we can get the residence time at queue i as

$$R_i' = V_i \times R_i = \frac{V_i \times S_i}{1 - U_i} = \frac{D_i}{1 - U_i}. \tag{9.3.3}$$

Using Little's Law, Eq. (9.3.2), and the Utilization Law again we can obtain the average number of requests at queue i as

$$n_i = U_i/(1 - U_i). \tag{9.3.4}$$

One common question in the analysis of client/server systems is "what is the maximum theoretical value of the arrival rate λ?" This question has an easy answer that depends solely on the service demands of all resources. Note that the service demand, the utilization, and the arrival rate are related by $\lambda = U_i/D_i$ for all resources i. Because the utilization of any resource cannot exceed 100%, we have that $\lambda \leq 1/D_i$ for all i's. The maximum value of λ is limited by the resource with the highest value of the service demand, called the bottleneck resource. Thus,

$$\lambda \leq \frac{1}{\max_{i=1}^{K} D_i}. \tag{9.3.5}$$

Example 9.1: A DB server has one CPU and two disks and receives requests at a rate of 10,800 requests per hour. Each request needs 200 msec of CPU and performs five I/Os on disk 1 and three I/Os on disk 2 on the average. Each I/O takes an average of 15 msec. What are the average response time per request, average throughput of the server, utilization of the CPU and disks, and the average number of requests at the server? What is the maximum theoretical arrival rate of requests sustained by this server?

The throughput, X_0, equal to the average arrival rate λ, is $10,800/3,600 = 3$ requests/sec. The service demand at the CPU, D_{CPU} is 0.2 sec. The service demands at disks 1 and 2 are computed as $D_{\mathrm{disk1}} = V_1 \times S_{\mathrm{disk}} = 5 \times 0.015 = 0.075$ sec, and $D_{\mathrm{disk2}} = V_2 \times S_{\mathrm{disk}} = 3 \times 0.015 = 0.045$ sec, respectively. From the Service Demand Law (see Sec. 3.5.3), $U_i = D_i \times X_0$. So, the utilization of the CPU and disks is given by $U_{\mathrm{CPU}} = D_{\mathrm{CPU}} \times X_0 = 0.2 \times 3 = 60\%$, $U_{\mathrm{disk1}} = D_{\mathrm{disk1}} \times X_0 = 0.075 \times 3 = 22.5\%$, and $U_{\mathrm{disk2}} = D_{\mathrm{disk2}} \times X_0 = 0.045 \times 3 = 13.5\%$, respectively. The residence times can now be computed as

$$
\begin{aligned}
R'_{\mathrm{CPU}} &= D_{\mathrm{CPU}}/(1 - U_{\mathrm{CPU}}) = 0.2/(1 - 0.60) = 0.50 \text{ sec} \\
R'_{\mathrm{disk1}} &= D_{\mathrm{disk1}}/(1 - U_{\mathrm{disk1}}) = 0.075/(1 - 0.225) = 0.097 \text{ sec} \\
R'_{\mathrm{disk\ 2}} &= D_{\mathrm{disk2}}/(1 - U_{\mathrm{disk2}}) = 0.045/(1 - 0.135) = 0.052 \text{ sec.}
\end{aligned}
$$

The total response time is just the sum of all residence times. So, $R_0 = R'_{\mathrm{CPU}} + R'_{\mathrm{disk1}} + R'_{\mathrm{disk2}} = 0.50 + 0.097 + 0.052 = 0.649$ sec. The average number of requests at each queue is given by

$$
\begin{aligned}
n_{\mathrm{CPU}} &= U_{\mathrm{CPU}}/(1 - U_{\mathrm{CPU}}) = 0.60/(1 - 0.60) = 1.5 \\
n_{\mathrm{disk1}} &= U_{\mathrm{disk1}}/(1 - U_{\mathrm{disk1}}) = 0.225/(1 - 0.225) = 0.29 \\
n_{\mathrm{disk2}} &= U_{\mathrm{disk2}}/(1 - U_{\mathrm{disk2}}) = 0.135/(1 - 0.135) = 0.16.
\end{aligned}
$$

The total number of requests at the server is given by $N = n_{\text{CPU}} + n_{\text{disk1}} + n_{\text{disk2}} = 1.5 + 0.29 + 0.16 = 1.95$ requests.

The maximum arrival rate is given by $1/\max\{0.2, 0.075, 0.045\} = 5$ requests/sec. Figure 9.3 shows how the average response time varies as the average arrival rate of requests increases. The curve shows the dramatic increase seen when the arrival rate approaches its maximum possible value.   ■ ·

9.3.2   Multiple-Class Open Queuing Networks

The expressions we derived for the single-class case can be generalized for the case where there are multiple classes of requests. The generalization on the notation used so far is quite obvious. We use the subscripts i, r to indicate variables associated with queue i and class r. For example, $R'_{i,r}$ stands for the residence time of class r requests at queue i. We use R for the number of classes. Different classes may have different values of the arrival rate λ_r. The set of all arrival rates $\lambda_1, \cdots, \lambda_r, \cdots, \lambda_R$ is denoted for convenience as the vector $\vec{\lambda} = (\lambda_1, \cdots, \lambda_r, \cdots, \lambda_R)$. Since all performance metrics depend on the values of the arrival rates, we extend our notation $R'_{i,r}$ to $R'_{i,r}(\vec{\lambda})$ to indicate that $R'_{i,r}$ is a function of the values of the arrival rates.

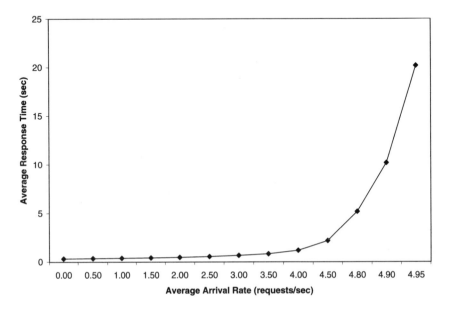

Figure 9.3. Response time vs. arrival rate for Ex. 9.1.

Figure 9.4 summarizes all equations for the multiple-class case of open QNs with no load-dependent resources. Readers interested in the detailed derivations of these formulas should refer to [6]. The equations for multiclass open QN models are implemented in the MS Excel workbook OpenQN.XLS that accompanies this book.

Example 9.2: A database server is subject to two types of transactions: query

---

Input Parameters:
$D_{i,r}$ and λ_r

Utilization:

$$U_{i,r}(\vec{\lambda}) = \lambda_r \times V_{i,r} \times S_{i,r} = \lambda_r \times D_{i,r} \tag{9.3.6}$$

$$U_i(\vec{\lambda}) = \sum_{r=1}^{R} U_{i,r}(\vec{\lambda}) \tag{9.3.7}$$

Average number of class r requests at resource i:

$$n_{i,r}(\vec{\lambda}) = \frac{U_{i,r}(\vec{\lambda})}{1 - U_i(\vec{\lambda})} \tag{9.3.8}$$

Average residence time of class r requests at resource i:

$$R'_{i,r}(\vec{\lambda}) = \begin{cases} D_{i,r} & \text{delay resource} \\[2ex] \dfrac{D_{i,r}}{1 - U_i(\vec{\lambda})} & \text{queuing resource} \end{cases} \tag{9.3.9}$$

Average class r request response time:

$$R_{0,r}(\vec{\lambda}) = \sum_{i=1}^{K} R'_{i,r}(\vec{\lambda}) \tag{9.3.10}$$

Average number of requests at resource i:

$$n_i(\vec{\lambda}) = \sum_{r=1}^{R} n_{i,r}(\vec{\lambda}) \tag{9.3.11}$$

Figure 9.4. Formulas for multiclass open QNs with no load-dependent resources.

and update. The arrival rate of query transactions is 5 tps and that of update transactions is 2 tps. The service demands for the CPU, disks 1 and 2, are given in the top part of Table 9.1. What are the response times, residence times, and utilizations?

Using the equations in Fig. 9.4 we obtain the utilizations per resource per class and the overall resource utilization. The residence times per resource per class depend on the service demands and on the overall resource utilizations. For example, the residence time of query transactions at the CPU is 0.50 sec. This number is obtained by dividing the CPU service demand for query transactions, 0.10 sec, by $(1 - U_{\rm CPU}) = (1 - 0.8) = 0.2$. The residence time is the time spent by a transaction at a resource, waiting or receiving service, over all visits to the resource. The sum of the residence times for all resources is the response time. So, the response time for query transactions is $0.50 + 0.40 + 0.16 = 1.06$ sec. ∎

9.4 Closed Models

The open-queuing network models we studied in the previous section do not place any limits on the maximum number of requests present in the system. There are situations where we want to model computer systems with a fixed and finite number of requests in the system. These situations arise when we want to model a system with a maximum degree of multiprogramming under heavy load, a client/server system with a known number of clients sending requests to a server, or a multithreaded server.

Table 9.1. Service Demands, Arrival Rates, and Performance Metrics for Ex. 9.2

	Queries	Updates
Arrival Rate (tps)	5	2
Service Demands (sec)		
CPU	0.10	0.15
Disk 1	0.08	0.20
Disk 2	0.07	0.10
Utilizations (%)		
CPU	50	30
Disk 1	40	40
Disk 2	35	20
Residence times (sec)		
CPU	0.50	0.75
Disk 1	0.40	1.00
Disk 2	0.16	0.22
Response times (sec)	1.06	1.97

Models that have a fixed number of requests per class are called *closed models*. The technique we present here to solve closed queuing networks is called Mean Value Analysis (MVA) [7]. It is rather elegant and intuitive. The first efficient technique to solve closed queuing network models is the convolution algorithm due to Buzen [4]. We first discuss MVA for single-class QNs and consider next the multiple-class case. The notation used for closed QN models is similar to the one used for open models with the exception that instead of denoting our variables as a function of the arrival rate, we denote them as a function of the number of requests, n, in the system. So, for instance, $R_i'(n)$ stands for the residence time at queue i when there are n requests in the system.

9.4.1   Single-Class Closed Models

Mean Value Analysis is based on recursively using three equations: the residence time equation, the throughput equation, and the queue length equation. We derive here these equations from first principles.

Consider a closed queuing network with n requests. Let us start by computing the response time, $R_i(n)$, per visit to resource i. As we know, the response time is the sum of the service time S_i, plus the waiting time $W_i(n)$. The waiting time is equal to the time to serve all requests found in the queue by an arriving request. This is equal to the average number, $n_i^a(n)$, of requests found in the queue by an arriving request multiplied by the average service time per request. So,

$$R_i(n) = S_i + W_i(n) = S_i + n_i^a(n) \times S_i = S_i \left[1 + n_i^a(n)\right]. \qquad (9.4.1)$$

An important result, the Arrival Theorem [7], [10], applied to closed QNs, says that the average number of requests seen upon arrival to queue i when there are n requests in the QN is equal to the average number of requests in queue i in a QN with $n - 1$ requests, i.e., with the arriving request to queue i removed from the queuing network. After all, the arriving request cannot find itself in the queue! Thus, from the Arrival Theorem we have that,

$$n_i^a(n) = n_i(n - 1). \qquad (9.4.2)$$

Combining Eqs. (9.4.1) and (9.4.2), we get that

$$R_i(n) = S_i \left[1 + n_i(n - 1)\right]. \qquad (9.4.3)$$

Multiplying both sides of Eq. (9.4.3) by V_i, we get the first equation of MVA:

$$R_i'(n) = D_i \left[1 + n_i(n - 1)\right]. \qquad (9.4.4)$$

If we add the residence time $R_i'(n)$ for all queues i we get the response time $R_0(n)$. Applying Little's Law to the entire QN we MVA's throughput equation:

$$X_0(n) = \frac{n}{R_0(n)} = \frac{n}{\sum_{i=1}^{K} R_i'(n)} \qquad (9.4.5)$$

To obtain the third equation of MVA, the queue length equation, we apply Little's Law and the Forced Flow Law to queue i. Hence,

$$n_i(n) = X_i(n) \times R_i(n) = X_0(n) \times V_i \times R_i(n) = X_0(n) \times R'_i(n). \qquad (9.4.6)$$

We repeat the three equations for single-class MVA in Fig. 9.5.

The residence time for n requests in the QN, $R'_i(n)$, requires that we know the value of the queue length for a QN with one less request, $n_i(n-1)$. But, $n_i(n-1)$ depends on $R'_i(n-1)$, which depends on $n_i(n-2)$, which depends on $R'_i(n-2)$, and so on. This indicates that we need to start with $n = 0$ and work our way up to the value of n we are interested in. Fortunately, the results for $n = 0$ are trivial because when there are no requests in the QN, the queue lengths are zero at all queues. So, $n_i(0) = 0$ for all i's. This allows us to compute $R'_i(1)$ for all i's. With the residence times for $n = 1$ we can use the throughput equation to obtain the throughput for $n = 1$. From the queue length equation we can obtain $n_i(1)$ since we now have $R'_i(1)$ and $X_0(1)$, and so on. This computation is illustrated in Fig. 9.6.

The MVA algorithm is very well suited for an implementation in a spreadsheet. The following example illustrates this.

Example 9.3: A database server receives requests from 50 clients. Each request to the database server requires that five records be read on the average from the server's single disk. The average read time per record is 9 msec. Each database request requires 15 msec of CPU to be processed. What is the throughput of the server, average time spent at the CPU and the disk by each request, average number of requests at the CPU and disk, and the average response time of requests as a

---

Residence time equation:

$$R'_i(n) = \begin{cases} D_i & \text{delay resource} \\[2mm] D_i\,[1 + n_i(n-1)] & \text{queuing resource} \end{cases} \qquad (9.4.7)$$

Throughput equation:

$$X_0(n) = \frac{n}{\sum_{i=1}^{K} R'_i(n)} \qquad (9.4.8)$$

Queue length equation:

$$n_i(n) = X_0(n) \times R'_i(n) \qquad (9.4.9)$$

Figure 9.5. Formulas for single-class MVA with no load-dependent resources.

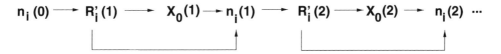

Figure 9.6. Sequence of computations for Mean Value Analysis.

function of the number of requests concurrently being executed at the server?

The service demand at the CPU is 15 msec and at the disk is $V_{disk} \times S_{disk} = 5 \times 9 = 45$ msec. Using the MVA equations, we obtain the values shown in Table 9.2 for the value n of concurrent requests from zero to seven. Note that the fourth column, the average response time R_0, is obtained by adding the two previous columns. For example, for $n = 3$, $R = 20.77 + 117.69 = 138.46$ msec. Column 5, the throughput, is obtained by dividing the value in column 1 by the value in column 4, the response time. For example, for $n = 3$, $X_0 = 3/138.46 = 0.0217$ requests/msec. The residence time for the CPU, R'_{cpu}, for $n = 3$ is computed as $D_{cpu}[1 + n_{cpu}(2)] = 15[1 + 0.385] = 20.77$ msec. As we can see, as the number of requests increases, the throughput saturates at a value of 0.0222 transactions/msec, or 22.2 tps. Figure 9.7 shows how the throughput in transactions per second varies as a function of the number of concurrent requests in the database server. ∎

Bounds for Closed QNs

Example 9.3 showed that the maximum achievable throughput is 22.2 requests/sec. This value happens to be equal to the inverse of the service demand at the disk $(22.2 = 1/0.045)$. The disk is the resource with the largest service demand and therefore is the bottleneck. So, the maximum throughput of the server is limited

Table 9.2. MVA Results for Ex. 9.3

n	R'_{cpu}	R'_{disk}	R_0	X_0	n_{cpu}	n_{disk}
0	0.00	0.00	0.00	0.0000	0.000	0.000
1	15.00	45.00	60.00	0.0167	0.250	0.750
2	18.75	78.75	97.50	0.0205	0.385	1.615
3	20.77	117.69	138.46	0.0217	0.450	2.550
4	21.75	159.75	181.50	0.0220	0.479	3.521
5	22.19	203.43	225.62	0.0222	0.492	4.508
6	22.38	247.87	270.25	0.0222	0.497	5.503
7	22.45	292.64	315.10	0.0222	0.499	6.501

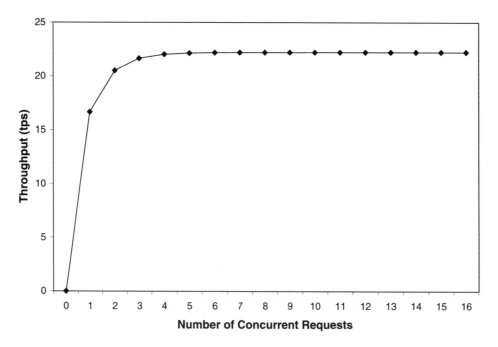

Figure 9.7. Throughput vs. number of request for Ex. 9.3.

by the device that is the bottleneck! Let us examine the bound on throughput in closer detail. Consider first the arguments we made to derive Eq. (9.3.5), which established a bound on the arrival rate of an open system. If we replace the arrival rate λ by the throughput $X_0(n)$, we get

$$X_0(n) \leq \frac{1}{\max_{i=1}^{K} D_i}. \tag{9.4.10}$$

Consider now the throughput equation of MVA and note that $R_i'(n) \geq D_i$ for all queues i. Thus,

$$X_0(n) = \frac{n}{\sum_{i=1}^{K} R_i'(n)} \leq \frac{n}{\sum_{i=1}^{K} D_i}. \tag{9.4.11}$$

Combining Eqs. (9.4.10) and (9.4.11), we get the following bound on the throughput of a closed QN:

$$X_0(n) \leq \min \left[\frac{n}{\sum_{i=1}^{K} D_i}, \frac{1}{\max_{i=1}^{K} D_i} \right]. \tag{9.4.12}$$

The bound given by Eq. (9.4.12) tells us that at the beginning, under light load, the throughput grows linearly at a rate equal to $1/\sum_{i=1}^{K} D_i$ and then flattens at a value equal to $1/\max_{i=1}^{K} D_i$. When the throughput reaches its maximum value, the response time becomes

$$R_0(n) \approx \frac{n}{\text{maximum throughput}} \quad \text{for large } n. \tag{9.4.13}$$

So, the response time grows linearly with n at a rate of $1/\text{maximum throughput} = \max_{i=1}^{K} D_i$. Thus,

$$R_0(n) \approx n \, \max_{i=1}^{K} D_i \quad \text{for large } n. \tag{9.4.14}$$

For very small values of n ($n = 1$), the response time is equal to the sum of the service demands for all resources, since there is no queuing. So, a lower bound for the response time is

$$R_0(n) \geq \max \left[\sum_{i=1}^{K} D_i, n \, \max_{i=1}^{K} D_i \right]. \tag{9.4.15}$$

Example 9.4: Consider the same database server of Ex. 9.3 Imagine the following scenarios: a) More indexes were built into the database to reduce the average number of reads per access from five to 2.5 b) The disk was replaced by a disk 60% faster, i.e., the average service time dropped to 5.63 msec c) The CPU was replaced by a CPU twice as fast, i.e., the service demand at the CPU dropped to 7.5 msec. What are the bounds on throughput for the following combinations of scenarios: a, b, c, a+b, and a+c?

We show on Table 9.3 the service demands at the CPU, disk, the sum of the service demands ($\sum D_i$), and the inverse of the maximum service demand ($1/\max D_i$). As shown in Table 9.3, the maximum throughput, 0.067 requests/msec or 67 requests/sec, is achieved for configuration "a+b". In that configuration, the CPU is the bottleneck, but its service demand is very close to that of the disk. Note that configurations "a" and "a+c" have the same maximum throughput even though configuration "a+c" uses a CPU that is twice as fast. Since the bottleneck in configuration "a" is not the CPU, upgrading the CPU contributes very little to improve performance. In fact, the maximum throughput remains unchanged. The only difference is that in the case of configuration "a+c", the throughput increases slightly faster with n than in configuration "a" ($1/30 = 0.0333$ for configuration "a+c" as opposed to $1/37.50 = 0.0267$ for configuration "a"). ∎

9.4.2 Multiple-Class Closed Models

The equations for multiclass closed models of QNs are very similar to those for single-class. There are some differences in notation though. As in the case of multiclass open QNs, we use the subscript i, r to indicate variables related to queue

Table 9.3. Table for Ex. 9.4

Scenario	D_{cpu} (msec)	D_{disk} (msec)	$\sum D_i$ (msec)	$1/\max D_i$ (req/msec)	Bottleneck
a	15	$2.5 \times 9 = 22.5$	37.50	0.044	disk
b	15	$5 \times 5.63 = 28.15$	43.15	0.036	disk
c	$15/2 = 7.5$	45	52.50	0.022	disk
a+b	15	$2.5 \times 5.63 = 14.08$	29.08	0.067	CPU
a+c	$15/2 = 7.5$	$2.5 \times 9 = 22.5$	30.00	0.044	disk

i and class r. In the case of multiclass QNs, there is a fixed number of requests, N_r, in the system for each class, which we represent conveniently by the load intensity vector $\vec{N} = (N_1, \cdots, N_r, \cdots, N_R)$. We use $\vec{1}_r$ as a notation to indicate a vector where all components are zero except for the rth component, which is equal to one. So, if the number of classes is three, $\vec{1}_2 = (0, 1, 0)$. Thus, $R'_{i,r}(\vec{N})$ stands for the residence time of class r requests at queue i when the number of class 1 requests in the system is N_1, the number of class 2 requests is N_2, $\cdots$, and the number of class R requests is N_R.

Figure 9.8 shows the MVA equations for multiclass QNs. The residence time equation for queuing resources shows a much more complex dependency on queue lengths for different load intensity values than in the single-class case. For example, consider a QN with two classes and assume that $\vec{N} = (2, 4)$. The computation of the residence time at queue i for class 1 for $\vec{N} = (2, 4)$ requires the queue length at queue i for $\vec{N} = (1, 4)$. The computation of the residence time for the same queue for class 2 and for the same load intensity vector $\vec{N} = (2, 4)$ requires the queue length for $\vec{N} = (2, 3)$. So, to compute the residence time values for a load intensity vector $\vec{N} = (2, 4)$, we need the queue length for $\vec{N} = (1, 4)$ and $\vec{N} = (2, 3)$. In general, to compute the residence time values for a load intensity vector $\vec{N} = (N_1, \cdots, N_r, \cdots, N_R)$, we need the queue lengths for the load intensity vectors $\vec{N} - \vec{1}_1, \vec{N} - \vec{1}_2, \cdots, \vec{N} - \vec{1}_r, \cdots, \vec{N} - \vec{1}_R$. Because of these dependencies, the number of computations for multiclass MVA grows very fast with the number of queues and classes.

To avoid this problem, Schweitzer [8] came up with a very nice approximation technique for the term $n_{i,r}(\vec{N} - \vec{1}_m)$ needed to compute $n_i(\vec{N} - \vec{1}_r)$ that appears in the residence time equation. It is based on the assumption that the number of class r requests in each queue increases proportionally with the number of class r customers in the QN. From this observation, it follows that

$$\frac{n_{i,r}(\vec{N} - \vec{1}_m)}{n_{i,r}(\vec{N})} = \frac{N_r - 1}{N_r} \qquad (9.4.20)$$

Residence time equation for class r at queue i:

$$R'_{i,r}(\vec{N}) = \begin{cases} D_{i,r} & \text{delay resource} \\ D_{i,r}[1 + n_i(\vec{N} - \vec{1}_r)] & \text{queuing resource} \end{cases} \tag{9.4.16}$$

Throughput equation for class r:

$$X_{0,r}(\vec{N}) = \frac{N_r}{\displaystyle\sum_{i=1}^{K} R'_{i,r}(\vec{N})} \tag{9.4.17}$$

Queue length equation for class r at queue i:

$$n_{i,r}(\vec{N}) = X_{0,r}(\vec{N}) \times R'_{i,r}(\vec{N}) \tag{9.4.18}$$

Queue length equation for queue i:

$$n_i(\vec{N}) = \sum_{r=1}^{R} n_{i,r}(\vec{N}) \tag{9.4.19}$$

Figure 9.8. Formulas for multiclass MVA with no load-dependent resources.

$$n_{i,r}(\vec{N} - \vec{1}_r) = \frac{N_r - 1}{N_r} \, n_{i,r}(\vec{N}). \tag{9.4.21}$$

So, using this approximation in the example just mentioned, we would get that

$$n_{i,2}((2,3)) = \frac{3}{4} \, n_{i,2}((2,4)). \tag{9.4.22}$$

This method avoids the computational complexity of the exact solution but requires an iterative approach to compute the performance measures. The reason is that $n_{i,r}(\vec{N} - \vec{1}_r)$ depends on $n_{i,r}(\vec{N})$. An easy way to solve this problem is to start with some (guessed) values for the queue lengths and refine these values in an iterative way. A good way to initialize the queue lengths is by equally distributing the number of requests per class over all queues visited by the class. So, if class r visits only K_r of the K queues, the initial value for $n_{i,r}$ would be N_r/K_r. We can now use the residence time equations, the throughput equation, and the queue length equations to obtain better estimates of the queue lengths. These estimates are used to obtain better values of the queue lengths. These iterations continue until the maximum relative error in the queue lengths between successive iterations is less than a tolerance specified by the user.

Figure 9.9 shows the algorithm used to implement approximate MVA for multiple classes. The MS Excel workbook ClosedQN.XLS that accompanies this book

Input Parameters:
$D_{i,r}$, N_r, and ϵ
Initialization
$\vec{N} = (N_1, N_2, \cdots, N_R)$
For $r := 1$ to R do
    For $i := 1$ to K do
        If $D_{i,r} > 0$ then $n_{i,r}^e(\vec{N}) = N_r/K_r$

Iteration Loop
Repeat
    Make the queue length estimates, $n_{i,r}^e(\vec{N})$, be the current queue length values.
    For $r := 1$ to R do
        For $i := 1$ to K do $n_{i,r}(\vec{N}) = n_{i,r}^e(\vec{N})$
    For $r := 1$ to R do
        Begin
            For $i := 1$ to K do
                Begin
                    Compute the queue length at queue i with one less class r request using Schweitzer's approximation.

$$n_i(\vec{N} - \vec{1}_r) = \frac{N_r - 1}{N_r}\, n_{i,r}(\vec{N}) + \sum_{t=1\ \&\ t\neq r}^{R} n_{i,t}(\vec{N})$$

                    Compute the residence time for class r at queue i.

$$R_{i,r}'(\vec{N}) = \begin{cases} D_{i,r} & \text{delay} \\ D_{i,r}\left[1 + n_i(\vec{N} - \vec{1}_r)\right] & \text{queuing} \end{cases}$$

                End;
            Compute the throughput for class r.

$$X_{0,r}(\vec{N}) = \frac{N_r}{\displaystyle\sum_{i=1}^{K} R_{i,r}'(\vec{N})}$$

        End;
    Compute new estimates for queue lengths.
    For $r := 1$ to R do
        For $i := 1$ to K do
            $n_{i,r}^e(\vec{N}) = X_{0,r}(\vec{N}) \times R_{i,r}'(\vec{N})$
Until $\max_{i,r} \left| [n_{i,r}^e(\vec{N}) - n_{i,r}(\vec{N})] / n_{i,r}^e(\vec{N}) \right| < \epsilon$

Figure 9.9. Approximate MVA algorithm for multiple-classes.

implements these equations and provides an easy way to model multiclass closed systems.

Example 9.5: Consider a database server subject to two types of workloads: query and update. The number of concurrent query transactions is five and the number of concurrent updates is two. The server has one CPU and two disks. The service demands at the CPU, disk 1, and disk 2 for queries and updates are given in Table 9.4. What are the response times and throughputs for query and updates? How would these numbers change if the number of concurrent query requests were to increase?

Table 9.5 shows the results obtained by applying the approximate MVA algorithm to this example. It shows that after 11 iterations, the maximum absolute relative error in the queue length values is less than 0.05%. The throughput in transactions per second for both query and update transactions is shown in the last two columns of the table. Note that the initial values of the queue lengths at the CPU, disk 1, and disk 2, are initialized as $5/3 = 1.6667$ for query and $2/3 = 0.6667$ for update transactions (see iteration 1). Table 9.6 shows the response times and throughput values for different values of the number of concurrent query transactions maintaining the number of update transactions fixed at two. These values are also shown as a graph in Fig. 9.10 illustrating that the throughput for query transactions increases at the expense of a decreased throughput of update transactions. Both throughput curves show that the value of the throughput saturates at a maximum and minimum value for query and update transactions, respectively. Figure 9.10 also shows the increase in response time for both types of transactions. Both query and update transactions experience an increase in response time as the number of query transactions increases. However, the rate of increase for update transactions is higher than that for query transactions.   ∎

9.5 Modeling Multiprocessors

The open and closed models described in the previous sections did not account for queues with multiple resources (see Fig. 9.11a). These types of queues are needed to model servers with multiple processors. As we discussed, one way to deal with this problem is to use load-dependent resources. Dealing with load-dependent

Table 9.4. Service Demands in msec for Ex. 9.5 (msec)

	Query	Update
CPU	20	40
Disk 1	80	160
Disk 2	32	48

Table 9.5. Approximate MVA Computations for Ex. 9.5

Ite-ration	Query				Update			
	Queue Length			TPUT	Queue Length			TPUT
	CPU	Disk 1	Disk 2	(tps)	CPU	Disk 1	Disk 2	(tps)
1	1.6667	1.6667	1.6667	12.63	0.6667	0.6667	0.6667	2.69
2	0.7576	3.0303	1.2121	10.18	0.3226	1.2903	0.3871	2.13
3	0.3927	3.8396	0.7678	9.22	0.1633	1.5911	0.2456	1.90
4	0.2725	4.1785	0.5489	8.88	0.1122	1.7152	0.1726	1.82
5	0.2363	4.3055	0.4582	8.77	0.0969	1.7601	0.1430	1.79
6	0.2255	4.3511	0.4235	8.73	0.0922	1.7760	0.1318	1.78
7	0.2221	4.3674	0.4106	8.71	0.0908	1.7816	0.1276	1.78
8	0.2210	4.3732	0.4059	8.71	0.0903	1.7836	0.1261	1.78
9	0.2206	4.3752	0.4042	8.70	0.0902	1.7843	0.1255	1.78
10	0.2205	4.3760	0.4035	8.70	0.0901	1.7846	0.1253	1.78
11	0.2205	4.3762	0.4033	8.70	0.0901	1.7847	0.1252	1.78

resources in closed multiclass models may pose some convergence problems to the iterative MVA solution method we described earlier. We offer here an approximation proposed by Seidmann et al. [9] that avoids convergence problems.

The basic idea is as follows. A queue with m resources and service demand D at each resource (see Fig. 9.11a) should be replaced in the QN model (open or closed) by two queues in tandem (see Fig. 9.11b). The first is a single resource queue with service demand D/m, that is, with a resource that works m times faster than any of the resources in the original multiple resource queue. The second is a delay resource, that is, no queuing takes place. The service demand for the delay resource is equal to $D (m-1)/m$. Under light load, there is virtually no queuing at the first queue and requests spend D/m seconds at this queue and $D (m-1)/m$ at the delay queue. So,

Table 9.6. Response Times (sec) and Throughput (tps) for Ex. 9.5

No. Query	R_{query}	R_{update}	X_{query}	X_{update}
5	0.6	1.1	8.70	1.78
10	1.0	1.9	10.32	1.05
15	1.4	2.7	10.98	0.74
20	1.8	3.5	⋅11.33	0.57
25	2.2	4.3	11.55	0.47
30	2.6	5.1	11.70	0.39
35	3.0	5.9	11.81	0.34

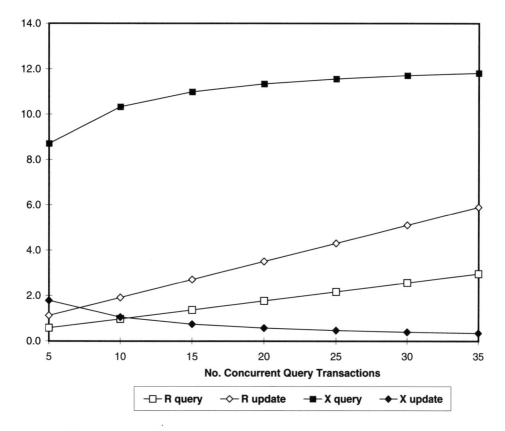

Figure 9.10. Throughput and response time curves for Ex. 9.5.

the total time spent by a request at these two queues is $D/m + D\ (m-1)/m = D$, which is the expected time spent in the original multiple resource queue under light load. Under heavy load, all resources will be busy most of the time and the multiple resource queue behaves as if it had a single resource that works m times faster. In this case, the time spent at the queue in the single resource queue dominates the time spent at the delay server. Thus, the approximation behaves well at both light and heavy loads. Experiments show that at intermediary loads, the error introduced by this approximation is small and increases as the service demand at the multiple resource queue increases with respect to the service demands at other queues. In these experiments, the error is smaller than 5% when the multiple resource queue has a service demand five times bigger than the other queues. The error approaches

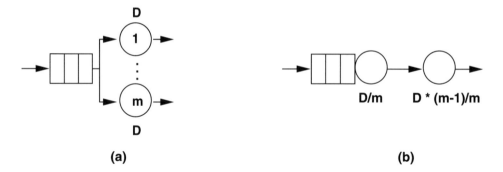

Figure 9.11. Approximation for multiple resource queues.

11% when the service demand at the multiple resource queue is ten times bigger than that of any other queue. The generalization of this approximation for the multiple-class case is straightforward: replace the m-resource queue i with service demands $D_{i,r}$ for class r by two queues in tandem: a single resource queue with service demand $D_{i,r}/m$ and a delay resource with service demand $D_{i,r} (m-1)/m$. One advantage of this approximation is that we can use the methods already presented to deal with multiple resource queues. This approach is implemented in both MS Excel workbooks `OpenQN.XLS` and `ClosedQN.XLS`.

Example 9.6: Consider again Ex. 9.2 where a single processor database server is modeled as an open QN. Consider now that we want to investigate the impact on response time of increasing the number of processors to 2, 3, and 4.

We use the approximation just described and the MS Excel workbook `OpenQN.XLS` to obtain the values of the response time for 2, 3, and 4 processors. As shown in Table 9.7, there is a significant improvement in response time when the number of processors increases from one to two. After that point, the improvement is negligible since the bottleneck shifts to disk 1 for both classes. ■

Table 9.7. Response times for Ex. 9.6 as a Function of Number of Processors

Number of	Response Time (sec)	
Processors	Query	Update
1	1.056	1.972
2	0.689	1.422
3	0.668	1.390
4	0.662	1.382

9.6 An Intranet Model

This section shows how the models presented in the previous sections can be used to model the performance of an intranet. Consider the intranet illustrated in Fig. 9.12 composed of three Ethernet LANs, one 16 Mbps Token Ring LAN, and a 100 Mbps FDDI ring backbone. A Web server that only serves clients within the intranet is located on LAN 3. The only Web-based application considered in this example is corporate training.

The training application is multimedia rich. A typical training session can be characterized by a user visiting an average of 20 text pages. Each page has an average of 2,000 bytes of text and five inline images averaging 50,000 bytes each. Links to higher resolution images, video clips, and audio files are also available. A user would typically request an average of 15 of these objects whose average size is 2,000,000 bytes. Users spend an average of 45 sec looking at the object retrieved before clicking on the next link.

Each LAN has a local NFS file server. Each client generates an average of 0.1 NFS requests/sec. Each request generates a transfer of 8,192 bytes on average through the LAN. We assume, for the sake of this example, that all file servers and

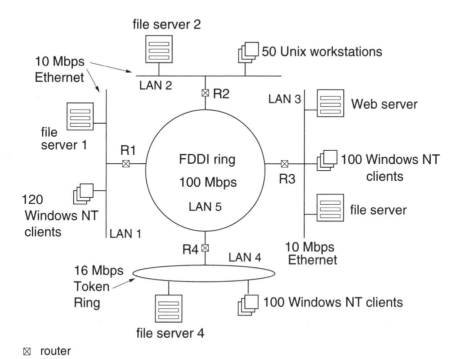

Figure 9.12. Example of an intranet.

the Web server have a single CPU and a single disk. We need to map the intranet depicted in Fig. 9.12 to a queuing network model. For that purpose, we need to take the following steps:

1. decide the goal of the performance modeling effort (e.g., are we interested in predicting the performance of a specific application, the response time of the Web server, or the network utilization?);

2. decide what kind of model, that is, open or closed, will be used;

3. determine the number of classes of the model and what they represent;

4. decide how the system components will be mapped into queues and decide on the type of queues (load-independent, delay, multiple resource queue) are used to represent each component;

5. compute the service demands for each queue and each class;

6. determine the number of requests per class for closed models and the average arrival rate of requests for open models.

For our specific example, we will use a closed model, given that we know the number of clients that generate load to the various servers. The model will be a multiclass model where a class is associated to the tuple (client group, application, server). For example, access to File Server 1 from clients in LAN 1 would be mapped to a class in the QN model. The client groups in LANs 1 through 4 are denoted by CL1, CL2, CL3, CL4, according to the LANs they are in. The applications considered in this example are FS for file server access and TR for training. The four NFS servers are denoted by FS1 through FS4 and the Web server is denoted as WebS. So, there are eight workloads labeled as (CL1, FS, FS1), (CL2, FS, FS2), (CL3, FS, FS3), (CL4, FS, FS4), (CL1, TR, WebS), (CL2, TR, WebS), (CL3, TR, WebS), and (CL4, TR, WebS).

We will use delay resources for the clients to represent the time spent by a request at the client before a new request to the server is made—the think time. Routers and the FDDI ring will also be modeled as delay resources due to the very low latency per packet at the routers and the very high bandwidth of the backbone. All other components, CPUs, disks, and LANS, are modeled as load-independent queues.

The computation of service demands is essentially done by using the $D_{i,r} = V_{i,r} \times S_{i,r}$ relationship for each class and queue. More specifically, we use the formulas developed in Chap. 3 for disk service times and network service times to compute the service demands at the disks and different networks. In fact, we used the MS Excel workbook `ServTime.XLS` that accompanies this book, which implements these service time formulas.

Some explanations are in order. For the Web Server access, we computed an average request size by considering that a typical training session generates 20

requests for text documents, 100 requests to inline images (= 20 text pages ×
5 inlines/text page), and 15 requests to other multimedia objects. So, the total
number of requests per training session is 135, distributed as 15% (= 20/135) for
text documents, 74% (= 100/135) for inlines, and 11% (= 15/135) for multimedia
objects. The average size of a document retrieved per HTTP request is calculated
as a function of the types of documents, their size, and frequency. Therefore, the
average document size is $0.15 \times 2,000 + 0.74 \times 50,000 + 0.11 \times 2,000,000 = 257,300$
bytes.

To compute disk service demands we assumed that accesses to text pages are
random requests and access to larger objects are sequential requests. The run
length for each sequential request is equal to the number of blocks to be read. In
this numerical example, we assumed all disks to be identical, with the following
characteristics: 9-msec average seek time, disk speed of 7,200 RPM, transfer rate
of 20 MB/sec, disk controller time of 0.1 msec, and block size of 2,048 bytes. Other
assumptions include 1 msec latency per packet at the routers, and 1-msec processing
time per HTTP request and per NFS request.

With these parameters and with the help of the `ServTime.XLS` workbook, we
obtained the service demands for each of the 23 queues (five networks, four client
groups, five CPUs, five disks, and four routers) and eight classes. The number of
requests per class is equal to the number of clients in the client group associated with
each class. So, the number of requests in class 1 is 120. Using the `ClosedQN.XLS`
MS Excel workbook, we solve the closed QN network and obtain the results shown
in Table 9.8.

If we add the throughput of all Web-based related classes, we get the throughput
of the Web server as 5.39 HTTP requests/sec. Considering a 24-hour day, this would
translate into 465,696 requests/day. If we analyze in more detail the outputs of the
solver in the `ClosedQN.XLS` workbook, we see that the bottleneck is LAN 3. In
fact, its utilization is 99.7%, the bulk of it attributed to the four Web classes. This

Table 9.8. Response Times and Throughputs for Intranet Model

Class	Throughput (req/sec)	Response Time (sec)
(CL1, FS, FS1)	11.35	0.57
(CL2, FS, FS2)	4.88	0.24
(CL3, FS, FS3)	9.27	0.80
(CL4, FS, FS4)	9.64	0.38
(CL1, TR, WebS)	1.63	28.51
(CL2, TR, WebS)	0.74	22.88
(CL3, TR, WebS)	1.57	18.59
(CL4, TR, WebS)	1.45	23.81

indicates that if we need to improve the throughput of the Web server to support more clients, we need to upgrade LAN 3 to a faster network, perhaps a 100-Mbps Ethernet.

9.7 Concluding Remarks

This chapter introduced powerful techniques to analyze the performance of C/S systems and intranets. These techniques are based on open and queuing network models. Some of the important results in the theory of queuing networks are worth noting here. One of them is the BCMP theorem [2], developed by Baskett, Chandy, Muntz, and Palacios, that specifies the combination of service time distributions and scheduling disciplines that yield multiclass product-form queuing networks with any combination of open and closed classes. Buzen developed the Convolution Algorithm—the first computationally efficient method to solve QNs [4]. Sevcik and Mitrani [10] developed the arrival theorem and Reiser and Lavenberg [7] developed Mean Value Analysis, which is based on the arrival theorem. Several approximations to QNs for the non product-form case were developed (see [1] and [5]).

The algorithms discussed here are backed by the MS Excel `OpenQN.XLS` and `ClosedQN.XLS` workbooks that accompany this book. They solve open and closed queuing networks, respectively, and provide results, such as utilization, residence times, queue lengths, per class and per device, as well as response times and throughputs per class. The next chapter discusses specific issues of Web performance modeling, such as modeling of burstiness, heavy-tailed distributions, and sizing aspects from the client and server sides.

BIBLIOGRAPHY

[1] S. AGRAWAL, *Metamodeling: A Study of Approximations in Queuing Models.* Cambridge, MA: MIT Press, 1985.

[2] F. BASKETT, K. CHANDY, R. MUNTZ, and F. PALACIOS, Open, closed, and mixed networks of queues with different classes of customers, *J. ACM*, vol. 22, no. 2, Apr. 1975.

[3] J. P. BUZEN, Operational analysis: an alternative to stochastic modeling, in *Performance of Computer Installations.* North Holland, June 1978, pp. 175–194.

[4] J. P. BUZEN, Computational algorithms for closed queuing networks with exponential servers, *Commun. ACM*, vol. 16, vo. 9, Sept. 1973.

[5] E. LAZOWSKA, J. ZAHORJAN, S. GRAHAM, and K. SEVCIK, *Quantitative System Performance: Computer System Analysis Using Queueing Network Models.* Upper Saddle River, NJ: Prentice Hall, 1984.

[6] D. A. MENASCÉ, V. A. F. ALMEIDA, and L. W. DOWDY, *Capacity Planning and Performance Modeling: From Mainframes to Client-Server Systems.* Upper Saddle River, NJ: Prentice Hall, 1994.

[7] M. REISER and S. LAVENBERG, Mean-value analysis of closed multi-chain queuing networks, *J. ACM*, vol. 27, no. 2, 1980.

[8] P. SCHWEITZER, Approximate analysis of multiclass closed network of queues, *Proc. Int. Conf. Stochastic Cont. Optimization*, Amsterdam, 1979.

[9] A. SEIDMANN, P. SCHWEITZER, and S. SHALEV-OREN, Computerized closed queueing network models of flexible manufacturing systems, *Large Scale Syst. J.*, North-Holland, vol. 12, pp. 91–107, 1987.

[10] K. SEVCIK and I. MITRANI, The distribution of queuing network states at input and output instants, *J. ACM*, vol. 28, no. 2, Apr. 1981.

Chapter 10

WEB PERFORMANCE MODELING

10.1 Introduction

In Chaps. 8 and 9 we discussed performance models that can be applied in general to client/server systems. Web server access is a special case of client/server interaction with very characteristic aspects such as the burstiness of Web traffic and heavy-tail distributions of file sizes as discussed in Chaps. 4 and 6. This chapter shows how these elements can be accounted for in performance models for the Web. It also shows how the performance models discussed in the two previous chapters can be specialized to take care of Web performance modeling.

10.2 Incorporating New Phenomena

The WWW workload exhibits two novel features: *burstiness* and *heavy tails*, introduced in Chap. 4. In this section, we show how to represent these features in the workload specification. In other words, we illustrate how we can modify the model input parameters to reflect these features. In particular, we show how to inflate service demands to account for burstiness and how classes of requests in QN models can be used to represent heavy tails.

10.2.1 Burstiness Modeling

In this section we offer an operational treatment [3] of the burstiness phenomenon and show how it can be reflected into a performance model. A characteristic of this approach is that all quantities are based on measured or known data. Our starting point is the HTTP LOG that records information about every access to a Web server.

   As pointed out in [2], bursts of traffic cause increased congestion on system resources. To account for this increase in congestion we modify the service demand at the bottleneck component using a *burstiness factor* that can be derived by analyzing the HTTP LOG as explained in what follows.

Defining a Burstiness Factor

Consider an HTTP LOG composed of L requests to a Web server. Let

- $\mathcal{T}$: time interval during which the requests of the HTTP LOG arrive at the Web server

- λ: average arrival rate of requests observed in the HTTP LOG, given by

$$\lambda \; = \; \frac{L}{\mathcal{T}}. \tag{10.2.1}$$

Consider now that the time interval $\mathcal{T}$ is divided into n equal subintervals of duration $\mathcal{T}/n$ called *epochs*. Let

- Arr (k): number of HTTP requests that arrive in epoch k

- λ_k: arrival rate of requests during epoch k given by

$$\lambda_k \; = \; \frac{\text{Arr } (k)}{(\mathcal{T}/n)} = \frac{n \times \text{Arr } (k)}{\mathcal{T}} \tag{10.2.2}$$

- Arr^+: total number of HTTP requests that arrive in epochs in which the epoch arrival rate λ_k exceeds the average arrival rate λ observed in the HTTP LOG. So,

$$\text{Arr}^+ = \sum_{\forall \; k \; \text{s.t.} \; \lambda_k > \lambda} \text{Arr } (k) \tag{10.2.3}$$

- Arr^-: total number of HTTP requests that arrive in epochs where the epoch arrival rate λ_k does not exceed the average arrival rate λ observed in the HTTP LOG. So,

$$\text{Arr}^- = \sum_{\forall \; k \; \text{s.t.} \; \lambda_k \leq \lambda} \text{Arr } (k) \tag{10.2.4}$$

Clearly, the number of requests in the HTTP LOG is equal to the number of requests in epochs with arrival rates exceeding the LOG average arrival rate plus the number of requests in epochs with arrival rates below or equal to the HTTP LOG average arrival rate. Thus,

$$L \; = \; \text{Arr}^+ \; + \; \text{Arr}^-. \tag{10.2.5}$$

We now review the definition of the burstiness parameter b given in Chap. 6 in light of the above operational definitions. The *burstiness parameter* b is defined as the fraction of time during which the epoch arrival rate exceeds the average arrival rate of the LOG. Hence,

$$b = \frac{\text{Number of epochs for which } \lambda_k > \lambda}{n}. \tag{10.2.6}$$

Note that if traffic is not bursty, i.e., is uniformly distributed over all epochs, $Arr(k) = L/n$, $\lambda_k = (L/n)/(\mathcal{T}/n) = L/\mathcal{T} = \lambda$ for all $k = 1, \cdots, n$. So, there are no epochs in which $\lambda_k > \lambda$. Thus, $b = 0$. We can now define the *above-average* arrival rate, λ^+, for the HTTP LOG as

$$\lambda^+ = \frac{\mathrm{Arr}^+}{b \times \mathcal{T}}. \tag{10.2.7}$$

We now redefine parameter a defined in Chap. 6 in light of the operational definitions above as the ratio between the above-average arrival rate and the average arrival rate computed from the LOG over the entire period $\mathcal{T}$. Thus,

$$a = \lambda^+/\lambda = [\mathrm{Arr}^+/(b \times \mathcal{T})]/(L/\mathcal{T}) = \mathrm{Arr}^+/(b \times L). \tag{10.2.8}$$

Since a and b are related through Eq. (10.2.8), we will use only b as an indicator of burstiness. The C program `burst.c` contained in the disk that accompanies the book can be used to compute the burstiness parameters a and b of an HTTP LOG (see Appendix B for a description of the program).

Example 10.1: Consider that 19 get requests are logged at a Web server at instants 1, 3, 3.5, 3.8, 6, 6.3, 6.8, 7.0, 10, 12, 12.2, 12.3, 12.5, 12.8, 15, 20, 30, 30.2, and 30.7 during an interval $\mathcal{T}$ of duration equal to 31 sec. Compute the burstiness parameter b for the LOG, considering that the interval $\mathcal{T}$ is divided into n subintervals, for values of n ranging from 21 to 30.

We show the computations for $n = 21$ and then show a plot illustrating the values of b for all values of n. Each epoch has duration equal to $\mathcal{T}/n = 31/21 = 1.48$ sec. The average arrival rate for the entire LOG is $\lambda = 19/31 = 0.613$ requests/sec. The number of arrivals in each of the 21 epochs are 1, 0, 3, 0, 4, 0, 1, 0, 4, 0, 1, 0, 0, 1, 0, 0, 0, 0, 0, 0, and 4. The arrival rate in the first epoch, $\lambda_1 = 1/1.48 = 0.676$ requests/sec, exceeds the average arrival rate of 0.613 requests/sec for the LOG. In eight of the 21 epochs, the epoch arrival rate λ_k exceeds the HTTP LOG arrival rate λ. So, the burstiness factor is $b = 8/21 = 0.381$. Figure 10.1 shows a graph of the burstiness factor for values of n ranging from 21 to 30. As it can be seen in the figure, the value of b oscillates around an average value of 0.39 with a maximum deviation around the mean equal to 13%. This is an expected behavior if the value of n is such that the epoch duration is close to the duration of the bursts. In this example, all requests arrive during epochs in which $\lambda_k > \lambda$. So, $\mathrm{Arr}^+ = L$ and $a = 1/b = 1/0.381 = 2.625$. ∎

Adjusting Service Demands to Burstiness

We present in this section an approximation that allows one to capture the effect of burstiness on the performance of Web servers. As shown in [2], the maximum throughput of a Web server decreases as the burstiness factor increases. We know from Chap. 9 that the maximum throughput is equal to the inverse of the maximum service demand or the service demand of the bottleneck resource. So, to account

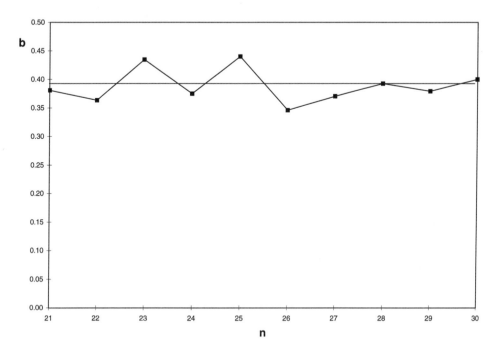

Figure 10.1. Burstiness factor vs. number of epochs.

for the burstiness effect, we will write the service demand, D, of the bottleneck resource as

$$D = D_f + \alpha \times b \qquad (10.2.9)$$

where D_f is the portion of the service demand that does not depend on burstiness and $\alpha \times b$, for $\alpha > 0$ is a term proportional to the burstiness factor b, used to inflate the service demand of the bottleneck component according to the burstiness of the arrival stream. The constant α can be determined using the procedure given below.

1. Consider a measurement interval $\mathcal{T}$ and let $\mathcal{L}$ be the HTTP LOG collected during this interval. Divide the interval into two subintervals of duration $\mathcal{T}/2$ each and let $\mathcal{L}_1$ and $\mathcal{L}_2$ be the HTTP LOGs corresponding to these two intervals.

2. During the interval $\mathcal{T}$, measure the utilization of all resources (e.g., CPU, disks, and communication links) of the Web server, the throughput, and the burstiness factor for each of the subintervals. Let U_1 and U_2 be the utilization

of the resource that is the bottleneck throughout both subintervals, respectively. The throughputs, X_0^1 and X_0^2 of subintervals 1 and 2, are computed from the two sub-LOGs $\mathcal{L}_1$ and $\mathcal{L}_2$ by dividing the number of successful requests in each sub-LOG by $\mathcal{T}/2$, the duration of each subinterval. Let b_1 and b_2 be the values of the burstiness factors computed for sub-LOGs $\mathcal{L}_1$ and $\mathcal{L}_2$ using the aforementioned approach.

3. For each of the two subintervals, we can use the Service Demand Law to write the service demand at the bottleneck resource as the ratio between its utilization and the system throughput during each subinterval. Thus,

$$U_1/X_0^1 = D_f + \alpha \times b_1 \tag{10.2.10}$$

and

$$U_2/X_0^2 = D_f + \alpha \times b_2. \tag{10.2.11}$$

We are assuming that the fixed service demand D_f is a function of the characteristics of the requests that arrive at the Web server and that the nature of the requests is fairly homogeneous during the entire period $\mathcal{T}$. The value of the constant α can be easily obtained by subtracting Eq. (10.2.11) from Eq. (10.2.10) and solving for α. Hence,

$$\alpha = \frac{U_1/X_0^1 - U_2/X_2^0}{b_1 - b_2}. \tag{10.2.12}$$

Example 10.2: Consider the HTTP LOG of Ex. 10.1. During the 31 sec in which the 19 HTTP requests arrived, the CPU was found to be the bottleneck component. What is the burstiness adjustment that should be applied to the CPU service demand to account for the effect of burstiness on the performance of the Web server?

The number of HTTP requests during each of the 15.5-sec subintervals is 14 and 5, respectively. Thus, the throughputs in each subinterval are $X_0^1 = 14/15.5 = 0.903$ requests/sec and $X_0^2 = 5/15.5 = 0.323$ requests/sec. The measured utilization of the CPU in each subinterval was 0.18 and 0.06, respectively. If we apply the procedure described in Sec. 10.2.1 to the two subintervals, we obtain $b_1 = 0.273$ and $b_2 = 0.182$, respectively. Thus,

$$\alpha = \frac{0.18/0.903 - 0.06/0.323}{0.273 - 0.182} = 0.149. \tag{10.2.13}$$

So, if we consider the entire HTTP LOG, the adjustment factor to the CPU service demand would be $\alpha \times b = 0.149 \times 0.381 = 0.057$ sec. ■

Figure 10.2 shows how the maximum system throughput varies with the burstiness factor. The figure assumes that the CPU is the bottleneck, that its fixed

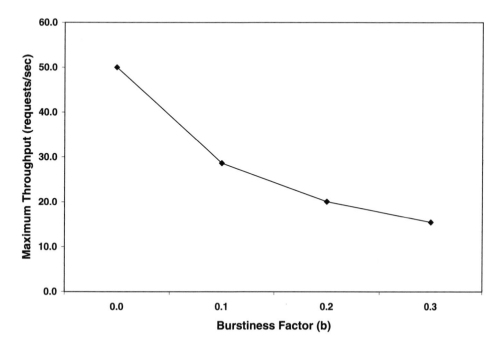

Figure 10.2. Maximum throughput vs. burstiness factor.

service demand D_f is 0.02 sec, and α has the value computed in Ex. 10.2, i.e., 0.149. Remember that the maximum system throughput is the inverse of the maximum service demand. As shown in the figure, the maximum throughput falls from 50 HTTP requests/sec to 15.5 requests/sec as we go from a nonbursty workload to a workload with a burstiness factor of 0.3.

10.2.2   Accounting for Heavy Tails in the Model

As discussed in Chaps. 4 and 6, Web traffic exhibits file-size distributions that decrease with a power tail [5]. In practical terms, this implies that we should expect to see a large percentage of HTTP requests for small documents and a small percentage of requests to documents that are one or two orders of magnitude larger than the small documents. Due to large variability of the size of documents, average results for the whole population of requests would have very little statistical meaning. Categorizing the requests into a number of classes, defined by ranges of document sizes, improves the accuracy and significance of the performance metrics.

The models we offer to address this situation are the multiclass queuing network models we discussed in Chap. 9. Different classes are associated with requests for documents of different sizes. The workload intensity parameters (e.g., arrival rates) per class reflect the percentage of requests for each file size.

Example 10.3: The HTTP LOG of a Web server was analyzed during 1 hour. A total of 21,600 requests were successfully processed during this interval. Table 10.1 shows the distribution of document sizes and the percent of requests in each category.

One can then build a multiclass QN model to represent the Web server. There are five classes in the model, each corresponding to the five file size ranges. The arrival rate for each class r is a fraction of the overall arrival rate $\lambda = 21,600/3,600 = 6$ requests/sec. So, $\lambda_1 = 6 \times 0.25 = 1.5$ requests/sec, $\lambda_2 = 6 \times 0.40 = 2.4$ requests/sec, $\lambda_3 = 6 \times 0.20 = 1.2$ requests/sec, $\lambda_4 = 6 \times 0.10 = 0.6$ requests/sec, and $\lambda_5 = 6 \times 0.05 = 0.3$ requests/sec. ∎

10.3   Client-Side Models

We consider here the performance perceived by a client browser and discuss models that can be used to answer some of the most important capacity and performance questions from the client's viewpoint such as

1. What should be the bandwidth of the link to the ISP to support Web traffic with acceptable performance?

2. What should be the bandwidth of the LAN to support Web traffic with acceptable performance?

3. Should I use a cache proxy server?

10.3.1   No Cache Proxy Server Case

The first environment discussed consists of a collection of M client workstations running Web browsers. These client workstations are connected to a LAN, which

Table 10.1. File Size Distributions for Ex. 10.3

Class	File Size Range	Percent of Requests
1	size < 5 KB	25
2	5 KB ≤ size < 50 KB	40
3	50 KB ≤ size < 100 KB	20
4	100 KB ≤ size < 500 KB	10
5	size ≥ 500 KB	5

is connected through a router to the Internet through an Internet Service Provider
(ISP) (see Fig. 10.3a).

The performance of a remote Web server, as perceived by a user, depends on
various factors including:

- performance characteristics of the client platform

- bandwidth of the LAN that connects the clients to the router

- bandwidth of the link that connects the router to the ISP

- router performance characteristics

- delays imposed by the Internet

- delays to retrieve the desired documents from the remote Web server

- delays at the ISP to which the client is connected

- workload characteristics of the requests generated by the clients

The Performance Model

Figure 10.4a shows the QN model that corresponds to Fig. 10.3a. It is a closed QN
model with the following six queues. Queue 1 is a delay queue that represents the

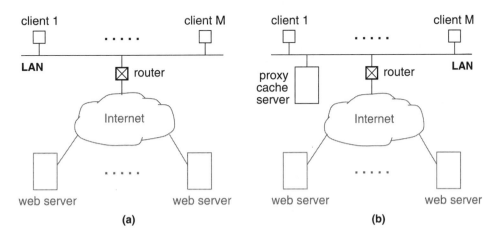

Figure 10.3. (a) Client access to Web servers without cache proxy server. (b)
Client access to Web servers with cache proxy server.

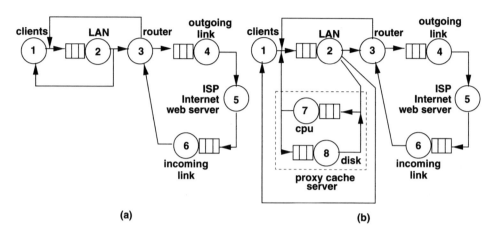

Figure 10.4. (a) Client-side QN model without cache proxy server. (b) Client-side QN model with cache proxy server.

set of clients. The time spent at this queue is the client think time which represents the time spent by a client between when it starts to receive a document until it requests a new document. Queue 2 is a load-independent queue that represents the LAN. The router is represented by a delay queue due to its relatively small latency when compared with the other delays involved. The link that connects the router to the ISP is a full-duplex link. This means that it can receive and transmit at the same time at the same bandwidth. Thus, we need to model the outgoing and incoming links separately as two separate load-independent queues—queues 4 and 6, respectively. Finally, the delays at the ISP, its link to the Internet, the Internet itself, and the remote servers, are represented by delay queue 5. The entities that flow through the QN model are HTTP requests.

We give now the general parameters to be considered and show how the service demands for the QN model can be computed.

- LANBandwidth: LAN bandwidth in megabits per second

- MaxPDU: maximum PDU size for the LAN's network layer protocol in bytes

- FrameOvhd: frame overhead of the LAN's link layer protocol, in bytes

- RouterLatency: router latency in microseconds per packet

- LinkBandwidth: bandwidth in kilobits per second of the connection to the ISP

- InternetDelayRTT: Internet average round trip time, in milliseconds

- InternetDataRate: Internet data transfer rate, in kilobytes per second

- BrowserRate: rate in HTTP operations/sec at which a browser requests a new document when the user is in think mode; the inverse of the user's think time

- NumberClients: number of client workstations

- PercentActive: percent of client workstations actively using the Web

- AvgSizeHTTPRequest: average size of the HTTP request sent by the browser to the server, in bytes

Besides the parameters listed above, we need to know the distribution of the sizes of the documents requested by the browsers. Let the document sizes be divided into R categories and consider the two following additional parameters:

- DocumentSize$_r$: average document size, in kilobytes, of category r $(r = 1, \cdots, R)$ documents

- PercentSize$_r$: percent of documents requested that are in category r $(r = 1, \cdots, R)$

The average document size, in kilobytes, over all requests issued by a client is given by

$$\text{DocumentSize} = \sum_{r=1}^{R} \text{DocumentSize}_r \times \text{PercentSize}_r. \qquad (10.3.1)$$

Computing Service Demands

We now compute all service demands, in seconds, based on the parameters given above. The service demand, D_{cl}, at queue 1 per HTTP request is given by

$$D_{\text{cl}} = 1/\text{BrowserRate}. \qquad (10.3.2)$$

To compute the service demand per request at the LAN, D_{LAN}, we need to remember that HTTP requests use TCP, and therefore we need to account for the overhead incurred by TCP and the underlying protocols, IP and the LAN link-level protocol, on top of which TCP is located. We use the service times equations given in Sec. 3.3.2, which we adapt to our case. Let NetworkTime (m) denote the LAN service time for a message m bytes long. Using the equations in Sec. 3.3.2, we have that

$$\text{NetworkTime} (m) = \frac{8 \times [m + \text{Overhead} (m)]}{10^6 \times \text{LANBandwidth}} \qquad (10.3.3)$$

where the TCP plus IP overhead due to sending an m-bytes long message is

$$\text{Overhead (m)} = \text{TCPOvhd} + \text{NDatagrams }(m) \times (\text{IPOvhd} + \text{FrameOvhd})$$
$$= 20 + \text{NDatagrams }(m) \times (20 + \text{FrameOvhd}) \qquad (10.3.4)$$

and the number of datagrams needed to send an m-bytes long message is

$$\text{NDatagrams }(m) = \left\lceil \frac{m + \text{TCPOvhd}}{\text{MaxPDU} - \text{IPOvhd}} \right\rceil$$
$$= \left\lceil \frac{m + 20}{\text{MaxPDU} - 20} \right\rceil. \qquad (10.3.5)$$

Thus, the LAN service demand can be computed by adding the LAN service time for the request from the browser to the server plus the service time from the server to the browser:

$$D_{\text{LAN}} = \text{NetworkTime (AvgSizeHTTPRequest)} +$$
$$\text{NetworkTime }(1,024 \times \text{DocumentSize}). \qquad (10.3.6)$$

The service demand at the router, D_{router}, is

$$D_{\text{router}} = [\text{NDatagrams }(1,024 \times \text{DocumentSize}) + 7] \times \text{RouterLatency} \times 10^{-6}. \qquad (10.3.7)$$

The term "7" in Eq. (10.3.7) accounts for three synchronization segments needed to establish a TCP connection, one TCP data segment to carry the HTTP request, and three TCP synchronization segments to close the connection [4]. The service demand per request, D_{OutL}, at the outgoing link is

$$D_{\text{OutL}} = \frac{8 \times [\text{AvgSizeHTTPRequest} + 5 \times (\text{TCPOvhd} + \text{IPOvhd})]}{1,024 \times \text{LinkBandwidth}}$$
$$= \frac{8 \times [\text{AvgSizeHTTPRequest} + 5 \times (20 + 20)]}{1,024 \times \text{LinkBandwidth}}. \qquad (10.3.8)$$

The term "5" that multiplies the TCP plus IP overhead in Eq. (10.3.8) is due to the fact that two TCP synchronization segments flow through the outgoing link to open a TCP connection, two synchronization segments close the connection, and one data segment carries the HTTP request itself.

The service demand D_{Int} at the Internet is the sum of the round trip time to establish the TCP connection with the server, plus 1/2 round trip time to send the HTTP request to the server, plus the data transfer delay to send the document from the server to the client. So,

$$D_{\text{Int}} = 1.5 \times \text{InternetDelayRTT}/1,000 + \text{DocumentSize}/\text{InternetDataRate}. \qquad (10.3.9)$$

Finally, the service demand per request, D_{InL}, at the incoming link is computed as

$$D_{\text{InL}} = \frac{8 \times (1,024 \times \text{DocumentSize} + \text{LinkOvhd})}{1,024 \times \text{LinkBandwidth}} \qquad (10.3.10)$$

where the TCP plus IP overhead, in bytes, in the incoming link is

$$\text{LinkOvhd} = \left\lceil \frac{1,024 \times \text{DocumentSize}}{65,535} \right\rceil \times (\text{TCPOvhd} + \text{IPOvhd})$$

$$= \left\lceil \frac{1,024 \times \text{DocumentSize}}{65,535} \right\rceil \times 40. \qquad (10.3.11)$$

The value 65,535 in the denominator is the maximum PDU size in bytes for TCP.

We now have all service demands for the QN model. The number of requests in the system is equal to NumberClients × PercentActive.

The following example shows how this model can be used to answer some useful capacity planning questions from the client side.

Example 10.4: A site has 150 PCs connected to an Ethernet LAN, which is connected to the Internet through a router that has a latency of 50 μsec/packet. The connection to the Internet is a 56-Kbps link. Ten percent of the clients are actively browsing the Web at any given time, and each user generates requests to external Web servers at an average rate of 0.3 requests/sec when they are in the thinking state. This includes requests to inline documents. The documents requested from clients were classified into four categories with average size and frequency of occurrence given by: 0.8 KB (35%), 5.5 KB (50%), 80 KB (14%), and 800 KB (1%). The average Internet round trip time to the sites most used by the clients in the site was measured to be 100 msec using the ping command (typical values for this parameter range from 89 to 161 msec [9]). The effective Internet transfer rate from these same remote servers was observed to be 20 KB/sec on average (typical values for this parameter range from 0.1 to 1 Mbps [9]). The average size of the HTTP requests sent by a browser to the remote servers is 100 bytes. What is the throughput in requests/sec for all clients, what is the bottleneck, and what is the average response time seen by each user?

The values of the input parameters are:

- LANBandwidth = 10 Mbps

- FrameOvhd = 18 bytes

- RouterLatency = 50 μsec/packet

- LinkBandwidth = 56 Kbps

- InternetDelayRTT = 100 msec

- InternetDataRate = 20 KB/sec

- BrowserRate = 0.3 requests/sec

- NumberClients = 150

- PercentActive = 0.1

- AvgSizeHTTPRequest = 100 bytes

The average document size is given by

$$\text{DocumentSize} = 0.8 \times 0.35 + 5.5 \times 0.5 + 0.14 \times 80 + 0.01 \times 800 = 22.23 \text{ KB.}$$

We can now compute the service demands for the QN model of Fig. 10.4a using the equations derived in this section:

$$
\begin{aligned}
D_{\text{cl}} &= 1/\text{BrowserRate} = 1/0.3 = 3.333 \text{ sec} \\
D_{\text{LAN}} &= \text{NetworkTime}\,(100) + \\
&\quad \text{NetworkTime}\,(22.23 \times 1{,}024) = 0.01884 \text{ sec} \\
D_{\text{router}} &= [\text{NDatagrams}\,(22.23 \times 1{,}024) + 7] \times 50 \times 10^{-6} = 0.00115 \text{ sec} \\
D_{\text{OutL}} &= \frac{[100 \ + \ 5 \ \times \ (20 + 20)] \times 8}{56 \times 1{,}024} = 0.04185 \text{ sec} \\
D_{\text{Int}} &= 1.5 \ \times \ 100/1{,}000 + 22.23/20 = 1.2615 \text{ sec} \\
D_{\text{InL}} &= \frac{(22.23 \times 1{,}024 + \lceil (22.23 \times 1{,}024)/65{,}535 \rceil \times 40) \times 8}{56 \times 1{,}024} = 3.18129 \text{ sec.}
\end{aligned}
$$

We now use the MS Excel `ClosedQN.XLS` workbook, which implements the performance model of Chap. 9, to solve the resulting QN model, using $150 \times 0.1 = 15$ requests as the effective number of clients. The results are shown in Table 10.2.

As shown in Table 10.2, the bottleneck is the link to the Internet. This resource is almost 100% utilized and limits the throughput. Most of the response time,

Table 10.2. Results for Ex. 10.4

	Residence Times (sec)	Utilizations (%)
LAN	0.019	0.59
Router	0.001	0.04
Outgoing Link	0.042	1.31
Incoming Link	43.403	99.29
Throughput: 0.3121 requests/sec		
Throughput: 55.5 Kbps		
Response Time: 44.7 sec		

43.4/44.7 = 97%, is spent in the incoming link. If we want to improve performance, i.e., increase the throughput and decrease the response time, we have two alternatives: use a faster connection to the Internet, which is more expensive, or decrease the demand on the incoming link by using a cache proxy server as discussed in the next subsection.   ■

The MS Excel workbook `WebModels.XLS` implements the equations to compute the service demands for the client-side under the no-proxy and proxy case.

10.3.2 Using a Cache Proxy Server

Figure 10.4b shows an environment similar to the one we analyzed in the previous section with the addition of a cache proxy server (see Chap. 4). Requests from clients go first to the cache proxy server, which holds copies of the most sought-after documents. If the requested document is in the cache, a *cache hit* is said to occur. In this case, the document is returned to the client; otherwise, the proxy server acts as a client, makes a connection to the originating Web server, requests the document, stores it into its cache, and then returns it to the client that requested it in the first place. Accessing documents that are found in the proxy server is generally much faster than accessing them from their originating servers. However, a document not found on the proxy server takes longer to retrieve because of the proxy server overhead. According to [15], a proxy server can speed up document access between two and ten times on cache hits and slow down document retrieval time by a factor of two on cache misses.

A QN model corresponding to the environment depicted in Fig. 10.3b is shown in Fig. 10.4b. The cache proxy server is modeled as having one CPU (queue 7) and one disk (queue 8). Extending the model to a multiprocessor cache server with multiple disks would be straightforward.

To model this situation, we need to add a few more parameters besides the ones discussed in Sec. 10.3.1.

- p_{hit}: fraction of requests that can be served from the proxy server's cache (typical values for p_{hit} range from 0.2 to 0.5 [13], [15])

- HitCPUTime: CPU time, in seconds, needed to process the request at the cache proxy server and return the document to the server when the document is found in the cache

- MissCPUTime: CPU time, in seconds, needed to process a request at the cache proxy server, request the document from the originating server, store it into the cache, run a cache replacement algorithm, if needed, and send the document to the client that originally requested it

- DiskTime: disk time per kilobyte at the cache proxy server, in milliseconds

The expressions for service demands derived in Sec. 10.3.1 have to be revised for the

LAN, router, Internet, and outgoing and incoming links. We use the superscript p to indicate service demands in the proxy server case.

The service demand at the LAN, D^p_{LAN}, is equal to the value computed in the no-proxy case, D_{LAN}, when the document is found in the proxy server. However, if there is a cache miss, the request has to flow through the LAN again to the router to be sent to the originating server. The document coming from the originating server will traverse the LAN twice: one from the router to the cache proxy server and the other from the cache proxy server to the client. Thus,

$$D^p_{\text{LAN}} = p_{\text{hit}} \times D_{\text{LAN}} + (1 - p_{\text{hit}}) \times 2 \times D_{\text{LAN}} = (2 - p_{\text{hit}}) \times D_{\text{LAN}}. \qquad (10.3.12)$$

Traffic will only go through the router, outgoing link, Internet, and incoming link when the document is not found in the cache proxy server. In this case, the service demand at these various queues is the same as in the no-proxy case. So,

$$D^p_{\text{router}} = (1 - p_{\text{hit}}) \times D_{\text{router}} \qquad (10.3.13)$$
$$D^p_{\text{OutL}} = (1 - p_{\text{hit}}) \times D_{\text{OutL}} \qquad (10.3.14)$$
$$D^p_{\text{Int}} = (1 - p_{\text{hit}}) \times D_{\text{Int}} \qquad (10.3.15)$$
$$D^p_{\text{InL}} = (1 - p_{\text{hit}}) \times D_{\text{InL}} \qquad (10.3.16)$$

The service demand at the CPU is given by

$$D^p_{\text{CPU}} = p_{\text{hit}} \times \text{HitCPUTime} + (1 - p_{\text{hit}}) \times \text{MissCPUTime}. \qquad (10.3.17)$$

The disk is used both in the case of cache hits and misses. In the first case, to retrieve the document from the cache and in the second, to store the document retrieved from a remote Web server into the cache. The average service demand, in seconds, at the disk is then

$$D^p_{\text{disk}} = \text{DiskTime} \times \text{DocumentSize}/1,000. \qquad (10.3.18)$$

Example 10.5: Consider adding a cache proxy server to the environment of Ex. 10.4. Consider that the CPU time per request at the cache proxy server is 0.25 msec in the case of a hit and 0.50 msec in the case of a miss. Consider also that the disk service time at the cache proxy server is 6 msec per kilobyte read. How do the throughput and response time vary as a function of the hit ratio?

Using the equations derived in this section and implemented in the enclosed MS Excel workbook WebModels.XLS, we compute the service demands for values of p_{hit} equal to 0.2, 0.3, 0.4, and 0.5. We then use the MS Excel workbook ClosedQN.XLS to solve the model for each set of values of the service demands. The results are summarized in Table 10.3. The throughput with a 50% hit ratio is 199% higher than the throughput obtained without a proxy server (see Table 10.2). The response time for the same value of the hit ratio drops to 47% of the value it had without the proxy cache. The link to the Internet continues to be the bottleneck and its utilization varies between 98.0% and 99.1%. ∎

Table 10.3. Results for Ex. 10.5

p_{hit}	Throughput (requests/sec)	Response Time (sec)
0.20	0.389	35.18
0.30	0.445	30.41
0.40	0.518	25.63
0.50	0.620	20.86

Example 10.6: Consider the parameters of Ex. 10.5 but assume that the link to the Internet is replaced by a T1 link (1.544 Mbps). Assume that the cache hit ratio is 40%. What is the throughput and the average response time, and which resource is the bottleneck?

Using the workbooks `WebModels.XLS` and `ClosedQN.XLS`, we obtain a throughput of 3.373 HTTP requests/sec, which translates into 361.1 ($= 3.373 \times (1 - 0.4) \times 22.3 \times 8$) Kbps over the T1 Link (the incoming link), which is now 24% utilized and is not the bottleneck any longer. The new bottleneck is the disk at the cache proxy server with a 45% utilization; the response time now dropped to 1.113 sec.   ∎

10.4 Server-Side Models

We now turn our attention to the server side and show the performance models that can be used to answer questions such as:

- What should be the bandwidth of the link that connects the Web server to the Internet so that acceptable service levels are provided?

- Should I have mirror sites? How many?

- Should I use a Redundant Array of Inexpensive Computers (RAIC) as opposed to a single powerful server?

- Should I use HTTP redirect as opposed to a distributed locally mounted file system shared by various Web servers?

- How do I assess the impact of relocating documents within my Web server? For example, moving inlines to disks different from the parent page.

- How do I assess the impact of adding much more multimedia contents to a Web site?

- How do I assess new strategies for server operation, including replicating popular documents in separate disks?

- What if I store my files on a RAID-5 disk rather than on regular disks? Should the HTTP LOG be on a non-RAID volume?

- What is the maximum throughput of my Web site?

- What is the impact of using compression on large multimedia objects?

- What is the impact of replacing CGI scripts with Java applets?

- What is the impact of using compiled CGI scripts versus interpreted CGI scripts?

- What are the performance impacts of using a multithreaded Web server versus using one that forks a new kernel level process per HTTP request?

This list is not exhaustive but gives an idea of the kind of concerns that a Web server administrator is faced with.

10.4.1 Single Web Server

Figure 10.5a shows a typical environment with a single Web server at the site. The Web server is connected to a LAN, which is connected to a router that connects the site to the ISP and then to the Internet. The document tree (set of documents served by the Web server) is stored at the same machine where the Web server runs.

The Performance Model

The queuing network model corresponding to Fig. 10.5a is shown in Fig. 10.6a. We are assuming here that we are dealing with a Web server that is publicly available on the Internet. Thus, there is a very large population of unknown size of clients that will access the Web server. Thus, we can only characterize the arrival rate of requests for various document sizes. Therefore, we will model the Web server as an open multiclass QN model. Different classes in the model correspond to HTTP requests of different size as discussed in Ex. 10.3. Let R be the number of classes and λ_r $(r = 1, \cdots, R)$ be the arrival rate of class r requests. As explained in Ex. 10.3, the average arrival rate is computed as

$$\lambda_r = \lambda \times \text{PercentSize}_r \tag{10.4.1}$$

where λ is the overall arrival rate of HTTP requests to the Web server.

As in Sec. 10.3, the incoming and outgoing links and the LAN are represented by load-independent queues and the router as a delay queue. The Web server is represented by two load-independent queues: one for the CPU and another for the disk. One could have many more disks and a multiprocessor CPU as well.

The parameters considered here include some of the parameters defined in Sec. 10.3, such as LANBandwidth, MaxPDU, FrameOvhd, RouterLatency, AvgSizeHTTPRequest, DocumentSize$_r$, and PercentSize$_r$, as well as the following additional parameters:

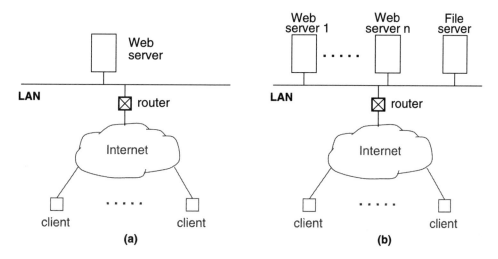

Figure 10.5. (a) Single Web server. (b) Mirrored Web servers with a shared file system.

- CPUTimePerHTTPRequest$_r$: total CPU time, in seconds, to process one HTTP request of class r

- DiskTime: disk time per kilobyte transferred, in milliseconds

Computing Service Demands

We now compute the service demands, in seconds, based on the parameters given above. The service demand, $D_{\mathrm{InL},r}$, at the incoming link is the same for all classes and has the same expression as the service demand for the outgoing link for the client side given in Eq. (10.3.8). Thus,

$$D_{\mathrm{InL},r} = \frac{8 \times [\mathrm{AvgSizeHTTPRequest} + 5 \times (20 + 20)]}{1{,}024 \times \mathrm{LinkBandwidth}}. \qquad (10.4.2)$$

The service demand at the router, $D_{\mathrm{router},r}$, for class r, is similar to Eq. (10.3.7) derived in Sec. 10.3, except that we now use the document size value for each class as opposed to the average document size. Thus,

$$D_{\mathrm{router},r} = [\mathrm{NDatagrams}\,(1{,}024 \times \mathrm{DocumentSize}_r) + 7] \times \mathrm{RouterLatency} \times 10^{-6}. \qquad (10.4.3)$$

The service demand at the LAN, $D_{\mathrm{LAN},r}$ is also very similar to Eq. (10.3.6) since in

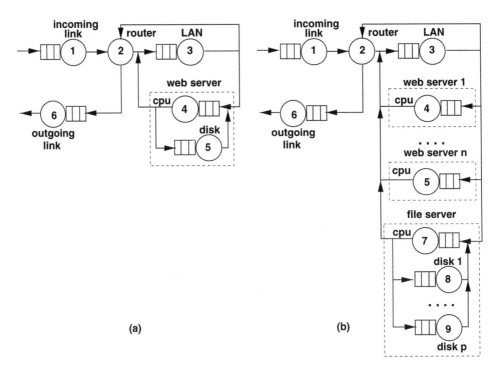

Figure 10.6. (a) QN model for a single Web server. (b) QN model for mirrored Web servers and a shared file system.

the client side and server side cases, the LAN is used to carry the HTTP requests and the documents retrieved as a result of the requests. Hence,

$$
\begin{aligned}
D_{\text{LAN},r} = {} & \text{NetworkTime (AvgSizeHTTPRequest)} + \\
& \text{NetworkTime } (1,024 \times \text{DocumentSize}_r).
\end{aligned}
\tag{10.4.4}
$$

The service demand at the outgoing link, $D_{\text{OutL},r}$, has the same expression as the service demand for the incoming link at the client side (see Eqs. [10.3.10] and [10.3.11]), except that now we specialize them per class as

$$
D_{\text{OutL},r} = \frac{8 \times (1,024 \times \text{DocumentSize}_r + \text{LinkOvhd}_r)}{1,024 \times \text{LinkBandwidth}}
\tag{10.4.5}
$$

where

$$
\text{LinkOvhd}_r = \left\lceil \frac{1,024 \times \text{DocumentSize}_r}{65,535} \right\rceil \times 40.
\tag{10.4.6}
$$

The service demand at the CPU, $D_{\text{CPU},r}$, for class r is given by

$$D_{\text{CPU},r} = \text{CPUTimePerHTTPRequest}_r + f(\overline{n}) \times \text{CPUOvhd} \qquad (10.4.7)$$

where $f(\overline{n})$ is a function f of the average number $\overline{n}$ of requests being processed at the server and CPUOvhd is the CPU overhead factor per request. The average number of requests $\overline{n}$ at the Web server is the sum of all requests of all classes at the CPU and disk. So,

$$\overline{n} = \sum_{r=1}^{R} (n_{\text{CPU},r} + n_{\text{disk},r}). \qquad (10.4.8)$$

The first term in Eq. (10.4.7) is called the *intrinsic* service demand and the second is called the *load-dependent* service demand. Processing overhead in networked environments depends on several factors, such as protocol, message sizes, number of simultaneous connections, and workload characteristics. There are several categories of overhead in network software. In [10], the authors propose seven categories: network buffer management, operating system functions, protocol-specific processing, checksum computation, data structure manipulations, data movement, and error checking. The same study shows that the categories of overhead for TCP/IP vary with message sizes. In [1], [11], measurement results show that more clients and larger files stress the Web server and operating system in different ways. For example, as the server load increases, the size of the system tables used to keep track of the processes and their TCP states grows larger. These tables consume CPU cycles to be searched on each packet arrival and to match the corresponding TCP state information.

Finally, the disk service demand, $D_{\text{disk},r}$, for class r is computed as

$$D_{\text{disk},r} = \text{DocumentSize}_r \times \text{DiskTime}/1,000. \qquad (10.4.9)$$

We are now ready to solve our open multiclass QN model since we have all the parameters. We can use the algorithms presented in Chap. 9 and the MS Excel workbook OpenQN.XLS. There is only one problem: The service demand at the CPU depends on the average number of requests at the Web server for all classes. But, this number can only be obtained once we solve the model. We can solve this problem by using an iterative procedure as explained later. Before we discuss how this should be done, we give an example of service demand computations.

Example 10.7: A Web server is connected to a 10-Mbps Ethernet, which is connected to an ISP through a router. The router has a latency of 50 μsec/packet and connects the LAN to the ISP through a T1 line (1.544 Mbps). There are four different types of workloads submitted to the Web server. Table 10.4 shows the main characteristics of the workload. The total arrival rate of HTTP requests is 6 requests/sec. Compute the service demands and arrival rates per class.

The arrival rates per class are $\lambda_1 = 6 \times 0.35 = 2.1$ requests/sec, $\lambda_2 = 6 \times 0.50 = 3.0$ requests/sec, $\lambda_3 = 6 \times 0.14 = 0.84$ requests/sec, and $\lambda_4 = 6 \times 0.01 = 0.06$

Table 10.4. Workload Parameters for Ex. 10.7

Class	Average File Size (KB)	% of Requests	CPU time per HTTP request (sec)
1	5.0	35	0.00645
2	10.0	50	0.00816
3	38.5	14	0.01955
4	350.0	1	0.14262

requests/sec . If we use the expressions given in this section and implemented by the MS Excel workbook `WebModels.XLS`, we obtain the service demands shown in Table 10.5. The CPU service demands shown in this table are the intrinsic service demands.   ■

We consider now the problem of computing the load-dependent service demands. If the overhead factor, CPUOvhd, in Eq. (10.4.7) is zero, then we can use an open multiclass QN models and the MS Excel workbook `OpenQn.XLS` to solve the model. But, if CPUOvhd is not zero, we can use the following iterative procedure:

1. Solve the open multiclass QN model, assuming CPUOvhd = 0, and obtain $\bar{n}$, the average number of requests at the server using Eq. (10.4.8).

2. Compute the new value of $D_{\mathrm{CPU},r}$ as

$$D_{\mathrm{CPU},r} = \mathrm{CPUTimePerHTTPRequest}_r + f(\bar{n}) \times \mathrm{CPUOvhd}. \quad (10.4.10)$$

3. Solve the model using the new value of $D_{\mathrm{CPU},r}$ and obtain a new value of $\bar{n}$.

4. If the absolute value of the relative error between the current and previous values of $\bar{n}$ exceeds a certain tolerance (say 10^{-3}), then go to step 2, else stop.

The following example illustrates this procedure.

Table 10.5. Service Demands for Ex. 10.7 (sec)

Component	1	2	3	4
LAN	0.0044	0.0085	0.0325	0.2942
Router	0.0006	0.0007	0.0017	0.0124
Outgoing link	0.0269	0.0535	0.2055	1.8679
Incoming link	0.0016	0.0016	0.0016	0.0016
Web server CPU	0.0064	0.0082	0.0196	0.1426
Web server Disk	0.0300	0.0600	0.2310	2.1000

Example 10.8: Consider that a fifth workload was added to the Web server of Ex. 10.7. This workload consists of requests to execute CGI scripts. The intrinsic service demand at the Web server's CPU for the new CGI workload is 0.35 sec. The new distribution of file sizes, percent of each type of request, and CPU time per class are given in Table 10.6. Assume that, according to measurements taken, the operating system and protocol management overhead at the CPU are linear with the number of requests being executed, and that the load-dependent portion of the service demand at the CPU can be characterized as $0.003 \times \bar{n}$ for all classes. This kind of behavior could be explained by the fact that many TCP implementations do sequential lookups on Protocol Control Block (PCB) tables [11]. So, the more TCP connections are open, the longer it takes to establish a new connection. What are the response times for each class?

Using the iterative procedure described in this section, we obtain the results shown in Table 10.7. Five iterations were needed to converge to an error of 0.03%. Column two of Table 10.7 shows the value of the average number of requests at the Web server. The response times per class are obtained in the last iteration.   ∎

10.4.2   Mirrored Web Servers

Let us start by considering the case where the environment of Fig. 10.5a is generalized in such a way that the Web server is mirrored (see Chap. 4) into n Web servers, that is, the document tree of the Web site is replicated into n identical Web servers. Let us examine how the model parameters need to be changed to reflect this situation. The arrival rates per class are clearly the same. The incoming link, router, LAN, and outgoing link demands are unchanged. However, the service demands at the CPU and disks of the Web server have to be divided by n, assuming the load will be equally split among all servers.

To understand why this is the case, remember that the service demand at a queue is the product of the average number of visits made by a request to the queue, multiplied by the average service time per visit. The service demand measured at any of the components (e.g., CPU, disks) of a server does not change by the addition of mirrored servers. But, the average number of visits to the queues that represent

Table 10.6. Workload Parameters for Ex. 10.8

Class	Average File Size (KB)	% of Requests	CPU time per HTTP request (sec)
1	5.0	25	0.00645
2	10.0	30	0.00816
3	38.5	19	0.01955
4	350.0	1	0.14262
5	1.0	25	0.35000

Table 10.7. Results for Ex. 10.8

Iteration	$\overline{n}$	% Error	Response Times (sec) per class				
			1	2	3	4	5
1	2.611	–	0.142	0.270	1.004	9.026	0.861
2	2.911	10.31	0.165	0.293	1.031	9.090	0.987
3	2.951	1.36	0.168	0.297	1.035	9.098	1.004
4	2.955	0.14	0.168	0.297	1.035	9.096	1.006
5	2.956	0.03	0.168	0.297	1.035	9.096	1.006

these components change due to the load balancing between the n mirrored servers. Consider a single class of requests, to simplify the notation, and let V_{server}^j be the average number of visits to Web server j ($j = 1, \cdots, n$). Let i be a component (e.g., CPU or disk) or Web server j, and let V_i^j be the average number of visits to queue i, given that a request is sent to Web server j. Note that V_i^j does not change because mirror servers are added. The average number of visits, V_i, to the queue that represents component i in the QN model is

$$V_i = V_{\text{server}}^j \times V_i^j \qquad (10.4.11)$$

since for every visit to the Web server, a request makes V_i^j visits, on the average, to component i. But since $V_{\text{server}}^j = 1/n$ for all Web servers,

$$V_i = V_i^j / n. \qquad (10.4.12)$$

Let S_i be the average service time of a request at component i. This value does not change with the number of Web servers. If we multiply both sides of Eq. (10.4.12) by S_i, we get that

$$V_i \times S_i = (V_i^j \times S_i)/n. \qquad (10.4.13)$$

But $V_i \times S_i$ is D_i, the service demand of component i in the QN that represents the mirrored server case, and $V_i^j \times S_i$ is the service demand of a request measured at the Web server, that is, the service demand for the single Web server case.

So, using the superscript m to indicate service demands in the mirrored case, we have that

$$D_{CPU,r}^m = D_{CPU,r}/n \qquad (10.4.14)$$

and

$$D_{\text{disk},r}^m = D_{\text{disk},r}/n. \qquad (10.4.15)$$

Example 10.9: Consider the parameters of Ex. 10.8. Assume that the arrival rate of requests is expected to increase from 6 to 8 requests/sec. The Web site administrator wants to know if two Web servers sharing the overall load would provide the same service levels as the ones currently offered.

To answer this question, we add two more queues to our QN model: the CPU and disk for the new server. Assume that the overall load will be equally split between the two servers. Therefore, the service demand at the CPU and disk of the original Web server has to be divided by two and assigned to the CPU and disk of each of the two servers as indicated in Eq. (10.4.15). If we solve the model again, we obtain the following response time for classes 1–5, respectively: 0.157 sec, 0.289 sec, 1.048 sec, 9.338 sec, and 0.643 sec. These numbers are very similar to the ones obtained in the previous example as seen in Table 10.7. This indicates that the two Web servers will be able to handle the increase in workload intensity while maintaining the same quality of service. ∎

Consider now the environment of Fig. 10.5b in which the document tree, instead of being replicated in all Web servers, is stored in a shared file system with P disks. This arrangement alleviates the problem of maintaining the mirrored copies' consistency. There is a penalty, though: The LAN and the file server are now shared among all Web servers and could potentially become a bottleneck if not adequately sized. Figure 10.6b shows the QN model that corresponds to Fig. 10.5b. We need an additional parameter CPUTimePerFSRequest that stands for the total CPU time in seconds per kilobyte accessed. Let us analyze how the service demands have to modified to account for the shared file server.

Each HTTP request uses the LAN to reach one of the n Web servers. The document specified in the URL is requested from the file server. The document uses the LAN to go to the requesting Web server and uses the LAN again to go to the router on its way to the outgoing link. So, if we neglect the short requests to the file server and consider the typically bulkier replies from the file server to the Web server, we have that

$$
\begin{aligned}
D^m_{\text{LAN},r} = \;& \text{NetworkTime (AvgSizeHTTPRequest)} + \\
& 2 \times \text{NetworkTime} \, (1{,}024 \; \times \; \text{DocumentSize}_r). \quad (10.4.16)
\end{aligned}
$$

The service demand, $D_{\text{FSCpu},r}$, at the file server's CPU for class r, is given by

$$
D_{\text{FSCpu},r} = \text{DocumentSize}_r \times \text{CPUTimePerFSRequest}. \quad (10.4.17)
$$

The service demand, $D_{\text{FSdisk},r}$, at each of the P disks of the file server, is

$$
D_{\text{FSdisk},r} = (\text{DocumentSize}_r \times \text{DiskTime}/1{,}000)/P. \quad (10.4.18)
$$

All equations for computing the service demands for Web servers with or without mirroring are in the MS Excel workbook `WebModels.XLS`.

Example 10.10: Consider the same parameters as in Ex. 10.9 with the difference that, instead of each of the two Web servers maintaining a replica of the document tree each, they use a shared file server with two disks. The arrival rate of requests is still 8 requests/sec. The Web site administrator wants to know what will be the impact on performance of using a shared file server.

The QN model has nine queues now: the incoming link, the router, the LAN, the two Web server CPUs, the file server CPU, the two file server disks, and the outgoing link. If we use the workbook `WebModels.XLS`, we obtain the service demands for this model. We can now use the workbook `OpenQN.XLS` to solve the model and answer the capacity planning question posed by the Web site administrator. Table 10.8 compares the response times for the nonshared file server case (Ex. 10.9) and the shared file server case considered in this example. The last row of the table shows the percent variation of the results. The first four classes—retrieval of HTTP documents—show an increasing percent variation on the response time. The maximum increase is 8.6% and is observed for class 4, the one with largest average document size. The main reason for the increase is increased congestion at the LAN. The last column of the table shows that the LAN utilization doubled because of the use of a shared file server. Class 5, the CGI script workload, exhibits a 3.0% decrease in response time. The reason is that the CPU processing associated with the file system has been moved from the Web server CPU to the CPU of the file server. Thus, the CGI scripts execute faster now.

By looking at the results of the QN model, one can see that in this case, the bottleneck is the outgoing link for classes 1–4 and the Web server CPU for class 5. The Web site administrator examined Table 10.8 and decided that using a shared file server would be advisable, despite the relatively small increase in the response time of some of the classes, since it would eliminate the problem of keeping the various copies of the document tree consistent.   ∎

10.5 Concluding Remarks

The performance models presented in this chapter specialize and extend the models presented in Chaps. 8 and 9 to deal with specific aspects of the Web, from the client and server sides. The chapter showed that the effects of burstiness of Web traffic can be incorporated into the models by inflating the service demands of the bottleneck resource by a factor proportional to a burstiness factor that can be obtained by analyzing the HTTP LOG. Heavy tails of file size distributions are handled by the performance models through the use of multiple classes that account for the different ranges of file sizes.

The client-side models presented here are closed QN models and allow for the

Table 10.8. Results for Ex. 10.10

	Response Times (sec) per Class					LAN Utilization (%)
	1	2	3	4	5	
No FS	0.157	0.289	1.048	9.338	0.643	10.4
Shared FS	0.162	0.306	1.130	10.138	0.624	20.7
% variation	3.1	5.6	7.8	8.6	-3.0	99.0

proper sizing of the bandwidth of the connection to the Internet, among other things. The server-side models are open multiclass QN models and can be used to analyze Web sites with many different configurations, including mirroring with and without shared file servers.

The examples given in the chapter are illustrative of scenarios that can be analyzed with these models. They are not in any way all encompassing. Many other situations can be analyzed by following the approach presented here.

To support the computation of service demands for the client and server sides, we developed MS Excel workbook `WebModels.XLS`, which computes the matrix of service demands from the values of the parameters. This matrix can be cut and pasted into the workbooks `ClosedQN.XLS` and `OpenQN.XLS` to conveniently solve the client- and server-side models, respectively.

A study of the performance impact of Web browsers on CPU and memory resources at the client side is given in [6]. Measurements of Web server resource CPU, disk, and memory, consumption are presented in [8]. Other modeling techniques, such as Layered Queuing Models [12], [14], have been used to model Web servers [7].

BIBLIOGRAPHY

[1] J. ALMEIDA, V. A. F. ALMEIDA, and D. YATES, Measuring the behavior of a World Wide Web server, *Proc. Seventh Conf. High Perform. Networking (HPN'97)*, IFIP, New York, April 1997.

[2] G. BANGA and P. DRUSCHEL, Measuring the capacity of a Web server, *Usenix Symp. Internet Technol. Syst.*, Dec. 1997.

[3] J. P. BUZEN, Operational Analysis: an Alternative to Stochastic Modeling, in *Performance of Computer Installations*. North Holland, June 1978, pp. 175–194.

[4] D. E. COMER, *Computer Networks and Internets*. Upper Saddle River, NJ: Prentice Hall, 1997.

[5] M. CROVELLA and A. BESTAVROS, Self-similarity in World-Wide Web traffic: evidence and possible causes, *Proc. 1996 SIGMETRICS Conf. Measurement Comput. Syst.*, ACM, Philadelphia, PA, May 1996.

[6] Y. DING and S. AGRAWAL, The performance impact of Web servers, *Proc. 1996 Comput. Measurement Group Conf.*, San Diego, CA, Dec. 8–13, 1996, pp. 62–73.

[7] J. A. DILLEY, R. J. FRIEDRICH, T. Y. JIN, and J. ROLIA, Measurement tools and modeling techniques for evaluating Web server performance, *Tech. Rep. HPL-96-161*, Hewlett Packard Labs, Dec. 1996.

[8] A. A. HAFEZ and Y. DING, Measuring Web server resource consumption, *Proc. 1997 Comput. Measurement Group Conf.*, Orlando, FL, Dec. 9–12, 1997.

[9] J. HEIDMANN, K. OBRACZKA, and J. TOUCH, Modeling the performance of HTTP over several transport protocols, *IEEE/ACM Trans. Networking*, vol. 5, no. 5, pp. 616–630, Oct. 1997.

[10] J. KAY and J. PASQUALE, Profiling and reducing processing overheads in TCP/IP, *IEEE/ACM Trans. Networking*, vol. 4, no. 6, Dec. 1996.

[11] J. MOGUL, Network behavior of a busy Web server and its clients, *Res. Rep. 95/5*, DEC Western Res. Lab., 1995.

[12] J. ROLIA and K. SEVCIK, The method of layers, *IEEE Trans. Software Eng.*, vol. 21, no. 8, pp. 689–700, Aug. 1995.

[13] M. R. STADELMAN, UNIX Web server performance analysis, *Proc. 1996 Comput. Measurement Group Conf.*, San Diego, CA, Dec. 8–13, 1996, pp. 1026–1033.

[14] C. M. WOODSIDE, J. E. NEILSON, D. C. PETRIU, and S. MAJUMDAR, *IEEE Trans. Comput.*, vol. 44, no. 1, Jan. 1995, pp. 20–34.

[15] N. YEAGER and R. MCCRATH, *Web Server Technology.* San Francisco, CA: Morgan Kaufmann, 1996.

Chapter 11

WORKLOAD FORECASTING

11.1 Introduction

Unprecedented demand for the newest product slows Web servers to a crawl. The company servers were overwhelmed on Monday as a torrent of customers attempted to download the company's new software product. Web services, in terms of responsiveness and speed, started degrading as more and more customers tried to visit the site. And it is clear that many frustrated customers simply stopped trying. This undesirable scenario shows how critical is workload forecasting for intranet and Internet Web sites. In particular, it emphasizes the importance of good planning and forecasting for online environments.

Can we forecast the number of visitors to our Web site in order to plan the adequate capacity to support the load? What is the expected workload for the electronic-commerce Web site of our company during the Christmas season? How will the number of messages processed by the e-mail server vary over the next year? These are typical questions that come up very often during the course of a capacity planning project. In fact, most successful implementation experiences of distributed systems, such as large client/server systems, rely on a careful planning process, a planning process that pays attention to performance and capacity right from the beginning. As was discussed in Chap. 5, planning the capacity of C/S systems requires a series of steps to be followed in a systematic way. One of its key steps is workload forecasting, predicts how system workloads will vary over the future.

Before discussing the techniques available to answer this kind of question, let us first examine why the workload changes. Let us take the example of e-mail traffic. It expands along three different dimensions: the number of users, the number of messages, and the size of messages. Compounding the problem, is the fact that the three dimensions expand at different growth rates. For instance, in company X, management has observed a threefold increase in the number of messages, but the size of the messages went up 20 times in the same period of time, because of attached graphics.

Workloads change; they may grow or shrink, depending on the business prospective and the technology evolution. The workload growth comes primarily from the following sources: new applications, increase in the volume of transactions and requests processed by existing applications, and enhancements of the application environment. Information technology moves fast. And so do the applications required by companies and users. New data base management systems, new security software systems, new multimedia software, and new versions of operating systems are examples of software resources usually incorporated to old systems. Usually, new software systems demand additional resources from servers, desktops, and networks; they increase the demand on system resources.

In Web-based environments, workload planning and forecasting play even more important roles. For instance, in electronic commerce applications, businesses must meet customers' expectation in terms of selection and presentation of products as well as in terms of the quality of the service delivered. If the Web site is slow, due to poor capacity or overload, customers may not return. Choices on the Web are numerous and customers can easily switch from one site to another. Forecasting peak demand periods is also a key issue. Providing high-level quality of service during peak periods matters. Companies do not want to lose customers that arrive at busy times. It is obvious that in online environments, performance problems must be anticipated. And a key step to avoid problems is to forecast the workload. This chapter discusses aspects and techniques for workload forecasting.

11.2 A Forecasting Strategy

Forecasting methods can be divided into two approaches, namely: quantitative and qualitative. The former relies on the existence of historical data to estimate future values of the workload parameters. The qualitative approach is a subjective process, based on judgments, intuition, expert opinions, historical analogy, commercial knowledge, and any other relevant information. There are methods to handle qualitative forecasting. One of them is the Delphi technique [1], which takes the best judgment estimate from experts concerning some medium-term or long-range events. Then, a process of seeking consensus among the experts is repeated several times to narrow down the initial forecast. As a final result, the Delphi method yields a consensus forecast for future events. Clearly, the difficulty associated with obtaining accurate forecasts from history is the relationship between the future and the past when technological paradigms change at an accelerated pace. This is why qualitative forecasting plays an important role in the forecasting process. A workload forecasting strategy combines both quantitative and qualitative approaches, as shown in Fig. 11.1. The main steps involved in a workload forecasting process are:

- *Determination of Forecasting Objectives:* Workload forecasting is an implicit phase of capacity planning. Therefore, the objectives of the forecasting phase are implicitly determined by the goals of the capacity planning project. What is the desired forecast span, that is, the time horizon for which forecasting is to be performed? How is the forecast to be used? What is the criticality (e.g., cost and expected benefits) of the decisions to be made on top of the forecast workload? These are typical questions that help one to establish the

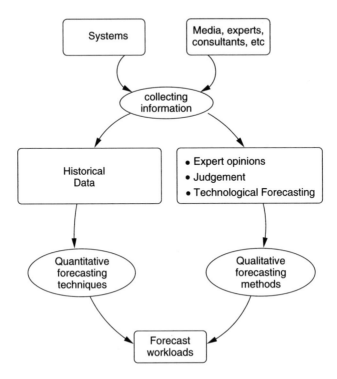

Figure 11.1. Forecasting strategy.

objectives of the forecasting phase.

- *Definition of Qualitative Forecasting:* Capacity planning projects need medium-range and long-term directions for information technology. Technological forecasting can help predict how the workload will change in the future. For example, new multimedia technology standards may have a strong impact on the network traffic of a company in the future. Estimates for the use of Java on the Internet for the next 5 years may influence the workload forecasting for some popular Web sites. Therefore, workload forecasting should take into account qualitative forecasting.

- *Analysis of Historical Data:* This step includes the specification of the several sources of historical data. For example, if the workload is described in business-oriented terms (e.g., number of orders), business statistics should be obtained. On the other hand, if the workload is characterized in terms of resource usage (e.g., processor time), then system logs should be the main source of historical data. Also, analysis of historical data should be carried out along the classes specified in the workload characterization process. For instance, if the workload is partitioned based on geographical orientation, then the historical data should also be organized in terms of geographical regions.

- *Selection of a Forecasting Technique:* Several criteria can be used for selecting forecasting techniques. The first one refers to the forecast span (e.g., short-range, medium-range, and long-term). Other criteria concern the availability of historical data, the data pattern, and the desired accuracy.

- *Workload Forecasting:* In this step, one should apply the selected forecasting technique to the historical data. After their validation, the quantitative results should be combined with qualitative forecasting to yield the forecast workload.

Several practical problems are commonly faced by a system administrator or capacity planner during the forecasting phase. First, it is difficult to obtain reliable information from users when they have to deal with terms they do not quite understand. For the purpose of performance modeling, workload characterization has been defined as the process of obtaining a set of parameters that specify the service demands and the load intensity. Those parameters are too vague for the end-user community. It is also hard to obtain resource usage information of new systems that have not been completely developed yet. Demands for new client/server applications are specially difficult to predict, because each C/S application is unique in terms of its configuration and workload. A framework for obtaining service demands for C/S systems under development is shown in [8].

Another problem refers to the *unpredictable demand*, which is a portion of the workload that shows up at random times and takes up all of the system capacity. This situation occurs in many Web sites in the Internet. For example, an unpredictable market crash can generate a huge increase in traffic to sites with financial news and analysis. It also spurs traffic spikes in the local area networks of companies involved with the stock market. The millions of host computers and users in the Internet create conditions for unexpected peaks of workloads. In order to avoid the undesirable problems caused by unexpected workloads, careful workload planning and forecasting must be performed in any capacity planning project.

11.3   From Business Processes to Workload Parameters

As specified in Chap. 6, the information required to characterize a workload is divided into two groups: component and load intensity. The former describes the service demands required by a component of a class (e.g., request, transaction, command, or job). The second group indicates the load placed on the several platforms of the system (e.g., client desktops, networks, and servers) by a workload class. Table 11.1 summarizes the modeling parameters that characterize a class of a workload.

The ultimate goal of a forecasting process is to determine the parameters of the estimated workload for the planning horizon. In other words, the forecasting process implies in answering questions such as:

Table 11.1. Class Parameters; λ is the Arrival Rate, M is the Number of Customers, and Z the Think Time

Class		Parameter	
Type	Component		
Open	Transaction	Demands	λ
Closed	Interaction	Demands	M and Z
Closed	Service	Demands	M

- What will be the intranet traffic next year?

- What will be the arrival rate of trivial transactions of the checking account application?

- What will be the number of visitors to the company's Internet site six months from now?

- What will be the average size of e-mails by the end of next year?

Answers to the above questions should then be converted to the typical workload parameters, shown in Table 11.1. These answers come primarily from the users. Hence, the first step in the workload forecasting process is to consult the user community to find out what are the estimates for the workload growth. Electronic questionnaires, on-line interviews and surveys over the Internet are useful tools for obtaining forecasting information. In general, questionnaires and interviews help to identify problems in online services, draw user profiles, and know future plans concerning information systems.

The major problem in contacting users is the nature of the information required by the workload forecasting process. The kind of information shown in Table 11.1 has nothing to do with the user world. Most users do not want to know what is behind the screen of their desktop. One can easily imagine the perplexity of a user trying to answer a question about the amount of bandwidth that his/her Web transactions will demand next year. It is clear that alternative ways should be used to obtain quantitative information on future workloads. Let us examine one approach that makes use of business-related information to predict workload growth.

In most companies, the business-critical applications account for the major part of the system resource usage. With direct relation to the business of a company, these applications perform functions such as inventory control, customer services, checking accounts, finances, e-mail, and telemarketing. The amount of system resources (e.g., server, network, and desktop computer) required by these applications can be associated with some kind of quantifiable business variables, called key value indicator (KVI), natural business unit (NBU), or forecasting business units (FBU) [5]. They provide a good indication of the volume of activity of a business or administrative function. Some examples of business units and their associated applications are shown in Table 11.2.

Methodologies based on business units assume that the volume of business activity in a company may be related to demands for system resources. Users estimate their computing needs in terms of business units, which are then converted to some form of resource requirements (e.g., client CPU demand, network bandwidth, and server I/O operations). The basic steps involved in workload forecasting by using business units are [11]:

1. Select the applications to be forecast. Look for the few major applications that account for most of the utilization of system resources. All other applications should be lumped together for forecasting purposes.

2. Identify the business units associated with the applications whose growth will be forecast. For example, the number of orders placed by customers is a good business unit for an order-entry application of an electronic bookstore.

3. Summarize the statistics (e.g., resource usage, number of transactions, and number of Web requests) of the selected applications. The frequency of execution of an application and the chosen time window determine the periodicity of the summarization. For instance, an order-entry transaction processing system should be analyzed on a daily basis. In particular, look at periods with peak loads.

4. Collect statistics concerning the chosen business units. In the electronic bookstore example, obtain the daily number of orders placed by customers.

5. Translate business units into computer demands. For example, divide the resource usage in the selected time window (e.g., peak period) by the number of orders processed in the same period. The result is an estimate of the amount of resources required by the system to handle a customer order.

6. Forecast the future resource demand as a function of the business units. In the example of an order-entry system, one should use a forecasting technique

Table 11.2. Natural Business Units

Application	Business Unit
E-mail	Number of users
E-commerce	Number of orders
Telemarketing	Number of calls
Checking account	Number of customers
Inventory	Number of stock lines
Rental car	Number of vehicles
Stock exchange	Number of shares traded

to estimate the growth in the number of customer orders—the business unit. Using some kind of translation technique, the capacity planner should be able to relate the future number of orders to the future workload demand. For example, one can use a multiple linear regression that takes the business units as independent variables and the resource demands to be forecast as dependent variables.

11.4   Forecasting Techniques

The literature [4]–[6] describes several forecasting techniques. In selecting one, some factors need to be considered. The first one is the availability and reliability of historical data. The degree of accuracy and the planning horizon are also factors that determine the forecasting technique. The pattern found in historical data has a strong influence on the choice of the technique. The nature of historical data may be determined through visual inspection of a plot of the data as a function of time. As displayed in Fig. 11.2, four patterns of historical data can be sharply identified: trend, cyclical, seasonal, and stationary. While the trend pattern reflects a workload that tends to increase (or decrease, in some cases), the stationary pattern does not show any sign of systematic increase or decrease (i.e., it exhibits a constant mean). Seasonal and cyclical patterns are similar with respect to the presence of fluctuations. The difference is the periodicity of the fluctuations exhibited by the seasonal pattern. The underlying hypothesis of forecasting techniques is that the information to be forecast is somehow directly related to historical data; this emphasizes the importance of knowing the pattern of historical data. Let us now examine in detail some forecasting methods. The most often applied techniques to workload forecasting are moving averages, exponential smoothing, and linear regression. There are many commercial packages (e.g., Matlab [7], S-PLUS [3]) that perform various methods of forecasting techniques.

11.4.1   Regression Methods

Regression models are used to estimate the value of a variable as a function of several other variables. The predicted variable is called a dependent variable and the others used to forecast the value are known as independent variables. The mathematical relationship established between the variables can take many forms. The most commonly used relationship assumes that the dependent variable is a linear function of the independent variables.

This section presents the simple linear regression analysis used to determine the linear relationship between two variables. The general equation for the regression line is

$$y = a + b \times x \tag{11.4.1}$$

where y is the dependent variable, x the independent variable, a the y-intercept, and b is called the slope of the line that represents the linear relationship between the two variables. The *method of least squares* determines the values of a and b that

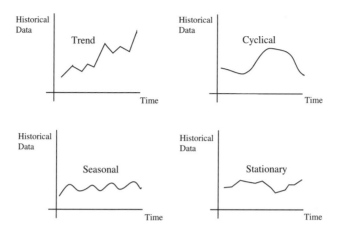

Figure 11.2. Historical data patterns.

minimize the sum of the squares of the error of forecasting. Thus,

$$b = \frac{\sum_{i=1}^{n} x_i \times y_i - n \times \bar{x} \times \bar{y}}{\sum_{i=1}^{n} x_i^2 - n(\bar{x}^2)} \qquad (11.4.2)$$

$$a = \bar{y} - b \times \bar{x} \qquad (11.4.3)$$

where (x_i, y_i), for $(i = 1, \cdots, n)$, are the coordinates of the n observed data points, $\bar{y} = \frac{1}{n}\sum_{i=1}^{n} y_i$, and $\bar{x} = \frac{1}{n}\sum_{i=1}^{n} x_i$.

Example 11.1: Advertiser-supported Web sites are usually analyzed by exposure and interactivity metrics. The former is represented by measures such as site hit counts and page access frequency. For the purpose of this example, let us consider hits as the number of pages and/or graphics requested by visitors. Web site interactivity is measured by metrics such as visit duration time and intervisit duration. In order to provide a high quality of service (e.g., fast response time) to its visitors, the Webmaster wants to know in advance what will be the number of visitors to the Web site during Christmas, that is, in December. Linear regression is used to forecast the number of hits. Let us examine the development of a simple linear regression model to forecast the number of hits. The number of hits represents the dependent variable (y) and the month the independent variable (x). From the data of Table 11.3, we have: $n = 12$, $\bar{x} = 6.50$, $\bar{y} = 62,863.67$, $\sum x_i^2 = 650.00$, $\sum x_i y_i = 5,071,498.00$, $n \times \bar{x}^2 = 507.00$, $n \times \bar{x} \times \bar{y} = 4,903,366.00$, $b = 1,175.74$, and $a = 55,221.30$. The expression for the linear relationship between the month (x) and the number of hits (y) is $y = 55,221.30 + 1,175.74 \times x$, as shown in Fig. 11.3. Thus, we can forecast the number of hits at the server for new values of x. For example, the next month of December is month 21, so the forecast number of hits

Table 11.3. Web Site Daily Activity by Month

Month	Actual Hits
April	53,110
May	61,222
June	62,345
July	57,312
August	57,897
September	63,544
October	52,856
November	68,932
December	78,932
January	66,280
February	68,932
March	63,002

is $y = 55,221.30 + 1,175.74 \times 21 = 79,911.84$.   ■

11.4.2 Moving Average

It is a simple forecasting technique that makes the value to be forecast for the next period equal to the average of a number of previous observations. When applied to nearly stationary data, the accuracy achieved by the technique is usually high [5]. A major disadvantage of simple moving averages comes from the fact that only one forecast value into the future can be calculated at a time. This technique is appropriate for short-term forecasting. The forecast value is given by

$$f_{t+1} = \frac{y_t + y_{t-1} + \cdots + y_{t-n+1}}{n} \qquad (11.4.4)$$

where

    f_{t+1}: forecast value for period $t+1$
      y_t: actual value (observation) at time t
      n: number of observations used to calculate f_{t+1}.

As can be noted from Eq. (11.4.4), a forecast value for time $t+2$ cannot be made until the actual value for time $t+1$ becomes known. One problem with this technique is the determination of n, the number of periods included in the averaging. One should try to select a value for n that minimizes the forecasting error, which is defined by the square of the difference between the forecast and actual values. The mean squared error (MSE) is given by Eq. (11.4.5). Different values of n may be tested to find the one that gives the smallest MSE:

$$\text{MSE} = \frac{\sum_{t=1}^{n}(y_t - f_t)^2}{n}. \qquad (11.4.5)$$

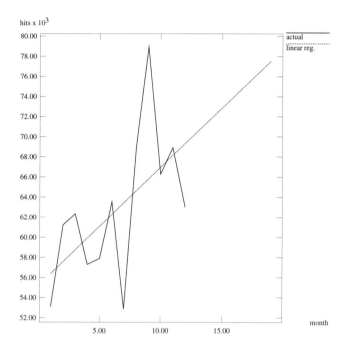

Figure 11.3. Forecasting Web-site hits.

Example 11.2: In many organizations, e-mail is considered a mission-critical application because of its ability to speed communications. In order to keep the expected level of service, e-mail volume, measured in number of messages, is constantly monitored. Column two of Table 11.4 displays the monthly number of message processed by the e-mail server in the last 17 months. To avoid performance problems (e.g., long backlogs of outgoing mails), the system administrator wants to know in advance what will be the number of messages processed in the next month. In particular, the administrator wants an estimate for September.

When applying the moving averages technique, three values of n were tried (3, 5, and 7) on the existing data. The use of three observations gives the smallest MSE. Thus, the number of messages for September is $f = (690,877 + 790,916 + 840,558)/3 = 774,117$. ∎

11.4.3 Exponential Smoothing

Historical trends can be analyzed using the exponential smoothing technique. It uses a weighted average of past observations to forecast the value of the next period. Exponential smoothing is similar to moving average with respect to the way

Table 11.4. E-mail Server Statistics

Month	Actual Number of Messages	Forecast Using Exponential Smoothing ($\alpha = 0.6$)
April	646,498.0	646,498.0
May	783,485.0	646,498.0
June	498,583.0	728,690.0
July	471,315.0	590,625.0
August	494,311.0	519,039.0
September	549,204.0	504,202.0
October	974,004.0	531,203.0
November	1,001,598.0	796,883.0
December	706,086.0	919,712.0
January	835,888.0	791,536.0
February	1,149,200.0	818,147.0
March	1,066,325.0	1,016,778.9
April	984,593.0	1,046,506.5
May	715,774.0	1,009,358.4
June	690,877.0	833,207.0
July	790,916.0	747,809.0
August	840,558.0	773,673.0

that both techniques calculate the forecast value. They both make the average of known observations equal to the forecast value. The difference is that exponential smoothing places more weight on the most recent historical data. The motivation for using different weights stems from the hypothesis that the latest observations give a better indication of the next future. As with moving averages, this technique is appropriate to data that present little variation and for short-term prediction. The forecast value is calculated as

$$f_{t+1} \;=\; f_t + \alpha(y_t - f_t) \tag{11.4.6}$$

where

    f_{t+1}: forecast value for period $t+1$
      y_t: actual value (observation) at time t
      α: smoothing weight ($0 < \alpha < 1$).

Example 11.3: Let us apply the exponential smoothing technique to the data shown in Table 11.4. The problem is to calculate the estimated number of messages for September, given that we have historical data composed of 17 observations. Column three of Table 11.4 shows the forecast values obtained by using the exponential smoothing technique with $\alpha = 0.6$ until August. Note that the forecast value for the first month (April) is set equal to the observed value, since there are no previous observations. The number of estimated messages for September is $f = 773,673.7 + 0.60\,(840,558 - 773,673.7) = 813,804.3.$ ■

11.4.4 Applying Forecasting Techniques

Before performing the forecasting, the selected technique should be validated on the available data. This can be done using only part of the historical data to exercise the model. The remaining data, which correspond to actual values, can then be compared to the forecast values to assess the accuracy of the method. Tests can be made to assess the MSE of each method under study, so that the one that gives the smallest MSE is selected. Figure 11.4 displays a plot of the observed number of messages processed by the e-mail server of Ex. 11.2. It also shows the forecast values obtained with moving averages (MA), exponential smoothing, and linear regression.

Let us go back to the example of e-mail workload. As we saw earlier in this

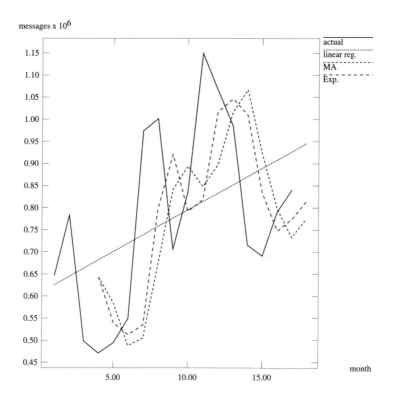

Figure 11.4. Forecasting values.

chapter, the e-mail workload varies along the following three dimensions: the number of users, the number of messages, and the size of messages. It has also been noted that the three dimensions expand at different rates of growth. Therefore, if we concentrate our estimate on a single dimension of the problem, important aspects may be missed. Suppose that in addition to the increase in the number of messages, it was observed that the size of the messages increased ten times in the same period of time, because of attached files. As a consequence, two workload parameters will change. The arrival rate changes as a function of the number of messages processed, and the service demand also increases, because larger messages consume more resources to be processed. The important issue here is that the process of workload forecasting should not be restricted to one specific parameter; it should cover all parameters that characterize the different demands of a workload.

Future workloads can be forecast in two different modes [5]: causal and trend. The causal mode uses business units as the independent variable and workload parameters as the dependent variable. For instance, a regression model can be used to estimate the future processor demand of an e-mail application as a function of the number of messages. The trend mode performs the forecast of a workload descriptor as a function of time, based only on historical data of the descriptor. In the same example, the future processor demand could be calculated by a forecasting technique using as input data the past application processor time recorded by the accounting logs.

11.5 Concluding Remarks

Workload forecasting is a key issue in any capacity planning project. In online environments, such as the Web or C/S systems, performance problems must be anticipated. An efficient way of avoiding problems is to have a good workload forecasting. The basic steps to workload forecasting are

- selection of the workload to be forecast

- analysis of historical data and estimation of the workload growth

- selection of a forecasting technique

- use of the forecasting technique on the historical data

- analysis and validation of forecast results

BIBLIOGRAPHY

[1] J. ARMSTRONG, *Long-Range Forecasting.* New York: Wiley, 1985.

[2] C. CHATFIELD, *The Analysis of Time Series: An Introduction.* 4th ed., Chapman & Hall, 1989.

[3] B. EVERITT, *A Handbook of Statistical Analyses Using S-PLUS.* Chapman & Hall, 1994.

[4] S. LAM, and K. CHAN, *Computer Capacity Planning: Theory and Practice.* London: Academic, 1987.

[5] H. LETMANYI, *Guide on workload forecasting, Special Public. 500-123*, Computer Science and Technology, National Bureau of Standards, 1985.

[6] R. JAIN, *The Art of Computer Systems Performance Analysis.* New York: Wiley, 1991.

[7] M. MARCUS, *Matrices and Matlab: A Tutorial*, Upper Saddle River, NJ: Prentice Hall, 1993.

[8] D. A. MENASCÉ, A framework for software performance engineering of client/server systems, *Proc. 1997 Computer Measurement Group Conf.*, Orlando, FL, Dec. 1997, pp. 460–469.

[9] D. A. MENASCÉ, V. A. F. ALMEIDA, and L. W. DOWDY, *Capacity Planning and Performance Modeling: From Mainframes to Client-Server Systems.* Upper Saddle River, NJ: Prentice Hall, 1994.

[10] J. MOHR and S. PENANSKY, A forecasting oriented workload characterization methodology, *CMG Trans.*, no. 36, The Computer Measurement Group, June 1982.

[11] D. SARNA, Forecasting computer resource utilization using key volume indicators, *AFIPS Conf. Proc.*, vol. 48, 1979.

Chapter 12

MEASURING PERFORMANCE

12.1 Introduction

Client/server environments are critical to everyday operations of many organizations. An ever-growing number of companies rely on the transaction- and Web-processing capacity of their computer systems. Measuring performance of network-based systems, such as on-line transaction processing and Web applications, is a key issue in the process of guaranteeing service-level agreements (SLA) and preventing problems. It is also an essential step for capacity planning because it collects data for performance analysis and modeling. Performance models aim at representing the behavior of real systems in terms of their performance. The input parameters for performance models describe the system configuration, the software environment, and the workload of the system under study. The representativeness of a model depends directly on the quality of input parameters. Before one starts collecting operational data for a performance model of a real system, three questions naturally arise:

- What are the information sources of performance data?

- What are the monitoring tools available for measuring response time and resource usage?

- What techniques are used to calculate model input parameters from typical performance data collected by standard measurement tools?

The main source of information is the set of performance measurements collected from different reference points, carefully chosen to observe and monitor the environment under study. Further performance information can also be obtained from product specifications (e.g., hardware, software, and network services) provided by manufacturers and industry standard benchmarks, described in detail in Chap. 7. Usually, typical performance data collected by standard monitoring tools do not match the type of information required as input by queuing network performance models. Usually, raw data collected by performance measurement tools need to be reworked to become useful for modeling.

This chapter presents first a framework for collecting performance data in network environments patterned after the client/server paradigm. Next, it discusses the main issues in the process of measuring performance of network-based systems. Because the particulars vary from system to system, we do not focus on any specific product or manufacturer. Instead, we present the information needed by performance models and then we discuss general procedures for transforming typical measurement data into input parameters. The procedures can be thought of as a set of major guidelines for obtaining input parameters for performance models.

12.2 Performance Measurement Framework

Performance models depend on quality measurement data to predict system behavior. Moreover, it is essential for capacity planning to base the models on application-oriented measurement data. After all, the workload is made up of applications. And application oriented measurement data is also important to management, who wants to keep track of application service levels. Usually, SLA outlines what users of an application can expect in terms of response time, throughput, system availability, and reliability. Information such as number of transactions per application, end-to-end response time, bandwidth per application, DBMS server time per application, and cost per application are some important indicators for cost $\times$ benefit analysis. Forecasting is also done on application basis. If one wants to estimate the workload growth, one will use business forecasting units that are related to specific applications. The bottom line here in this section is the importance of the availability of application-oriented measurement data. Needless to say, that although system usage information is important, it does not fill out all of the capacity planning needs.

By and large, measurement data has three main uses in performance management: operation problem detection, performance tuning, and capacity planning [3]. To find out what is really happening, system operators rely on runtime monitors. These tools continuously collect measurement data from the system and display the status of some key variables that may indicate potential problems, such as CPU utilization, paging activity, memory usage, error rate, number of concurrent users accessing the database server, link utilization, and packets per second. Operators need global measurement data that help them draw a big picture of the system and check if something goes wrong. Values considered high for these variables trigger alarms.

The second use of measurement data is for performance tuning purposes. Analysts examine performance historical data (e.g., logs and traces) to pinpoint possible causes of performance problems that may harm the system operation. Usually, the first level of tuning occurs at the operating system, based also on system measurements. According to performance data, one can tune a UNIX system by changing some of its parameters. For example, if measurements indicate that the file system is slow, one can change the size of the file system buffer cache to speed up I/O operations. Other forms of tuning or optimization are also possible. Suppose that one measures the performance of a Windows NT server. By examining the *NT Performance Monitor* results, one concluded that the system was suffering from lack of memory. Before recommending to upgrade the system and add more memory, the following optimizations could be tried: scheduling memory-intensive applications to off-peak hours and distributing memory-consuming programs across multiple servers on the network.

Capacity planning makes use of measurement data to develop models to predict the performance of future system configurations or to anticipate problems, such as service-level degradation. Performance models that are user-oriented (e.g., models that calculate user response time) must rely on application-oriented measurement data.

Performance management of network-based environments involves monitoring networks (i.e., LANs, WANs, and routers), systems (i.e., servers, clients, and proxies) and links to determine response times, resource utilizations, and traffic issues. A performance measurement framework aims at providing a big picture of the quantitative behavior of C/S systems and the corresponding network infrastructure that supports them. The framework should be able to provide the variety of measurement data required by the three functions of performance management, i.e., operation problem detection, performance tuning and capacity planning. In this chapter, the discussions of performance measurement are driven by the need to obtain the input parameters for performance models of network-based computing environment.

Figure 12.1 shows the main elements of a network-based environment with triangles representing reference points from which measurement data are usually collected. Consider the example of a corporate intranet spread over different locations of the country. A measurement framework should be able to monitor traffic in LAN segments where Web servers are located and to send the data to a centralized measurement system for performance analysis. At measurement point A, a monitoring API could be embedded directly into the application code to measure end-to-end response time. A vendor-neutral API, called Application Response Measurement (ARM), provides a method for tracking response time of transactions for which the source code is available [8]. At points B and E, it is possible to collect utilization measurements of the two LAN segments that make up the C/S environment. Network sniffers can be installed at points C and D to inspect network traffic at the links that connect the LANS to a WAN. At point F, operating system tools should be able to measure the server performance. These tools provide network managers with global information about traffic load, end-to-end response time and system utilization that can be used to calculate input parameters for performance models.

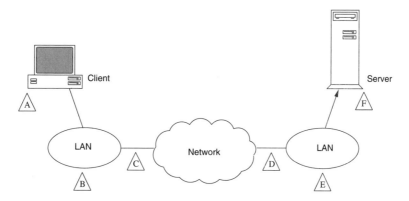

Figure 12.1. Measuring C/S performance.

12.3 Measurement Techniques

What are the most used resources of a given system? Network bandwidth? Server I/O? Client desktop processor time? What is the average end-to-end response time of stock trading transactions? How much CPU time does the e-mail server consume daily? How much bandwidth of the enterprise network is being consumed by Internet traffic? These are examples of typical questions that managers of information technology resources frequently face. To answer quantitative questions about the behavior of computers and networks, one has to measure them. But what does this really mean? System measurement can be viewed as a process that observes the operation of a system over a period of time and registers the values of those variables that are relevant for a quantitative understanding of the system [18]. As illustrated in Fig. 12.2, a measurement process involves four major steps:

1. *Specify Reference Points:* This is the first step toward measuring network-based computing environments. One has to specify the points from which performance data will be collected. As an example, one could determine that the starting point to measure the system is to collect traffic data that go through the LAN where the Web server is located.

2. *Specify Measurements:* In this step, one should decide on the performance variables to be measured. For example, consider an Ethernet network. Statistics that represent its behavior include measurements such, as packets per second and collisions per second. As another example, suppose that we are interested in developing a model for analyzing the behavior of a virtual memory manager of an operating system. Performance variables, such as page fault rate and throughput of paging disks, will certainly be among those required by the model.

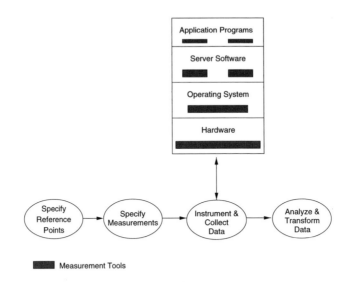

Figure 12.2. A representation of the measurement process.

3. *Instrument and Collect Data:* After selecting variables to be observed, one should install measurement tools to monitor the system. This involves configuring the tools so that the specified variables are measured during the observation period and the required information is recorded. A computer system can be viewed as a series of layers that create an environment for the execution of application programs, as shown in Fig. 12.2. According to the variables selected, one may have to install several measurement tools across the layers. For instance, if one were interested in obtaining the packet rate on the Ethernet, a LAN analyzer (composed of a network interface, a programmable hardware filter, and a PC-based system), would have to be connected to the Ethernet under observation.

4. *Analyze and Transform Data:* Measurement tools gather huge amounts of raw data, which correspond to a detailed observation of the system operation. Usually, raw data specify time intervals, event counts, and percentages that have to be related to the logical functions of a system. To be useful, these bulky data must be analyzed and transformed into significant information. For instance, logs generated by software measurement tools typically include a record for each Web request serviced during the monitoring period. These records must be then summarized to yield useful results such as average size of requested files, number of accesses, and file popularity.

In any performance measurement process, the key point is to understand what is being measured and how accurate and reliable are the resulting numbers. Thus, it is essential to know the measurement tools, their capabilities, and their limitations. Measurement techniques used to collect data can be divided into two categories: event mode and sampling mode.

Event Mode

An I/O interrupt that indicates the arrival of a network packet can be viewed as an *event* that changes the state of a system. The state of a system is specified by a set of variables. At the operating system level, the state of the system is usually defined as the number of processes that are in the ready-queue, blocked-queue, and running. Examples of events at this level are: a call to operating system modules, a clock interrupt, and an I/O request. At a higher level, where the number of transactions in memory represents the state of the system, the completion of a transaction can also be considered an event. In the *event mode*, information is collected at the occurrence of specific events. Usually, an event-based measurement tool consists of special codes inserted at specific points of the operating system. Upon detection of an event, the special code calls an appropriate routine that generates a record containing information such as date, time, and type of the event. In addition to that, the record contains some kind of event-related data. In general, measurement tools record the information corresponding to the occurrence of events in buffers, which are later transferred to disk. For example, in UNIX systems, a process record is entered in the accounting log upon process completion.

When the event rate becomes very high, the event handling routines are executed very often, which may introduce a large overhead in the measurement process. The overhead corresponds to the load placed by the measurement tool on system resources. Depending on the events selected, the event rate, and the amount of data collected, the overhead may reach unbearable levels, such as 30%. Overheads up to 5% are regarded as acceptable for measurement activities [7]. As the event rate cannot be controlled by the software routines, the measurement overhead becomes unpredictable, which constitutes one of the major shortcomings of this class of measurement tools. Overhead in the case of event-based monitoring may not be a problem for network sniffers used in promiscuous mode. In this case, the monitor runs in a dedicated PC configured to receive all packets sent between any two stations.

Sampling Mode

In the *sampling mode*, information about the system is collected at predefined time instants. Instead of being triggered by the occurrence of an event, the data collection routines of a sampling software tool are activated at predetermined times, specified at the start of the monitoring session. The sampling is driven by timer interrupts, based on a hardware clock. The overhead introduced by a sampling tool depends on two factors: the number of variables measured at each sampling point and the size of the sampling interval. With the ability of specifying both factors, a sampling monitor is also able to control its overhead. On one hand, large sampling intervals result in low overhead. On the other hand, if the intervals are too large, the number of samples decreases and reduces the statistical significance of the variables of interest. The uncertainty of the measured variables depends on the number of samples. Statistical methods can be used to assess the confidence in the measured values [11]. Therefore, one has to play with both the size of the sampling and monitoring interval to obtain low overhead and good accuracy . There exists a clear tradeoff between overhead and accuracy of measurement results. The higher the accuracy, the higher the overhead. When compared to event trace mode, sampling provides a less-detailed observation of a computer system [9].

12.4   Data Collection Tools

Monitors are tools used for measuring the level of activity of a system, being it a network, a server, or a client computer. The main function of a monitor is to collect data regarding the system's operation. Ideally, a monitor must be an observer of the system under study (e.g., network devices, server, and desktop client), and not in any way a participant. The monitoring activity must be done in such a way as to not affect the operation of the system being measured. This means that the monitoring process should minimally degrade the performance of the monitored system. Two attributes characterize a monitor: mode and type. As we saw in the previous section, monitors perform data collection in two different modes: event trace and sampling. There are three types of performance monitors, depending on their implementation approach: hardware, software, and hybrid.

12.4.1   Hardware Monitor

A *hardware monitor* is a measurement tool that detects events within a computer system by sensing predefined signals. A hardware monitor examines the state of the computer system under study via electronic probes attached to its circuitry and records the measurements. The electronic probes can sense the state of hardware components of the system, such as registers, memory locations, and I/O channels. There are advantages to hardware monitors. As they are external to the measured system, they do not consume resources from the system. This means that hardware monitors typically do not place any overhead on the monitored system. Another feature is portability. Usually, it is possible to move a hardware monitor to different types of computing environments, since they do not depend on the operating system. There are also potential difficulties associated with the use of hardware monitors for capacity planning. They usually do not access software-related information, such as the identification of a transaction that triggered a given event. Thus, it is difficult to use a hardware monitor to obtain performance measurements that are related to applications or workloads.

12.4.2 Software Monitor

A *software monitor* consists of a set of routines embedded in the software of a system with the aim of recording status and events of the system [18]. The routines gather performance data about the execution of one or more programs and about the components of the hardware configuration. They can be activated either by the occurrence of specific events or by timer interrupts, depending on the mode of the monitor. The combination of hardware and software monitors results in a *hybrid monitor*. For instance, many network performance tools are hybrid monitors that combine hardware and software monitoring facilities.

Software monitors basically record any information that is available to programs and operating systems. This feature, along with a great flexibility to select and reduce the amount of performance data, makes software monitors a powerful tool for analyzing computer systems. However, in order to run their routines, software monitors use the same resources they are measuring and may interfere significantly with the system. Depending on the level of overhead introduced, monitoring may yield meaningless results. Some tools, such as the NT Performance Monitor [4], allow users to control the overhead, letting them select the time interval for sampling. Software monitors are generally easy to install and easy to use. The main shortcomings are the overhead and the dependency on the operating system. Measurement data, commonly provided by current monitors, can be grouped into two categories, according to the information scope.

- *System-level measurements:* show system-wide resource usage statistics. Examples include global CPU and disk utilization, total number of physical I/O operations, page fault rate, and total traffic through a router. This kind of information is usually provided by software monitors that run at the operating system level. As a rule, system-level monitors do not collect statistics by class of application programs.

- *Program-level measurements:* show program-related information. Examples include program identification, elapsed time, CPU time, number of I/O operations per execution, physical memory usage, and application traffic (i.e., packets per second per application). Accounting systems constitute the most common source of program execution information.

There are some classes of tools that may be regarded as software monitors, in the sense that they monitor, via a set of appropriate routines, the behavior of hardware and software systems. However, due to their specific uses, they receive special names: accounting systems, log generators, and program analyzers.

Accounting Systems

Accounting systems are intended primarily to collect information to be used as a means of apportioning charges to users of a system [5], [7]. These tools are usually an integral part of most multiuser operating systems (e.g., UNIX process accounting log). Although their main purpose is billing, accounting systems can be used as a data source for capacity planning studies. Accounting systems are the easiest way to gather some very important performance information. They allow management to find out what applications users run, how much CPU time is spent with user applications, and how much system time is used by the applications. They should be viewed as the first recourse when one begins a measurement effort. In general, accounting data include three groups of information: identification (e.g., process, user, or application), resource usage indicators (e.g., CPU time, I/O operations, and memory usage), and execution times, showing the start and completion times of the processes. Although accounting systems provide a lot of useful data, there are some problems with the use of their data for performance modeling. They do not capture the use of resources by the operating system, i.e., they do not include any unaccountable system overhead.

Another problem refers to the way that accounting systems view some special programs such as database management systems (DBMS) and transaction processing monitors. These programs have transactions and processes that execute within them and therefore are not visible to the accounting system. For example, an Oracle server runs in Unix as a single process. Because the **sar** command views Oracle as single entities, it does not collect any information about what is being executed inside the Oracle process, such as the transactions processed by the database management system. However, if one wants to model transaction response time, one needs to obtain information about individual transactions. This information is not collected by the accounting system. Hence, special monitors are required to examine performance of some special programs, such as Oracle.

Program Analyzers

Instead of monitoring the whole system, *program analyzers* are software tools especially designed to collect information about the execution of individual programs. They can also be used as an optimizer tool, pinpointing those parts of a program that consume significant system resources. For example, most of the workload of large corporations is due to TP, which is usually controlled by single programs known as transaction processing monitors (e.g., Tuxedo, TopEnd, Encina, and CICS). For performance modeling purposes, the information provided by the accounting logs and operating system facilities is not sufficient. Both types of tools do not look inside the TP environment and only capture global resource usage data. Thus, what is needed is a tool capable of observing and recording events internal to the execution of specific programs. In the case of transaction processing monitors, program analyzers provide information such as transaction count, average transaction response time, mean CPU time per transaction, mean number of I/O operations per transaction, and transaction mix. Examples of program analyzers include monitors for database management systems and transaction processing software, such as Oracle, Informix, Sybase, DB2, CICS, Tuxedo, and others.

Logs

Log files contain information about the services requested from a system, the responses provided, and the origin of the requests. The NT Performance Monitor [4] places performance data in a log file that can be exported for further processing and reporting. The analyst can choose the objects to log and specify the monitoring interval and the time interval for sampling.

In the case of the World Wide Web, servers keep a log of their activities. Web server logs are text files that contain information about the server activity. Web logs are organized into four separate types, namely: access, referrer, agent, and error. The log used for analyzing performance and behavior of Web servers is the access log, which contains lines with the following types of information:

- *host:* contains the client host name or IP address

- *identification:* shows the identity of the user; no longer used

- *login name or authorization:* contains the authorization user ID used to access protected portions of the site

- *date, time, and zone:* instant at which the request was completed

- *request:* contains the name of the requested file and the operation or method performed (e.g., "GET/HTTP/1.0")

- *status:* specifies the response status from the server; may indicate, for instance, if the request was successful or if the client requested an unauthorized or nonexistent file

- *file size:* indicates the number of bytes transferred in response to a file request

There are many tools, both commercial and public domain, for analyzing Web server logs. For instance, over the Internet, one can find *wwwstat*, script provide performance statistics such as, total bytes transmitted during a period of time and number of requests per unit of time. There are also a number of commercial products that measure Web site activity [17]. They typically provide measures that indicate the degree of exposure and interactivity of a Web site. Some of the metrics used are: number of site accesses per day, number of page accesses per day, average visit duration time, average inter-visit duration time, and average page duration time

Example 12.1: Figure 12.3 displays the access log of a Web site, that was collected during a very short time interval. From the log, we want to derive performance measures, such as average arrival rate and average file size of the documents requested from the server. The log entry for a normal request is of the form:

```
hostname - - [dd/mmm/yyyy:hh:mm:ss tz] request status bytes
```

```
perf.xyz.com - - [24/Jan/19xx:13:41:41 -0400] "GET i.html HTTP/1.0" 200 3185
perf.xyz.com - - [24/Jan/19xx:13:41:41 -0400] "GET 1.gif HTTP/1.0" 200 1210
h0.south.com - - [24/Jan/19xx:13:43:13 -0400] "GET i.html HTTP/1.0" 200 3185
h0.south.com - - [24/Jan/19xx:13:43:14 -0400] "GET 2.gif HTTP/1.0" 200 2555
h0.south.com - - [24/Jan/19xx:13:43:15 -0400] "GET 3.gif HTTP/1.0" 200 36403
h0.south.com - - [24/Jan/19xx:13:43:17 -0400] "GET 4.gif HTTP/1.0" 200 441
cs.uni.edu - - [24/Jan/19xx:13:46:45 -0400] "GET i.html HTTP/1.0" 200 3185
cs.uni.edu - - [24/Jan/19xx:13:46:45 -0400] "GET 2.gif HTTP/1.0" 200 2555
cs.uni.edu - - [24/Jan/19xx:13:46:47 -0400] "GET 3.gif HTTP/1.0" 200 36403
cs.uni.edu - - [24/Jan/19xx:13:46:50 -0400] "GET 4.gif HTTP/1.0" 200 98995
sys1.world.com - - [24/Jan/19xx:13:48:29 -0400] "HEAD index.html" 400 -
```

Figure 12.3. Web access log.

For example, the first line of the log of Fig. 12.3 indicates that the request came from
the host perf.xyz.com at 13:41:41 Eastern time on January 24, 19xx. The requested
document, the index page, and the status code 200 indicates a successful response by
the server. The code 400 indicates an unsuccessful request due to a client error. The
size of the file transferred from the server was 3185 bytes. Although Web logs can
help in workload characterization, they do not provide all of the information needed
by performance models. For instance, there is no information about the elapsed time
required for a document transfer. Also, the log does not show information on the
complete set of documents available on the server; it only shows the documents
accessed during the measuring interval.

The measuring interval T is equal to $(13:48:29 - 13:41:41) = 408$ sec. The
number of requests is 11 and the arrival rate is 11/408 requests/sec. The average
size of the transferred files is $188,117/10 = 18,811.7$ bytes. We also note that the
minimum and maximum file sizes are 441 and 98,995 bytes, respectively. Once we
have a big difference in file sizes it would be useful to group the documents into
classes, to reduce the variability of the measurements, as discussed in Chap. 6.
Thus, we could classify the documents into two types: small and large. The former
would have documents up to 4,000 bytes. Thus, this workload would have a class
for small documents with seven requests and average file size equal to 2,330.9 bytes.
The class of large documents has three requests and average size of 57,267 bytes.■

12.5 Performance Model Parameters

The input parameters for performance models describe the hardware configuration,
the software, and the workload of the system under study. This section presents a
series of steps for specifying what the parameters are and how to estimate values
for the parameters of performance models. These parameters include four groups
of information:

- queues or devices

- workload classes

- workload intensity

- service demands

12.5.1 Queues

The first step in obtaining input parameters is to define of the queues that make up the model. The scope of the capacity planning project helps to select which queues are relevant to the performance model. Consider the case of a distributed system composed of file servers and workstations connected via a LAN. The capacity planner wants to examine the impact caused on the system by the replacement of the uniprocessor file server by a four-processor server. For example, the system under study could be well represented by an open queuing network model consisting of three queues, which correspond to the file server configuration: one processor and two disks. The workstations are implicitly represented by the arrival rate of read and write requests generated by the workstations. A different performance model, with other queues, would be required if the planner were interested in studying the effect of the LAN utilization on the performance of the distributed system. Thus, the specific focus of the project may be used to define the components of a performance model.

12.5.2 Workload Classes

To increase the model's representativeness, workloads are partitioned into classes of similar components, as described in Chap. 6. Programs with comparable resource usage may be grouped into the same workload class. Depending on the way a class is seen by a system, it may be classified as *open* or *closed*. The second step in determining the input parameters for a performance model is to define class types. The nature of the real workload is the main factor that influences the choice of class type. A class that represents the set of read and write requests that arrive at a file server may naturally be classified as an open class. Another example of open class is that of a workload generated by Web users. Although the nature of the real workload is important in determining the class type, it is not the only factor to be considered. Performance modeling considerations are equally important. Consider the case of a Web server in an intranet. All employees of the company request documents, videos, and graphics from the Web server. At first sight, one would classify the workload as closed because of the fixed number of customers (i.e., employees) and due to the nature of the work carried out by the employees (i.e., they submit requests and wait for the responses). However, for capacity planning purposes, it would be preferable to view the workload as open. The open type is specially suited for estimating future workload, because the forecast can be performed in terms of business units. It is also useful when the number of customers is not known in advance. Suppose that the company of our example decided to sell online training to other companies. It would be difficult to predict the number of simultaneous users of the service. It would be much easier to estimate the arrival rate of requests based on the correlation between historical arrival rates and the number of employees.

12.5.3 Workload Intensity

Workload intensity parameters give an indication of the number of transactions, requests, processes, customers, or jobs that contend for the resources of a network-based computing environment. The arrival rate (λ) indicates the intensity of an open class. Both the number of active customers (M) and the average think time (Z) specify the intensity of a closed class. Also, the average number of customers in a system is an indication of the load intensity of a closed class.

12.5.4 Service Demands

Queuing network (QN) models represent resources of a computer system. Although QNs may be used to model software resources (e.g., database locks), queuing networks have most frequently been applied to represent hardware resources. However, in modern computer systems, application programs do not see the hardware resources directly. Instead, they view the computer system as a set of services, provided by various layers of software. Clearly, there exists a gap between the application program view and the representation provided by a queuing network model. For example, a file server attached to a LAN provides a common service to all other systems on the LAN. The primary service of the file server is to provide the file management capabilities found on time-sharing systems. Thus, when a user program running on a networked workstation executes a command to read a file, it does not need to know where the file is stored. Several pieces of software implement a network file system that provides the service requested by a read command. Then, the following question arises: How are the services provided by software systems represented in a queuing network model? The answer lies in the full understanding of the concept of service demand.

By definition, the service demand of a request at a queue specifies the total amount of service time required by the request during its execution at the queue. It is worth repeating that service demand refers only to the time a request spends actually receiving service. It does not include waiting times. Recall that V_i denotes the average number of visits that a request makes to queue i and S_i represents the mean service time per visit to queue i. The service demand of a request at queue i is given by $D_i = V_i \times S_i$.

Another view for service demand is that derived from measurement data. Consider that a system is monitored for a period of time $\mathcal{T}$. During that period, the utilization of device i was U_i, which means that the system was busy $U_i \times \mathcal{T}$ units of time. If the count of completed requests during the period is C_0, then we can write that $D_i = U_i \times \mathcal{T}/C_0$.

Let us examine how the services provided by software layers of a computing environment may be represented by service demand parameters. Looking at the definition of service demand, $D_i = U_i \times \mathcal{T}/C_0$, we note that U_i is the only factor amenable to different interpretations, according to the specific environment. The meaning of U_i is key to understanding the concept of service demand in different execution environments. The effects of the various software layers are incorporated into the service demands through the way the utilization is calculated.

Example 12.2: Consider a Web server running on top of a UNIX/AIX system. The server operation was monitored during a period of $\mathcal{T} = 10$ min using a built-in trace facility [10] that captures the system activity while the Web server is running. From the trace, a summary report that gives several performance measurements, including processor utilization by the Web server and the UNIX kernel, was generated. It was observed that the CPU was 90% busy. It was also noted that 10% of the CPU time was spent on the execution of HTTP code (i.e., %user) and 80% on the operating system kernel (i.e.,%system) [1]. The CPU time spent on the kernel includes the work done by the file system, the network system, and other activities, such as interrupt handling, scheduling, and memory management. The number of HTTP requests counted in the HTTP log was 30,000. We want to calculate the service demand of an HTTP request.

Let $U_{\text{cpu}}^{\text{total}}$ be the total CPU utilization measured by the system monitor. $U_{\text{cpu}}^{\text{HTTP}}$ and $U_{\text{cpu}}^{\text{kernel}}$ denote the CPU utilization by the HTTP processes and OS kernel, respectively. The total CPU utilization is then composed of two parts:

$$U_{\text{cpu}}^{\text{total}} = U_{\text{cpu}}^{\text{kernel}} + U_{\text{cpu}}^{\text{kernel}}.$$

Thus, the CPU service demand can be compute as

$$D_{\text{cpu}} = U_{\text{cpu}}^{\text{total}} \times \mathcal{T}/C_0 = (0.80 + 0.10) \times (10 \times 60)/30,000 = 0.018 \text{ sec}.$$

We can note from the above expression that the CPU service demand of an HTTP request includes the services done by the operating system on its behalf. ■

The resource usage by the operating system is known as *overhead*. It can be viewed as composed of two parts: a constant one and a variable one. The former corresponds to those activities performed by an OS that do not depend on the system load, such as the CPU time to handle an I/O interrupt. The variable component of overhead stems from activities that are closely associated with the system load. For instance, as the number of processes in memory increases, the work done by memory management modules also increases. Another example of variable cost is the processing overhead of a network software, that depends on message size.

Basically, there are two approaches for representing overhead in performance models. One approach uses a special class of the model for representing the overhead of the OS activities performed on behalf of application programs (i.e., I/O, network, and security). There are problems associated with this approach. Because of its variable component, service demands of the special class have to be made load-dependent. Thus, whenever the intensity parameters (e.g., number of customers and arrival rate) of the application classes change, the service demands of the overhead class have to be modified too. The interdependency between overhead parameters and execution mix may make this approach impractical. Unless the operating system load is itself a subject of the performance analysis, it is not a good modeling assumption to represent overhead as an independent class of the model. The alternative and more common modeling approach attempts to distribute the overhead among the various classes of application programs.

12.5.5   Parameter Estimation

Parameter estimation deals with the determination of input parameters from measurement data. Many times, monitors do not provide enough information for calculating the input parameters required by a performance model. Therefore, inferences have to be made to derive the desired parameters. This section discusses general procedures for estimating input parameters.

Once the performance model has been specified and the solution techniques selected, the analyst faces the problem of estimating input parameters for the model. This section outlines the basic steps for obtaining the most common input parameters for performance models. The techniques presented here attempt to use, to the maximum extent possible, the data which are commonly provided by current commercial monitors.

1. *Identify the type of execution environment.* In other words, the analyst has to find out what software layers are underneath application programs and on top of the hardware. The type of environment determines the way of estimating the workload service demands.

2. *Specify the measurement process.* Once the environment has been typified, the next step involves basic definitions concerning the monitoring tools to be used, the data to be obtained, and the measurement interval (i.e., starting time and duration).

3. *Monitor the system and collect performance data.* The measurement data will be used to estimate the input parameters.

4. *Estimate input parameters.* According to the type of environment and measurement data obtained, calculate input parameters using the appropriate techniques and formulas described in the next sections.

We show now how service demands are computed from measurements obtained from a combination of operating system utilities and program analyzers. Consider Fig. 12.4 which illustrates a server process (e.g., file server, database server, or HTTP server) running on top of the operating system. The figure also shows various types of requests $(R_1 - R_n)$ running on top of the server process. In many cases, the operating system is not directly aware of the requests that are running

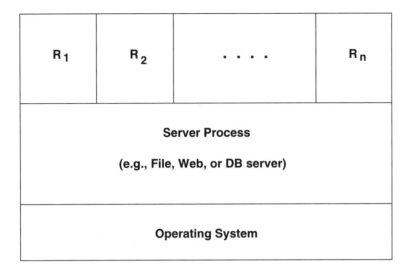

Figure 12.4. Layers for computing service demands.

on top of the server and can only provide measurements related to the server as an aggregate viewed as a single process.

Remember that, from the Service Demand Law, the service demand $D_{i,r}$ of a request of class r at a resource i is given by

$$D_{i,r} = U_{i,r}/X_{0,r}. \tag{12.5.1}$$

It turns out that the operating system monitoring tools do not provide, in general, the utilization of several resources on a per-request basis. These tools provide the utilization of the server process. Then, we need to combine information provided by program analyzers with information provided by the OS to derive the utilization for each type of request. We use the information provided by program analyzers to distribute the overall utilization of the server process as measured by the OS to the various types of requests. Consider that we want to obtain the service demands at the CPU for class r requests and that we have the following measurements:

- $U^{\text{os}}_{\text{cpu,server}}$: utilization of the server process at the CPU measured by an OS utility

- TotalCPUTime$_r$: total CPU time for requests of class r measured by a program analyzer at the server level

- $X_{0,r}$: throughput of class r requests measured from a log generated by the server process or from a program analyzer at the server level

Then, the utilization of class r requests at the CPU is

$$U_{\text{cpu},r} = U_{\text{cpu,server}}^{\text{os}} \times \frac{\text{TotalCPUTime}_r}{\sum_{s=1}^{n} \text{TotalCPUTime}_s} \qquad (12.5.2)$$

and the service demand at the CPU for class r requests is

$$D_{\text{cpu},r} = U_{\text{cpu},r}/X_{0,r}. \qquad (12.5.3)$$

Example 12.3: Consider that an HTTP server received 21,600 requests during 1 hour as measured from the HTTP log. An analysis of this log places the requests in three categories according to file sizes: small (up to 10KB), medium (from 10KB to 100KB), and large (larger than 100KB). Table 12.1 shows the total CPU time for each class of request as obtained from an instrumented HTTP server. It also shows the total number of requests processed in each category. These numbers are obtained from an analysis of the HTTP log. If the overall CPU utilization measured by the OS was 86% and the machine was dedicated to being a Web server, what is the service demand at the CPU for each class of request?

The throughputs per class are

$$\begin{aligned}
X_{\text{small}} &= 12,960/3,600 = 3.60 \ \text{requests/sec} \\
X_{\text{medium}} &= 6,480/3,600 = 1.80 \ \text{requests/sec} \\
X_{\text{large}} &= 2,160/3,600 = 0.60 \ \text{requests/sec}.
\end{aligned}$$

The utilizations per class are

$$\begin{aligned}
U_{\text{cpu,small}} &= 0.86 \times \frac{1,555}{1,555 + 972 + 389} = 0.46 \\
U_{\text{cpu,medium}} &= 0.86 \times \frac{972}{1,555 + 972 + 389} = 0.29 \\
U_{\text{cpu,large}} &= 0.86 \times \frac{389}{1,555 + 972 + 389} = 0.11.
\end{aligned}$$

Thus, the service demands per class of HTTP request are

$$\begin{aligned}
D_{\text{cpu,small}} &= U_{\text{cpu,small}}/X_{\text{small}} = 0.46/3.60 = 0.13 \ \text{sec} \\
D_{\text{cpu,medium}} &= U_{\text{cpu,medium}}/X_{\text{medium}} = 0.29/1.80 = 0.16 \ \text{sec} \\
D_{\text{cpu,large}} &= U_{\text{cpu,large}}/X_{\text{large}} = 0.11/0.60 = 0.18 \ \text{sec}. \qquad \blacksquare
\end{aligned}$$

Table 12.1. Measurements for Ex. 12.3

File Size Range	Total CPU Time (sec)	No. of Requests
file size ≤ 10 KB	1,555	12,960
10KB < file size ≤ 100KB	972	6,480
file size > 100KB	389	2,160

12.6 Collecting Performance Data

As shown in Fig. 12.1, measurements of network-based computing environments should be collected at various points, including networks, servers, and clients. This section presents some tools available for collecting performance data on these elements.

12.6.1 Network

A network management system is a collection of tools for measuring and monitoring the behavior of a network. It provides a big picture of the entire network. The Simple Network Management Protocol (SNMP) provides the basis for collecting performance data from network devices, such as servers, routers, and switches. The SNMP architecture consists of a manager and an agent [2]. The network management application runs on a network management workstation and sends information requests to the managed devices. An agent that runs on the device receives the request, collects the requested measurement, and sends it back to the manager application that keeps the SNMP historical performance database. The information collected by the agents is organized in a tree structure known as Management Information Base (MIB). The performance variables are logically grouped into branches of the tree structure, such as the interface, IP, and TCP. For instance, performance information about routing is found in the IP branch. Most network management products comply with MIB standards.

Individual LAN segments can be monitored with LAN analyzers, which are a combination of specialized hardware and software or, simply, software. Most monitors, such as Network General Sniffer and HP Network Advisor, consist of a LAN interface, a hardware filter, and a portable PC-based system. These monitors operate in promiscuous mode, examining all frames that pass through the segment. Frames that match given specifications (e.g., destination, source, and port number) are selected and have their information recorded for later analysis. Statistics produced by LAN analyzers for Ethernet networks include metrics such as packets per second, collisions per second, utilization, and CRC errors. Because of the volume of data, LAN analyzers collect only a few minutes of traffic measurements. Packet traces collected by this type of monitor are more useful for operations personnel and network specialists.

When it comes to remote segments, monitor devices gather real-time performance information about a LAN network segment. The Remote Monitoring MIB (RMON) specification provides an industry standard basis to many real-time commercially available network monitors, such as Tivoli TME, HP OpenView, SunNet Manager, Optimal, BMC, and Econet. The RMON specification includes the following goals: offline operation from the central network management system, preemptive monitoring, problem detection and reporting, and value-added data. The

RMON probe is also able to interpret the collected data. RMON devices can respond to multiple network management systems. RMON specifications, though, do not include application-oriented measurement data [3], [12].

Usually, most network performance monitors focus primarily on measurement data needed by operations and performance tuning. Network monitor tools display information such as traffic intensity on various network segments (i.e., LAN and WAN), bandwidth usage, and server utilizations. They do not collect data on application basis. Although sniffers or LAN analyzers provide detailed measurement data, they do not operate continuously, which limits their use in capacity planning. For capacity planning purposes, it requires higher level information that indicates how the system behaves for longer periods of time. Commercial network monitors can provide part of the measurement data required by analytical models of network-based systems.

Example 12.4: Consider a C/S environment where a database server is accessed by 60 client workstations through a dedicated LAN. The network traffic consists only of the database requests submitted by the clients and the replies sent back by the server. Using a LAN analyzer, the performance analyst monitored the network several times during the peak periods. The average network utilization was 16%. During the same monitoring period, the database performance monitor measured a total transaction rate of 2.0 tps. The analyst wants to know the average service time spent by a C/S transaction at the LAN. Note that the average service time per transaction is equal to the average service time for the request plus the average service time for the reply. The average service time per transaction includes all the frames exchanged plus the protocol overheads. From the operational laws (see Chap. 3), we know that

$$D_{\text{network}} = U_{\text{network}}/X_0 = 0.16/2.0 = 0.08 \text{ sec}$$

where D_{network} is the average network service demand of a C/S transaction and X_0 the server throughput. ∎

12.6.2   Server

A server is a combination of hardware platform, operating system, and functional server software, such as HTTP server, DBMS server, file server, and application server. A quantitative description of the server behavior can be obtained through measurements collected at the different layers of the system, as depicted in Fig. 12.5.

A number of system resources need to be monitored to obtain input data for performance models. The resources that have the most impact on server performance are memory, processor, disk, and networking subsystems. In order to develop performance models, different monitor tools are needed to collect data at the different layers of the server. The combination of several tools provides global performance data as well as application oriented measurement data. This section discusses some of the standard performance tools that come with the two most popular operating systems for C/S environments: Windows NT and UNIX.

Windows NT

Windows NT provides a set of performance tools that can be used to collect and display performance information of any computer in a distributed environment. The main tool to collect data and analyze performance is the NT Performance Monitor [4], which comes with NT. Performance Monitor measures the behavior of computer objects. In the NT environment, an object is a standard mechanism for identifying and using a system resource. The objects represent processes, threads, memory, and physical devices. Objects that always appear in Performance Monitor include Cache, LogicalDisk, Memory, PagingFile, PhysicalDisk, Process, Processor, System, and Thread. Each object type can have several instances. For example, a system that has multiple processors will have multiple instances of the Processor object type. The Logical Disk object type has two instances if the physical disk has two logical partitions. Some object types (Memory and Server) do not have instances. If an object type has multiple instances, each instance produces the same set of statistics.

The concept of a counter is fundamental to understand NT performance. A counter is an entity for which performance data are available. Counters are organized by object type. A unique set of counters exists for each object, such as processor, memory, logical disk, processes, and other object types that produce statistical information. Performance Monitor collects data on various aspects of software and hardware performance, such as use, demands, rates, and used space. They represent measures such as processor utilization, number of processes waiting for disk, number of network packets transmitted per second, number of visits to a device, and available bytes.

A counter defines the type of data available to a particular counter object. On hardware devices, such as disks, counters count visits to the devices and provides, in many cases, the average device service time. Each object can have multiple counters. There are three types of counters. Instantaneous counters exhibit the most recent measurements. Averaging counters represent a value over a time interval and display

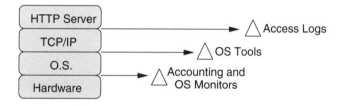

Figure 12.5. Collecting server performance data.

the average of the two last measurements. Difference counters show the difference between the last measurement and the previous one. Counters are usually expressed as rates per second or fraction of time a device is used (i.e., utilization expressed in percentage). Table 12.2 displays some counters that indicate system resource usage information.

There are different ways to view the data collected by Performance Monitor, namely: chart, report, alert, and log. Chart displays the value of a counter over time. A report view shows the value of a counter and an alert view triggers an event when the value of a counter reaches a specified threshold. These three views are more useful for operation problem detection and performance tuning. Capacity planing makes use of the log view, which records the counters on disk. Log files can be retrieved by Performance Monitor at a later time for charting and reporting. This tool can be used to gain a better understanding of how efficiently a system is working and what the problems might be if it is performing poorly. Despite its wide applicability, Performance Monitor does not answer capacity planning questions and does not provide basic input data required by analytical models. Another problem is that NT does not have an intrinsic definition of a basic component of a workload, such as transaction, request, interaction, or job. With the standard performance tools available in NT, it is difficult to obtain measurements that would characterize real workloads in terms of interactions or applications. The concept of transaction or interaction is important because it is meaningful from the end-user's viewpoint. It is a key element to define, characterize, and forecast workloads. Thus, if developers want to measure transaction processing times in NT, they must write their code to instrument the applications or base their applications on packages that implement and keep track of transactions or any other unit of work. Another difficulty with the Performance Monitor is that it does not save information about processes [3]. Once a process stops running, its execution information disappears from the system.

Example 12.5: Let us consider a Windows NT Web server running the Internet Information Server (IIS) that provides several Internet services, such as HTTP,

Table 12.2. NT Performance Monitor Counters

Object	Counter	Description
System	% Processor time	Average utilization
System	Processor queue length	Number of requests in queue
Processor	% Processor time	Average processor utilization
Processor	% Privileged time	Operating system service time
Processor	% User time	User service time
Memory	Pages/sec	Pages read and written per sec
Network interface	Bytes/sec	Network throughput
Physical disk	% Disk time	Average disk utilization

FTP, and telnet. The system was monitored during a period of time $T = 900$ sec. Performance Monitor and IIS collected information about the the system performance and resource usage, as shown in Table 12.3. The "GET Request" counter indicates the number of HTTP GET requests received by the Web server during the monitoring period. Let us denote by C_{www} the number of GET requests. Let us also consider that the WWW workload was composed only of GET requests. Thus, our model has two classes. One class represents the WWW service (i.e., HTTP) that handles the GET requests. The second class refers to other services provided by the NT operating system. Based on the values displayed on Table 12.3, we want to calculate the processor service demand for class WWW, made up of GET requests.

The counter "Thread" indicates the processor time used by the threads of the *Inetinf* process that implements the WWW service. We note from Table 12.3 that the processor time attributed to the processes do not add up to the total processor time measured for the system object. It happens that the portion of time captured by monitors varies with both the nature of the workload and the type of operating system. The proportion of total CPU time that is captured by measurement tools is known as *capture ratio*. Although the concept of capture ratio has been defined for CPU time, it also applies to other resource categories. In a more general way, we can define the resource usage capture ratio as the ratio of the resource usage accounted to programs to the resource usage measured by system monitors.

The reason for the difference between total processor time and total process time in this example stems from the fact that the time spent in interrupts are not charged to the processes that were running. However, this time is counted in the overall processor usage. So, to calculate the service demand, we need to distribute the amount of unaccounted time to the two classes. We do that by distributing the total time in proportion to the accounted time displayed in Table 12.3. The CPU

Table 12.3. NT Performance Monitor Results

Object	Counter	Value
System	% Total processor time	74.7
System	Processor queue length	2.0
Processor	Interrupts per sec	989.6
User disk	% Disk time	44.8
System disk	% Disk time	10.2
Memory	Page faults per sec	55.3
Thread: WWW	% Processor time	41.21
Process: others	% Processor time	6.55
HTTP service	GET requests	8,120

utilization of class r is given by

$$U_{\text{cpu},r} = U_{\text{cpu}}^{\text{total}} \times f_{\text{cpu},r}$$

where $U_{\text{cpu}}^{\text{total}}$ is the total CPU utilization and $f_{\text{cpu},r}$ is the fraction of the total CPU utilization that can be attributed to class r (i.e., it is equivalent to the capture ratio) which is given by

$$f_{\text{cpu},r} = \frac{U_{\text{cpu},r}^{\text{os}}}{\sum\limits_{\forall \text{ class } s} U_{\text{cpu},s}^{\text{os}}}$$

where $U_{\text{cpu},r}^{\text{os}}$ is the CPU utilization of class r measured by an accounting system or monitor facility of the OS. So, the service demand, $D_{\text{cpu},www}$, for class WWW is given by

$$D_{\text{cpu},www} = \frac{U_{\text{cpu},www}}{C_{\text{www}}/\mathcal{T}} = \frac{U_{\text{cpu}}^{\text{total}} \times f_{\text{cpu},www}}{C_{\text{www}}/\mathcal{T}}.$$

Plugging the numbers from Table 12.3 into the above expressions, we obtain

$$D_{\text{cpu},www} = 0.747 \times \frac{41.21}{41.21 + 6.55} \times 900/8120 = 0.071 \ \text{ sec}$$

In other words, the execution of a typical GET request demands 0.071 sec of CPU time. ∎

Further considerations on modeling and collecting data for Windows NT are given in [6].

UNIX

A UNIX system can be viewed as a combination of several resources: processor, memory, disks, kernel, network, and graphics. There exist system tools that measure and yield statistics about the behavior of each class of resource. Performance measurement facilities provide global and per-process results. In this section, we examine some of the standard UNIX measurement facilities. Different UNIX versions (i.e., versions derived from Berkeley BSD and System V) have different monitoring tools. It is worth mentioning that no single tool provides all the information required by performance models.

A useful tool for workload characterization is System Activity Reporting (sar), which is included in many UNIX versions. It is a sampling mode tool that records cumulative and average system activity data, as maintained by the UNIX kernel. sar offers several options and reports, as shown in Table 12.4 which displays results of CPU utilization, stratified by system, user, wio, and idle percentage. The results came from the execution of the sar command at 3:36 PM. The meaning of each metric is the following: *sys* corresponds to the percentage of time spent executing code in the system state (i.e., kernel), *usr* refers to the percentage of time spent executing code in the user state, *wio* is the amount of time spent waiting for blocked I/O, and *idle* represents the percentage of time the CPU was idle.

Table 12.4. System-Wide **sar** Statistics

Time	%sys	%usr	%wio	%idle
3:36:00	28	41	25	6
3:41:00	27	48	20	5
3:46:01	26	42	26	6
3:51:00	27	60	12	1
3:56:00	29	59	11	1
4:01:00	28	60	12	1
4:06:01	19	58	12	1
4:11:00	29	55	15	1
4:16:01	29	54	16	1

Example 12.6: Consider that a UNIX based Web server was monitored for 40 min and that 14,400 HTTP requests were processed during this period as measured from the HTTP log. During the same period, **sar** was active and provided the measurements given in Table 12.4. If the machine is dedicated to being a Web server, what was the average service demand at the CPU during the measurement period?

The server throughput X was $14,400/(40 \times 60) = 6$ requests/sec. The average CPU utilization can be obtained from Table 12.4 by averaging the values of (100 − %idle) over the interval. This gives us $U_{cpu} = 877/9 = 97.4\%$. From the Service Demand Law (see Chap. 3) we get that $D_{cpu} = U_{cpu}/X = 0.974/6 = 0.162$ sec. ∎

There are other commands that provide information on how the system is performing. For instance, **ps** reports information about processes running on the system. The **vmstat** command (i.e., virtual memory statistics) informs about virtual memory, disk accesses, and CPU utilization. The **iostat** command provides I/O statistics, such as bytes per second, transfers per second, and milliseconds per seek. Information about networking can be obtained with the command **netstat**. It lists the state of all network connections and provides information about the number of packets (e.g., TCP, IP, and UDP) processed by the system.

Different versions of UNIX have accounting systems that differ in a number of respects [5], [13]. The UNIX operating system periodically updates resource usage information for each active process. When a process terminates, the performance information is recorded in the process accounting log file. For UNIX versions derived from System V, the log file is **pacct**. BSD-derived versions have a similar log file, but with a different format. Special commands (e.g., **acctcom** and **sa**) generate several reports from the entries recorded in the accounting log files, as shown in Table 12.5. *Command Name* gives the name of the program. *Number of Commands* indicates the number of times the program was executed during the interval of time covered by the report. The total amount of CPU time accumulated during all executions of the program is given by *Total CPU*. The total amount of elapsed time is denoted by *Total Real*. The average CPU time used to execute the program is *Mean CPU*. *Hog Factor* is the total CPU time divided by the total elapsed time. The unit of time in Table 12.5 is minutes.

Example 12.7: Consider that the results displayed in Table 12.5 are the summary of the log of a 24-hour period of a database server. Suppose that the average CPU utilization reported by the `sar` command for the same period of time is 63.2%. What is the CPU capture ratio for the measurements in Table 12.5? In other words, we want to know much CPU time was captured by the processes recorded in the accounting log. Recall that the capture ratio was defined

$$f_{\text{cpu}} = \frac{U_{\text{cpu}}^{\text{acct}}}{U_{\text{cpu}}^{\text{os}}}$$

where $U_{\text{cpu}}^{\text{acct}}$ is the utilization measured by the accounting system and $U_{\text{cpu}}^{\text{os}}$ is the CPU utilization measured by a system-level monitor. Considering that the accounting system shows a "Total CPU" of 783.06 min in a 24-hour (i.e., 1,440 min) period, the calculated utilization is then $U_{\text{cpu}}^{\text{acct}} = 783.06/1,440 = 54.38\%$. Thus, the capture ratio or the portion of time captured by the accounting system is $f_{\text{cpu}} = 54.38/63.20 = 86\%$. ∎

Once we have obtained the capture ratio, it is easy to estimate the true utilization per class. A detailed analysis of capture ratios and on the method to distribute all unaccounted resource usage among classes of a workload can be found in [16].

12.7 Concluding Remarks

Performance models are useful tools for understanding and predict the quantitative behavior of network-based environments, such as C/S systems, intranets, and the Internet. However, the representativeness of a model depends directly on the quality of input parameters. There are two key issues in the process of obtaining input

Table 12.5. Total Command Summary (Times in min)

Command Name	Number of Commands	Total CPU	Total Real	Mean CPU	Hog Factor
oracle	15	421.11	1880.24	28.07	0.22
mail	150	96.23	319.67	0.64	0.30
grep	300	250.88	1609.45	2.17	0.16
ls	322	9.09	112.33	0.03	0.08
cd	98	5.75	90.01	0.05	0.06
hline Total	885	783.06	4011.70	4.53	0.19

parameters for performance models: performance measurement and parameter estimation. With regard to the measurement process, it is essential to understand what is being measured, how accurate the measurements are, and how reliable the resulting numbers are. This chapter discussed several aspects of the measurement process in a network-based environment and showed techniques and tools used for collecting performance data of a system.

Parameter estimation deals with the determination of input parameters from measurement data. Many times, monitors do not provide enough information for calculating the input parameters required by a performance model. In most cases of real systems, assumptions have to be taken about the behavior of the system and inferences need to be made to derive the desired parameters.

Although this chapter does not focus on any particular product or manufacturer, it provides a set of general guidelines for transforming typical measurement data into typical input parameters. The guidelines can be applied to real problems in a straightforward manner. Because of the uncertainties associated with the process of estimating parameters, it is necessary to validate the model. An in-depth discussion of validation and calibration techniques is found in [16]. The main thrust of this chapter was on how to obtain parameters for existing C/S server systems. However, if C/S are under development, one needs to estimate service demands using different techniques. A framework for doing this is given in [15].

BIBLIOGRAPHY

[1] J. Almeida, V. A. F. Almeida, and D. Yates, Measuring the behavior of a World-Wide Web server, *Seventh Conf. High Perform. Networking (HPN)*, IFIP, Apr. 1997, pp. 57–72.

[2] J. Blommers, *Practical Planning for Network Growth.* Upper Saddle River, NJ: Prentice Hall, 1996.

[3] J. P. Buzen and A. N. Shum, Beyond bandwidth: mainframe style capacity planning for networks and Windows NT, *Proc. 1996 Comput. Measurement Group (CMG) Conf.*, Orlando, FL, Dec. 8–13, 1996, pp. 479–485.

[4] R. Blake, *Optimizing Windows NT.* Microsoft, 1993.

[5] J. Bouhana, UNIX workload characterization using process accounting, *Proc. 1996 Comput. Measurement Group Conf.*, San Diego, CA, Dec. 8–13, 1996, pp. 379–390.

[6] J. P. Buzen and A. N. Shum, Considerations for modeling Windows NT, *Proc. 1997 Comput. Measurement Group Conf.*, Orlando, FL, Dec. 9–12, 1997, pp. 219–230.

[7] J. Cady and B. Howarth *Computer System Performance Management and Capacity Planning.* Australia: Prentice Hall, 1990.

[8] Y. Ding, Performance modeling with application response measurement (ARM): pros and cons, *Proc. 1997 Comput. Measurement Group Conf.*, Orlando, FL, Dec. 9–12, 1997, pp. 34–45.

[9] P. Heidelberger and S. Lavenberg, Computer performance methodology, *IEEE Trans. Comput.*, vol. C-33, no. 12, Dec. 1984.

[10] D. Helly, *AIX/6000 Internals and Architecture.* New York: McGraw-Hill, 1996.

[11] R. Jain, *The Art of Computer Systems Performance Analysis.* New York: Wiley, 1991.

[12] A. LEINWAND and K. CONROY, *Network Management: A Practical Perspective.* Reading, MA: Addison-Wesley, 1996.

[13] M. LOUKIDES, *System Performance Tuning, A Nutshell Handbook.* O'Reilly & Assoc., 1991.

[14] D. A. MENASCÉ, K. NGUYEN, and D. NGUYEN, Performance modeling of a Unix communications server, *Proc. 1997 Comput. Measurement Group Conf.*, Orlando, FL, Dec. 9–12, 1997, pp. 211-218.

[15] D. A. MENASCÉ, A framework for software performance engineering of client/server systems, *Proc. 1997 Comput. Measurement Group Conf.*, Orlando, FL, Dec. 9–12, 1997, pp. 460–469.

[16] D. A. MENASCÉ, V. A. F. ALMEIDA, and L. W. DOWDY, *Capacity Planning and Performance Modeling: From Mainframes to Client-Server Systems.* Upper Saddle River, NJ: Prentice Hall, 1994.

[17] T. NOVAK and D. HOFFMAN, New metrics for new media: toward the development of web measurement standards, *World Wide Web J.*, Winter, vol. 2, no. 1, 1997.

[18] C. ROSE, A measurement procedure for queueing network models of computer systems, *Computing Surveys*, vol. 10, no. 3, Sept. 1978.

Chapter 13

WRAPPING UP

Information technology and networking are key elements of modern electronic societies. These elements have reshaped the way people and business interact and operate. Computers are ubiquitous and are connected to millions of other computers by world wide networks. New applications have been devised and proposed as a result of the high degree of connectivity enabled by the Internet. Examples include electronic commerce, digital libraries, distance training and education, Web-based banking, and other multimedia-rich applications that use Web-related technologies. As a consequence, demands on computing and communications resources have grown exponentially, stressing servers, routers, and networks to the limit of their capacity. This has resulted, in many cases, in extremely degraded performance, unsatisfied users, and financial losses. Trends point toward ever-increasing demands on IT resources. Thus, capacity problems will continue to exist in the future and will likely become more prevalent as new network-based applications are planned and deployed and more and more users gain network access.

Capacity planning techniques are needed to avoid the pitfalls of inadequate capacity and to meet users' performance expectations in a cost-effective manner. This book gives the reader the foundations required to carry out capacity planning studies for intranets and client/server systems. The main steps are based on two models: a workload model and a performance model. The first model results from understanding and characterizing the workloand and the second from a quantitative description of the system behavior.

A key aspect of this book is the use of a quantitative approach to analyzing client/server and Web-based systems. This approach lends itself to the development of performance-predictive models for capacity planning. Instead of relying on intuition, ad hoc procedures, and rules of thumb, we provide in this book a uniform and formal way of dealing with performance problems. The performance models discussed here are based on the theory of queuing networks. Delays in networked environments consist of two parts: service times and waiting times. The former are defined as the time spent using resources such as processors, routers, disks, communication links, and LAN segments. Waiting times arise when several requests contend for the use of a finite-capacity resource. Performance models are used to compute waiting times from service times and from load intensity parameters. This book focuses on explaining how to compute service times and on how to use them to build and solve performance models that calculate waiting times. Other performance metrics of interest are also derived from the solution of these models. Metrics include throughput, utilization, response time, and average queue lengths.

The methods used to compute service times for the various types of network, processing, and storage elements are derived from abstractions of the behavior of these elements and from intrinsic performance and functional characteristics. For example, disk service times can be computed from seek times, latency, block size, and transfer rates. Message service times through a LAN segment depend on the LAN bandwidth, message size, and Protocol Data Unit sizes of the protocols involved. The book shows how to compute service times for single disks, disk arrays, routers, LANs, and WANs. The procedures used for these cases can be easily generalized to deal with cases not specifically covered here. As an example, the performance impact of using cryptography for message transmission can be assessed by properly adjusting network and processing service times to reflect the change in message size due to the cryptographic transformations and the processing time needed to encrypt and decrypt messages. Other security techniques, such as the use of network authentication protocols and firewalls [4] can be treated similarly.

Waiting time computations are based on the solution of queuing models. Two broad categories of models were considered in this book: system- and component-level models. System-level models treat a subsystem as a black box. Only the input, represented by the arrival rate of requests, and the output behavior, represented by the throughput, are considered at this level. System-level models are represented by the set of possible states a system can be found in, along with the possible transitions between states and the rates at which they occur. For example, a system-level model of a Web server looks only at the arriving HTTP requests and the corresponding HTTP responses. On the other hand, to examine the impact of the Web server components (e.g., disks, processors, and network links) and its architecture on its throughput, one needs to explicitly represent the components and architecture. This can be accomplished by a component-level model based on single and multiclass queuing networks, in which components are represented by queues. Connections between queues reflect the system architecture and the flow of requests between the components. The component-level models presented here capture the essential behavior of the main elements of network-based environments and represent the effect of contention for shared resources. Detailed models of specific networking technologies, such as LAN access protocols or ATM switches, can be found in [1], [6]. These models can be integrated with queuing network models through the use of load-dependent servers as discussed in [5].

This book shows how queuing network models can be used to account for Web-specific workload characteristics. In particular, the burstiness of the Web traffic can be incorporated into the models by properly inflating the service demands by a burstiness factor computed from measured operational data. Heavy-tailed distributions of document sizes are modeled through the use of multiple classes in a queuing network model. For example, requests for large files and requests for small HTML documents would form two different classes, modeled according to their specific resource usage. Class attributes can be used to differentiate the access frequency for different types of objets.

System- and component-level models can be further classified into open and closed models, depending on the size of the population. Open models have an unknown and potentially infinite population. This is the case of a public Web site on the Internet. On the contrary, a closed model is characterized by a known and finite population. For example, the intranet Web site of a company is only available to its employees. Therefore, the population of users of this server is known and finite.

Performance models can be used to answer typical what-if questions frequently faced by managers of IT resources. Examples of the application of performance models are discussed throughout the book. Some questions that can be answered by these models are, "Is the capacity of the servers and networks adequate to handle load spikes?" "Is the corporate network able to sustain the intranet traffic?" "Should the company Web site have mirror sites?" "How do I assess the impact of multimedia contents in a Web site?" and "What should be the bandwidth of the link that connects the Web server to the Internet so that acceptable service levels are provided?"

Performance has been a concern in the design of many important systems for the past 30 years. The past and future of system performance evaluation have been discussed in several meetings and forums [2], [3], [7]. Four critical areas were identified in the area of performance evaluation and analysis of computer and networked systems [3]:

1. the increasing complexity of today's systems,

2. the need to bridge the gap between theoretical and practical work,

3. the need to better educate engineers and analysts on performance issues, and

4. the need for industry to accept and integrate performance evaluation techniques as a standard practice in system design and implementation.

This book is an attempt to provide answers to these questions.

BIBLIOGRAPHY

[1] D. BERTSEKAS and R. GALLAGER, *Data Networks*. 2nd ed., Upper Saddle River, NJ: Prentice Hall, 1992.

[2] CMG, *Proc. 22nd Int. Conf. Resource Management Perform. Evaluation Enterprise Comput. Syst.*, San Diego, CA, December 8–13, 1996.

[3] G. HARING, C. LINDEMANN, and M. REISER, eds., Performance evaluation of computer systems and communication networks, *Dagstuhl-Seminar-Report; 189, 15.05.-19.09.97 (9738)*, Schloss Dagstuhl, Sept. 1997.

[4] S. GARFINKEL and G. SPAFFORD, *Practical UNIX & Internet Security*. 2nd ed., O'Reilly, 1996.

[5] D. A. MENASCÉ, V. A. F. ALMEIDA, and L. W. DOWDY, *Capacity Planning and Performance Modeling: From Mainframes to Client-Server Systems*. Upper Saddle River, NJ: Prentice Hall, 1994.

[6] R. O. ONVURAL, *Asynchronous Transfer Mode Networks: Performance Issues*. Norwood, MA: Artech House, 1994.

[7] SIGMETRICS, *Proc. 1997 ACM Sigmetrics Int. Conf. Measurement Modeling of Comput. Syst.*, Seattle, WA, June 15–18, 1997.

Appendix A

GLOSSARY OF TERMS

ACID The basic transaction properties of atomicity, consistency, isolation, and durability.

Accounting Systems Tools intended primarily as means of apportioning charges to users of a system.

ADSL See *Asymmetric Digital Subscriber Line*.

AIM Proprietary benchmark suites used to evaluate UNIX system performance.

Analytic Model Set of formulas and/or algorithms used to generate performance metrics from model parameters.

Arrival Theorem The number of customers seen by an arriving customer to a system is equal to the mean number of customers found in steady-state if the arriving customer were removed from the system.

Artificial Models Models that do not make use of any basic component of the real workload. Instead, these models are constructed out of special-purpose programs and descriptive parameters.

ARPA See *Defense Advanced Research Projects Agency*.

Asymmetric Digital Subscriber Line A variation of Digital Subscriber Line, designed for an upstream data flow (client-to-server), which is a fraction of the downstream data flow (server-to-client).

Asynchronous Transfer Mode A method for dynamic allocation of bandwidth using a fixed size packet, called cell.

Availability Metric used to represent the percentage of time a system is available during an observation period.

Average Degree of Multiprogramming Average number of transactions or customers that are concurrently in execution in a system.

ATM See *Asynchronous Transfer Mode.*

Bandwidth Specifies the amount of data that can be transmitted over a communications link or network per unit of time, usually measured in bits per second.

Baseline Model Performance model of a computer system in its current situation (i.e., before any modifications on the parameters are investigated). The baseline model must be calibrated and validated using measurements of performance metrics from the actual system.

Basic Component Generic unit of work that arrives at a system from a external source.

Batch Class of programs executed in batch mode, which can be described by its multiprogramming level.

Benchmarking Running a set of standard programs on a machine to compare its performance with that of others.

Bottleneck Resource that saturates first as the workload intensity increases. It is the resource with the highest service demand.

Bridge A device that forwards traffic between network segments based on data link layer information.

Browser A program that allows a person to read hypertext.

Burstiness A characteristic of the WWW traffic that refers to the fact that data are transmitted randomly, with peak rates exceeding the average rates by factors of 8 to 10.

Cache A small fast memory holding recently-accessed data, designed to speed up subsequent accesses to the same data. Although caching techniques have been most often applied to processor-memory access, they also have been used for a local copy of data accessible over a network.

Calibration Technique used to alter the parameters (either the input or the output parameters) of a base model of an actual system, so that the output parameters of the resulting calibrated model matches the performance of the actual system being modeled.

Capacity Planning Process of predicting when future load levels will saturate the system and of determining the most cost-effective way of delaying system saturation as much as possible.

Capture Ratio Proportion of total CPU time that is captured by measurement tools, such as accounting systems or monitor tools.

Carrier Sense with Multiple Access/Collision Detection The access method used by local area networking technology, such as Ethernet.

CGI See *Common Gateway Interface.*

Class Concept used in a performance model to abstract the parameters of a workload that are relevant to performance.

Class Population Maximum number of customers of a class.

Client Process that interacts with the user and is responsible for (1) implementing the user interface, (2) generating one or more requests to the server from the user queries or transactions, (3) transmitting the requests to the server via a suitable interprocess communication mechanism, and (4) receiving the results from the server and presenting them to the user.

Client/Server (C/S) The client/server computing model is predicated on the notion of splitting the work to be performed by an application between two types of processes—the client and the server. The server accepts requests for data from a client and returns the results to the client.

Client Think Time Average time elapsed between the receipt of a reply from the server and the generation of a new request.

Closed Model Queuing model of a system with a fixed number of customers. Customers circulate among the system resources. The number of customers in the system at all times is fixed and the number of possible system states is finite.

Clustering Analysis Process by which a large number of components are grouped into clusters of similar components.

Command Unit of user-submitted work in an interactive system.

Common Gateway Interface A protocol for processing user-supplied information through Web server scripts.

Conservation of Total Probability Equation Equation that specifies that the sum of the steady-state probabilities is 1. That is, the system must always be in one of the known system states.

Convolution Algorithm An iterative technique for efficiently finding the solution of closed queuing networks.

Cryptography The study of techniques for encrypting and decrypting data, i.e., encoding data so that they can only be decoded by specific individuals.

C/S See *Client/Server.*

CSMA/CD See *Carrier Sense with Multiple Access/Collision Detection.*

Customer Entities that flow through a system receiving service from its various queues.

DARPA See *Defense Advanced Research Projects Agency.*

Database Management System Collection of programs that enable users to create and maintain a database.

DBMS See *Database Management System.*

Defense Advanced Research Projects Agency An agency of the U.S. Department of Defense responsible for the development of new technologies for use by the military.

Delay Queue Queue in which no queuing is allowed.

Disk Controller Device that decodes the device-specific I/O commands (e.g., seek and transfer) into control signals for the associated disks.

Dhrystone A synthetic benchmark program intended to be representative for system programming, with emphasis on integer and string operations.

Disk Array A storage system that consists of two or more disk drives designed to improve performance and/or reliability.

DNS See *Domain Name Server.*

Domain Name Server The DNS is a distributed, replicated, data query service that provides host IP address based on host names.

FDDI See *Fiber Distributed Data Interconnect*

Fiber Distributed Data Interconnect A high-speed (100 Mbps) LAN standard, whose underlying medium is fiber optic.

Effective Capacity Largest system throughput at which response time remains within the service levels.

Elapsed Time Total time spent by a job from its submission until its completion. This corresponds to the response time concept, except that it is generally used for batch workloads.

Event-Based Monitor Monitor that collects information at the occurrence of specific events.

Flow Equilibrium Assumption Principle that equates the customer's rate of flow into a system state to the customer's rate of flow out of the system state.

File Transfer Protocol A service to transfer files to and from one host to another over a network.

Firewall Mechanism used to protect data and computers from activities of untrusted users.

FTP See *File Transfer Protocol.*

Functional Characterization Description of the programs or applications that make up the workload.

Global Workload Set of transactions or jobs submitted to a computer system.

Heavy-tailed Distribution A random variable X follows a heavy-tailed distribution if $P[X > x] \sim x^{-\alpha}$, as $x \to \infty$ for $0 < \alpha < 2$.

Homogeneous Workload Assumption All requests that make up the workload are assumed to be statistically identical.

HTML See *Hypertext Markup Language.*

HTTP See *Hypertext Transfer Protocol.*

Hypertext Markup Language A language that allows authors to specify the appearance and format of multimedia documents, in particular Web documents.

Hypertext Transfer Protocol The protocol used by the World Wide Web, that defines how client browsers and Web servers communicate with each other over a TCP/IP connection.

Integrated Services Digital Network A technology that combines voice and digital network services in a single medium, making it possible to offer this combination of services through a single wire.

Interactive Class On-line processing class with components generated by a given number of PCs or workstations with a given think time.

Internet The global set of interconnected networks that uses TCP/IP.

Internet Protocol The protocol that defines the format of packets used on the TCP/IP Protocol Suite and the mechanism for routing a packet to its destination.

Internet Service Provider A company that provides other companies or individuals with access to, or presence on, the Internet.

Intranet A private Internet deployed by an organization for its internal use and not necessarily connected to the Internet. Intranets are based on TCP/IP networks and Web technologies.

IP See *Internet Protocol.*

ISAPI Microsoft's programming interface between applications and their Internet Server.

ISDN See *Integrated Services Digital Network.*

ISP See *Internet Service Provider.*

IT Information Technology.

I/O path Physical connection between memory and an I/O device.

Java An object-oriented, distributed, interpreted, architecture-neutral, portable, multithreaded, dynamic, programming language developed by Sun Microsystems.

LADDIS A benchmark suite that measures NFS server performance, by generating a synthetic load of NFS operations.

LAN See *Local Area Network.*

Little's Result Fundamental and general result that states that the number of customers in a system is equal to the product of the arrival rate of customers to the system and the mean time that each customer stays in the system (i.e., the customer's mean response time).

Linpack A benchmark that measures the performance of two routines of a collection of routines that solve various systems of simultaneous linear algebraic equations.

Load-Dependent Queue Queue whose rate of service delivery is not constant but rather is a function of the number of customers in the queue.

Local Area Network A network intended to serve a small geographic area.

Management Information Base The set of named items an SNMP management station can query or set in the SNMP agent of a device. To monitor a remote device, such as a router, a manager fetches values from MIB variables.

Maximum Degree of Multiprogramming Maximum number of transactions or customers of a class that can be in execution at a given time.

Maximum Transmission Unit The largest amount of data that can be sent across a given network using a single packet.

Mean Value Analysis Elegant iterative technique for solving closed queuing networks. It iterates over the number of customers.

MIB See *Management Information Base.*

Mission-Critical Applications Those applications that are fundamental to running the business.

Model Validation Process of verifying if a model captures accurately key aspects of a system. As a rule of thumb, if a model can accurately predict various changes to the system, the model is termed "validated."

Model Calibration Process of modifying a model so that it can be validated.

Modification Analysis Analysis of the variation of the performance behavior of a system as a function of the variation of its workload, hardware, and software parameters.

Monitors Tools used for measuring the level of activity of a computer system.

MTU See *Maximum Transmission Unit*

Multiclass Models Models where customers may be partitioned into different classes. Each class has unique device service demands and routing behavior.

MVA See *Mean Value Analysis.*

Natural Business Unit A quantifiable business variable that gives an indication of the volume of activity of a business.

NBU See *Natural Business Unit.*

Neal Nelson's Business Benchmark A proprietary benchmark suite used for performance evaluation of large UNIX-based systems.

Network File System A protocol developed by Sun Microsystems, which allows a computer to access files over a network as if they were on its local disks.

Network Interface Card An adapter circuit board installed in a computer to provide a physical connection to a network.

NFS See *Network File System.*

NIC See *Network Interface Card.*

NSAPI Netscape's programming interface between applications and their Web Server.

Open Model Queuing model of a system with an infinite customer population. Customers arrive from the outside world, receive service, and exit. The number of customers in the system at any one time is variable. Usually, infinite buffer sizes are assumed and the number of possible system states is infinite.

Operational Analysis Assumes that the input parameters of the system model are all based on measured quantities.

Overhead System resources (e.g., processor time and memory space) consumed by activities that are incidental to, but necessary to, the main tasks. Examples include the operating system overhead involved in user program execution or the Web server overhead needed to process HTTP requests.

Packet Switching A communication paradigm in which data units of a maximum size, packets, are individually routed between hosts, with no previously established communication path.

PDU See *Protocol Data Unit.*

Performance Model A system's representation used for predicting the values of performance measures of the system.

Physical I/O Operations Operations that correspond to actions performed by an I/O subsystem to exchange blocks of data with peripherals.

Prediction Model Model that, once calibrated, is used to answer "what if" performance prediction questions.

Program Analyzers Software tools intended to collect information about the execution of individual programs.

Protocol A set of formal rules describing how computers interact, especially across a network.

Protocol Data Unit An international standard denomination for packet.

Proxy Server It is a special type of World Wide Web server that acts as an agent, representing the server to the client and the client to the server. Usually, a proxy is used as a cache of items available on other servers that are presumably slower or more expensive to access.

Queue Set composed of a resource and its associated waiting queue.

Queue Length Number of customers in the system, including both customers in service as well as enqueued customers.

Queuing Network Set of interconnected queues.

RAID See *Redundant Arrays of Inexpensive Disks.*

Real Workloads All original programs, transactions, and commands processed during a given period of time.

Redundant Arrays of Inexpensive Disks A storage system that provides improved availability and/or performance.

Resource Saturation State that occurs when the utilization of a resource reaches 100%.

Reliability Measures of the occurrence of failures during the processing of services.

Remote Procedure Call A paradigm for implementing the client/server model. In general, a program invokes service across a network by making modified procedure calls.

Residence Time Total time spent by a request, transaction, or program at a resource.

Resource-Oriented Characterization Description of the consumption of the system resources by the workload.

Response Time Time from when a customer arrives to a system until the customer completes service and exits the system.

ROT See *Rules of Thumb.*

Round Trip Time A measure of the current delay on a network, found by timing a packet bounced off some remote host.

Router A device that forwards traffic between networks, based on network layer information and routing tables.

RPC See *Remote Procedure Call.*

RTT See *Round Trip Time.*

Rules of Thumb A method of procedure based on experience and common sense.

Sampling-Based Monitor Monitor that collects information about the system at predefined instants of time.

Scheduling Policies Policies responsible for assigning customers to be executed by a server over time in order to reach system objectives, such as minimizing average response time or maximizing throughput.

Server Process Process, or set of processes, that collectively provide services to clients in a manner that shields the client from the details of the architecture of the server's hardware/software environment. A server does not initiate any dialogue with a client; it only responds to requests. Servers control access to shared resources.

Service Demand Sum of the service times at a resource (e.g., CPU, disks) over all visits to that resource during the execution of a transaction or request.

Service Level Agreements It is a contract between the service provider (e.g., IT department or ISP) and the end user or business unit. It sets specific goals for response time, throughput, overall uptime, and cost.

Service Time Time spent at a resource (e.g., CPU, disks) receiving service from it each time a transaction or request visits that resource.

Shortest Positioning Time First A disk scheduling policy in which the request chosen to be serviced is the one that yields the shortest positioning time (i.e., seek + rotational time).

Shortest Seek Time First A disk scheduling policy in which the request chosen to be serviced is the one that yields the shortest seek time.

Simple Network Management Protocol The Internet standard protocol developed to manage nodes on an IP network.

Simulation Model A computer program that mimics the behavior of a system and provides statistics on the performance metrics of the system under study.

Single-Class Models Models where all customers are indistinguishable with respect to their device service demands and routing behavior.

SLA See *Service Level Agreements.*

SMDS See *Switched Multimegabit Data Service.*

Software Performance Engineering Process of constructing software systems that meet performance objectives.

SNMP See *Simple Network Management Protocol.*

SPEC See *Standard Performance Evaluation Corporation.*

SPECmark The term used to collectively refer to the CPU ratio speed metrics.

SPECrate A throughput metric based on the SPEC CPU benchmark, that measures the capacity of a system for processing specific jobs in a given time interval. It is also used to evaluate how much work one or more processors can accomplish.

SPECratio Measures how fast a given system might be. It is obtained by dividing the elapsed time that was measured for a system to complete a specified job by the reference time. The reference time is the amount of time that a particular benchmark requires to run on a given reference platform.

SPECweb A standardized benchmark developed by SPEC to measure a system's ability to act as a Web server.

SPTF See *Shortest Positioning Time First.*

SQL See *Structured Query Language.*

SSTF See *Shortest Seek Time First.*

Standard Performance Evaluation Corporation SPEC is an organization of computer industry vendors dedicated to developing standardized benchmarks and publish reviewed results.

Steady State Long-term average behavior after any initial transient effects have dissipated.

Structured Query Language The standard language for defining and accessing relational databases.

Switched Multimegabit Data Service An emerging high-speed datagram-based public data network service developed by Bellcore.

Synthetic Models Models that are constructed using basic components of the real workload as building blocks.

System Monitors Monitoring tools (hardware or software) that collect global performance statistics (i.e., do not attempt to distinguish among workload classes).

T1 A term for a digital carrier facility that transmits at 1.544 Mbps.

T3 A term for a digital carrier facility that transmits at 44.736 Mbps.

TCP See *Transmission Control Protocol.*

TCP/IP The protocol suite used in the Internet.

Telnet The Internet standard protocol for remote login service, that runs on top of TCP/IP.

Theoretical Capacity Maximum rate at which a computing system can perform work.

Think Time Interval of time that elapses since the user receives the prompt until he/she submits a new transaction.

Throughput Rate at which customers depart from the system measured in number of departures per unit time.

Time Windows Intervals of time during which the system, the workload, and the performance indexes are observed.

Token Ring A type of LAN with ring topology that uses token passing for access control.

TPC See *Transaction Processing Performance Council.*

TPC-C An on-line transaction processing (OLTP) benchmark suite. Order-entry provides a conceptual model for the benchmark.

TPC-D A benchmark suite to assess cost/performance of a particular system processing decision support applications. TPC-D models a decision support environment in which complex and adhoc business-oriented queries are submitted against a large database.

Transaction On-line processing class that groups components that arrive at a computer system with a given arrival rate.

Utilization of a Device Fraction of time that the device is busy, or equivalently, the percentage of time that at least one customer is in the system receiving service.

Transaction Processing Performance Council A nonprofit corporation founded to define transaction processing and database benchmarks.

Transmission Control Protocol The most common transport layer protocol used on the Internet as well as on Ethernet LANs.

UDP See *User Datagram Protocol.*

URL See *Uniform Resource Locator.*

Uniform Resource Locator A syntactic form used for identifying documents on the Web.

User Datagram Protocol It is a connectionless protocol that uses the Internet Protocol (IP) to deliver datagrams.

Validation Desirable characteristic of a model, seldom achieved in practice. A validated model of a system accurately mimics the actual behavior of the system in all aspects and can be used to predict the performance of the system under system or workload changes. The only truly validated model of a system is the system itself.

WAN See *Wide Area Network.*

Web A common short name for the World Wide Web.

Web server A combination of a hardware platform, operating system, server software and contents.

Webstone A configurable client/server benchmark for HTTP servers.

Whetstone A small benchmark program for measuring floating point calculations.

Wide Area Network A network, usually built with serial lines, that covers a large geographical region.

Workload Characterization Process of partitioning the global workload of a computer system into smaller sets or workload components composed of transactions or jobs having similar characteristics, and assigning numbers that represent their typical resource demand and intensity.

Workload Model Representation that mimics the real workload under study.

Workload Saturation State that is said to have been reached for a given workload when the service level for that workload is violated.

Workstation Response Time Time interval elapsed between the instant a transaction or command is submitted until the answer to it begins to appear at the user's workstation.

World Wide Web A client/server architecture that integrates various types of information on the global Internet and on IP networks.

WWW See *World Wide Web*.

Zipf's Law States that if one ranks the popularity of words (denoted by ρ) in a given text by their frequency of use (denoted by f), then $f \sim 1/\rho$.

Appendix B

ABOUT THE CD-ROM

The CD-ROM that comes with the book contains several MS Excel workbooks that implement the various formulas and algorithms described in the book. The CD-ROM also contains a sample of an HTTP log and a program to compute the burstiness factor of an HTTP log.

B.1   The Workbooks

The MS Excel workbooks in the CD-ROM can be opened in any version of Excel from 5.0 on and can be found in the folder xls. All of them have Visual Basic modules associated with them. A Help worksheet in each workbook provides details about the operation of the workbook. All worksheets have cells that contain input parameters and cells that contain computed values from the input parameters. Different colors are used to distinguish between the two types of cells. Also, the workbook structure and computed cells are password-protected to prevent the workbook from being unintentionally damaged. We recommend that you always work on a copy of the workbook and never on the original. If you want to modify the copy, you can use the password "1998" to unprotect the workbook. The workbooks are:

ServTime.XLS contains the formulas needed to compute service times on single disks, disk arrays, networks, as well as the operational laws. The material relevant to this workbook can be found in Chap. 3.

Cost.XLS contains a template for computing startup and operational costs in C/S systems as described in Chap. 5.

SysMod.XLS implements various system models discussed in Chap. 8, including

- infinite population, fixed service rate, and unlimited queue size
- infinite population, fixed service rate, limited queue size
- infinite population, variable service rate, and unlimited queue size
- infinite population, variable service rate, and limited queue size

309

- finite population and fixed service rate

- finite population and variable service rate

OpenQN.XLS implements the algorithm to solve multiclass open queuing networks as described in Chap. 9 and provides utilizations, queue lengths, residence times, and response times.

ClosedQN.XLS implements the algorithm to solve multiclass closed queuing networks as described in Chap. 9 and provides utilizations, queue lengths, residence times, response times, and throughputs.

WebModels contains worksheets to compute service demands for performance models for the Web as discussed in Chap. 10. In particular, this workbook contains worksheets for computing service demands for the client side with and without a proxy cache and for the Web server side. Once the service demands are computed, they can be copied and pasted into the proper location of the ClosedQN.XLS (for the client side) and OpenQN.XLS (for the server side) workbooks for model solving.

B.2   HTTP Log Sample and Program

The web folder in the CD-ROM has two files: httplog.txt and burst.c. The first is a sample of an HTTP log with 20,000 lines. Host ids were eliminated from the log to preserve the privacy of the clients of that particular site. The file burst.c is a C program that computes the burstiness parameters a and b according to the algorithm described in Chap. 10. This program has three parameters:

- -f <name>: name of the file containing an HTTP log

- -e <number>: number of epochs, i.e., the number of equal subintervals of the interval during which the log was obtained

- -r <number>: number of requests to be processed in the log. If this parameter is not specified, it is assumed to be equal 10,000, the value of the variable "maxreq" in the program burst.c

For example, if we wanted to compute the burstiness parameters for the sample log provided in the CD-ROM for 50 epochs, we would invoke the program as:

```
burst -f httplog.txt -e 50 -r 20000
```

SUBJECT INDEX

LICENSE AGREEMENT AND LIMITED WARRANTY

READ THE FOLLOWING TERMS AND CONDITIONS CAREFULLY BEFORE OPENING THIS CD PACKAGE. THIS LEGAL DOCUMENT IS AN AGREEMENT BETWEEN YOU AND PRENTICE-HALL, INC. (THE "COMPANY"). BY OPENING THIS SEALED CD PACKAGE, YOU ARE AGREEING TO BE BOUND BY THESE TERMS AND CONDITIONS. IF YOU DO NOT AGREE WITH THESE TERMS AND CONDITIONS, DO NOT OPEN THE CD PACKAGE. PROMPTLY RETURN THE UNOPENED CD PACKAGE AND ALL ACCOMPANYING ITEMS TO THE PLACE YOU OBTAINED THEM FOR A FULL REFUND OF ANY SUMS YOU HAVE PAID.

1.   **GRANT OF LICENSE:** In consideration of your purchase of this book, and your agreement to abide by the terms and conditions of this Agreement, the Company grants to you a nonexclusive right to use and display the copy of the enclosed software program (hereinafter the "SOFTWARE") on a single computer (i.e., with a single CPU) at a single location so long as you comply with the terms of this Agreement. The Company reserves all rights not expressly granted to you under this Agreement.

2.   **OWNERSHIP OF SOFTWARE:** You own only the magnetic or physical media (the enclosed CD) on which the SOFTWARE is recorded or fixed, but the Company and the software developers retain all the rights, title, and ownership to the SOFTWARE recorded on the original CD copy(ies) and all subsequent copies of the SOFTWARE, regardless of the form or media on which the original or other copies may exist. This license is not a sale of the original SOFTWARE or any copy to you.

3.   **COPY RESTRICTIONS:** This SOFTWARE and the accompanying printed materials and user manual (the "Documentation") are the subject of copyright. The individual programs on the CD are copyrighted by the authors of each program. Some of the programs on the CD include separate licensing agreements. If you intend to use one of these programs, you must read and follow its accompanying license agreement. If you intend to use the trial version of Internet Chameleon, you must read and agree to the terms of the notice regarding fees on the back cover of this book. You may not copy the Documentation or the SOFTWARE, except that you may make a single copy of the SOFTWARE for backup or archival purposes only. You may be held legally responsible for any copying or copyright infringement which is caused or encouraged by your failure to abide by the terms of this restriction.

4.   **USE RESTRICTIONS:** You may not network the SOFTWARE or otherwise use it on more than one computer or computer terminal at the same time. You may physically transfer the SOFTWARE from one computer to another provided that the SOFTWARE is used on only one computer at a time. You may not distribute copies of the SOFTWARE or Documentation to others. You may not reverse engineer, disassemble, decompile, modify, adapt, translate, or create derivative works based on the SOFTWARE or the Documentation without the prior written consent of the Company.

5.   **TRANSFER RESTRICTIONS:** The enclosed SOFTWARE is licensed only to you and may not be transferred to any one else without the prior written consent of the Company. Any unauthorized transfer of the SOFTWARE shall result in the immediate termination of this Agreement.

6.   **TERMINATION:** This license is effective until terminated. This license will terminate automatically without notice from the Company and become null and void if you fail to comply with any provisions or limitations of this license. Upon termination, you shall destroy the Documentation and all copies of the SOFTWARE. All provisions of this Agreement as to warranties, limitation of liability, remedies or damages, and our ownership rights shall survive termination.

7.   **MISCELLANEOUS:** This Agreement shall be construed in accordance with the laws of the United States of America and the State of New York and shall benefit the Company, its affiliates, and assignees.

8. **LIMITED WARRANTY AND DISCLAIMER OF WARRANTY:** The Company warrants that the SOFTWARE, when properly used in accordance with the Documentation, will operate in substantial conformity with the description of the SOFTWARE set forth in the Documentation. The Company does not warrant that the SOFTWARE will meet your requirements or that the operation of the SOFTWARE will be uninterrupted or error-free. The Company warrants that the media on which the SOFTWARE is delivered shall be free from defects in materials and workmanship under normal use for a period of thirty (30) days from the date of your purchase. Your only remedy and the Company's only obligation under these limited warranties is, at the Company's option, return of the warranted item for a refund of any amounts paid by you or replacement of the item. Any replacement of SOFTWARE or media under the warranties shall not extend the original warranty period. The limited warranty set forth above shall not apply to any SOFTWARE which the Company determines in good faith has been subject to misuse, neglect, improper installation, repair, alteration, or damage by you. EXCEPT FOR THE EXPRESSED WARRANTIES SET FORTH ABOVE, THE COMPANY DISCLAIMS ALL WARRANTIES, EXPRESS OR IMPLIED, INCLUDING WITHOUT LIMITATION, THE IMPLIED WARRANTIES OF MERCHANTABILITY AND FITNESS FOR A PARTICULAR PURPOSE. EXCEPT FOR THE EXPRESS WARRANTY SET FORTH ABOVE, THE COMPANY DOES NOT WARRANT, GUARANTEE, OR MAKE ANY REPRESENTATION REGARDING THE USE OR THE RESULTS OF THE USE OF THE SOFTWARE IN TERMS OF ITS CORRECTNESS, ACCURACY, RELIABILITY, CURRENTNESS, OR OTHERWISE.

IN NO EVENT, SHALL THE COMPANY OR ITS EMPLOYEES, AGENTS, SUPPLIERS, OR CONTRACTORS BE LIABLE FOR ANY INCIDENTAL, INDIRECT, SPECIAL, OR CONSEQUENTIAL DAMAGES ARISING OUT OF OR IN CONNECTION WITH THE LICENSE GRANTED UNDER THIS AGREEMENT, OR FOR LOSS OF USE, LOSS OF DATA, LOSS OF INCOME OR PROFIT, OR OTHER LOSSES, SUSTAINED AS A RESULT OF INJURY TO ANY PERSON, OR LOSS OF OR DAMAGE TO PROPERTY, OR CLAIMS OF THIRD PARTIES, EVEN IF THE COMPANY OR AN AUTHORIZED REPRESENTATIVE OF THE COMPANY HAS BEEN ADVISED OF THE POSSIBILITY OF SUCH DAMAGES. IN NO EVENT SHALL LIABILITY OF THE COMPANY FOR DAMAGES WITH RESPECT TO THE SOFTWARE EXCEED THE AMOUNTS ACTUALLY PAID BY YOU, IF ANY, FOR THE SOFTWARE.

SOME JURISDICTIONS DO NOT ALLOW THE LIMITATION OF IMPLIED WARRANTIES OR LIABILITY FOR INCIDENTAL, INDIRECT, SPECIAL, OR CONSEQUENTIAL DAMAGES, SO THE ABOVE LIMITATIONS MAY NOT ALWAYS APPLY. THE WARRANTIES IN THIS AGREEMENT GIVE YOU SPECIFIC LEGAL RIGHTS AND YOU MAY ALSO HAVE OTHER RIGHTS WHICH VARY IN ACCORDANCE WITH LOCAL LAW.

ACKNOWLEDGMENT

YOU ACKNOWLEDGE THAT YOU HAVE READ THIS AGREEMENT, UNDERSTAND IT, AND AGREE TO BE BOUND BY ITS TERMS AND CONDITIONS. YOU ALSO AGREE THAT THIS AGREEMENT IS THE COMPLETE AND EXCLUSIVE STATEMENT OF THE AGREEMENT BETWEEN YOU AND THE COMPANY AND SUPERSEDES ALL PROPOSALS OR PRIOR AGREEMENTS, ORAL, OR WRITTEN, AND ANY OTHER COMMUNICATIONS BETWEEN YOU AND THE COMPANY OR ANY REPRESENTATIVE OF THE COMPANY RELATING TO THE SUBJECT MATTER OF THIS AGREEMENT.

Should you have any questions concerning this Agreement or if you wish to contact the Company for any reason, please contact in writing at the address below.

Robin Short
Prentice Hall PTR
One Lake Street
Upper Saddle River, New Jersey 07458

ABOUT THE CD-ROM

Platform required

The CD-ROM is written in a format that can be read by a computer running Microsoft Windows 95 or NT or by an Apple Macintosh computer.

Software required to use the CD-ROM

The CD-ROM contains directories xls and web. Directory xls contains various MS Excel workbooks useful in planning the capacity of Web and C/S systems. You will need MS Excel version 5.0 or higher to use these workbooks. Directory web contains a C program to compute burstiness parameters from an HTTP log file, as well as an example of a log file. To compile the program you will need an ANSI C compiler.

Installation instructions

Copy the files you need from directories xls and web to your hard disk. Detailed instructions on the use of the program and Excel workbooks are available in Appendix B.

Prentice Hall does not offer technical support for this software. However, if there is a problem with the media, you may obtain a replacement copy by emailing us with your problem at discexchange@phptr.com